The relational turn and group seems so obvious that you w such an integration! The und unconscious, intersubjectivity, "the third" provide the theoretical scaffolding for synthesis, or at the very least engaged dialogue and mutual learning. With the publication of this book, Grossmark and Wright take the lead in bringing together cutting-edge theorists and clinicians who "stand in the spaces"—"building bridges"—between individual, relational, and group psychotherapy. Relational psychoanalysis provides particularly fertile ground for systematic and thoughtful psychotherapy integration, and this book will invigorate the movement toward such clinical creativity.
   —**Lewis Aron**, *PhD, Director, New York University Postdoctoral Program in Psychotherapy and Psychoanalysis*

This book is much needed in the contemporary group psychotherapy field. It breaks new theoretical ground, approaching group psychotherapy from the many perspectives that come together under the relational umbrella. With abundant clinical examples, it is an integrative, evocative, and very helpful volume for all who practice or have an interest in group psychotherapy.
   —**Jeffrey Kleinberg**, *PhD, Fellow and Former President of the American Group Psychotherapy Association, and Professor Emeritus, LaGuardia Community College, City University of New York*

It is at the very heart of the revolution in psychoanalytic thought that is relational theory that human beings must be understood in the context of the web of relationships that frames their lives. Yet relational practice has been very largely confined to work with individuals and to the context of the two-person relationship in the consulting room. This book represents an important extension of relational thinking, both in theory and in practice, and should be read widely by anyone interested in how people live in the wider contexts that characterize so much of our lives.
   —**Paul L. Wachtel**, *PhD, Distinguished Professor, Doctoral Program in Clinical Psychology at City College and the Graduate Center of the City University of New York, Co-founder of the Society for the Exploration of Psychotherapy Integration, and author of* Therapeutic Communication *and* Relational Theory and the Practice of Psychotherapy

This book is essential reading for anyone interested in group psychotherapy, and for anyone interested in the application and expansion of relational theory to the practice of group therapy.
   —**J. Scott Rutan**, *PhD, Past President and Distinguished Fellow of the American Group Psychotherapy Association, and author of* Psychodynamic Group Psychotherapy

The One and the Many

The One and the Many: Relational Approaches to Group Psychotherapy applies advances in relational psychoanalysis to the theory and practice of group psychotherapy. In this volume, Robert Grossmark and Fred Wright bring together leading writers in the group psychotherapy field, both psychoanalysts and group therapists, who have integrated ideas from contemporary relational psychoanalysis. Together, they constitute a vibrant and dynamic new wave in group psychotherapy and psychoanalysis that challenge much accepted wisdom and practice in the field, including classic group psychotherapy ideas regarding the therapist's role, the group-as-a-whole, and unconscious processes in group.

In this book, Grossmark and Wright show how the development of relational psychoanalysis has had a transformative impact on the field of psychoanalysis that has reverberated in the group psychotherapy world. The contributors illustrate how the broadening scope of the contemporary relational scene offers much that coheres with and amplifies the theory and practice of group treatment. The focus on dissociation, enactment, trauma, mutuality, and intersubjectivity in the clinical setting, the foregrounding of sub-symbolic communication and implicit relational knowing, the registration of mutual containment and mutual regulation, all open new and exciting vistas for understanding the process and healing properties of group treatment.

The One and the Many expands the theory and practice of group psychotherapy, offering innovative and refreshing ways to understand group interaction and to formulate interventions in both large and small groups. This book will be of interest and practical help to all who practice group psychotherapy, group process, psychoanalysis, and psychotherapy in general, including all mental health practitioners, psychoanalysts, psychotherapists, psychiatrists, social workers, counselors, and pastoral counselors.

Robert Grossmark is a psychoanalyst in private practice in New York City. He teaches at the National Institute for the Psychotherapies, the Eastern Group Psychotherapy Training Program, and the Doctoral Program in Clinical Psychology at the City University of New York (CUNY). He supervises in the New York University Postdoctoral Program in Psychoanalysis, the National Institute for the Psychotherapies, and the CUNY Clinical Psychology Doctoral Program. He is the co-editor of *Heterosexual Masculinities: Contemporary Perspectives from Psychoanalytic Gender Theory* (Routledge, 2009) and writes on psychoanalytic process.

Fred Wright is Emeritus Professor of Psychology at the John Jay College of Criminal Justice of the City University of New York. He has practiced psychotherapy in New York City for forty years, writing and publishing on the topics of shame and guilt in human experience as well as violence and antisocial behavior. He is also co-editor of the book *Forensic Psychology and Psychiatry* (New York Academy of Sciences, 1980).

PSYCHOANALYSIS IN A NEW KEY BOOK SERIES
DONNEL STERN
Series Editor

When music is played in a new key, the melody does not change, but the notes that make up the composition do: change in the context of continuity, continuity that perseveres through change. Psychoanalysis in a New Key publishes books that share the aims psychoanalysts have always had, but that approach them differently. The books in the series are not expected to advance any particular theoretical agenda, although to this date most have been written by analysts from the Interpersonal and Relational orientations.

The most important contribution of a psychoanalytic book is the communication of something that nudges the reader's grasp of clinical theory and practice in an unexpected direction. Psychoanalysis in a New Key creates a deliberate focus on innovative and unsettling clinical thinking. Because that kind of thinking is encouraged by exploration of the sometimes surprising contributions to psychoanalysis of ideas and findings from other fields, Psychoanalysis in a New Key particularly encourages interdisciplinary studies. Books in the series have married psychoanalysis with dissociation, trauma theory, sociology, and criminology. The series is open to the consideration of studies examining the relationship between psychoanalysis and any other field—for instance, biology, literary and art criticism, philosophy, systems theory, anthropology, and political theory.

But innovation also takes place within the boundaries of psychoanalysis, and Psychoanalysis in a New Key therefore also presents work that reformulates thought and practice without leaving the precincts of the field. Books in the series focus, for example, on the significance of personal values in psychoanalytic practice, on the complex interrelationship between the analyst's clinical work and personal life, on the consequences for the clinical situation when patient and analyst are from different cultures, and on the need for psychoanalysts to accept the degree to which they knowingly satisfy their own wishes during treatment hours, often to the patient's detriment.

Vol. 21
The One and the Many: Relational Approaches to Group Psychotherapy
Robert Grossmark & Fred Wright (eds.)

Vol. 20
Mended by the Muse: Creative Transformations of Trauma
Sophia Richman

Vol. 19
Cupid's Knife: Women's Anger and Agency in Violent Relationships
Abby Stein

Vol. 18
Contemporary Psychoanalysis and the Legacy of the Third Reich: History, Memory and Tradition
Emily A. Kuriloff

Vol. 17
Love and Loss in Life and in Treatment
Linda B. Sherby

Vol. 16
Imagination from Fantasy to Delusion
Lois Oppenheim

Vol. 15
Still Practicing: The Heartaches and Joys of a Clinical Career
Sandra Buechler

Vol. 14
Dancing with the Unconscious: The Art of Psychoanalysis and the Psychoanalysis of Art
Danielle Knafo

Vol. 13
Money Talks: In Therapy, Society, and Life
Brenda Berger & Stephanie Newman (eds.)

Vol. 12
Partners in Thought: Working with Unformulated Experience, Dissociation, and Enactment
Donnel B. Stern

Vol. 11
Heterosexual Masculinities: Contemporary Perspectives from Psychoanalytic Gender Theory
Bruce Reis & Robert Grossmark (eds.)

Vol. 10
Sex Changes: Transformations in Society and Psychoanalysis
Mark J. Blechner

Vol. 9
The Consulting Room and Beyond: Psychoanalytic Work and Its Reverberations in the Analyst's Life
Therese Ragen

Vol. 8
Making a Difference in Patients' Lives: Emotional Experience in the Therapeutic Setting
Sandra Buechler

Vol. 7
Coasting in the Countertransference: Conflicts of Self Interest between Analyst and Patient
Irwin Hirsch

Vol. 6
Wounded by Reality: Understanding and Treating Adult Onset Trauma
Ghislaine Boulanger

Vol. 5
Prologue to Violence: Child Abuse, Dissociation, and Crime
Abby Stein

Vol. 4
Prelogical Experience: An Inquiry into Dreams & Other Creative Processes
Edward S. Tauber &
Maurice R. Green

Vol. 3
The Fallacy of Understanding & The Ambiguity of Change
Edgar A. Levenson

Vol. 2
What Do Mothers Want? Contemporary Perspectives in Psychoanalysis and Related Disciplines
Sheila F. Brown (ed.)

Vol. 1
Clinical Values: Emotions That Guide Psychoanalytic Treatment
Sandra Buechler

The One and the Many

Relational Approaches to Group Psychotherapy

Edited by
Robert Grossmark
and Fred Wright

NEW YORK AND LONDON

First published 2015
by Routledge
711 Third Avenue, New York, NY 10017

and by Routledge
27 Church Road, Hove, East Sussex BN3 2FA

Routledge is an imprint of the Taylor & Francis Group, an informa business

© 2015 Taylor & Francis

The right of the editors to be identified as the authors of the editorial material, and of the authors for their individual chapters, has been asserted in accordance with sections 77 and 78 of the Copyright, Designs and Patents Act 1988.

All rights reserved. No part of this book may be reprinted or reproduced or utilized in any form or by any electronic, mechanical, or other means, now known or hereafter invented, including photocopying and recording, or in any information storage or retrieval system, without permission in writing from the publishers.

Trademark notice: Product or corporate names may be trademarks or registered trademarks, and are used only for identification and explanation without intent to infringe.

Library of Congress Cataloging in Publication Data
The one and the many : relational approaches to group psychotherapy / [edited by] Robert Grossmark and Fred Wright.
pages cm. -- (Psychoanalysis in a new key book series ; vol. 21)
Includes bibliographical references (pages).
1. Group psychotherapy. 2. Object relations (Psychoanalysis) 3. Interpersonal relations. 4. Psychoanalysis. I. Grossmark, Robert, editor of compilation. II. Wright, Fred, 1935- editor of compilation.
RC488.O54 2014
616.89'152--dc23
2014003000

ISBN: 978-0-415-62180-9 (hbk)
ISBN: 978-0-415-62181-6 (pbk)
ISBN: 978-1-315-76511-2 (ebk)

Typeset in Times New Roman
by Saxon Graphics Ltd, Derby

Printed and bound in the United States of America by Publishers Graphics, LLC on sustainably sourced paper.

For Carina, Tomas, and Sophia
Robert Grossmark

For Phyllis, Julie, and Chris
Fred Wright

Contents

	List of Contributors	xiii
	Introduction ROBERT GROSSMARK AND FRED WRIGHT	1
1	**Personal Reflections on Hugh Mullan: Existential Group Therapist** FRED WRIGHT	12
2	**Being Seen, Moved, Disrupted, and Reconfigured: Group Leadership from a Relational Perspective** FRED WRIGHT	27
3	**The Group as an Inevitable Relational Field, Especially in Times of Conflict** HAIM WEINBERG	38
4	**The Edge of Chaos: Enactment, Disruption, and Emergence in Group Psychotherapy** ROBERT GROSSMARK	57
5	**Repairing the Irreparable: The Flow of Enactive Engagement in Group Psychotherapy** ROBERT GROSSMARK	75
6	**Developing Nuclear Ideas** RICHARD M. BILLOW	91
7	**Progressing While Regressing in Relationships** RONNIE LEVINE	112

8	**Use and Impact of Empathic, Other-Centered, and Self Listening/Experiencing Perspectives in Analytic Group Psychotherapy** JAMES L. FOSSHAGE	128
9	**Interventions at an Impasse: Vulnerability, the Group Leader's Use of Self, and Sustained Empathic Focus as a Bridge Between Theory and Practice** MARTY LIVINGSTON	145
10	**Group Psychotherapy and Neuro-Plasticity: An Attachment Theory Perspective** PHILIP J. FLORES	168
11	**Using a Systems Lens to Illuminate the Intersubjective Field in Group** BARBARA R. COHN	188
12	**Rethinking Tavistock: Enactment, the Analytic Third, and the Implications for Group Relations** GREGORY S. RIZZOLO	215
13	**Relational Experiences in Large Group: A Therapeutic and Training Challenge** ROSEMARY SEGALLA	242
	Index	263

Contributors

Richard M. Billow, PhD (ABPP, CGP), is a clinical psychologist, psychoanalyst and group analyst, with over fifty publications in analytic and group journals, and the author of *Relational Group Psychotherapy: From Basic Assumptions to Passion* (Kingley, 2003), *Resistance, Rebellion and Refusal in Groups: The 3Rs* (Karnac, 2010), and *Relational Group Psychotherapy: Developing Nuclear Ideas* (Karnac, 2014). He is a Clinical Professor at the Derner Postgraduate Programs (Adelphi University, Garden City, New York), and Director of the Group Program. He practices combined individual-group psychotherapy in Great Neck, New York.

Barbara R. Cohn, PhD, ABPP, LFAGPA, is Associate Professor of Medical Psychology, Columbia University College of Physicians and Surgeons. She is former Director of Psychology Education and Training St. Lukes Roosevelt Hospital Center in New York City where she coordinated the psychology internship and a psychology fellowship programs with a concentration in group theory and technique. Dr. Cohn is co-director of the Eastern Group Psychotherapy Society group training program. She has published several journal articles and book chapters on issues such as gender, couples and the application of systems theory to organizational and therapeutic situations. She also edited a special edition of GROUP on women and group. Currently she teaches and supervises and has a private practice in New York City.

Philip J. Flores, PhD, ABPP, CGP, FAGPA, is a Fellow of the American Group Psychotherapy Association (AGPA) and is a Diplomate in Group Psychology. He is Adjunct Faculty at Georgia State University, the Georgia School of Professional Psychology at Argosy University and is supervisor of group psychotherapy at Emory University. He produced two books, *Group Psychotherapy With Addiction Populations* (Haworth Press, 2007, 3rd edn.), and *Addiction as an Attachment Disorder* (Jason Aronson, 2011). He is the lead author on the American Group Psychotherapy Association's treatment manual, *Group Psychotherapy of Substance Abuse and Addiction*. He was Consensus Panel Chair for Substance Abuse Treatment: Group Therapy, A Treatment Improvement Protocol (TIP #41) issued by the U.S. Department of

Health & Human Services, and is co-chair and contributing member of the Science to Service Task Force of American Group Psychotherapy Association that produced the Clinical Practice Guidelines for Group Psychotherapy. His latest book, *Addiction as an Attachment Disorder*, was the 2005 Gradiva Award Winner issued by The National Association for the Advancement of Psychoanalysis. He has presented numerous workshops nationally and internationally on these two subjects. He and his wife, Lisa Mahon, PhD, continue to run several outpatient psychotherapy groups a week in their private practice in Atlanta, Georgia.

James L. Fosshage, PhD, is Founding President, International Association for Psychoanalytic Self Psychology; Clinical Professor of Psychology, New York University Postdoctoral Program in Psychotherapy and Psychoanalysis (Co-founder, Relational Track); Co-founder, Board Director, and Faculty, National Institute for the Psychotherapies; Founding Faculty, Institute for the Psychoanalytic Study of Subjectivity; Editorial Board member on seven journals and author of over 100 psychoanalytic publications, including seven books. He has been among PEP's "Top 100 Authors Downloaded" since 2010. His website is www.jamesfosshage.net.

Robert Grossmark, PhD, teaches at the National Institute for the Psychotherapies, the Eastern Group Psychotherapy Society, the Clinical Psychology Doctoral Program at CUNY, and the University of New Mexico Medical School. He is clinical supervisor, NYU Postdoctoral Program in Psychoanalysis, Doctoral Program at City University; the Psychoanalytic Training Program and the National Training Program at NIP. He co-edited *Heterosexual Masculinities: Contemporary Perspectives from Psychoanalytic Gender Theory*, and has published numerous psychoanalytic articles.

Ronnie Levine, PhD, is a graduate of the NYU Postdoctoral Program in Psychotherapy and Psychoanalysis, a Diplomate in Group Psychology and a Fellow of the American Group Psychotherapy Association, (AGPA). She serves on the EGPS Board and is on the faculties of the EGPS Group Training Program and the Center for Group Studies. She is also on the Board of the AGPA. She conducts an ongoing training group in Austin, TX. She has conducted many workshops and institutes for AGPA and for EGPS on Managing Love and Hate, Barriers to Intimacy, Resiliency, and the Therapist's Effective Use of Uncomfortable Feelings. She has published articles on clinical issues in group therapy and was honored by EGPS in 2011 for outstanding achievement in the field of group psychotherapy. Her private practice, which is in New York, includes individual, couples, group psychotherapy and individual and group supervision.

Marty Livingston, PhD, is the former director of the Group Therapy Department, Postgraduate Center for Mental Health and the former editor of GROUP (The Journal of the Eastern Group Psychotherapy Society). He is the author of

Vulnerable Moments:Deepening the Psychotherapeutic Process (Jason Aronson, 2001) and two other books as well as about thirty journal articles and chapters.

Gregory S. Rizzolo, MA, NCC, LPC, is a candidate in psychoanalytic training at the Chicago Institute for Psychoanalysis and a doctoral student in psychoanalytic studies at the University of Essex. In addition, he is a Visiting Lecturer at the Institute for Clinical Social Work in Chicago.

Rosemary Segalla, PhD, CGP, has been conducting, teaching and publishing about group psychotherapy for thirty-five years. She presents frequently on group psychotherapy both nationally and internationally. Her primary focus is on self-psychological, intersubjective and relational themes as they apply to working with groups. She is on the faculty of the Group Psychotherapy Training Program of the Washington School of Psychiatry, Washington, DC. She is cofounder and director emeritus of the Institute of Contemporary Psychotherapy and Psychoanalysis, Washington, DC where she also serves on the faculty. She is also a member of the International Association of Psychoanalytic Self Psychology governing council.

Haim Weinberg, PhD, is a clinical psychologist and group analyst in private practice in California. Director of International Program at the Professional School of Psychology, Sacramento, California. Adjunct Professor at the Wright Institute, Berkeley and at the Alliant International University, Sacramento. A faculty member of the Group Facilitators Training Program in Tel-Aviv University. Former president of the Northern California Group Psychotherapy Society and of the Israeli Association of Group Therapy, a former member of the Board of the International Association of Group Psychotherapy and Group Processes. Co-edited books on the Large Group and on the Social Unconscious.

Fred Wright, PhD, is Emeritus Professor of Psychology at the John Jay College of Criminal Justice, the City University of New York. He is also on the editorial board of *The International Journal of Group Psychotherapy* and is in the private practice of individual and group psychotherapy in New York City.

Introduction

Robert Grossmark and Fred Wright

Psychoanalysis has always had a tentative relationship with the field of group psychoanalysis and group psychotherapy. Few psychoanalytic institutes include courses on group treatment in the curriculum and even fewer would regard group psychoanalysis as a partner treatment to individual work. Group psychotherapists have tended to eschew psychoanalytic treatment as too intellectualized and rarefied, perhaps even disconnected from the real lives of patients. Both of us editors are psychoanalysts who work with individual patients and conduct group treatment. Where others may have found disparate worlds, we have often found convergence and overlap. It seems to us that this convergence has grown even more clear and meaningful in the last three decades with the emergence and growth of relational psychoanalysis. The growth of the relational perspective has transformed the worlds of both psychoanalysis itself and group psychotherapy. Furthermore many have noted with great excitement the elements of group theory that are echoed in relational theory and practice.

However, there has yet to be a concerted attempt to spell out this convergence and integration. It is our belief that many group psychotherapists will gain much insight from the contemporary relational world and likewise that many psychoanalysts of all persuasions will be pleased to find that current thinking in the group psychotherapy field has much to offer them. In this volume we have brought together leading writers in the group psychotherapy field who have integrated ideas and perspectives from contemporary relational psychoanalysis. Some are psychoanalysts who conduct group psychotherapy; some are group psychotherapists who have integrated relational theory into their own theory and practice. Together, we believe, they constitute a vibrant and dynamic new wave in group psychotherapy and psychoanalysis.

Relational Psychoanalysis and Group Treatment

The emphases of relational psychoanalysis on the continuous and non-linear emergence of experience in the psychotherapeutic dyad, the focus on the relationship as both constituting and constitutive of the dyad, and the value placed on the analyst's experience and its thoughtful communication to the patient, all seem to relate in a potentially telling way to the group therapy setting and to cohere with the central thrust of all group therapies. The recognition that it is the emotional communication and intersubjective engagement between people that can facilitate the formulation of previously unformulated and dissociated experience and lead to new experience of the self and other, has a paramount application to the theory and practice of group psychoanalysis. Relational psychoanalysts and group therapists have privileged the engagement with the *other*, in relation both to others and to the others within ourselves. This is a tone exemplified by the British group analyst Malcolm Pines, who embellishes upon Michael Bakhtin's idea of alterity: "we gain ourselves only through our dialectical relationship with others; we need others to aid in the creation and completion of ourselves" (Pines, 1998, p. 24). And certainly this is a view familiar to relational psychoanalysts summed up by Jessica Benjamin: "Intersubjectivity theory postulates that the other must be recognized as another subject in order for the self to fully experience his or her subjectivity in the other's presence" (Benjamin, 1999, p. 186).

Moreover, the broadening scope of the contemporary relational scene offers much that coheres with and amplifies the theory and practice of group treatment. The focus on dissociation, enactment, and trauma, mutuality in the clinical setting, the foregrounding of sub-symbolic communication and implicit relational knowing, the registration of mutual containment and mutual regulation, all open new and exciting vistas for understanding the process and healing properties of group treatment. Likewise the consideration of how these processes unfold in the group setting offer expansions of the concepts themselves.

Similarly there is much work in the group psychotherapy field that will be eye-opening and stimulating for the readers who come from the field of psychoanalysis. The history of group therapy has always valued the understanding of the individual in context and has emphasized the impoverishment of a psychology that only talks of an isolated mind. Relational psychoanalytic readers will find many surprising convergences between the work of many of the pillars of the group therapy field such as Foulkes, the founder of the group analytic movement in the UK, and Hugh Mullan, whose work is described by Wright (Chapter 1, this volume); and the relational perspectives of Steven Mitchell, Lew Aron, and many others.

In recent years both relational psychoanalysis and the group therapy field have begun to integrate non-linear dynamic systems theory into theory and practice. Just as traditional views of psychological development, human interaction, and the process of therapeutic change have been challenged and expanded by ideas of non-linearity and complexity, the foundational ideas of group process and interaction, and the role and task of the group leader have all been productively problematized by these new and exciting developments.

The classical conception of the group leader as neutral and removed from the dynamics and unconscious processes of the group and therefore able to utilize interpretation as the major promoter of the therapeutic action of the group has been deconstructed and reconfigured by developments in relational practice that emphasize the intersubjective engagement of the analyst. As well as group transferences, we can now understand group process from the perspective of mutual enactments that involve all group members and the group leader in multiple conscious and unconscious ways.

The One and the Many

The title of this book deserves some explanation. "The One and the Many" is a phrase from Aristotle's *Metaphysics*. It captures the essential human dialectic: we are both individual and intrinsically a part of something greater—society, community. Aristotle introduces this aspect of human life in terms of political reality and also, most crucially for us, in terms of human ontology, our *being*. This volume is in no further way oriented to Aristotelian philosophy, but in raising the question about *being*, this phrase, "the One and the Many," does introduce the issue and highlights that working with patients in group and building a theory that appreciates the individual *one* as always situated in the context of the *many*, and as both constituted by and constitutive of this *many* gets at the heart of the relational understanding of the human individual. Along with Foulkes and other group theorists, Sullivan and Mitchell questioned the value of speaking of the psychology of the "individual," of the *one*. We are all more than *one* whether we speak of the world of internal objects, "the we of me" (McCullers, 1946), or the world of cultural embeddedness that is sedimented (Gadamer, 1975) inside of us.

"The One and the Many" also describes the patient's individual self in the context of the group and the continual fluid shifting of figure and ground between the individual and the group that the group therapist and the group members experience. There is the *one* group, which often indeed acts as if it had one mind. There is the "mathematical" multiplicity of the group; it comprises many (most commonly eight) individuals. But more central to our theoretical and clinical concerns in this volume is the kaleidoscopic nature of the group when one takes into account the multiplicity inherent in each of the individuals in the group. Philip Bromberg assumes that we all comprise multiple self-states and that these are exclusive to each other to the degree that dissociative sequestering of one or many self-states from the others is required to maintain self continuity (Bromberg, 2006). The group therapy situation is perfectly constructed to illustrate and to open up for change the multiple *ones* and *manys* in the group at any one time.

There is also the issue of the many perspectives of group treatment. When running a group we ask the members to talk as openly as possible with each other about their experience of each other as it is happening. The idea is to create an environment where multiple perspectives are valued; where there is never one voice—the therapist—that holds the one truth or interpretation. Such an approach creates a fluid and dynamic environment where the questions need not fold into rigid either/or dichotomies, but rather promote an inclusive and continually shifting both/and culture. In this environment members can think new thoughts and experience surprise rather than continually repeat the rigid and deadened "familiar chaos" (Stern, 1997) of the enactment of unformulated and dissociated experience.

"The One and the Many" also captures the multiple theories of group therapy that we hope the reader will find in this volume. Relational psychoanalysis itself is not a homogenous approach. It may be best regarded as a large tent that encompasses different perspectives that each bring their own emphasis in both clinical thinking and practice. Our volume reflects this "many" as well. The reader will find chapters that construct a relational approach to group psychotherapy while emphasizing and integrating ideas from self psychology, intersubjectivity theory, enactment and dissociation, trauma theory, post-Bionian psychoanalysis, systems theory, neurophysiology, attachment theory, modern psychoanalysis, and more.

Organization of the Book

We begin our volume with an essay by Fred Wright that outlines the clinical ideas of Hugh Mullan and illustrates the growth of ideas in the group therapy field that have great resonance with the developments that were to characterize the relational movement in psychoanalysis. Having been a member of a group psychotherapy with Hugh Mullan in the 1960s, Wright offers both a personal and a clinical overview of the prescient ideas of Mullan. Like many others in the group field, Mullan was inspired by existential thinking and emphasized the ongoing and impactful relationship between the group members as the primary source of change in treatment rather than interpretation offered from a non-involved analyst. In fact many contemporary relational readers will be surprised to find Mullan describing individual treatment as an encounter between two vulnerable humans, both of whom inevitably change in the course of their work together. Eschewing the psychic determinism that dominated psychoanalysis at that time, Mullan emphasized spontaneity and immediacy of interaction as the hallmarks of the treatment process. He proposed that the subjectivities of patients *and* group therapists are at the center of group treatment and argued for mutuality and non-rational thinking as core ingredients in facilitating change. Like so many relational psychoanalysts to come, he valued the use of the therapist's subjectivity and the use of self disclosure, spontaneity, and honesty on the part of the group therapist. Wright outlines the uncanny resonance between Mullan's approach and contemporary relational writers such as Aron, Benjamin, Bromberg, D.B. Stern, Wilner, and others.

In Chapter 2, "Being Seen, Moved, Disrupted and Reconfigured: Group Leadership from a Relational Perspective," Wright examines his own development as a relational group therapist and builds on the personal and theoretical influence of Hugh Mullan outlined in Chapter 1. This chapter, reprinted here, was one of the first to introduce some of the core contributions of the relational shift in psychoanalysis to the group therapy field. Embellishing Mullan's foregrounding of therapist participation, authenticity, and engagement, Wright introduces contemporary relational ideas on the understanding of unformulated and inchoate experience in group psychotherapy via enactments within the group. Unlike more traditional writers in the group theory field, such as Irving Yalom (1975), Wright foregrounds a focus on the therapist's own internal process as a key to the resolution of group enactments and highlights the relational reformulation of transference as perspective and adaptation rather than as distortion. He captures the relational focus on in vivo recognition within a context of mutuality as crucial to the development of patients' subjectivity and agency, and emphasizes the need for therapist authenticity and personal resonance in the clinical moment.

Wright also addresses the skepticism and even outright opposition often encountered in the fields of psychotherapy and psychoanalysis toward group treatment. Indeed this volume is an attempt to speak to some of the hesitation toward group treatment often encountered. Wright is interested in the degree to which the emotional work of group therapy from a relational perspective that values leader participation and authenticity is tremendously emotionally challenging. The group leader is asked to confront much potential emotional pain, disruption, shame, and humiliation. In the spirit of mutuality, the openness and flexibility required to work relationally within a group, offers all participants, including the leader, the opportunity to grow and "reconfigure."

The emotional work required to work with groups relationally is captured by Haim Weinberg in Chapter 3, "The Group as an Inevitable Relational Field, Especially in Times of Conflict." Approaching the group from an intersubjective/relational point of view he places enactment at the center of group dynamics and conceptualizes traditional psychodynamic concepts such as transference and resistance as co-created by group therapists and members. Weinberg calls upon the foundations of group therapy literature (Foulkes, 1964) and foregrounds the group matrix and the power of the group interactions. He offers a powerful vignette of a supervision group in Israel to illustrate the confusion, anxiety, and heightened emotions that he and the group members experience when drawn into a painful enactment, and the group therapist's work of continuing to process the emotions and develop an understanding of the enactment. Weinberg's work focuses on building mutual acknowledgment of the subjective experiences of those involved in the conflict, including himself, despite overwhelming emotional intensity, and illustrates Foulkes's (1964) axiom that interpretation follows change rather than precedes it. Weinberg's vignette highlights the relational appreciation and inclusion of social and political context within the group setting.

Chapters 4 and 5 by Robert Grossmark continue the theme of enactment in group psychotherapy and constitute an application of the central relational focus on trauma, dissociation, and the multiplicity of self-states (Bromberg, 1998; Stern 1997, 2010) to the theory and practice of group psychotherapy. In Chapter 4, "The Edge of Chaos: Enactment, Disruption and Emergence in Group Psychotherapy," Grossmark outlines the emphasis on therapy *by* the group rather than therapy *in* the group. The therapist's task is to help the group itself become the agent of change. He conceives of the group as comprising many multiple selves. The process of group psychotherapy unfolds through enactments that involve the whole group and the group therapist entering into the grip of repetitive and unmentalized self-states. Grossmark looks to the group itself for help in resolving these enactments. With the therapist's help and containment, the members can access alternative self-states that allow for new and unformulated experience to emerge. He utilizes dynamic systems theory to understand the dialectical movement between the rigid "familiar chaos" of enactment and the reflective and related states that allow working through. Grossmark describes a group session that involves a painful enactment. It illustrates how the therapist allows the enactment to unfold by holding and containing intense affect, and how the group members are helped to find their own meaning and new experience in interaction with each other.

In Chapter 5, "Repairing the Irreparable: The Flow of Enactive Engagement in Group Psychotherapy," Grossmark combines the idea of group free association as articulated by Foulkes (1964) and other original group psychotherapy pioneers with a contemporary idea of the flow of enactive engagement, where the free unimpeded flow into and out of group enactments of trauma is the fulcrum of group process and change. For Grossmark, the foregrounding of the concept of enactment enables an uncoupling from the often pejorative resistance approach to treatment that tends to focus on what is being avoided and not being addressed. He finds more utility in the constant focus on what is being enacted and what hitherto unthinkable story of trauma is unfolding in the group process. This work emphasizes the creative and meaning-making properties of the group that are often eclipsed by the focus on the negative and destructive qualities of regressive forces in groups.

Richard Billow has been an exponent of a contemporary application of Bion's theory of thinking to group treatment. In numerous articles and two books (Billow, 2003, 2010), Billow has grappled with the dilemmas of thinking and relating that lie at the core of Bion's work. In Billow's work, the pain and terrors of thinking new thoughts, of connecting to others, and of engaging in a group are constant struggles for every group member, group leader, and the group as a whole. In Chapter 6, Billow outlines and explains his main orienting concepts based on Bion's (1963) ideas of L, H, and K links: that the group is always involved in a search for emotional truth which involves connecting to basic feelings of curiosity, love, and hate. In this chapter he advances a new concept of "developing nuclear thoughts" that takes as its springboard a close reading of his own reverie and thought process while leading a group. Deeply relational in its focus on the internal process of the embedded group analyst, Billow shows how his reverie and the sharing of his own perceptions with the group moves various kinds of groups from non-conscious thinking to conscious thinking, to greater relatedness and aliveness, and to the creation of new meaning.

The challenges of working in group with non-verbal and unformulated states are further addressed by Ronnie Levine in Chapter 7. Integrating a diversity of psychoanalytic theories in her approach, Levine foregrounds the influence of modern psychoanalysis and in particular the work of Louis Ormont. These are influences that may be obscure for many relational readers. Based on the work of Spotnitz (1969), the modern school of psychoanalysis modified psychoanalytic technique to work with patients previously regarded as unanalyzable, emphasizing a focus on pre-verbal and non-symbolized experience as well as valuing the emotional communication in the treatment relationship. Ormont (1992) applied these ideas to group work and developed concepts of "bridging" and "joining" that help create groups that work with dynamism and immediacy in the here-and-now. Levine's chapter illustrates her application of this approach within the contemporary relational context. Conceptualizing regression as a relational phenomenon, her chapter focuses on the movement into and out of regressed states in group therapy. She outlines the great treatment opportunities that arise as group members regress to less related, less coherent, and less intersubjective states. Levine offers an extended case vignette that illustrates the intensity of a dynamic group therapy that focuses on emotional communication between members and the open and feelingful sharing of her own emotional reactions in the group. She illustrates how group therapy can be a powerful tool in achieving greater self–other separateness and relatedness, growth in reflective function, increased ability to recognize the subjectivity of the other, more solid self cohesion, and the more resilient ability to shift into and out of different self-states.

In the following two chapters we hear voices from two prime exponents of the contemporary blend of relational psychoanalysis and Kohut's self psychology. In Chapter 8, James Fosshage describes psychoanalytic development from the initial objectivism of Freud to the contemporary environment where both therapist's and patient's subjectivities are regarded as mutually constructing the dynamics of the treatment, and the consequent shift from the focus on intrapsychic dynamics to the relational field. Fosshage draws on Kohut's (1959, 1982) conceptualization of the empathic mode of observation and suggests that analysts experientially oscillate between the empathic, other-centered and analyst's self listening perspectives. He shows how group therapists' and group members' empathic listening is filtered through the protagonist's subjective experience. Whether within the individual or group setting, listening perspectives affect the protagonists' experience, inquiries, and impact on one another. Fosshage outlines when other-centered listening is preferred for an individual or group therapist and when it is most useful to utilize the therapist's self perspective. Arguing that all group members oscillate between these different listening perspectives, he suggests that group members can be greatly helped by appreciating their own listening perspectives and can therefore understand their own internal organizing patterns and hence their contribution to interpersonal difficulties. In this way group members enhance their reflective awareness as well as understanding of self, other, and self-with-other.

In Chapter 9, Marty Livingston presents a self psychology/intersubjective approach to group therapy. Livingston makes a distinction between a group leader's specific interventions on the one hand, and the attitudes and behaviors conveyed in an ongoing fashion by the leader *throughout* the treatment, on the other hand. He indicates that it is these attitudes and beliefs, functioning in the background that create safety for patients and allow the therapeutic process to unfold and deepen. He also stresses the importance of what he calls a "sustained empathic focus" on the patient's emotional vulnerabilities. This should be an experience-near, affective focus in the here-and-now allowing unmet developmental needs to emerge and be attended to, thereby allowing growth to proceed and affect regulation skills to develop. These attitudes and focuses by therapists facilitate the appearance of what Livingston calls "vulnerable moments," which are moments when the person is open to affective experiences. He proposes that such emotional vulnerability is necessary not only for the group patient but also for the group leader. The vulnerable involvement of the group therapist, he says, plays a key role in promoting change. This idea is a significant departure from the classical psychoanalytic position that therapists should keep their own subjective experience out of the unfolding interaction and maintain a blank-screen position.

In Chapter 10 Philip Flores addresses the findings of neuroscience and describes the profound impact psychotherapy has on the brain. More specifically he describes how ongoing relationships powerfully influence the brain's plasticity and development, and, contrary to earlier notions, establishes that the brain is malleable throughout the lifespan. He outlines the value of attachment theory in deepening our understanding of the impact relationships have on neurobiology. He says that it's not so much particular techniques or leader style or approach that advances treatment but rather it's the development of strong emotional bonds with another or others that can take place in a therapy group that will lead to success. Additionally, he points out that attachment is a primary drive and that its establishment in the therapeutic relationship is absolutely necessary for successful treatment. Further, attachment allows for mentalization to develop. This term refers to people's ability to understand the mental states of self and others, skills essential for functioning in a complex social world.

Meaningful talk with others in the context of emotional arousal, attunement and strong emotional bonds will alter brain mechanisms. Flores indicates that all forms of psychotherapy that accomplish this task will enhance growth in the structure and function of the brain.

Barbara Cohn reviews systems theory in Chapter 11, in an effort to integrate the rich notions from this perspective with the existing collection of relational theories and findings regarding group theories and group therapy. She points out that applying systems thinking provides new meaning within small groups and also the larger context, which, in turn, provides group patients with more enduring self-experiences as well as enhancing the location of meaning in the social surround. She says systems theory also provides a language that expands clinician consciousness but does not contradict other understandings. Rather it presents a meta view that adds new meanings. Additionally and importantly, she identifies it as a tool that helps clinicians extract themselves from enactments.

Focusing on the intersubjective by definition calls attention to therapist subjectivity and the part it plays in the unfolding system. This attention to therapist countertransference is a most important contribution of systems thinking. This accords with Cohn's aim to expand clinician consciousness to further illuminate the intersubjective field, which by definition, calls for recognition of therapist subjectivity in the therapeutic endeavor. It also leads to an understanding that events in the group are not necessarily lodged in any one group member but rather may be the result of complex and non-linear interactions between and among group members and levels in the system. This way of thinking helps counter the scapegoating of individuals or sub-groups that groups are prone to.

Finally, Cohn offers an excellent discussion of the topic of "context," an issue often ignored by clinical writers. She notes that therapists working in their private offices tend to let the larger context, the world outside their office, slip out of mind. She presents a vignette illustrating how economic matters outside the group contributed to a group resistance. When the group finally attended to the matter, it opened the group system to new and important internal work.

We complete our volume with two chapters that bring a relational and intersubjective approach to larger group process. Greg Rizzolo offers a critique of the Tavistock group relations epistemology and methodology and Rosemary Segalla describes her work with a large group from an intersubjective perspective.

Since the pioneering work of Bion, the "group relations" or Tavistock approach to the study of group process has been the predominant mode for the psychoanalytic study of group process. Bion (1961) proposed three "basic assumptions"—fight/flight, dependency, and pairing—that characterize and dominate the unconscious and dynamic life of groups and impede the work group, that is, the group's ability to stay focused on its primary task (Grinberg et al., 1993). Over fifty years of group relations conferences have offered people from many professions the chance to experientially learn about these group dynamics. In the UK, they have been termed "Tavistock" groups after the clinic where Bion conducted his group work (Bion, 1961). In the USA, the A.K. Rice Institute has been the focal organizer of these group learning events.

In Chapter 12 Rizzolo suggests that the group relations model continues to depend on the questionable metaphor of the isolated mind as a container of reified mental contents, which can be passed around by means of projective identification. Furthermore, it continues to invoke the notion of a neutral analyst or consultant with privileged insight into the group's unconscious fantasy life. Through a critical discussion of this approach, Rizzolo attempts to begin a dialogue about intersubjectivity and its implications for the study and practice of group relations. He argues that an intersubjective approach requires one to look not at how reified mental contents are being moved around within a given group, but rather at how intersubjective experiences can be co-created by the group members and their conference consultants. He focuses on how enactments between all of these participants can lead to a transformation of self and other through the experience of mutual subjugation and the emergence of a shared third space. In addition, he introduces the concept of the alien group self—a shared identity that the group can form to accommodate to the mindset of its consultants.

In Chapter 13 Rosemary Segalla describes her work as both a co-leader and member of a large group team that has been operating for over twenty years in the Washington School of Psychiatry, Group Psychotherapy Institute. She has observed how the shifts in psychoanalytic theory have filtered into the workings of this large group. She approaches the large group from an intersubjective position integrating self psychology and relational psychoanalysis. Rather than Freudian and Kleinian group relations approaches to large groups, addressed by Rizzolo in the previous chapter, which foreground the regressive, aggressive and projective qualities of group life, Segalla primarily focuses on the positive, health-seeking, and self-organizing qualities of large group processes that seek to maintain connection and engagement between members. Creatively adapting Kohut's theory, Segalla suggests that group members seek a "groupobject experience," an affiliation with a larger group or tribe. Embodying a hermeneutics of trust (Orange, 2011), group leaders seek to "humanize the group" (de Mare et al., 1991) and maintain an empathic focus on the dilemmas and difficulties of maintaining connectedness and self-cohesion in the swirl of the larger culture and the personal inner world for engagement, like "a dream in dialogue" (ibid.).

Taken together these chapters capture the shift that is emerging in group psychotherapy and in psychoanalysis away from the reliance on interpretation by a neutral group or individual analyst toward an emphasis on engagement with the other or others as the primary fulcrum for change and growth. These chapters represent many voices and perspectives on this shift and taken together they open up new and vibrant pathways for both patients and analysts to expand their experience of themselves, of their patients, and of other group members. We thank all the contributors for their generosity and effort. In particular we thank Donnel Stern, the editor of the book series *Psychoanalysis in a New Key* for inviting us to add this volume to a wonderful sequence of books that represent the exciting and expanding world of contemporary psychoanalysis.

References

Benjamin, J. (1999) Recognition and destruction: An outline of intersubjectivity. In S.A. Mitchell & L. Aron (eds.) *Relational Psychoanalysis: The Emergence of a Tradition*. Hillsdale, NJ: The Analytic Press.

Billow, R.M. (2003) *Relational Group Psychotherapy: From Basic Assumptions to Passion*. London and Philadelphia: Jessica Kingsley Publishers.

Billow, R.M. (2010) *Resistance, Rebellion and Refusal in Groups: The 3 Rs*. London: Karnac Books Ltd.

Bion, W.R. (1961) *Experiences in Groups*. London: Tavistock Publications, Chapters 1, 2, and 3, pp. 29–75.

Bion, W.R. (1963) *Elements of Psycho-analysis*. London: Heinemann.

Bromberg, P.M. (1998) *Standing in the Spaces: Essays on Clinical Process, Trauma and Dissociation*. Hillsdale, NJ: The Analytic Press.

Bromberg, P.M. (2006) *Awakening The Dreamer: Clinical Journeys*. Mahwah, NJ: The Analytic Press.

De Mare, P., Piper, R., & Thompson, S. (1991) *Koinonia*. London: H. Karnac (Books) Ltd.
Foulkes, S.H. (1964) *Therapeutic Group Analysis*. London: George Allen & Unwin.
Gadamer, H.-G. (1975) *Truth and Method*. Trans. G. Barden and J. Cumming. New York: Seabury Press.
Grinberg, L., Sor, D., & Tabak de Bianchedi, E. (1993) *New Introduction to the Work of Wilfred Bion*. Northvale, NJ: Jason Aronson Inc., Chapter 1, "Groups."
Kohut, H. (1959) Introspection, empathy, and psychoanalysis. *J. Amer. Psychoanaly. Assn.*, 7: 459–483.
Kohut, H. (1982) Introspection, empathy, and the semicircle of mental health. *Internat. J. PsychoAnal.*, 63: 395–408.
McCullers, C. (1946) *The Member of the Wedding*. New York: Houghton Mifflin.
Orange, D.H. (2011) Persons in context. In R. Frie & W. Coburn (eds.) *Beyond Individualism: Philosophical Contributions of Buber, Gadamer and Levinas*. New York: Routledge.
Ormont, L. (1992) *The Group Therapy Experience: From Theory to Practice*. New York: St. Martin's Press.
Pines, M. (1998) The self as a group: The group as a self. In I.N.H. Harwood & M. Pines (eds.) *Self Experiences in Group: Intersubjective and Self Psychological Pathways to Human Understanding*. London and Philadelphia: Jessica Kingsley Publishers.
Spotnitz, Hyman (1969) *Modern Psychoanalysis of the Schizophrenic Patient: Theory of the Technique*. New York: Grune & Stratton.
Stern, D.B. (1997) *Unformulated Experience: From Dissociation to Imagination in Psychoanalysis*. Hillsdale, NJ: The Analytic Press.
Stern, D.B. (2010) *Partners in Thought: Working with Unformulated Experience, Dissociation and Enactment*. New York: Routledge.
Yalom, I.D. (1975) *The Theory and Practice of Group Psychotherapy*. New York: Basic Books.

Chapter 1

Personal Reflections on Hugh Mullan
Existential Group Therapist

Fred Wright

The primary purpose of this chapter is to review the approach to group psychotherapy of Hugh Mullan, MD (1912–2003). Hugh was among the few practitioners of the mid-twentieth century to apply concepts derived from existential and phenomenological philosophy to the conduct of group therapy (cf. Shaffer & Galinsky, 1989). An innovative and unorthodox psychiatrist, he was described by Saiger (2008), in a survey of the schools of group psychotherapy, as one of the pioneers of this discipline. A second purpose is to show how Hugh Mullan's work foreshadowed that of many contemporary practitioners of psychotherapy, and how his ideas continue to enrich theoretical development in the field.

Hugh was a graduate of the United States Naval Academy and the Cornell University School of Medicine. He served in World War II as a medical officer in the US Army. Subsequently, he trained in psychiatry at the New York State Psychiatric Institute and in psychoanalysis with Karen Horney at the Association for the Advancement of Psychoanalysis. He served as president of the AGPA from 1956 to 1958. After many years in private practice in New York City, Hugh moved to New Orleans in 1967 to become chief of psychiatry at the New Orleans Veterans Administration, and taught at Tulane University. In the early 1970s, he settled in Washington, DC, where he taught group therapy at Georgetown University and the Washington School of Psychiatry, and continued in private practice until his retirement in 1986.

This brief professional profile scarcely conveys the compelling manner and relentless intelligence of the man and the clinician. I was a patient in group therapy with him from 1960 through 1964, and directly experienced how Hugh, with his penetrating blue eyes, could make the timely, appropriate disclosure or even a personal gesture in a group that would remain with the patient for a lifetime. As a therapist and mentor, Hugh's influence on me was enduring, as I gratefully acknowledge here. He modeled living fully and spontaneously in the moment, courage in the face of adversity and mortality, and the healthy questioning of established belief.

In 1964, Hugh Mullan, with Iris Sangiuliano, co-authored *The Therapist's Contribution to the Treatment Process*. In a section titled the "Foundations for a new Direction" (p. 8), they described an emerging paradigm that has since become a dominant model in contemporary psychotherapy. At the time, it verged on blasphemy. Mullan and Sangiuliano questioned Freud's and his associates' deep grounding in scientific pragmatism and positivism. The challenge by new schools of psychotherapy to the views of the early classical psychoanalysts, they said, corresponded to changes taking place in science with the development of the Quantum Theory and Relativity. This was also mirrored in philosophy with existentialism's emphasis on one's relationship to self and other. The philosopher Martin Buber, for example, contended that the fundamental reality of human life lies in the relationship between one being and another (2002). Mullan and Sangiuliano envisioned a similar development in psychotherapy. It was no longer to be seen as a "fixed scientific procedure in which reason is deified and the *only* search is for intellectual solutions to man's difficulties" (p. 8). Psychotherapy would be understood as a powerful and life-changing emotional meeting between vulnerable humans (both patient and therapist) who communicated one with another.

In two subsequent publications (Mullan & Rosenbaum, 1978; Mullan 1992), Hugh again vigorously eschewed logical positivist thinking, since it emphasized determinism as distinct from the human capacity to choose. He argued that a positivist mentality projects a mechanized, linear view of the person and of living, rather than an awareness of non-linear processes and the many *immeasurable* aspects of life which positivism cannot address. He saw classical psychoanalysis as an expression of this mentality in that it posited the notion of intrapsychic determinism, in contrast to the existential philosophical approach that "insists that human behavior is indeterminate and subject only to the individual's will" (Mullan & Rosenbaum, 1992, p. 453).

Existential therapy, therefore, emphasizes the patient's freedom and responsibility to choose. Hugh believed that decisions were to be made by the individual, and not the therapist or the group; he considered decisions made by others for the individual to be non-therapeutic. In a 1981 article, he stated that "central to existential philosophical belief is the fact that one's freedom of choice negates all predictions of one's future behavior. This point contradicts all the social sciences, including dynamic psychology, which hold that behavior *is* predictable" (p. 55).

In addition, Hugh emphasized the central importance of the therapeutic relationship and the emotional *experience* of treatment, as distinct from a more linear and linguistically grounded approach to analyzing content. That is, the focus he argued should be on promoting and processing the emotional experience of the moment, rather than eliciting and interpreting content (1981, p. 63). He passionately repudiated approaches that allowed techniques, methods and systems to dominate the therapeutic process, overshadowing the individuality of the patient (1981).

This way of thinking was prescient, and only much later recognized as part of a longer historic trend. Frie (2003), for example, discussing the origins of existential and relational thinking in psychoanalysis, points out that such a view was implicit and explicit in the work of earlier clinicians and theorists such as Ludwig Binswanger, Medard Boss, Erich Fromm, Frieda Fromm-Reichmann, Karl Jaspers, and Ronald Laing. It also resembles the ideas of contemporary psychoanalysts including self psychologists and interpersonal, relational, and intersubjective psychoanalysts, who emphasize that experience cannot be understood outside of the context in which it is formed and expressed.

Hugh espoused other ideas that were sharply at odds with the mental health community of his time. He contended for example that group therapy, rather than individual therapy, was the most effective psychological treatment method. He firmly proposed that the intense intimate emotional interaction among therapy group members, including the group leader, was the very source of psychological healing (Mullan & Rosenbaum, 1978). This stood in direct opposition to the rather rigidly held belief, during most of his years in practice, that interpretation formulated by the therapist was the key to psychological change. Hugh further asserted that the therapist as well as the patient must be altered by the therapeutic process; he held the still somewhat unconventional position that the patient's change is *contingent* on change in the therapist.

In a paper published late in his career, "Inherent Moral Practice in Group Psychotherapy" (1991), Hugh approached yet another controversial topic. The moral quality to which he referred was the almost instinctive move toward the mutual self-help he observed in patients in group treatment, and the respect displayed early on for co-members when all share the right and power to speak and act freely. Hugh proposed that this "love of neighbor" or altruistic phenomenon motivates all participants in the group situation. Indeed, he saw morality, that is to say moral agency, as "inherent not alone in the patients and therapist but *in the process itself*" (emphasis added, p. 197).

In addition to fertile notions such as the above, three issues especially important to Hugh have emerged as central to many of the new generation of psychotherapy theoreticians and practitioners. Subjectivity, mutuality, and non-rational (or non-teleological) experience will be reviewed here to illuminate the confluence between Hugh Mullan's and contemporary thinking on these topics.

Subjectivity

As is commonly acknowledged, Freud and the classical or early psychoanalysts aimed for analytic neutrality and objectivity. The purity, even sterility, of the interpersonal field in the consulting room was expected to be cultivated and preserved, well into the 1960s when Hugh was developing his own approach and testing it in practice. He emphatically rejected the orthodox model, and stressed the importance of subjectivity for therapists and patients alike. The term implies reflection on one's interior life, dreams, fantasies, personal values, and so on (Atkins, 2005). Hugh saw subjectivity as the channel to a person's individuality, developmental history, and perspective on the world. In a 1992 paper, he stated that subjectivity was "the essence of therapy" (p. 454), and particularly emphasized the importance of the *therapist's* subjectivity in the change process.

For Hugh, the fact of the therapist as a person was a consistent focus, an inescapable reality. As he put it, "the therapist *persists* in revealing his humanness" (emphasis added, 1981, p. 68). The therapist was to be there openly and honestly, without role playing, status maneuvers, or emotional distancing; his or her actual direct lived experience was central to the efficacy of the process.

Many psychotherapy theorists have critiqued this approach due to concern about destructive "acting-out" on the part of the therapist. This is certainly a legitimate concern. However, when working with Hugh, his self-disclosures were always expressed in the context of the therapeutic task which he personified and at all times was about the matter of taking one's life seriously and living it fully and constructively.

Furthermore, Hugh took the rather startling position that, since each therapist will function in a unique manner, theoretical systems of therapy do not make sense and are thus of limited usefulness in and of themselves. He would, for example, have found manual-guided therapy profoundly unacceptable since as he saw it each therapist will find his or her unique subjectivity, as will each patient (Mullan & Rosenbaum, 1978). Decisions must be made independent of the judgment of others, or of abstract paradigms. Looking to others or to a particular theory to determine how to conduct your practice (or your life) is futile, because no formula will remain constant. Therapists needed to accept this, Hugh advised, instead of attacking themselves for deviating from the "right way to do therapy." According to Hugh: "The nature of the therapist's participation, his or her words and expression of emotion, is idiosyncratic and marks the group as his or her own" (Mullan & Rosenbaum, 1978, p. 456).

He gave Freud due credit for recognizing the subjective in the phenomenon of countertransference. But, he saw Freud's view as limited, because the construction of countertransference referred solely to the therapist's neurotic response to the patient. Hugh believed that Freud did not appreciate the *appropriate* subjectivity embodied in countertransference. As he and Sangiuliano described their emerging concept:

> The psychotherapist as an objective observer, or even as a participant-observer, has been supplemented by the psychotherapist as the *subjective interactor* ... The therapist's inner and many times unconscious self, along with his objective perceptions, is more and more becoming a meaningful element in the treatment transaction.
>
> (1964, p. 16)

This view of subjectivity also meant that the therapist's inner consciousness, mood, intuition, dreams, and fantasies were very important, and should be employed and shared with patient and group alike to move the therapy forward. We cannot expect the patient to be subjective if the therapist will not also be subjective. In Hugh's words, "the therapist's inner consciousness is most significant—his mood at the beginning and end of each session, the presence of personal problems that tend to distract him, and his dreams and fantasies" (Mullan & Rosenbaum, 1978, pp. 387–388) all have their place in the healing process.

The notion that the therapist ought to be objective and emotionally neutral, according to Hugh, meant that the *patient* would be objectified, and perceived as an object to be "done to" through the use of interventions and techniques determined ahead of time. Rather, he believed that therapist and patient must meet face to face, and come to know each other as two (or more) interacting human beings. This meant that the therapist's personal involvement and personal evolution was central. Therapists should not attempt to conceal their uniqueness, but be authentic and present in the moment. Their own flights of mood and daily concerns were elements to be openly experienced and coped with, rather than denied. For Hugh, the therapist was the agent of change, neither the messenger nor the message (1992).

Existential philosophy, he believed, impacts each therapist personally, demands that they be awakened, different, and unique. "Individuality stands out as the essential characteristic of all existentialists. In varying degrees, freedom to choose, dignity, personal love, and creativity are traits which they extol. These qualities must first be found in the therapist if patients likewise are to discover them in themselves" (Mullan & Rosenbaum, 1978, p. 380). This is why, he suggested, existential group therapists are inclined to ignore contemporary treatment technologies and find themselves out of the mainstream of current approaches, to work in their own singular fashion. Reliance on data, quantification, and verification do not appeal to them. They prefer subjectivity to objectivity, connectedness to detachment, and emotionality to intellectuality. They "know that emotion, compassion, kindness and concern cannot be parceled out by formula" (Mullan & Rosenbaum, 1978, p. 380).

Again, Hugh emphasized that any *system* of treatment, with its built-in actions and codified responses, is not authentic: it is role playing. This, according to Mullan and his existential cohorts, is artificial. It prevents the group members and therapist from appropriately responding to the patient's emergency, and cannot be depended upon. The real despair of the patient must be met by equally *genuine* care and responsibility, warmth, and feeling from the therapist. A system approach is problematic, especially in the group setting, because the group is not a facsimile of life outside, but *is* life in all its intensities and nuances. No system can contain or accommodate it. To go one step further with Hugh, the group meeting is not only an essential part of the patient's real life, but also an essential part of the therapist's life (Mullan & Rosenbaum, 1978).

Mullan and Sangiuliano argued that willingness to change and venture were possibly the therapist's greatest assets. A realization of therapeutic potential is, therefore, intimately linked with the therapist's changing relationship to self, to others, and to the world. Despite any protestations to the contrary, it is understood that the patient seeks treatment because he wishes to retain his status quo. The therapist's capacity to change, then, is critical. If the therapist is genuinely evolving, the patient, although at first reluctant, is forced or maneuvered into a field of forces which are far from fixed. To remain in this therapeutic setting, by definition a state of flux, the patient also must move. Each participant in the therapeutic session fundamentally changes as his and the other's behavior becomes more relevant to who he actually is in the passing moment (Mullan & Sangiuliano, 1964).

Hugh's early elaboration of subjectivity in the psychotherapy process aligns him with many contemporary theoreticians who have moved away from the classical insistence on objectivity. There is currently a rich and ongoing discussion of this topic in the psychotherapy literature (e.g., Aron, 1996; Bromberg, 2006; Beebe, Knoblauch, Rustin, & Sorter, 2005; Burston & Frie, 2006; Coburn, 2001; Wright, 2004). For example, Aron (1996), in a highly regarded publication presenting key ideas from the relational psychoanalytic school of psychotherapy, maintains that subjectivity is central to the treatment process. Bromberg (2006), another influential writer, states that "the analyst's use of his subjective experience ... is the critical factor in promoting a patient's self-growth ... The heart of the work ... is negotiation between subjectivities, not interpretation" (p. 72).

In a 2001 paper Coburn said:

> one's embeddedness in one's subjectivity actually facilitates the reciprocal and mutual processes of emotional resonance and unconscious communication ... The emphasis on the analyst's ... subjective experience in contemporary psychoanalysis provides vital theoretical and clinical insights about what is constitutive and transformative for the patient.
>
> (pp. 304–305)

Teicholz (2009), summarizing Kohut's thinking on this matter, observes that he too questioned the ideal of scientific objectivity. He emphasized the importance of the subjective vantage point variously labeled "vicarious introspection" or "empathic immersion" (p. 75). The desirability, indeed the possibility of pure objectivity, grows dim in Kohut's vivid terminology.

Beebe and colleagues (2005) illustrate how the thinking on this topic has grown in complexity. In their review, they agree that today a great many theorists see attention to subjectivity as crucial to the work of therapy. However, they also note that theorists often differ in their view of the location of its influence in the therapeutic action itself. For example, Benjamin (1992) emphasizes the importance of the patient's experience and developing ability to recognize the therapist's subjectivity. Ogden (1994), like Hugh, values particularly the therapist's experience of subjectivity, while Stolorow, Atwood, and Brandchaft (1994) underscore the significance of the therapist's impact on the patient's subjective experience within the therapeutic field. The emerging importance of subjectivity to contemporary psychotherapy is perhaps most dramatically exemplified by the popular and prominent "Institute for the Psychoanalytic Study of Subjectivity" in

New York City. Its founding in 1987, just a year after Hugh's retirement from practice, and its longevity confirm widespread acceptance and appreciation of what many today consider central to the work of psychotherapy.

Mutuality/Status Denial

Discussions of subjectivity often take place in tandem with the term "intersubjectivity," which is very much at the forefront of current theorizing and literature of psychotherapy (e.g., Aron, 1996; Frie 1997; Beebe et al., 2005). The coinage of the term "intersubjectivity" in clinical circles is uncertain; wide usage likely dates from the emergence of relational theory. Hugh Mullan never used it, but he did refer to "mutuality" extensively. This word denotes shared experience or reciprocity between two or more minds. There is overlap between the two terms but there are points of distinction as well. Aron (1996), for example, distinguishes between mutuality of regulation and mutuality of recognition; the former refers to the co-regulation that takes place between interactors, while the second refers to the recognition of similarities and commonalities that interactors share. Aron indicates that the latter definition is what clinicians usually mean by "intersubjectivity"; it is also what "mutuality" meant to Mullan.

In their 1964 discussion of new directions, Mullan and Sangiuliano said "Psychotherapists now focus their attention upon the combination of 'therapist–patient' rather than the single isolated patient" (p. 10). This meant developing a relationship with the patient based on mutuality rather than one based on traditional assumptions about authority and hierarchy. They described the therapeutic meeting as "oriented toward mutual discovery, [and that] patient and therapist have a common human struggle to find meaning" (p. 32). In their 1978 book, Mullan and Rosenbaum put special emphasis on the importance of patient and therapist facing life's paradoxes *together*.

Mullan and Sangiuliano pointed out that patients will be inclined to place the therapist in a fixed role, such as "magic helper," in order to avoid responsibility for their own existence. They stressed that it is the therapist's job not to collude with such maneuvers, and recommended that therapists practice "status denial" which meant to avoid playing the role of omnipotent and omniscient "Doctor." By mutuality between therapist and patient, they further meant that the interaction was bi-directional. There were to be mutual interventions, mutual discoveries, and mutual growth; all group members were responsible for what transpired in the therapy, not just the group therapist. Here again, Mullan and Sangiuliano contended that the therapist's evolution and personal change was as important as the patient's.

They placed special value on the care and maintenance of the therapist in the work of therapy. It was their idea that when therapists see themselves as more like the group members than not, when they rely on each member to help them with the other members, and when they are also scrutinized in the group, it will motivate reexamination of themselves as well. This is very much in accord with current thinking in regard to therapists paying close attention to their part in unfolding and unconscious interactions. This kind of engagement is now referred to as attending to "enactments," and is similar to the notion of "intersubjectivity" in that it is referring to the shared and often non-conscious experience of all participants in the therapeutic field. The topic of enactments is currently the focus of much attention by psycho-dynamically oriented clinicians such as Ellman and Moskowitz (1998), D.B. Stern (1997), and Wright (2005).

Mullan and Sangiuliano maintained that therapists who are able to set aside their sense of expertise gain in therapeutic acumen and in treatment ability as well. No longer must they be clever, overly intellectual and isolated. They further said that:

> Our belief in the need for the therapist and patient to engage and *change together* has given us a new vector which is continuously present. This is the element of the therapist's satisfaction during the time that he is with the patient. Like other creative efforts we contend that the therapist not only has the right to gain satisfaction from his activity but if he doesn't he is actually jeopardizing the therapeutic outcome.
>
> (1964, p. xiv)

This way of thinking about the therapists' involvement has widespread support today. Maroda (2005), in enthusiastic agreement, says:

> I am convinced that every successful treatment was inherently a mutual event that irrevocably changed, gratified, pained, and enlivened both participants … The treatment relationship is essentially asymmetrical, but also essentially symbiotic. It is my hope that we can reduce the incidence of abuse and countertransference dominance through admitting that we need our patients and that they potentially enhance and transform our lives.
>
> (p. 385)

Faculty and theoreticians of the Relational–Cultural Therapy approach to therapy located at the Stone Center's Jean Baker Miller Training Institute at Wellesley University also place a heavy emphasis on the importance of mutuality as a mutative factor in psychotherapy. They point out that it is particularly important that therapy relations proceed with clarity about power; they stress specifically that it is essential to pay attention to how power is constructed and used in relationships, including the therapeutic relationship. Additionally, they say change cannot occur unless therapists are open to influence by patients as well (Walker & Rosen, 2004).

A significant number of practitioners today also focus on different *facets* of mutuality in the therapy experience. Infant-caregiver researchers such as Lachmann and Beebe (1996) and intersubjective systems theorists such as Stolorow and colleagues (1987) stress mutual influence and co-regulation between patient and therapist. Relationally oriented psychoanalysts, however, emphasize mutual recognition. For instance, Benjamin (1992) highlights the need of the self to be recognized by another, which means being acknowledged by another as "an equivalent center of experience" (p. 28) who has meaning and has had an impact. She underscores the particular importance in the change process of the patient's developing ability to recognize and be responsive to the subjectivity of the therapist.

Burke (1992) has also addressed the matter of mutuality and contrasts it to what he calls the asymmetry position. The former calls for uninhibited self-expression by the therapist, and the latter recommends that the therapist hold back, observe, interpret, and not disclose countertransference subjectivity. Burke's main point is that therapist self-expression may be a source of important information that needs to be made known to patients when striving to clarify the configuration of roles and behaviors under analysis. He cautions, however, that total mutuality may be in some instances counter-productive and thus not appropriate, at times. Slochower (1996), a relational psychoanalyst, agrees. She contends that therapist subjectivity needs to be set aside for some patients until they are developmentally more advanced and can tolerate subjectivities different from their own. Thus, she suggests, we need to vary our responsiveness to patients according to the specific situation.

The matter of therapist self-expression also links to an ongoing debate in the field regarding therapist self-disclosure (cf. Teicholz, 2009). The matter is further complicated by the common clinical experience where therapists are misunderstood due to patients' transference experience, no matter how cautious therapists may be regarding self-disclosure. The group itself may be of special value in helping group therapists address this problem. If the therapist is unable or unwilling to be present in his or her full, authentic subjectivity, either because of personal style or theoretical position or countertransference blockage, or if an individual member has a toxic response to the therapist's raw subjectivity, other group members may be able to be help make sense of what's going on. This is exactly what Hugh meant by the notion of group *members* helping with the work of therapy, as well as his idea that therapists must also allow themselves to be scrutinized.

Hugh so valued the therapeutic acumen of group members that he advocated for the use of a method called "alternate group meetings." Group members would meet a second time during the week, but in each other's homes and without the therapist. Radical as this was, a number of Hugh's contemporaries saw value in the approach and adopted it as well (e.g., Kadis, Krasner, Winick, & Foulkes, 1963; Wolf, Schwartz, McCarty, & Goldberg, 1970). These writers suggested that alternate group meetings, as well as post-meetings and pre-meetings, countered dependency on omnipotent parental figures, such as the group therapist, and provided patients with the opportunity to assume a responsible adult role, which according to Kadis and colleagues was the "strongest single element in growth and maturation" (1963, p. 113). This also accords with Yalom and Leszcz's (2005) recognition of the therapeutic value of therapy patients' exercising altruism by facilitating fellow group members' growth, an opportunity that is unique to group therapy.

The Non-Rational/Non-Teleological

In their survey of the historical development of psychotherapy, Burston and Frie (2006) distinguish between what they describe as rationalist and irrationalist theoreticians of psychotherapy. Rationalists emphasize the primacy of reason, while irrationalists argue that the human intellect is limited and imperfect, and that there are other ways of finding the truth such as faith, love, and imagination. Further, the irrationalists argue, there are ambiguities and uncertainties in the human experience that cannot be captured by language or the intellect alone. Unequivocally, Hugh Mullan kept company with the latter group. He stressed the search for meaning in an essentially paradoxical and non-rational world, and contended that meaning can only be gleaned from the raw experience of living (Mullan & Rosenbaum, 1978, p. 384).

In their 1964 publication, Mullan and Sangiuliano said that "Communication in psychotherapy is essentially directed to reach the non-rational, unrealized and unexpressed experiences of the individual" (p. 33). This echoes a 1956 paper in which Hugh emphasized the value of what he called the "non-teleological" in the process of psychotherapy, defined as that which is "without known future purpose" (p. 480). The term connotes a logical, preverbal, non-verbal and non-symbolized experience. He de-emphasized the usefulness of linear and academic reporting of past events, and placed greater value on report of dreams, fantasies, unfamiliar feelings, spontaneous associations, and unreal thought which weave in and out of the members' communications (Mullan & Rosenbaum, 1978). In service of this, psychological or philosophical jargon was rarely used in the context of Hugh's group sessions, and was in fact discouraged, as patients were to rely upon their common daily speech. As Hugh described his goal, "existential therapy uses no technique ... Sessions are not planned, and the interaction which occurs is neither known nor even contemplated beforehand" (Mullan & Rosenbaum, 1978, p. 392).

Mullan and Sangiuliano (1964) challenged the traditional model of psychotherapy that searched for causes and explanations of the "why" or the "how" of a patient's life. They said:

> It is quite apparent that the logical explanation objectively rendered although allaying the *therapist's* anxiety is futile as far as changing the patient is concerned. For the therapist and patient to set about to *try* to solve the problem is not to solve. The rigidity of the patient who perceives himself and his world in a fixed manner is not moved by logical explanations. More often than not the patient's seeking to *solve* his problem is the problem ... the therapist and patient esteem their unrehearsed moments together over the explanations offered and even the patient's talking about himself.
>
> (p. 13)

They added:

> The therapeutic process receives added impetus through the therapist's spontaneous and changing thought, feelings and acts. Such changes profoundly effect all the patients.
>
> (p. 18)

They found that the existential writer Eugene Ionesco best articulated this idea, for he too emphasized the importance of whatever the spontaneous imagination might produce. Ionesco contended that insisting on lucidity *first* is to dam up the sluice-gates, and that "the waters must be allowed to come flooding out, but *afterwards* comes the sorting, the controlling, the understanding, the selecting" (Coe, 1961, p. 6, cited in Mullan & Sangiuliano, 1964, p. 21).

To summarize Hugh's position: the therapist's and the patient's spontaneous emotional response is central. It comes from within, rather than from a theory of technique, and it shows in a deep emotional involvement between therapists and patients. Feelings and experience are privileged over analysis; making sense of that experience is more important than interpretation.

The non-rational was exuberantly given full play by Hugh. His behavior in session was often quite unorthodox. He would tell his own dreams, disclose feelings, make non-logical associations, and, at times, act in a fashion that was puzzling, "not nice," and even weird from a conventional perspective. In response to a patient's question regarding the fastest way to do therapy, he might answer "How fast are you?" "Where are you going in such haste?" "Why not take us with you?" Or, "Why can't you be with us?" (Mullan & Sangiuliano, 1964, p. 35).

Hugh's "non-teleological" approach resembles the work of a number of current relationally oriented psychoanalysts. For instance, Wilner (2006) discusses the value of "emergent and unbidden experience" (p. 13) that he sees arising from the therapist's unconscious embeddedness in the immediate clinical context. He indicates that working in this fashion honors one's "felt sense" or intuition. Emphasis is placed on the analyst's openness to whatever inadvertent and imaginative experience may come to mind in the patient's presence because everything that comes to mind has something to do with the patient.

Wilner, like Hugh, advocates moving beyond a linguistic framework for understanding human experience to what he calls a "direct experience" approach that complements the need for reflection and understanding of meaning. Wilner says there is a dimension of experience over which we have no control. When we try to assume

> conscious control, we are not in a good position to resonate experientially and behaviorally with the unconscious contextual forces in the immediate clinical moment; … we should be attuned to this unconscious dimension of experiencing more fully in our work before invoking our more consciously informed efforts to account for, understand, and direct what is happening.
>
> (2006, p. 17)

This approach is deeply resonant with the thinking advanced by Mullan and Sangiuliano over forty years ago, and throughout Hugh Mullan's later writings.

D.B. Stern's (2003) elaboration of the notion of unformulated experience is also well suited to appreciating the role of unbidden, non-rational, non-conscious and un-symbolized experience, and its important role in psychodynamic psychotherapy. Stern indicates that it emerges out of the therapist's and patient's bidirectional processes of empathic resonance. He sees progress in therapy as not simply the removal of distortion to reveal preexisting truths, but rather as a reflection of an increased willingness to attend to new experience and to value imagination and freedom of thought. He further recommends that in order to be open to new experience, we need to be capable of *not knowing* what will come next, that is, to be able to tolerate uncertainty. He suggests allowing language to take its own shape and encouraging vague senses to take their own meaningful form rather than forcing them in a particular direction because it feels familiar, and therefore safer. Stern, and others writing from this perspective, also say that the unconscious does not have one predetermined meaning, and that meaning is formulated in interpersonal interaction: it is co-created in relationship with others.

Like Hugh and the newer writers cited above, researchers of neuroscience now posit the importance of non-linear, non-rational affective experience. They tell us this comes from right-hemisphere brain functions that are centrally involved in the psychotherapy process (Bucci, 2002; Schore, 2003, 2008). Their investigations show that the right hemisphere of the brain mediates feeling, sensing, and non-linguistic information processing, while the left is more linked with higher executive functioning and is thought to be the "interpreter" of experiences. This suggests that focusing on right-brain experience is an important part of the healing process in psychotherapy. Additionally, it appears that right-brain functions operate beneath the conscious awareness of both patient and therapist, that is to say beneath the exchanges of language and explicit cognitions. These are the non-conscious processes essential to bringing about change through psychotherapy. The group cohesion or bonding experience so highly valued by students of the therapeutic factors in group therapy (e.g., Yalom & Leszcz, 2005) appears, then, to be a right-brain activity.

Schore (2003, 2008), who is both a neuroscientist and psychoanalyst, sees in these findings a significant paradigm shift taking place in our understanding of the mutative factors in psychotherapy. He says that they "alter our conception of the clinical expert from one who creates insight via interpretations that make the unconscious conscious, to one who optimally processes and regulates patients' unconsciously communicated bodily-based affective states in order to facilitate development of the unconscious." He adds that the "therapist's right brain generates essential components of this expertise, not the left" (2008, p. 3). According to Schore, the shift in perspective is toward a psychotherapy not defined by what the therapist explicitly and objectively *does* for the patient, or *says* to the patient. Rather, the key mechanism of the work is how to implicitly and subjectively *be* with the patient, especially during affectively stressful moments. Schore goes on to assert that "psychotherapy is not the "talking cure," but the "affect communication and regulation cure" (2008, p. 12). It must be recognized that Hugh Mullan and his colleague, Iris Sangiuliano, advocated this very position many years ago.

Conclusion

This review of Hugh Mullan's innovative approach to group psychotherapy demonstrates his ardor to contribute to the development of a discipline, still in its infancy, and to promote the most useful and dynamic qualities inherent in it. These lie in the crucial role that the therapist's emotional, subjective self plays in the therapy process. Although trained as a medical doctor, Hugh certainly did not see psychological problems as medical in nature. He saw relationship factors as the basis for fostering therapeutic change, and was vigorous in his advocacy of this point of view. Hugh clearly understood the impact effective psychotherapy had on therapists as well as their patients, and the need for ongoing self-processing and personal change. While his thinking ran against the grain of his contemporaries, he fully recognized that disrupting the status quo was intrinsic to the work of the therapist, both in the consulting room and in the psychotherapy profession itself.

A potent and charismatic figure, Hugh was also modest about the role he played bringing out the best in others and promoting their growth. As mentioned, I was a patient of his in the early 1960s and I still remember and value the gift he gave me in a therapy group meeting on the occasion of my marriage. Such acknowledgment (a Tiffany candy dish) of a significant milestone offered in the context of a psychotherapy session was understood in those days to be a radical departure from the clinical norm. Years passed with virtually no contact between me and Hugh after I left the group until we met at an American Group Psychotherapy Association conference in 1990. We were both presenters on the same panel and I said to the audience "I am very proud to be on this dais with Hugh Mullan who helped me so much so many years ago." Hugh gave me a quiet nod and his blue eyes smiled.

Acknowledgments

I would like to thank Hugh Mullan's son, Fitzhugh Mullan, MD, for providing me with some of Hugh Mullan's publications which were very helpful in preparing this article. I would also like to thank Sy Rubenfeld, PhD for reminding me of the importance of the topic of morality in Mullan's thinking about the psychotherapy process. Finally, thanks to Iris Sangiuliano, PhD for consulting with me about her experiences working with Hugh Mullan.

References

Aron, L. (1996) *A Meeting of Minds*. Hillsdale, NJ: Analytic Press.
Atkins, K. (ed.) (2005) *Self and Subjectivity*. Malden, MA: Blackwell Publishing.
Beebe, B., Knoblauch, S., Rustin, J., & Sorter, D. (2005) *Forms of Intersubjectivy in Infant Research and Adult Treatment*. New York: Other Press.
Benjamin, J. (1992) Recognition and destruction: An outline of intersubjectivity. In N. Skolnick & S. Warshaw (eds.), *Relational Perspectives in Psychoanalysis* (pp. 43–60). Hillsdale, NJ: Analytic Press.
Bromberg, P. (2006) *Awakening the Dreamer*. Mahwah, NJ: Analytic Press.
Buber, M. (2002) *Between Man and Man*. 2nd edn. New York: Routledge.
Bucci, W. (2002) The referential process, consciousness, and the sense of self. *Psychoanalytic Inquiry*, 5: 766–793.
Burke, W. (1992) Countertransference disclosure and the asymmetry/mutuality dilemma. *Psychoanalytic Dialogues*, 2 (2): 241–271.
Burston, D. & Frie, R. (2006) *Psychotherapy as a Human Science*. Pittsburgh, PA: Duquesne University Press.
Coburn, W. (2001) Subjectivity, emotional resonance and the sense of the real. *Psychoanalytic Psychology*, 18: 303–319.
Coe, E. (1961) *Eugene Ionesco*. New York: Evergreen Pilot Books, Grove Press.
Ellman, S.J. & Moskowitz, M. (eds.) (1998) *Enactment: Toward a New Approach to the Therapeutic Relationship*. Northvale, NJ: Jason Aronson.
Frie, R. (1997) *Subjectivity and Intersubjectivity in Modern Philosophy and Psychoanalysis: A Study of Sartre, Binswanger, Lacan and Habermas*. Lanham, MD: Rowman and Littlefield.
Frie, R. (ed.) (2003) *Understanding Experience: Psychotherapy and Postmodernism*. London: Routledge.
Kadis, A., Krasner, J., Winick, C., & Foulkes, S.H. (1963) *A Practicum of Group Psychotherapy*. New York: Harper and Row.
Lachman, F. & Beebe, B. (1996) Three principles of salience in the organization of the patient–analyst interaction. *Psychoanalytic Psychology*, 13: 1–22.
Maroda, K. (2005) Legitimate gratification of the analyst's needs. *Contemporary Psychoanalysis*, 3 (41): 371–387.
Mullan, H. (1956) The nonteleological in dreams. *Journal of Hillside Hospital*, 5 (3–4): 480–487.
Mullan, H. (1981) Subjectivity in existential group psychotherapy. *Group and Family Therapy* (annual): 54–69.
Mullan, H. (1991) Inherent moral practice in group psychotherapy. *International Journal of Group Psychotherapy*, 2 (41): 185–197.
Mullan, H. (1992) "Existential" therapists and their group practice. *International Journal of Group Psychotherapy*, 4 (42): 453–468.
Mullan, H. & Rosenbaum, M. (1978) *Group Psychotherapy: Theory and Practice*. New York: Free Press.
Mullan H. & Sangiuliano, I. (1964) *The Therapist's Contribution to the Treatment Process: His Person, Transactions and Treatment Methods*. Springfield, IL: Charles C. Thomas.
Ogden, T. (1994) *Subjects of Analysis*. Northvale, NJ: Jason Aronson.
Saiger, G. (2008) Some thoughts on the existential lens in group psychotherapy. In G. Saiger, S. Rubenfeld, & M. Dluhy (eds.), *Windows into Today's Group Therapy* (pp. 153–167). New York: Routledge.

Schore, A. (2003) *Affect Regulation and the Repair of the Self*. New York: W.W. Norton.

Schore, A. (2008) A regulation model of clinical expertise: Working with attachment trauma and right brain unconscious affect. Paper presented at the Affect Regulation: Development, Trauma, and Treatment of the Brain-Mind-Body Conference, New York, November.

Shaffer, J.B. & Galinsky, M.D. (1989) *Models of Group Therapy*. Englewood Cliffs, NJ: Prentice Hall.

Slochower, J. (1996) Holding and the fate of the analyst's subjectivity. *Psychoanalytic Dialogues*, 6: 323–353.

Stern, D.B. (1997) *Unformulated Experience: From Dissociation to Imagination in Psychoanalysis*. Hillsdale, NJ: Analytic Press.

Stolorow, R., Atwood, G., & Brandchaft, B. (1994) *The Intersubjective Perspective*. Northvale, NJ: Jason Aronson.

Stolorow, R.D., Brandchaft, B., & Atwood, G.E. (1987) *Psychoanalytic Treatment: An Intersubjective Approach*. Hillsdale, NJ: Analytic Press.

Teicholz, J.G. (2009) A strange convergence: Postmodern theory, infant research and psychoanalysis. In R. Frie & D. Orange (eds.) *Beyond Postmodernism: New Dimensions in Clinical Theory and Practice* (pp. 69–91). New York: Routledge.

Walker, M. & Rosen, W.B. (2004) *How Connections Heal*. New York: Guilford Press.

Wilner, W. (2006) The analyst's embeddedness and the emergence of unconscious experience. *Contemporary Psychoanalysis*, 1 (42): 13–29.

Wolf, A., Schwartz, E., McCarty, G., & Goldberg, I. (1970) *Beyond the Couch: Dialogues in Teaching and Learning Psychanalysis in Groups*. New York: Science House.

Wright, F. (2004) Being seen, moved, disrupted and reconfigured: Group leadership from a relational perspective. *International Journal of Group Psychotherapy*, 54 (2): 235–250.

Wright, F. (2005) Valuing enactments in group therapy: Discussion of three case studies. *Group*, 29 (4): 399–406.

Yalom, I.D. & Leszcz, M. (2005) *The Theory and Practice of Group Psychotherapy*. New York: Basic Books.

Chapter 2

Being Seen, Moved, Disrupted, and Reconfigured

Group Leadership from a Relational Perspective

Fred Wright

I entered group therapy with Hugh Mullan in 1960 and he and the group had a profound impact on my life. I was a young man of twenty-four at that time and was having difficulty getting along with people, particularly successfully connecting with women. These problems were due to a number of family and cultural factors, chief amongst those being the dissonant nature of my relationship with my mother.

There were two sources of help for me in the group: the group itself, of course, and Hugh. There were a number of psychologically sophisticated members in the group, two women in particular, who, shall we say, vigorously de-constructed my conflicts and fears regarding women and intimacy. Hugh's help came largely from the way he behaved in the group. This was the heyday of classical orthodox psychoanalysis and the blank screen, or non-involved, "objective" therapist. Hugh, however, was no blank screen. To the contrary, he was open, emotional, and very spontaneous. He would do things that at that time in the evolution of psychotherapy were quite unorthodox. He would act in a fashion that could appear puzzling, "not nice," and even weird from a conventional perspective. For example, he would tell his own dreams, disclose feelings, make non-logical associations and in other ways reveal his own raw subjectivity. He modeled unguarded, authentic, affective involvement. His way of behaving was, oddly enough, comforting for me in that it established that I was not alone in my own "weirdness." Or in a more benevolent way of saying it, I was not alone with my own unique subjectivity. Using the language of contemporary psychotherapy, I felt "held" by his behavior.

One event took place with Hugh that I believe was especially helpful for me. One day he was sitting in group next to another group member, a woman, with his eyes closed and looking very relaxed; in fact he looked like he could be asleep. A group member commented to him, "You look very comfortable Hugh, why's that?" He opened his eyes and immediately responded with "Because I'm sitting next to a woman." Now I don't remember how other members responded to that unguarded, apparently very spontaneous expression of his, nor do I know what he might have been responding to that was going on in the group process at that time. In fact he didn't appear to be concerned about the group process at all. He looked like he was, as he said, simply enjoying his own inner experience of sitting next to a woman. I do, however, know his response had a big impact on me and continues to do so to this day as demonstrated by my addressing it in this chapter over forty years later.

Here was a high-status psychiatrist who personified and occupied the role-defined hierarchical aspect of the therapeutic relationship that Hoffman (1998) discusses, openly revealing, in a professional situation with a number of people looking at him, that sitting next to a woman made him feel comfortable enough to close his eyes and rest. This really impressed me because up to that point I could never have admitted in public that I had such feelings about women, or even have admitted such feelings to myself for that matter. I had concluded that women could only be sources of comfort in a sexual way. Beyond that they were trouble and needed to be kept at a distance. Hugh's response in that context stimulated a whole new way of thinking and feeling in me, namely that it's safe to relax in mixed company, if you will. When I first joined the group, I had concluded in a semi-conscious fashion that I would probably never marry since marriage didn't work as vigorously demonstrated by many of the members of my original family. However, I did know I had to find a way to get along with people, particularly women since I definitely needed and wanted them. When I left the group five years later, I was solidly married and have stayed married to the same woman to this day.

Let it be noted that this interaction with Hugh, that turned out to be so important for me, could not have occurred in individual therapy because there would not be a woman present for Hugh to respond to. His willingness to reveal his own feelings with such directness presented me with a real-life drama that stimulated me to move in new directions, directions that were out of conscious consideration until this event happened.

Mullan's willingness to do this—disclose his unguarded subjectivity—made us equals in our humanness and need to be connected, and this approach is consistent with notions of contemporary relational authors such as Aron (1996), Benjamin (1992), Hoffman (1998), Mitchell (1988), and Miller (1976). To my mind the incident I just described and other aspects of Hugh's work including his publications shows that he was ahead of his time. He was already functioning as a relationalist and moreover was doing it in group therapy. With regard to the latter, he was even ahead of the contemporary relationalists just mentioned in that he understood that a relational approach to therapy could be practiced in group therapy in addition to individual therapy, something most of the relational writers have not addressed at all. Thus the model I am presenting here is not so new after all. Gifted or intuitive therapists like Mullan have been practicing it all along. It was just not as codified or formally worked out as it has been in the last fifteen to twenty years.

As mentioned, the notions developed by the relationalists have not been fully applied to group therapy and I would like to select and review some of the ideas coming from this school that I think are particularly applicable to the conduct of analytic group therapy. An analytic group, as distinguished from other kinds of groups designed to help people with psychiatric problems (e.g., social skills training groups), is one that focuses on dysfunctional relationship patterns and the goal is to bring about personal change and particularly change in the way group members relate to other people.

A notion of central importance to many relational theoreticians is that of enactment. It is hard to know exactly when this term started to be used in psychotherapy discourse. Eagle, Jacobs, Kohut and McLaughlin have all been credited as using it starting in the late 1970s and/or 1980s (Ellman & Moskowitz, 1998). There is no agreed-upon definition in the field and the term appears to mean different things across different theoretical positions. For example, psychoanalysts tend to see it as a difficulty, while others view it as a desirable event in the therapeutic interaction. The school of thought I am reviewing here falls into the "enactment as desirable" category.

An enactment is typically defined as an automatic, unformulated, non-reflective moment involving all participants in the therapeutic interaction. It can be deleterious or beneficial, repeating old traumas or advancing new experiences of growth. It differs from acting out in that it is mainly an interactive concept reflecting what occurs in the relationship between patient(s) and therapist, that is, it refers to the ways in which patient and therapist act upon one another verbally and non-verbally in the therapy setting. It is also thought of as the only way available to the patient to communicate an inner inchoate experience that he/she wants to address in therapy. In addition, it is stressed that the therapist is usually unconsciously involved in the process. The interpersonal psychoanalysts Levenson (1983) and Wolstein (1993) emphasize this part of the process and describe therapists as "unwitting coparticipants" in the interaction. This notion of unwitting or unconscious participation by therapists gets to the heart of the matter for relationalists. They espouse the inevitability of therapists using and communicating their own subjectivities, or, to use the more traditional term, countertransference, in the therapeutic interaction. Thus from this school of thought enactments are inevitable, bidirectional, and mutual and contain great therapeutic potential.

Davies (1999), a leading relational writer, says the relational model is most accurately defined in terms of continual movement from one enactment to the next, that is, in doing relational psychoanalytic psychotherapy we move from enactment to enactment because that is the way the unconscious reveals itself. We only "know" the territory we have "left" because we have some perspective on it. But we have far less knowledge of the territory we now "occupy" because we are right smack in the middle of it and can't yet feel its borders. Therapy from this perspective then is the ongoing examination or processing of these enactments or "unwitting" interactions between patients and therapists. This means both parties must not only be willing to be observed or seen, but also that it is inevitable: it is beyond the therapist's control. However, the therapist does know about enactments and inevitable countertransferential reactions and is therefore prepared to step back and examine the interactions. This is the observing part of the notion of "observing participation," which portrays the therapist as both in and outside the interaction.

Group therapists have known about this matter of examining the interaction for some time and have addressed it through what Yalom (1985) calls "process commentary." Here he is referring to the analysis of the here-and-now interactions and behaviors that unfold between group members and between the leader and members during a group session. He's distinguishing between attending to the verbal content of a discussion on the one hand and the nature of the relationship between individuals who are interacting with one another on the other hand. This, of course, is a core procedure in analytic group therapy. Yalom, however, does not attend very thoroughly to the issue of the subjectivity of the group therapist and how that may manifest in the interactions with the group or individual members. This appears to be the case generally in the group therapy literature with the exception of the work of Hugh Mullan, as mentioned earlier.

Writers from the relational perspective also conceive of transference and countertransference in non-traditional ways. Transference has usually been understood in the context of psychopathology and treatment and has been seen as a *distortion* of reality, a carrying over of representations and anxieties from the past into present life and especially into the treatment situation. The relationalists (e.g., Aron, 1996) have re-defined it, emphasizing perspectivism, the philosophical view that the world may be understood through a variety of belief systems and that there is no one true vision of reality. From this point of view, transference is not thought of as distortion, but rather one way amongst many to perceive and understand experience. Each view is a plausible construction. That is, there is no one authoritative independent view of reality, but many plausible versions other than one's own.

Relationalists (e.g, Slavin, 1994), in addition, define transference positively as a developmental and adaptive phenomena. Looked at this way, transference can be seen as an effort by patients to induce or compel a complementary response from others to meet their needs, that is, it's an effort to regulate the other. Humans, due to developmental experiences, are striving to maneuver others to provide the gratifications they need. So from this angle it is not a distortion of the present by the past but rather a *creation* of a past reality in the present and it may serve either adaptive or destructive purposes depending on how it fits with the present social environment.

Thus people engage in mutual efforts to "pull" each other, or try to pull each other, into some sort of response that matches preconceived wishes, expectations and needs. In sum we try to make present others more like the people we have known in the past. People do this to their therapists and we describe this as transference. When the therapist inevitably responds to the pull, often in a complementary fashion, we call that countertransference and the interaction is called an enactment.

This way of looking at transference, as well as the perspectivist view, puts us in a better position to understand its resolute and determined nature and the consequent powerful impact patients can have on therapists and the groups we place them in. As Slavin (1994) puts it, "we're targets, and we put ourselves there" (p. 269). Improvising on this metaphor, it might then be said that doing group therapy is a bit like putting oneself in front of a firing squad. However, and to paraphrase Aron (1996), since our goal is to facilitate patients' awareness of their impact on us and our awareness of our impact on them and, when doing group therapy to facilitate members' awareness of their impact on each other, we therapists must be prepared to be closely examined, analyzed, and influenced by patients in the service of *their* psychological needs.

From this perspective, group therapy might be thought of as a sensible effort by therapists to get help in coping with these powerful transference maneuvers and the resulting emotional or countertransference responses. Thus not only is group treatment helpful for many of the reasons discussed in the group literature such as providing multiple sources of feedback rather than relying only on the therapist's ability to understand, but it also provides additional "eyes" to see what's going on if and when the therapist's vision is impaired by her or his own inevitable subjectivity.

Additionally, it can be argued that the blank-screen approach to therapy as well as other technical strategies such as assigning homework, hypnosis, structured group exercises and sitting out of sight of the patient are, at least partially, efforts to avoid what the patient is trying to do to the therapist. That is, they can be regarded as attempts to defend against the powerful and often distressing and disruptive feelings stimulated by unfettered transferences.

From a relational point of view, then, the primary therapeutic task is not so much striving to gain genetic insight as it is an effort to offer patients a safe place and enough genuine concern so that their inevitable effects on the people they are relating to can be examined and processed. This stance does not require a deliberate courting of enactments or undisciplined self-disclosure by the therapist. It does require, though, that therapists' responses be seen as part of a complex relational situation in which the patients' efforts to influence and the complementary responses to those efforts be sorted out. The central matter is not the origins of the therapists' countertransference but the therapist's *capacity* to make the entire process examinable and not simply unconsciously enacted. In dyadic analytic therapy, interaction is limited, by definition, to two participants. Analytic *group* therapy has the advantage of providing a forum where a variety of transferential perspectives and consequent interactions can emerge for examination—for example, peer transferences as well as authority transferences.

Also one of the reasons for examining members' and leaders' relational enactments and associated beliefs, needs, and expectations is to create doubt in group members' minds regarding their perspectives on how to relate and/or develop relationships. The therapy group is especially valuable in such an enterprise because so many different perspectives on relating are revealed during group interaction, that is, there is a pluralism of perspectives on display. As the group culture comes to reflect the norm that all perspectives are subject to examination, members, including leaders, have the chance to re-visit and reconsider their own idiosyncratic constructions of reality.

In addition, this processing or examining of all the group interactions, including the leader's, serves to model mutuality to all members. Mutuality is prized by the relational school. It refers to the fact that all parties in the therapy setting are undergoing experiences and reactions, and that each influences and is being influenced by the other or others in an ongoing fashion. In mutuality one extends oneself out to the other and is also receptive to the impact of the other. In short, the therapeutic process is reciprocal.

Writers (e.g., Miller, 1976) associated with the Stone Center at Wellesley College have developed a theory relevant to this discussion called the Relational–Cultural Model of human development. They especially emphasize therapy as a process that helps build mutuality or, to use one of their related terms, relational competence. According to them, developing mutuality skills means seeing the self as interactive and growing through relations with others rather than developing a separate, cut-off, autonomous self. Relational competence skills include the abilities to integrate while vulnerable, to negotiate and work through conflict while in relationship, and to be responsive rather than defensively closed to others.

Jessica Benjamin (1992) has addressed this matter of responsivity to others through her notion of mutual recognition. This refers to the need of the self to be recognized by another. Being recognized means one is acknowledged by another person as "an equivalent center of experience" (p. 28), and begins, "with the other's confirming response, which tells us that we have created meaning (and) had an impact" (p. 33). Group therapy is a particularly apt way to develop these skills. Members learn mutuality skills by observing them in action between members and between leaders and members. These skills, or ineptness at such, are always on display or being demonstrated in unstructured, primary groups. The analytic therapy group is designed to promote enactment and examination of the mutual impact people have on each other.

Pollack and Slavin (1998) use the notion of agency to discuss this matter of recognition in some detail. They say agency is represented by the internalized experience of being able to have an impact on one's relational world and that the disruption of this experience is the source of emotional trouble. The idea is that the therapist must be *seen* as seeing or recognizing the patient and also being moved or affected by the patient. This facilitates patients' development of a sense of personal agency, a sense that "I matter." They and Benjamin are describing an oscillation that takes place between an assertion of personal agency and self-interest and a state of mutual recognition and vulnerability. This takes place on both sides of the therapy relationship. In order to establish a real connection, both parties must have an impact on each other, that is, both must allow the other to have an impact on one's self.

From this perspective therapists must relate to patients in a fully authentic way that reveals or exposes parts of themselves. Any obfuscating by the therapist "undermines the patient's chance to regain not only a sense of the potential accuracy of her own perceptions but also of her agency as a perceiver and as an agent in the real interpersonal world" (Pollack & Slavin, p. 866). Further, the validation must be real and authentic rather than a self-conscious attempt to attune oneself to the patient's perceptions. The authors add that when therapists act in a way that is not congruent with their own experience, they rob patients of their sense of agency because therapists are immersed in their own agenda about what is in the patients' best interests. This amounts to a refusal to let the patient have an impact on the therapist, rather than entering into an authentic negotiation of responsibility and agency. They argue that a blank-screen approach and other technical innovations are efforts by therapists to guard against the patient's impact and ways to avoid being moved in real, unpremeditated ways, that is, they are defenses against vulnerability. Mullan's behavior, in the clinical vignette described initially, accords with this point of view. His willingness to allow a member of the group to impact him, and to allow that impact to be seen, turned out to be quite beneficial for me.

This raises the controversial issue of therapist self-disclosure which is presently under discussion by many schools of therapy, and it also refers to a significant difference between self psychologists on the one hand and relational psychoanalysts on the other. These two models of psychoanalytic psychotherapy have much in common but differ on this matter of therapist self disclosure. The position of Pollack and Slavin (1998) just summarized represents the thinking of a number of the relational analysts cited here.

Other contemporary psychoanalytic writers challenge this position, however. Teicholz (1999), for example, has discussed this matter in considerable detail. She reviews a debate now taking place between self psychologists and analysts from the relational school. (She refers to the latter group as "the postmoderns.") The latter, as described above, call for the spontaneous expression of the therapist's subjectivity arguing that it is in the patients' best interest for therapists to be seen by them as they really are. Patients' active exploration of the therapist's subjectivity, according to this view, is required for the patient to develop his or her own subjectivity. Self psychologists (as well as some relational analysts, e.g., Slochower, 1996), however, contend that therapist subjectivity needs to be "set aside" for some patients until they are developmentally more advanced and can tolerate subjectivities different from their own. They say we need to vary our responsiveness to patients accordingly, lest it be experienced as traumatic impingement.

This is a debate that is complicated and may never be fully resolved given the complex and varying nature of human personalities. As group therapists, however, we may consider the possibility that the group approach may help us address this dilemma. If the therapist is unable or unwilling to be present in his or her full, authentic subjectivity, either because of personal style or theoretical position, or if an individual patient in a group cannot tolerate the therapist's raw subjectivity, there may be others in the group who may be able to be there for the patient in the way that is needed. For example, counterdependent group members, as a consequence of their particular transference, often find relating to an authority figure like the group leader to be quite a toxic experience, no matter how the leader behaves. They often can only get the kind of connection they need to continue the work of therapy through bonding with peers, people who do not have any kind of authority over them.

There's another variable to consider when thinking about the disagreements over the matter of therapists' disclosing their subjectivity to patients. It is possible that patients may vary as a function of their character structure or defense style regarding which of these approaches they may need. Or patients may vary in the course of their therapy, requiring one approach at one stage in their therapy and the other at some other point in time.

McWilliams (1991) has presented some related ideas that may help with this dispute. She has written on mothering and fathering processes in psychoanalytic treatment, and, according to her, patients emphasize the *attitude* of the therapist when describing what helped. Specifically, they distinguish between a mothering attitude that emphasizes the expression of understanding, affective resonance, and flexibility of technique and a paternal attitude that stresses the importance of boundaries, interpretation, expertise, and distance from contaminating countertransference.

She says that, in fact, both attitudes are necessary and that effective therapists, irrespective of actual gender, are able to express both attitudes when necessary. Patients often need one or the other at different times and the therapist may need to respond accordingly. Thus self-disclosure may be helpful at one point in therapy, but not at another. It's also interesting to note that these two attitudes parallel the evolution of psychoanalytic therapy with the early classical model resembling the paternal style and the more contemporary relational style corresponding to the maternal.

As illustrated by my history I regard group therapy highly. However, from time to time over the years I have run into psychotherapists, often psychoanalysts, who have a very negative, even hostile, attitude toward group therapy. For example, one very prominent and senior analyst at the psychotherapy training program I attended in the 1970s said to me upon learning that I was conducting a therapy group, "You do *that*?" As she uttered "that" the expression on her face contorted into one of great horror. This was an attitude that prevailed then and still does to this day.

I'd like to explore some of the possible sources of this defensive reaction on the part of many therapists to group work and also point out that even group therapists have considerable resistance to doing group therapy. Billow (2000) makes the point that the kind of "emotional thinking" that accompanies examining or analyzing enactments in therapy hurts, and, I would add, doing it in group can amplify the hurt. He describes a universal tendency to avoid suffering the process of meaning making, and further says "the therapist, as well as the group and its members, ambivalently approach emotional thinking since it causes mental pain, and (the group) makes unconscious 'decisions' at various moments to evade or modify the meaning-making process" (p. 245). In short, thinking hurts both group members and the group therapist and may lead to evasive action.

Emotional thinking leads to changing, disrupting and/or re-organizing one's emotional and psychological structures. Said again, analyzing enactments and one's part in them is a thinking/meaning-making activity and this hurts. Revealing or exposing one's self in public (i.e., in group) runs the risk of setting oneself up for shame and humiliation. It's noteworthy that many of the interactions around fees, payment of money, and scheduling between clients and other professionals in our society like medical doctors, dentists, and lawyers are often handled by the professional's secretary. These professionals therefore are protected from the conscious and unconscious feelings both parties bring to such transactions, particularly money transactions. These are exactly the interactions and associated feelings and possible enactments that may well need to be observed and analyzed by psychotherapists and therapy groups. Calling attention to enactments around such matters, catching people off guard if you will, can stimulate anxiety and even rage.

Billow (2001) also notes that forming a new group or adding new members can stir difficult feelings for all involved. For example, adding new members to an ongoing group causes disruptions of the status quo for all members of the group, including the leader. New enactments are inevitable, thereby forcing new analytic work to take place. The group leader, in particular, has to stretch and accommodate to the new interactions and face her or his own "unwitting coparticipations" and accompanying emotional experiences.

The notion of complementarity is helpful here. New patients and new group members evoke new parts of the self and cause internal and external reconfigurations for all. Further, new members lead to different sub-group combinations, which, in turn, may well pull new parts from the therapist that were not induced in the old combination of patients. All of this of course may unconsciously be enacted by the group therapist in front of group members, thus compounding the therapist's exposure to being seen as possibly "wrong" or "foolish" by many as opposed to only one. When dealing with only one observer, we may be able to get away with covering it up (or possibly summoning the distortion view of transference to rescue us), but when there are many eyes seeing us, we are likely to stand revealed and have to face our own contributions to the unfolding, possibly very tumultuous, drama.

Being seen making mistakes or doing "bad" can be shame and guilt producing. Shame, guilt, and humiliation are some of the most painful affects humans can suffer. Also the chances of being "caught" in an enactment are much greater in group because there are so many more people observing the leader. Said another way, and in the spirit of postmodernism, there are many more possible constructions of the leader by the group.

One can also feel guilty over disrupting the status quo in striving to foster growth by undoing through analysis the stability individuals and groups work hard to attain. Additionally, there is the fear that can emerge when the de-stabilized group directs its rage at the leader for disrupting them. The group can threaten him or her with loss of control and/or aggression.

Another unattractive feeling we group therapists can experience (and perhaps being observed experiencing it) is envy of smart, insightful group members who may pick up on things we do not. Group members often have greater wisdom on topics unfamiliar to us. Although we think of the increase in the number of observer/analysts as one of the advantages of group therapy as mentioned earlier, it may also generate competition and envy in us.

In sum, examining enactments disrupts the status quo, and the quest for certainty and freedom from anxiety and unpredictability is undone. Stimulating or creating new social configurations means we must be prepared to tolerate the anxiety and stress that accompanies these new arrangements or new internal and external structures. Finally, these emotional experiences can be amplified or inflamed for the group and therapist by whole group processes such as emotional contagion, groupthink, deindividuation and group polarization dynamics.

Given all this we might consider the possibility that therapists may select people for their groups who fit what Mitchell (1988) has called our "internalized relational configurations" in order to minimize discomfort. To what extent do we select members for our groups who are consciously and unconsciously familiar to us and thus "safe"? Might we select according to ethnic, racial, sexual orientation, or religious similarity? Or could we select people with personality styles or defense mechanisms and/or needs that complement our own, thereby protecting ourselves from being seen, moved, and re-organized?

Dedication and Acknowledgments

This chapter is dedicated to the memory of Hugh Mullan, MD. He died on March 22, 2003. The text was originally presented as a paper at a conference sponsored by the National Group Psychotherapy Institute of The Washington School of Psychiatry on April 4, 2003.

The author would like to thank Drs. Robert Friedman and Les Greene for their editorial comments.

References

Aron, L. (1996) *A Meeting of Minds: Mutuality in Psychoanalysis*. Hillsdale, NJ: Analytic Press.

Benjamin, J. (1992) *Recognition and Destruction: An Outline of Intersubjectivity*. Hillsdale, NJ: Analytic Press.

Billow, R.M. (2000) Relational levels of the "container-contained" in group therapy. *Group*, 24: 243–259.

Billow, R.M. (2001) The therapist's anxiety and resistance to group. *International Journal of Group Psychotherapy*, 5: 83–100.

Davies, J. (1999) Dissociation, therapeutic enactment and transference-countertransference process. *Gender and Psychoanalysis*, 2: 241–259.

Ellman, S.J. & Moskowitz (eds.) (1998) *Enactment: Toward a New Approach to the Therapeutic Relationship*. Northvale, NJ: Jason Aronson.

Hoffman, I.Z. (1998) *Ritual and Spontaneity in the Psychoanalytic Process*. Hillsdale, NJ: Analytic Press.

Levenson, E.A. (1983) *The Ambiguity of Change: An Inquiry into the Nature of Psychoanalytic Reality*. New York: Basic Books.

McWilliams, N. (1991) Mothering and fathering processes in the psychoanalytic art. *Psychoanalytic Review*, 78: 525–545.

Miller, J.B. (1976) *Toward a New Psychology of Women*. Boston: Beacon Press.

Mitchell, S.A. (1988) *Relational Concepts in Psychoanalysis: An Integration*. Cambridge, MA: Harvard University Press.

Pollack, L. & Slavin, J.H. (1998) The struggle for recognition: Disruption and reintegration in the experience of agency. *Psychoanalytic Dialogues*, 8: 857–873.

Slavin, J. (1994) On making rules: Toward a reformulation of the dynamics of transference in psychoanalytic treatment. *Psychoanalytic Dialogues*, 4: 253–274.

Slochower, J. (1996) Holding and the fate of the analyst's subjectivity. *Psychoanalytic Dialogues*, 6: 323–353.

Teicholz, J.G. (1999) *Kohut, Loewald and the Postmoderns*. Hillsdale, NJ: Analytic Press.

Wolstein, B.J. (1993) Sandor Ferenczi and the American interpersonal relationship. In L. Aron & A. Harris (eds.) *The Legacy of Sandor Ferenczi* (pp. 379–388). Hillsdale, NJ: Analytic Press.

Yalom, I. (1985) *Theory and Practice of Group Psychotherapy*. 3rd edn. New York: Basic Books.

Chapter 3

The Group as an Inevitable Relational Field, Especially in Times of Conflict

Haim Weinberg

Introduction

Participants in a therapy group interact with one another and the relationships formed through the group process become a transformational vehicle. Yalom (1995) defines the process as "the nature of the relationship between interacting individuals" (p. 130). As the group progresses, group members interact more intimately with one another and deeply explore their relationships with the group leader as well, not only through analyzing transferential distortions but also as expressions of authentic relationship (Berman & Weinberg, 1998). The quality of therapeutic relationship in itself is critical in predicting positive therapeutic outcome. This important factor, found in evidence-based literature (Norcross, 2002), only strengthens the focus put on relationship in most group theories.

Group psychotherapy is, in its essence, a relationship-based treatment. But is it enough to say that group members interact and relate to one another and to the group therapist in order to perceive group therapy as relational therapy?

Differences in Traditional Psychoanalytic and Relational/Intersubjective Terms

Before exploring the implications of the relational approaches to group therapy, let me summarize the differences between traditional psychoanalytic and relational ideas in general. This summary might seem basic to some readers, but it is necessary as a way to set the scene and describe the frame of reference for the group leader. So what differentiates the relational/intersubjective approaches from other theories?

> Relational theory is based on the shift from the classical idea that it is the patient's mind that is being studied (where mind is thought as independently and autonomously within the boundaries of the individual) to the relational notion that mind is inherently dyadic, social, interactional, and interpersonal.
> (Aron, 1996, p. x)

If the mind is inherently interactional, nothing is created only by one individual, and we need to look at all the phenomena in therapy as created by both therapist and patient (or, in a group, by all participants). The therapist cannot avoid becoming a participant in this process and should examine his or her contribution to what is going on in the session as well as the patient's contribution.

Transference and Countertransference

In traditional psychoanalysis, transference is considered a distortion, due to the projection of the past onto the present. In relational approaches transference is not regarded as a distortion but as a different view of the world based on one's history and unique needs. The therapist's countertransference, which in traditional psychoanalysis is perceived as a response to the patient's transference, can actually be seen as the therapist's transference. As we are talking about what is going on between the two participants in the session, labeling transference and countertransference as different processes, originating from different sources, is no longer legitimate.

Resistance

Resistance is defined as whatever interrupts the progress of analysis or therapy. Traditionally it always resides within the patient, arising because something in the patient's psyche must be kept from awareness. But is it not possible that what looks like resistance is actually a response to some uncaring acts or miss-attunement of the therapist? Not all resistant behaviors "originate" from the patient. Resistance has an interpersonal meaning and, in individual therapy, can be understood as the outcome of collusion between the therapist and the patient. In the group it might involve the group as a whole.

Interpretation and Change

In the traditional approach, interpretation is seen as the vehicle of change. According to this approach, good interpretations, given at the right timing, help the patient give up previous faulty perceptions and adopt new ways of understanding of the world, thus impacting the patient's behavior. Interpretations are offered by the therapist from what seems like an objective perspective. These assumptions are criticized by relational writers both for impossibility of an objective point of view and for being the only way to change.

If interpretation is not the only vehicle of change, what other mechanisms contribute to change in therapy? Stern et al. (1998) explored "non-interpretive mechanisms of change," discussing "moments of meeting" as a mutative phenomenon. These moments consist of instances where the therapist's responses are fully in attunement with the patient's emotional and psychological state, providing the patient an experience of being deeply understood. It seems that in addition to interpretation, other mutative mechanisms exist, leading to growth and change.

Enactment

In relational psychology, enactment is the focus of attention more than the notion of resistance, transference, and countertransference that governed the scene in traditional psychodynamic approaches. Enactment is defined as an automatic, unformulated, non-reflective moment involving all participants in a therapeutic interaction (Wright, 2004, p. 238). The relational theoreticians argue that therapists will inevitably be drawn into enactments with their patients, and that processing or analyzing enactments is a major component of the therapy. We can conclude that enactments express, variously, resistance, transference, countertransference, unconscious individual, interpersonal, group, and social processes, and that the analysis of enactments should include the acts of both the patients and the therapist.

Dissociation

Enactment cannot be discussed without mentioning the role of dissociation, for what is enacted is that which is dissociated. Dissociation means that some experience that is incompatible with how one ordinarily sees oneself is split off. It refers to whole experiences, thoughts, or self-states that are not admitted into experience. Therefore they are not thought about, and when they stem from a traumatic nature, they are not even registered. We all have "islands of dissociation" and thus dissociation is seen as an inevitable aspect of being human. However, the greater the degree of dissociation, the more contradictory, unstable, and confusing is the sense of self. Dissociation is different from repression because the latest acts upon experiences that have been conscious. The therapist's subjective experience during the session can contain aspects of the patient's experience that have been dissociated. Thus, the patient enacts the dissociative parts, and as long as the therapist cannot reflect on his or her experience and reactions, he or she will participate in the enactment.

Relational vs. Intersubjective Approaches

These approaches are usually mentioned interchangeably. The difference between them lies more on the focus of attention. We can focus on the relational aspect, namely the contribution of both partners to the interaction, or the intersubjective aspect, namely how the subjective experiences of the partners interact. Intersubjective approaches stress that in every meeting there are at least two subjective experiences that meet, each of them with a need for recognition of their subjectivities. Beliefs and theories about the self and others are regarded as phenomenological rather than objective and are most productively viewed as context-related. The two subjectivities of the therapist and the patient come together in the therapeutic session. The patient needs acknowledgment and recognition of his or her subjective experience (Benjamin, 1995).

Of course, there is a difference between Benjamin's and Stolorow's approach. Benjamin (1999) proposes that intersubjectivity depends upon not only correspondence but also difference, and not only upon mutual regulation but also mutual recognition. Stolorow and his colleagues (Stolorow, Brandchaft, & Atwood, 1987) are more interested in the analytic context and see intersubjectivity as constituted by the intersection of two subjectivities: the reciprocal influence of the conscious and unconscious subjectivities of the people in a relationship. For the sake of this chapter, I will use more Benjamin's ideas about mutual recognition as the ability both to recognize and to be recognized by another: we will see how difficult it becomes when we deal with conflict.

Intersubjective theories follow Stern's (1985) observations and research about the importance of mother–infant optimal attunement and mutuality. Updated neuroscience research (Cozolino, 2006) even shows how right-hemisphere networks of attachment, social relationships, and affect regulation are built during childhood in an experience-dependent manner through the attunement of parent and child. Self and interactional regulations (Beebe & Lachmann, 2002) are the result of internalizing secure attachment schemas, and their balance is essential to a person's wellbeing. In therapy, reintegration of these self and other regulation mechanisms is achieved through the therapist–patient attunement. Thus, another important tenet of these approaches is that optimal attunement to the patient's experience, recognizing the other's subjectivity, is most healing to the patient. This notion started with self-psychology which emphasized the importance of empathy in the therapeutic process, but contrary to self-psychology, where the therapist serves as a self-object for the patient, which means that the therapist becomes functional for the patient's developmental needs, in intersubjective approaches the therapist's subjectivity is important as well. This does not necessarily mean an equal relationship, because the focus is still on what serves therapy and the patient's growth, but the therapist might become more transparent and look more carefully at the way he or she contributes to the therapeutic situation.

The advantage of intersubjective and relational approaches is that by highlighting the inescapability of mutual reciprocal influence, they enable therapists to be more aware and accept their contribution to the therapeutic relationship, and provide therapists with an attitude that produces a collaborative response to the inevitable enactments.

Foulkes as a Forerunner of Relational Group Therapy

Foulkes, the founding father of group analysis in Britain, can be considered the pioneer of relational approaches. Long before the distinction between one- and two-person psychologies emerged, he defined group analysis as "the analysis by the group, of the group, including its conductor" (Foulkes, 1975, p. 3). The inclusion of the conductor (the group analyst, in Foulkesian terms) in the analysis introduced the notion that the group therapist's behaviors, thoughts, and feelings are part of the group process and that the therapist is not only the therapist "of" the group, but also "in" the group.

Group analysis preceded its time by emphasizing such intersubjective concepts as multiplicity, mutuality, and radical openness. The idea of the analysis of the group by the group and not by the group analyst grants the group itself a therapeutic position that equals the therapist's position, and redefines the role of the group therapist. The spirit of group analysis conveys an egalitarian view of the group and its leader.

In traditional psychoanalysis, the interpretation of transference and resistance acquires a central role in the mobilization of change. In his radical approach, Foulkes (1964) argued that interpretation follows change rather than precedes it. Instead of interpretation as a primary technique, Foulkes claimed that the group conductor's primary goal is to facilitate the participation in group life by the members of the group. By placing patients face to face in a group, it had become clear to him that the minds of all group members are connected in a web of relationships through which unconscious material flows. The shift from the couch to the group is not only a technical change: think of how projection differs in a group from individual therapy, that is, when a group member holds the disowned parts for another member, rather than the therapist.

Foulkes (1964) introduced several new concepts to the group situation that underscore the importance of group interaction and subjective experience, such as mirroring and resonance:

> Mirror reactions are characteristically brought out when a number of persons meet and interact. The person sees himself, or part of himself—often a repressed part of himself—reflected in the interactions of other group members. He sees them reacting in the way he does himself, who [sic] are in contrast to his own behaviour. He also gets to know himself … by the effect he has on others and the picture they form of him.
>
> (p. 81)

Pines (2003) described resonance as the individual responses that group members make to shared events, each responding at their own level of attunement to the predominant affect in the group. In both concepts the relational aspect is predominant: resonance and mirroring heavily depend on the interactions, relationship, and subjective experiences of the group members to the shared group events.

Wilke (2007) summarizes Foulkes's core ideas pertinent to relational theories in the following sentences:

> First, there is the idea that the individual mind is not self-enclosed but has a translucent boundary through which the 'We' of the belonging group can be

internalized and projected outwards. The second idea suggests that all of us are linked to a shared and invisible network of minds that Foulkes called a matrix.

(p. 429)

Group Therapy and Relational Theory

It seems natural to apply the relational approaches to the group, focusing not just on the relations between the therapist and the patient. In groups we focus on the relationships developing between members, and between therapist and participants. In addition, the more group work deepens, the more we have the possibility to deepen the exploration, expression, recognition, and acknowledgment of the members' subjective experiences. Surely the way to study and explore this social-interactional mind is in the concrete space where interactions are revealed—the group

Gergen (1994) stresses the relational nature of the human mind. He claims that meaning is produced by and located in the context of continuing relationships. Psychotherapy, from this perspective, is dedicated to mutual exploration of the interpersonal milieu. If we want to explore this interpersonal milieu and the relationships of more than two people (that one of them is automatically positioned as an authority), we need to move from the dyad to the group arena. All the relational ideas, from exploring relationships in vivo to finding how both therapist and group member participate and contribute to the interaction, are best addressed in the group.

Another advantage of the group from the intersubjective point of view is the ability and easiness of revealing the subjective experience of the participants. The group inevitably creates a conflict between the members' need to assert themselves and the others' need for their subjectivity to be recognized. There is a continuous contrast between joining/similarity vs. subjectivity/individuality: we vs. me. These contrasting needs are in the center of any relationship and become a major focal conflict in the group. Sometimes they are more in the background. Other times, like in instances of conflicts in the group, they are in the eye of the storm. Benjamin (1995) pointed out that intersubjectivity is about these simultaneously existing conflicting needs, and that healthy relationships prevail when both partners' subjectivities are recognized and acknowledged. Where else can we strive to achieve this goal if not in a group? In every group session the patient is called upon not only to express his or her subjective thoughts and feelings but also to relate to the problems and personalities of the other members, being sensitive to their needs too. In short, the patient is asked to bring forward one's subjective experience, while simultaneously serving as a quasi-therapist to the other, recognizing the other's subjective experience. Finding a way to do both can be best learned in a group, where group members are peers whose individualities should be taken into consideration.

The group is also a suitable space to witness and experience multiple self-states. According to the intersubjective approach, we have multiple parts or states of mind that possess varying degrees of compatibility with one another. Different relational contexts reveal different self-states. Because the group is rich with possibilities for different interactions and relations, we can easily explore how a member's different self-states emerge in response to others in the group.

Billow (2003) uses Bion's concepts and ideas to illuminate intersubjective processes in the group. He claims that "the concept of container-contained describes relationships that are dynamic and fluctuating, cognitively multilevel, and interpersonally multidimensional. We come to learn about and represent intersubjective experience at various developmental levels of thought" (p. 112). Billow relates especially to the relational nature of projective identification as described by Bion (1962). According to Bion, the normally empathic mother introjects her baby's projections, elaborates, processes, deciphers, and communicates them back to the infant aspects of his or her psychic experience beyond his or her cognitive and emotional capacity. This prototype of projective identification is communicative in nature and involves two persons.

But describing Bion's approach in groups as relational is quite misleading. It is true that the container-contained concept is relational, but apart from this stance (which was not attributed by Bion specifically to the group leader), Bion describes the group therapist as a "bizarre object" (Bion, 1967), positioned outside the group circle, illuminating the group processes with a beam of darkness. The group leader is not perceived as participating in the group process at all, in contrast to the Foulksian approach mentioned before.

Apart from Billow's book (2003), only a few papers connecting group therapy to relational approaches have been published, although their number is beginning to increase. A selection of these papers and their main focus follows.

Weegman (2001) demonstrates some of the obstacles and defensiveness arising from the more classical analytic tradition, whether applied to individuals or to groups, and suggests that intersubjectivity theory illuminates group as well as individual processes. He is one of the first to demonstrate the similarity between group analytic ideas and intersubjective ones.

Wright (2004) focused on the concept of enactment and its importance in intersubjectivity and applied it to groups. Enactment typically involves the two partners in therapy. The therapist is unconsciously entrapped in this enactment and contributes to its creation, existence, and maintenance. As relational psychotherapy in practice involves moving from enactment to enactment, the group is *the* arena for enactments. All the group members and the therapist participate both in creating these enactments and in their exploration.

Grossmark (2007) conceives groups as being composed of many multiple selves, and the process of group psychotherapy as unfolding through enactments that involve the whole group and the group therapist. He focuses on the group therapist's role of holding and containing intense affect throughout these enactments.

The issue of "the difficult patient in groups" can explain how in relational terms the patient can be seen in a less pathologizing way as understandably protecting himself in the group situation. The term "difficult patient" has come to refer in the group therapy literature, at the very least, to those with borderline and narcissistic personality disorder (Roth, Stone, & Kibel, 1990). Often it refers to a range of severe personality disorders, including schizoid, paranoid, histrionic, avoidant, dependent, and sometimes even anti-social personalities. Many of these show elements of borderline and narcissistic pathology, including projection of blame, distrust or paranoid thinking, and narcissistic rage, and have a range of narcissistic fantasies. However, Gans and Alonso (1998) applied intersubjective theory to the understanding of the difficult patient in the group. They argue that from this perspective, therapist and group members construct together the difficult patient, without appreciating how they themselves contribute to this construction and what it serves in the group. Their paper demonstrates how intersubjective/relational ideas can be successfully applied to specific phenomena in group therapy, while still avoiding the trap of a radical position that a difficult patient does not exist. Rather than conceptualizing the dynamic as stimulated by the patient's narcissism, inability to tolerate criticism is seen as context dependent.

The traditional ways of recognizing and disentangling from one's countertransference in individual therapy are self-reflection, supervision, and the therapist's own therapy. But when entering the complicated field of enactment, these ways may not be enough: the therapist should be exceptionally thoughtful and honest in understanding his or her own contribution to this mutual dance of transference–countertransference enactment. Bringing the situation to supervision tackles the difficulty of telling the story only from one point of view. The same problem goes for the therapist's therapy: the patient is not in the room, and the therapist's therapist cannot observe the interaction in the here-and-now.

But when we move to group therapy, the solution to this problem lies at hand, and is right in front our eyes. The group itself is there to witness the interaction and comment on it. The therapist does not have to tell the supervisor what happened, because the group, serving as a covert supervisor, can help both sides explore and understand the process. Wright (2005) has written that "the group therapist is particularly fortunate, for, in addition to these methods of discovery, the group therapist has the group" (p. 400). Of course, the group therapist who wants to use the group members' minds for analyzing the process, including the therapists' contributions, should drop defensiveness and be open to the participants' comments. Allowing oneself to participate in the enactment together with the group members, and then non-defensively listening to what the members have to say, and verbalizing the therapist's subjective self-experience, can be a very powerful tool in the group process.

The Role of the Group Therapist in Relational Group Therapy

Yalom (1995) counts three fundamental tasks of the group therapist: creating and maintenance of the group, culture building, and activation and illumination of the here-and-now. Rutan and Stone (2007) mention that the most useful activities of the group therapist are internal ones, such as feeling, empathizing, and hypothesizing in order to further understanding for group members. Although we can find many lists of group leadership skills needed for group therapy or group counseling (see Corey, 1995, for a list of twenty-two detailed skills), in general, we can talk about the cognitive roles of the therapist (thinking, analyzing, interpreting) vs. the emotional roles (feeling, empathizing, containing).

These two aspects of the group leader's role connect with the two tiers Yalom (1995) mentions in relation to the here-and-now: the experiencing tier, and the illumination of the process level. "Accordingly, the therapist has two discrete functions in the here-and-now: to steer the group into the here-and-now and to facilitate the self-reflective loop (or process commentary)" (p. 130). Unfortunately, Yalom does not discuss the emotional involvement of the therapist in the here-and-now as associated with the experiencing tier. He sees the therapist's task as "steering" the group, usually by focusing on the interactions and how people feel one toward the other.

Fortunately, other authors did relate to the therapist's emotional involvement as important in the progress of the group. This is especially true of Ormont who wrote: "the worst therapists are those out of touch with their feelings ... the best therapists experience a great range of feelings. They let themselves feel nearly everything" (1992, p. 52). Ormont assumes that it is simply a question of whether therapists let themselves feel. He seems to ignore the existence of feelings that therapists are unaware of, and these are very much what the relational approach deals with.

Actually, the role of the group therapist is deeply connected with the theory that the therapist holds. In the traditional psychodynamic theories, the group therapist is a transference object and should interpret the underlying emotional themes around this transference as well as the unconscious dynamics taking place in the group (such as the basic assumptions according to Bion, 1962). When it comes to relational/intersubjective theories, the presence of the therapist as a subject and the quality of the therapeutic relationship is more important for change than insight acquired through interpretations. Interpretations made in the absence of the therapeutic relationship are probably not very useful, although they certainly are significant in patients consolidating the gains they have made and an understanding of what has happened to them in their therapeutic relationship. The empathic attunement of the therapist is crucial to the healing process.

Stone (2001) emphasizes the role of the therapist's affect in conducting treatment, and recounts many sources for the therapist's emotional responses, whether they arise from the therapist, the relationship between therapist and patient, the patient, social and cultural values, and so on. The group introduces additional pressures that have a powerful impact upon clinicians' feelings. When enactment in the group unfolds, the therapist must be able to contain and hold the group through this process. The strong enactments that groups create call for adding a different role of the group leader: "Such a group leader is effective by being engaged, moved, and changed along with the group" (Grossmark, 2007, p. 495). Group therapists should not (actually cannot) avoid being drawn into these enactments, but they need to let the emotions flow through them, staying in touch with the feelings, even living a short period of confusion, anxiety, and instability, while emerging from this process with more understanding of what is happening in the enactment.

The above statements do not mean that group therapists should totally give up confrontation, interpretation, or analysis of group processes and even resistance. For example, when an anti-group phenomenon occurs (Nitsun, 1996), the therapist should point out the destructive forces and help the group change this process and use them in a creative way. When scapegoating governs the group scene, it is imperative for the group therapist to intervene in order to prevent damage for both the excluded-attacked member and the other group participants. Still, this could be done from an intersubjective point of view. (For an example of an intersubjective perspective of scapegoating, see Cohen & Schermer, 2002.) Some enactments are worthy of limit-setting, confrontation, and interpretation, although these therapist-based responses are also intersubjective responses and enactments in their own right.

Some readers might wonder whether the idea of mutuality, central to relational theories, does not mean that the group therapist becomes one of the group members. Aron (1996) stresses that mutuality does not equate symmetry or equality. He explains the word mutuality as a sharing in common or a sharing between people. He brings the example of mutual admiration between a teacher and a student, while each maintains the status and position.

The Task of the Group Leader in Times of Conflict

In times of group conflict, the safe space is threatened. An intense conflict between two or more group members, usually breaking out suddenly and escalating very quickly, can become very distressful for both the members participating in the fight and the observing group members. Such a conflict, if unresolved satisfactorily, may lead to the emotional withdrawal of some of the members (both those involved and those who did not seem to be part of the conflict) and even to premature group termination of one of the parties involved (usually feeling hurt and misunderstood). It might create more caution of group members around self-disclosure or giving authentic feedback, and can have a long-standing impact on the group, demonstrated in a kind of an impasse as if the group is stuck. Sometimes, even months after the event seems to be forgotten, the group is still conflict-avoidant and tiptoes around any expression of difference of opinions.

The development of such a conflict usually involves massive mechanisms of projections, splitting, and projective identification. Both partners feel misunderstood and misinterpreted. Usually, the outburst of the conflict is not only due to difference of opinions or simple disagreement (that can regularly be resolved by discussion and negotiation), but also involves hurt. One group member usually feels deeply hurt by the other (whether for justified "objective" reasons or as a result of narcissistic vulnerable self). As a result, this member retaliates and attacks the other person, believing that this attack is justified, and in an effort to hurt the other in return. The end result is that both parties are deeply hurt and as the conflict evolves, it does not matter any more who started the fight. They see the other as their "enemy" and project on him or her the characteristics of a bad object. The "other" is perceived as mean, full of negative intentions, untrustworthy, and threatening. Just as it happens in social conflicts, perceiving the "other" as such means that we focus on how different and better we are, leading to depersonalizing and even dehumanizing the person with whom we have a fight. When happening in the group, the fact that other members observe the scene exerts more pressure on the conflict-participating partners. Both feel that they are totally right and the other is totally wrong. More than that, they feel that injustice is done to them and they demand justice. They might become righteous and fight viciously to prove their justice. Because this struggle takes place in front of the others, an element of shame and "saving face" is added to the fight, and each of the partners becomes sensitive, counting how many people support them and how many do not. Group members who do not support them are easily considered against them, and when someone gives any negative feedback to one of the partners in conflict, he or she belongs to the "enemy" side. Each partner tries hard to convince the group that they are right and to recruit more group members to support them. Thus, splitting becomes prevalent and an atmosphere of Us and Them governs the scene (Berman, Berger, & Gutmann, 2000). Similar processes are observed in social conflicts, and can easily be analyzed in large groups (Weinberg & Schneider, 2003). They are strongly personified in a small group.

Using Ghent's (1999) terms of submission and surrender, we can say that in times of conflict described above, each partner is stuck in a submission position. In this situation there is no ability to move and the participants are locked and submit to their subjective experiences. Laor (2009) describes submission in a way that is very relevant to conflict situations: "In such situations, each partner is driven (unconsciously) to an "I am Right" position, *I am the victim of the situation, I only wanted what was best*, and so on" (p. 489). In contrast, surrender "convey a quality of liberation and expansion of the self as corollary to the letting down of defensive barriers" (Ghent, 1999, p. 213).

What is the role of the group therapist in these incidents from the intersubjective point of view? Apparently, the therapist should help the participants move from submission to surrender. The task is to restore the safe space as a place of reflection and processing. The main difficulty of such conflicts is that the participating partners lose the ability to see one another's subjectivity (Benjamin, 1998), and unless this ability is restored, each of them continues to be convinced that they are holding the "objective" truth, while only the other is inflicting pain and creating injustice. Hurt and pain make people very self-centered and disable their ability to see that the other suffers as well. From an intersubjective perspective, these group members (and sometimes all the others actively or passively involved in the conflict) fall into the trap of believing that injustice is done only to them and that they themselves are not doing any injustice. It is almost impossible to keep in mind the relativity and subjectivity of the experience, and, moreover, it is very difficult to remember that the other's subjectivity is legitimate. This is where the group leader is called upon to intervene. Perhaps in times of conflict the group therapist should move slightly and temporarily from being a participant in the interaction, to standing outside of the action. The therapist can use a different part of his/her self in order to restore the group safety. The concrete task of the leader is to help the parties see the other's subjective experience, acknowledge the legitimacy of the different points of view, confirm the fact that all partners involved are hurt, and gently help them to take responsibility for the pain they inflicted upon the other. Mutual recognition of the other's suffering and hurt is the best end-result of such a conflict. The therapist can still use a reflective expression of his or her own subjectivity to enable participants to shift their self-states.

In order to achieve this end-result, the group therapist cannot stay passive. This is the time for a very active effort to help both partners express their feelings. Usually, when a group member feels injured, the last thing they want to do is to express the hurt, as they feel so vulnerable and try to avoid exposing themselves to repeated attack. The group therapist should stay attuned to the sound of pain beyond the expression of anger and sometimes rage, and bring those sounds to the forefront. It is a difficult and delicate task to help people who suffer, to open their mouth to express their hurt, to open their ears to listen to the suffering of the other, to open their eyes to see the subjective experience of the other, and especially to open their hearts to acknowledge and recognize the other's pain.

But what happens when the therapist is one of the partners involved in the conflict? The above perspective may not actually work in practice, as the therapist is drawn to enactment, becomes involved in the anger, and often has trouble hearing the pain.

A Group Vignette Analyzed According to Two Different Approaches

> In a supervision group I had led in Israel for group facilitators, the only Islamic member, Mustafa, started behaving in a very defiant way. It happened after he had talked about an event from his work: he was leading a group of battering men and one of his group members became angry with him, after he had cut him off when the man monopolized the group session. Mustafa received some feedback from the supervision group members focusing on how he probably contributed to this situation at work. The group members said that he could have responded to this monopolizer in a gentler way, and tried to convince him how his reaction to the battering man might have come across as

aggressive. Mustafa could not listen. My subjective feeling was that our group members gave him legitimate feedback in a way that I saw as constructive and that Mustafa could learn from these responses, and I said that in the group. Mustafa clearly did not see it this way. He said nothing about the feedback, but withdrew into silence and passive compliance, although he had been more active in the group before this event. When other group members asked him what is happening, Mustafa dismissed them and said that nothing has happened, although it was clear that his behavior in the group has changed. Some of the members tried to tell him about the distance that they feel in their relationship with him, that were warmer before, but he dismissed that too, and said that he does not want to talk about it. I became more and more annoyed at him. I tried to approach him in any possible and creative way I could think of: I asked him if he needs some help to get out of his silence. I suggested that he was hurt from something that occurred in the group. I looked for a parallel process between what happened in our supervision group and his group for battering men. I talked about the possibility that he felt criticized by me or the group. All in vain: Mustafa stayed silent and irresponsive to any of the interventions. He also adopted what seemed like passive-aggressive patterns, such as leaving the group ten minutes earlier without explanation and when asked by group members, he gave a practical excuse about it. In fact his behavior was quite provocative, suggesting that he was holding the group hostage—he could abandon them at any moment.

I decided that I could not ignore him and I made a final attempt to approach him. On one session, two group members discussed a conflict that had occurred in their groups. When the timing seemed appropriate, I turned to Mustafa, assuming that the issue of conflict relates to him and his group too, and suggested that he joins the discussion. Mustafa said that he is not inclined to do that. I responded that I respect his decision, but I wonder if he can share with us what is the reason for that. He said that there is no reason. He just does not want to do it.

At this point I lost my patience and harshly told him that this is going nowhere and that maybe he should leave the group because he does not seem to benefit from it any more. He clarified that he is not ready to do that either. We had some stormy moments of interaction: he accused me of being very demanding and expecting more from him than from any other group member. The other group members helped me to get back to my group leader's position, by commenting that I seemed very angry and that I was drawn to engage in an unproductive interaction. When I asked Mustafa why he thinks that I behaved the way I did, he blamed me with racism and said that it is probably because he is a Muslim. We processed the group reactions until the end of the meeting.

Before describing how we resolved the situation later in the group, let us analyze this vignette from two points of view: a traditional psychodynamic one and a relational one. Practically, these approaches are not necessarily so extremely contradictory, but for didactic reasons I will emphasize and exaggerate the differences.

In the traditional approach, Mustafa's behavior shows maladaptive ways of handling negative feedback, hinting to narcissistic personality features and vulnerability. His withdrawal and passive-aggressive attitude could be understood as representing a fragile self, with internalized persecutory objects. We can conclude that he holds a lot of aggression inside of himself. His response toward me after I lost my temper clarifies his projections, unresolved issues with authority, to the extent of distortion of reality (if we assume that my behavior and reactions toward him had nothing to do with his social or religious identity). My angry reaction can be interpreted as countertransference, either as an objective one—assuming that any group leader might become frustrated and angry with such a member's defiant behavior—but probably with a subjective element due to my inappropriate comment that maybe Mustafa should leave the group. I was clearly not acting only in the best interest of Mustafa or the group. We can also speculate about projective-identification mechanism working in the background that pushed me to express overt anger and intense feelings while he was avoiding expressing his anger and feelings. Perhaps I identified with his projected feelings? Parallel processes around ways of expressing and responding to anger might also exist between what happened to Mustafa with his member in the battering men's group, and between Mustafa and me.

But what if we look at this vignette intersubjectively, and analyze the relational interchange, focusing on how each of the participants jointly created this escalating event? Although we can analyze the chain of events as starting and resulting from the group members' initially commenting on Mustafa's work, at least from a certain point in the interaction, it looks as if the impasse was not created due to a specific member's (Mustafa's, group members' or leader's) contribution. Mustafa probably felt that he needs to protect himself from the members' and leader's pressures and expectations, and did the best that he could to avoid further communication that might lead to more criticism and dissatisfaction with him. We can also say that he had his own issues with aggression and did act in a provocative and not just protective manner, but according to self-psychology, aggression is considered more a reaction to narcissistic hurt and in the service of protecting the self. Adding now the relational perspective, this behavior triggered more pressure from group members to get him out of his protective silence. It is interesting to note that no one seemed to *identify* with him, which means that he probably represented something to the group members, which they did not want to own. My addressing Mustafa was a sign for him that I joined the group pressure and that he needs to be more cautious and protective of himself. The group acted upon the assumption that he is angry with them, while I thought that he is hurt, and tried to find ways to connect with him, but for him it just seemed more threatening.

More than that: the more I tried, the more it seemed that he withdrew because he felt attacked by my good intentions, using the only patterns he knew—being defiant and provocative. As I became more and more frustrated, I started reacting also out of my hurt because my benevolent intentions were rejected. The situation escalated into a powerful enactment of a clash between Mustafa and authority, to which we both contributed. It was a co-created explosion.

At this point, some readers might wonder whether any clash is "co-created": whenever a conflict escalates, both parties are hurt, both become angry too and retaliate. This is very true. As I described in the previous section about the therapist role in times of conflict, the mechanisms of splitting, projection, and projective-identification are very active when a clash occurs. Unfortunately, when you are part of the conflict, you cannot see the incident as created by both participants, and a therapist entering such a situation in a group is no exception. Being a therapist and looking for the patient's maladaptive patterns, might blind the therapist to her or his own contribution. In the above example, the interpretation handy for the therapist was that Mustafa's behavior is defiant and passive-aggressive, thus labeling it as pathological and residing inside the patient.

To support the notion of a co-created conflict, let me share with you some of the thoughts, feelings, and associations that went through my mind during and after these events. Mustafa's behavior felt like a threat to my leadership, and a challenge to my therapeutic skills. I felt as if all the group members are observing our interaction, hoping that I will find a way to deal with this conflict, expecting me to do something extraordinary to resolve the situation. I was under a lot of pressure. I tried to understand the source of this pressure and was reminded of my mother's expectations of me to excel. When it became clearer to me, I embarrassedly had to recognize and own my dissociated parts in this enactment.

In addition, there was a political context to consider. Biran (2003), following Bion's concepts, showed how difficult it is to transform Beta-type elements to Alpha-type elements in the case of two societies (large groups) in conflict, which blocks dialogue between Israelis and Palestinians. The same thing happened in my group. In fact, trying to keep a balanced-liberal attitude, I did everything to avoid relating to Mustafa differently from the other (Jewish) group members. In an effort to stay "objective" and avoid prejudgments, I tried hard not to see his behavior as having anything to do with his being the only Arab in a Jewish group led by a Jewish leader, or with being a minority in Israel. At the same time, from time to time a stereotyped thought crept into my mind: "All Arabs have a problem with authority." I was reminded of a famous sentence that right-wing politicians used to repeat: "Arabs understand only the language of power." I was ashamed with these thoughts that did not suit my self-image and political attitude and tried to ignore them. Was I just angry at Mustafa or also with myself and my denied and dissociated thoughts?

Enactment involves the therapist as participant caught up in the relationship rather than observing it. It is also accompanied by some dissociated and disowned parts. The group acted as a good enough consultant, pointing out my futile anger, and I was able to listen to them. The ability to analyze the events the way I presented above helped me free myself from the enactment. Looking at the situation the relational way, I could get back to the group and describe the chain of events from the intersubjective point of view, admitting my mistake, and normalizing Mustafa's behavior as an act of self-protection. I also said that maybe we can learn how conflicts escalate by misinterpreting the other's behavior as hostile and (sometimes passive-)aggressive, when in fact the other subjectively sees it as legitimate ways of self-defense (which can probably be broadened to the social context of the Israeli–Arab conflict). In response, Mustafa tearfully thanked me and described how, as a minority, he was expected by his father to be better than others (interesting how this reflected my subjective experience of the pressure to excel!), and how much he had to face misunderstandings from authority figures during his life in Israel, developing caution when approached by authority (perhaps an almost anti-thesis of my pre-conscious stereotypes about Arabs and authority). He remembered a traumatic encounter from his childhood with an Israeli policeman, where he was humiliated and called nasty names by this policeman while other kids were watching, although he had done nothing wrong. We could now better understand Mustafa's reaction to me and to the group.

The group members joined in, by reflecting on their subjective experience both when they could not reach Mustafa, during the intense encounter where we had our strong conflict, and now, after it seems that communication was restored in the group. They were relieved that peace was restored but did not ignore Mustafa's considerable aggression and its effects on all group members. In the new atmosphere of mutual acknowledgments, some of them talked about their fear of aggression, either their own or the other's anger. Mustafa himself began exploring his passive-aggressive ways and their impact on the other group members.

Conclusion

The above example demonstrates well the usefulness of the relational paradigm in group therapy. The group leader in that vignette carries a double burden, both being drawn to an enactment which emotionally impacts his reactions and participating in a conflict with a group member, thus losing the ability to see the subjective experience of the other for a while. He was unconsciously caught in a submissive position (Ghent, 1999). The group served as a good supervisor, helping the therapist restore his therapeutic role and observing ego and moving into a surrendering position. Only when understood from an intersubjective point of view and analyzing the shared contribution of both the leader and the participant(s) to the situation, we could resolve the conflict in the group. One of the influences of the relational approach on the therapeutic relationship, as manifested in this vignette, is the effective negotiation of conflicts and differences, facilitating the repair of disruptions. Insisting on a traditional object relations point of view, this group member would have been labeled a difficult patient.

Gans and Alonso (1998) have already clearly described how group therapists and group members can co-create a difficult patient in a group.

The political context of this vignette needs more consideration, as clearly the attempt of the therapist to avoid acknowledging the fact that Mustafa was the only Muslim in the group and ignoring the impact of this fact on the group, only complicated the situation. As a minority in the group, more was asked of Mustafa all the time, so it was not only his imagination but also some real enactment of his father's expectations by the group. Furthermore, we can connect the events in the group to the larger political situation, and see them as an enactment of a moment of cultural trauma: Mustafa is isolated by the group who puts all the aggression in him and then attacks it. Suchet's article (2010) shows how the therapist cannot avoid the political and social environment, even against her will: "As the work unfolded I find myself thrust into a psychic and social space I had not wanted to inhabit, into the Israeli–Palestinian conflict and the turmoil of Jewish identity" (p. 158). Actually, it is always there, as part of the Social Unconscious (Weinberg, 2007; Hopper & Weinberg, 2011).

In retrospect, the enactment with Mustafa seems to be an enactment of trauma, part cultural and part personal, and contained some thoughts, feelings, and processes that were traumatic and dissociated in that group.

In addition, this vignette shows how strong enactments in a group can become, drawing into intense emotional involvement group members and even experienced group therapists. The group therapist cannot (and should not) escape participation and the emotional impact of the enactment, but needs to examine the process and understand it from a relational point of view. The therapist can be helped by the group members who are not involved in the enactment to point out what is happening and help the therapist out of the "trap." Thus the group serves as the best supervisor.

A possible difficulty arises when the whole group participates in this enactment process. It might be almost impossible for the therapist to distance himself or herself and examine the situation more from a distance and in such a situation external supervision might be helpful. If this supervision is done in a group setting, it is probably very useful to pay attention to the parallel processes and explore the repeating enactment in the supervision group, thus enlivening and deeply understanding the situation in the original therapy group.

References

Aron, L. (1996) *A Meeting of Minds*. Hillsdale, NJ: Analytic Press.
Beebe, B. & Lachmann, F. (2002) *Infant Research and Adult Treatment: Co-constructing Interactions*. Hillsdale, NJ: Analytic Press.
Benjamin, J. (1995) *Like Subjects, Love Objects*. New Haven, CT: Yale University Press.
Benjamin, J. (1998) *Shadow of the Other: Intersubjectivity and Gender in Psychoanalysis*. New York: Routledge.
Benjamin, J. (1999) Recognition and destruction: An outline of intersubjectivity. In S. Mitchell & L. Aron (eds.) *Relational Psychoanalysis: The Emergence of a Tradition*. Hillsdale, NJ: Analytic Press.

Berman, A. & Weinberg, H. (1998) The advanced-stage therapy group. *International Journal of Group Psychotherapy*, 48: 499–518.

Berman, A., Berger, M., and Gutmann, D. (2000) The division into Us and Them as a universal social structure. *Mind and Human Interaction*, 11 (1): 53–72.

Billow, M.R. (2003) *Relational Group Psychotherapy: From Basic Assumptions to Passion.* London: Jessica Kingsley.

Bion, W.R. (1962) *Learning from Experience.* London: Heinemann.

Bion, W.R. (1967) *Second Thoughts: Selected Papers on Psychoanalysis.* London: Jason Aronson.

Biran, H. (2003) The Difficulty of Transforming Terror into Dialogue. *Group Analysis*, 36 (4): 490–502.

Cohen, B.D. & Schermer, V.L. (2002) On scapegoating in therapy groups: A social constructivist and intersubjective outlook. *International Journal of Group Psychotherapy*, 52 (1): 89–109.

Corey, G. (1995) *Theory & Practice of Group Counseling.* 4th edn. Pacific Grove: Brooks/Cole Pub.

Cozolino, L. (2006) *The Neuroscience of Human Relationships.* New York: W.W. Norton.

Foulkes, S.H. (1964) *Therapeutic Group Analysis.* London: George Allen & Unwin.

Foulkes, S.H. (1975) *Group Analytic Psychotherapy, Method and Principles.* London: Gordon & Breach.

Gans, S.J. & Alonso, A. (1998) Difficult patients: Their construction in group therapy. *International Journal of Group Psychotherapy*, 48 (3): 311–326.

Gergen, K.J. (1994) *Realities and Relationships.* Cambridge, MA: Harvard University Press.

Ghent, E. (1999) Masochism, submission, surrender: Masochism as a perversion of surrender. In S.A. Mitchell & L. Aron (eds.) *Relational Psychoanalysis: The Emergence of a Tradition* (pp. 211–243). Hillsdale, NJ: Analytic Press.

Grossmark, R. (2007) The edge of chaos: Enactment, disruption, and emergence in group psychotherapy. *Psychoanalytic Dialogues*, 17 (4): 479–499.

Hopper, E. & Weinberg, H. (2011) *The Social Unconscious in Persons, Groups and Societies: Mainly Theory.* London: Karnac Books.

Laor, I. (2009) The Holy See: The individual and the group-intersubjective meetings. *Psychoanalytic Dialogues*, 19 (4): 486–501.

Nitsun, M. (1996) *The Anti-Group: Destructive Forces in the Group and Their Creative Potential.* London: Routledge.

Norcross, J.C. (ed.) (2002) *Psychotherapy Relationships that Work: Therapist Contributions and Responsiveness to Patient Needs.* New York: Oxford University Press.

Ormont, L.R. (1992) *The Group Therapy Experience.* New York: St. Martin's Press.

Pines, M. (2003) Social brain and social group: How mirroring connects people. *Group Analysis*, 36 (4): 507–513.

Roth, B.E., Stone, W.N., & Kibel, H.D. (eds.) (1990) *The Difficult Patient in Group: Group Psychotherapy with Borderline and Narcissistic Disorders.* American Group Psychotherapy Association Monograph Series No. VI. Madison, CT: International Universities Press.

Rutan, S.J. & Stone, W.N. (2007) *Psychodynamic Group-Psychotherapy.* 4th edn. New York: Guilford Press.

Stern, D. (1985) *The Interpersonal World of the Infant: A View from Psychoanalysis and Developmental Psychology.* New York: Basic Books.

Stern, D.N, Sander, L.W., Nahum, J.P., Harrison, A.M., Lyons-Ruth, K., Morgan, A.C., Bruschweilerstern, N., & Tronick, E.Z. (1998) Non-interpretive mechanisms in psychoanalytic therapy: The 'something more' than interpretation. *International Journal of Psychoanalysis*, 79: 903–921.

Stolorow, R., Brandchaft, B., & Atwood, G. (1987) *Psychoanalytic Treatment: An Intersubjective Perspective*, Northvale, NJ: Jason Aronson.

Stone, W.N. (2001) The role of the therapist's affect in the detection of empathic failures, misunderstandings and injury. *Group*, 25: 3–14.

Suchet, M. (2010) Face to face. *Psychoanalytic Dialogues*, 20: 158–171.

Weegmann, M. (2001) Working intersubjectively: What does it mean for theory and therapy? *Group Analysis*, 34 (4): 515–530.

Weinberg, H. (2007) So what is this social unconscious anyway? *Group Analysis* 40 (3): 307–322.

Weinberg, H. & Schneider, S. (2003) Introduction: Background, structure and dynamics of the large group. *The Large Group Revisited: The Herd, Primal Horde, Crowds and Masses* (pp. 13–26). London: Jessica Kingsley.

Wilke, G. (2007) 31st S.H. Foulkes annual lecture: Second generation perpetrator symptoms in groups. *Group Analysis*, 40 (4): 429–447.

Wright, F. (2004) Being seen, moved, disrupted, and reconfigured: Group leadership from a relational perspective. *International Journal of Group Psychotherapy*, 54: 235–251.

Wright, F. (2005) Valuing enactments in group therapy: Discussion of three case studies. *Group*, 29 (4): 399–406.

Yalom, I.D. (1995) *The Theory and Practice of Group Psychotherapy*. 4th edn. New York: Basic Books.

Chapter 4

The Edge of Chaos

Enactment, Disruption, and Emergence in Group Psychotherapy

Robert Grossmark

<blockquote>
To jump into the unknown from what is known, but intolerable.

Bela Bartok
</blockquote>

Introduction

In this chapter I will introduce an approach to group therapy that is based on the idea that group psychotherapeutic process and change involves a constant movement into and through enactments that involve the group as a whole, the group analyst, and each group member. It is a truism in the group therapy field that a group is always interacting. This group interaction is the primary unique resource of group psychotherapy. It is out of this interaction that each group develops its particular group culture and the "group matrix" (Foulkes, 1975) from which change and growth emerge. As the group members engage with each other and bring in their whole personalities, enactments are unavoidable, and just like interaction, inevitable. In this chapter I will examine the process of these enactments from the perspective of current relational theorizing that emphasizes the presence of multiple self-states in the group and the embeddedness of the group analyst within the group enactments. These enactments are constantly unfolding and involve the group as a whole and the group analyst in repetitive and unmentalized states. Therapeutic action, in part, involves the ongoing work on the part of the group analyst and group members in attempting to understand what is going on in the group. This is achieved by accessing alternative self-states that allow the therapist or group members to think about and try to understand what is happening and thus turn unmentalized (Fonagy et al., 2002), "un-understandable" (Pines, 1998) and painful interaction into psychological learning and development. This process often involves the group and the group analyst entering into difficult and sometimes painful passages of group process together. With the therapist's help in containing the painful and disowned affect, new experience and meaning can emerge for the group members from the unmentalized, unformulated, and rigid repetitive self-states that characterize the enactments.

The primary dynamic of change is conceptualized as a constant dialectical movement into and out of the "familiar chaos" (Stern, 1997) of the self-states engaged in the enactments and the more reflective and related self-states that enable working through. In order to describe this process and to outline the experience of the analyst's embeddedness, I will look to dynamic systems theory that offers a conceptualization of change and emergence that seems to capture the experience of these enactments both systemically and metaphorically and is beautifully captured by Stuart Kauffman's notion that "life exists at the edge of chaos" (Kauffman, 1995), to hermeneutic psychoanalysis that emphasizes the emergence of meaning from dialogic interaction and to relational psychoanalytic ideas of enactment, dissociation, and multiplicity.

The Work of the Group and Enactment

As the group therapist, my task is primarily to create and maintain the safe, productive, and transformational space within which the group can do its work. I set the boundaries of the group and help and encourage the group members to work together to create a dynamic group that is itself the agent of change. Rather than therapy *in* the group I am working toward a situation where there is therapy *by* the group (Foulkes, 1975).

It is not uncommon for the group to engage in what feels like chaotic, painful, or numbing interactions with each other and with me. Most often these interactions are variations on the very damaging, deadening, and mystifying dynamics of the group members' lives and minds. When these internalized modes of experiencing themselves and others unfold, it is often as familiar, repetitive patterns in relationships that are experienced as unthought "things that happen." They leave the individuals with a dead and helpless feeling about themselves and the sense that this is "just the way things are." At times there is tremendous pain and turbulence generated for the individual and the whole group by these ways of being. These interactions are versions of early trauma to the self that has taken place before there was sufficient language or cognitive ability to mentalize and thus construct a meaningful narrative, or later trauma that has been dissociated and has not been available for mental processing. This kind of damage to the mind and its relations to the world is not amenable to being talked about. It can only find expression via projective identification and enactment. My work is to help the group find what is meaningful and coherent in these chaotic interactions and to allow the emergence of what has until now been unformulated (Stern, 1997) and stuck in the realm of what cannot be thought and felt.

Rather than overcoming resistances or lifting repressions so that the unconscious can be made available, I see this work as the facilitating of a creative and emergent interactive group process wherein what was unformulated can take shape and find meaning. I help the group members work together such that the multiple and sometimes incompatible parts of themselves come to be enacted in the group.

These enactments always involve the individual members themselves, the group as a whole, and the therapist. Everyone is involved.

Time and the Emergence of Meaning in Group Therapy

Group therapists almost universally talk about the focus on the "here-and-now" in group therapy (Ormont, 1992; Rutan & Stone, 2001; Yalom 1975). Patients are encouraged to talk about their experience in the here-and-now. Often focus on past events or on future hopes is questioned as an avoidance or flight from what is going on in the here-and-now (Ormont, 1992). My focus on the emergence of unformulated experience in group enactments takes a somewhat different view to the trajectory of time in group psychotherapy. The focus is on what is *happening* in the group and what will *emerge*. The distinctions between past, present, and future dissolve when the focus shifts to the finding of meaning in the what-is-about-to-emerge. Whether group members are talking about past experience or their feelings in the moment, is less relevant. The point is that either way, they and the other members are, or soon will be, doing something with each other that may itself contain the pieces of unformulated experience that need to be allowed to emerge and take shape within the group. Hans Loewald (1980) used the phrase "near future" to capture the curious transference enactments wherein the past is continually lived as an about-to-be future. It seems useful to think of the life of the group as taking place in the transformational space that is the "near future," or as the French poet Yves Bonnefoy puts it, "the ever next" (Bonnefoy, 1982).

The work of finding meaning rather than repetitive deadness is itself a reparative and restorative endeavor. The British group analyst Malcolm Pines (1998) has eloquently described how the group evokes the primary mother–infant emotional environment and can become a space and an object in and of itself that contains the qualities of mirroring, relatedness, and reparation. Group members respond to and internalize these qualities over time. My hope is that they not only find situations that promote the making of meaning out of their empty and unthought experience, but will also internalize and develop for themselves the reflective function and the ability to mentalize that emerge within the group (Fonagy et al., 2002). These capacities are initially embodied in my being, presence, and attitude in the group.

The Hermeneutic Circle and Unformulated Experience in Group

From a hermeneutic and constructivist approach to group psychoanalysis the unconscious is not regarded as a storehouse of complete and inert memories, objects, and experiences waiting to be unearthed and brought to consciousness via interpretation (Hoffman, 1998; Orange, 1995; Stern, 1997). Rather, the meaning of behavior emerges through the group interactions and dialogue. The hermeneutic contribution to psychoanalytic process builds on Gadamer's conception of the hermeneutic circle (Gadamer, 1975, 1976). Meaning is conceived as "an activity, an event" that "can only take place in interaction" (Stern, 1997, p. 212). Although originally applied to textual analysis, the relevance to group interaction is compelling. Meaning emerges as we test our assumed understanding in dialogue with an other. Our understanding shifts as our preconceptions have to be adjusted to account for what we do not yet understand or only partially understand. One way to think about the interaction of group psychoanalysis is a version of the hermeneutic circle wherein the members are trying to be understood and are trying to understand the others in the groups. Gadamer (1976) has emphasized that the act of trying to understand a text or an other is transformative in itself. There is an ongoing process of adjusting and re-adjusting perceptions and assumptions in order for a shared meaning to emerge.

This transformation of the self and creation of meaning is the very process that has broken down for the patients who come to group. Rather than being open to alternative perspectives about their own ways of being and an openness to know the other group members fully, we find that they are locked in a repetitive "familiar chaos." This is a phrase that Donnel Stern (1997) borrowed from Paul Valery. He describes a "state of mind cultivated and perpetuated in the service of the conservative intention to observe, think and feel only in the well worn channels—in the service, actually of the wish not to think" (p. 51). Such a state of mind feels familiar and therefore a comfort, and yet is chaotic in that experience and thoughts are yet to be developed or formulated. It is a state of mind that is dissociated in that there is a failure to construct or make sense of what is happening. Things just happen. Such a conceptualization is not far from Bion's concept of "-K" or "anti-thought" (Bion, 1962). The as yet unformulated experience is not accessed through interpretation, because there is nothing there yet to interpret. The unformulated experience can only be known if allowed to emerge in the group process, and to take shape and meaning in that emergence.

In group psychotherapy there is a constant dialectical movement between enactments of the familiar chaos of the patients' lives and the search to find the meaning in these enactments. (In truth, the word "multilectic" would be more appropriate, given that "dialectic" implies a dialogic pattern between two poles— as in Hegel's thesis and anti-thesis—while in the group therapy situation we are looking at a situation where the multiple self-states of the group and its members intertwine in a multitude of enactments and reflective states at any given time). The leader is often involved unconsciously in the enactments along with the other group members, either in a dyadic manner or in terms of a group-as-a-whole enactment. The task of the leader and the group is to try to notice when these enactments are occurring—in everyday speech, "to figure out what's going on"— to describe the experience and then to try to make sense of it. The exercise of making and finding meaning in the enactments gives shape to what is unformulated as it is emerging and is transformative in itself.

Complexity and Multiple Self-States in Group

This constant movement between the rigidity of dissociated repetitiveness and the freedom to think new thoughts and find meaning finds resonance in the application of complexity theory, or dynamic systems theory to psychoanalysis (Galatzer-Levy, 2004; Ghent, 2002; Harris, 2005; Palombo, 1999) and group therapy (Rubenfeld, 2001). Outlined in an ever-expanding literature (Gleick, 1987; Lewin, 1999; Waldrop, 1992), complexity theory offers a way of thinking about the clinical experience of group and individual psychoanalysis that goes beyond linear and binary explanations (Harris, 2005). The group may be viewed as a self-organizing eco-system that is subject to the processes of all biological systems, and like all biological systems any perturbation to the system will cause changes to the whole system. A group like any open system will settle into attractor states that offer relative stability. These attractor states can be shallow and therefore vulnerable to complete reconfiguration in response to perturbations or can be deep and far more resistant to disruption.

Rubenfeld (2001) points out that unlike earlier notions of General Systems Theory (Agazarian, 1989; Durkin, 1981; von Bertalanffy, 1966) that conceptualized a group, like all living systems as drawn toward equilibrium and homeostasis, complex systems—and a psychotherapy group is a superb living example—must maintain *dis*equilibrium and *in*stability in order to adapt to changes in the internal and external environment. Rather than seeing a group as always engaged in maintaining homeostasis, this view sees groups as always engaged in adapting to new and changing circumstances. In particular, perturbations to an open system cause destabilization and turbulence that then open up the opportunity for change.

In the group therapy situation, there are manifest perturbations to the system, such as the arrivals and departures of members, vacations, and the like. (There are also constantly more subtle and perhaps smaller perturbations such as the shifts in self-states within the group members from one moment to the next.) As the vignette to be described below illustrates, such events can cause terrific personal and group turbulence, and powerful opportunities for change and growth. It is in the most turbulent times that vulnerable group members are more prone to rely on the more rigid and known patterns of their own "familiar chaos" as a first-order adaptation. Familiar and protective self-states are called upon to manage the terrors of change. It is out of these self-states that enactments are born, as the whole group and the therapist may get pulled into a dissociated self-state that does not allow access to other more adaptable and flexible self-states that would allow for the formulation of the experience. As we will see below, a self-state that allows thought and mentalization can be a rare and precious commodity at a time of such turbulence.

Stuart Kauffman's (1995) concept that "life exists at the edge of chaos" highlights the ongoing tension in all living systems between rigidity and sameness on the one hand and disruptions, chaos and change on the other. This is what happens in group psychotherapy when there are perturbations to the system and when the old familiar ways of coping that involve the dissociation of more flexible self-states operate. From this perspective enactments involve a cleaving to a familiar and worn pathway of being and not formulating experience (i.e., dissociating), in the face of turbulence.

Both complexity theory and contemporary relational psychoanalysis offer us ways to focus on the fine-grained moments when there are shifts from one state to another, from dissociation and enactment to reflection and the creation of meaning. In the field of complexity and mathematics, there has been a shift from the prior held truth that there are three classes of behavior—fixed point, periodic, and chaotic—to the addition of a fourth class—an intermediate class between fixed and chaotic (Lewin, 1999). Lewin (1999) describes how these ideas were adapted to the world of cell life and then to eco-systems by Kauffman (1995) and others. It appears that all biological life is sweetly poised at the "edge of chaos" where "chaos and stability pull in opposite directions" (Lewin, 1999, p. 51). What is so compelling to psychoanalysts and group analysts is the idea that it is the intermediate area between order and chaos that offers maximal information processing, change and creativity (Lewin, 1999, p. 51). This area is termed the "edge of chaos."

In systemic terms, the group and the individual members involved in trying to find their way through an enactment are poised in that fourth zone between the fixed and chaotic—within and between dissociation and the formulation of experience—and it is here that there is tremendous opportunity for powerful emotional experience and change. Such a moment can also be conceptualized as the "phase transition" (Lewin, 1999, p. 20) where the disruption has been sufficient to shift the system out of one attractor state and the system has yet to settle into the next one.

The phrase "the edge of chaos" also speaks eloquently to the phenomenology of these situations. As the vignette described below hopefully conveys, for the group members and the therapist there is an exquisite alchemy of pain, disruption, and new insight and experience when an enactment is allowed to emerge and is worked through.

From within the field of relational psychoanalysis, Philip Bromberg's (1998) image of "standing in the spaces" within and between different self-states also speaks to the phenomena of enactments in group psychotherapy. I suggest that this resonates with the above idea of the fourth zone of experience that is between the fixed and the chaotic. The very task of interacting with each other and living out the group interactions whilst simultaneously engaging with the task of figuring out what's going on asks the group therapist and the group members to inhabit at least two self-states at once, and the space between them: one that permits an immersion in the experience of the moment with the other members and the other that seeks to mentalize, to find the meaning and shape of that experience. In other words of Bromberg, how do we "stay the same while changing?" Bromberg has given us many compelling clinical examples that highlight the immense value of careful attention to the shifts in self-states in the patient and in himself in individual work (Bromberg, 1998, 2006). Similarly, the work of group therapy is conducted right "at the edge of chaos," that is, when there are shifts in the self-states of the group-as-a-whole, the members, and the group analyst.

The Group Analyst and Enactment

Often when the group-as-a-whole is engaged in a blind and total way, the group analyst is unable to maintain his or her analyzing function and stay in the self-state that will offer insight or at least some connection to the task of the group to try to understand their experience. Unlike other approaches to group-as-a-whole phenomena and to group therapy, a relational approach does not assume that the group analyst can stay outside of the enactment with the clarity that enables accurate and meaningful interpretations of the group process. Indeed the idea that the group therapist is immune to group-as-a-whole processes and can maintain clarity of consciousness while the group members are swept away in the unconscious group process is seen from a relational perspective as both undesirable and actually impossible. Steven Mitchell (1993, 1997) has persuasively reconsidered the analyst's authority and knowledge as entirely mediated by the analyst's own experience and subjectivity. It is only by becoming lost in the total experience of the group, or as Donnel Stern (1997) puts it, the "grip of the field," even if that involves a temporary destruction of thought processes (Hinshelwood, 1994; Gordon, 1994), that one can find and create meaning in the enactment. In situations such as this, the analyst has to work hard to help the group stay in touch with the task and to try to find one or some parts of some of the members who can begin the process of mentalizing and reflective function that will guide the group out of their temporary darkness. Experiences such as these are drenched in pain and struggle for the group members and the group analyst, but are the *sine qua non* of a group therapy experience that will be real and vital and will actually bring about change.

In order for this kind of process to emerge, to be "lived out," as Betty Joseph (1985) would say, the group therapist must be able to contain and hold the group while the enactment unfolds. Premature interpretation, the rush to know something before it has come to be, in the group—or in Betty Joseph's words, to turn the experience into analytic "material"—can impinge and constrict the group's potential to live through and find their own meaning and grounding in the experience that unfolds. The hermeneutic approach values the idea that there is no one correct meaning to the group's behavior, and I would always value the meaning that the group comes to from within their own struggle together, over any interpretation I might be able to offer.

An Enactment of Disruption and Emergence in a Group Session

As by now will be clear, my approach to group psychotherapy embraces the idea of disruption and turbulence. Far from being a problem to be overcome, disruptions to the group mind-set and to the group itself are seen as opportunities for growth and for the shifting of self-states. What follows is part of a session of an ongoing group in which we will see the group's response to another disruption in a sequence of disruptions. The session will illustrate the dialectics of enactment: the rigid repetition of "familiar chaos" as a response to disruption and turbulence, on the one hand, and the emergence of new and invigorating meaning from within that enactment, on the other. Here is a group living at "the edge of chaos."

This is a weekly psychotherapy group that has been ongoing for ten years. There are six current members, two of whom have been in the group for the duration. The most recent member, Karen, joined approximately nine months ago, and both the membership and the feeling in the group in that time has been one of increasing solidity and stability.

Two months prior to this session, I moved office after eight years in the same office. This was a major disruption in the life and minds of the group. There were various enactments of the loss of object constancy and going-on-being that this event called up in the group members. For instance, Victor forgot about the existence of Karen, and Gladys insisted that she would leave the group and that I was "a fucking bastard" for "dragging her around." As is often the case during disruptions such as the move, there really is a feeling of living on the edge of chaos. At one and the same time there is a feeling of the re-living of all the past traumas, and also of new and durable experience being made as the group goes-on-being and survives the storm.

The following session takes place four weeks after the move to the new office. All six members are present.

> It is in the group's culture to make all announcements at the beginning of the group. Accordingly I announce that there will be a new member coming to the group soon. There is a swirl of energy in the room mostly centering around curiosity as to whether the new person will be a man or a woman. Karen (the most recent member) is upset and says "Oh no; I was just beginning to open up. I hope it's not someone with an eating disorder. Those eating disorder groups are so competitive and insane. I'm thinking of doing DBT. But I don't have to do it on Wednesday night (group night)." By way of background, Karen is in her mid-thirties and has had years of treatment after a massively traumatic childhood. She has struggled for years with all the disorders of trauma and neglect; difficulties in self-regulation, self-injury, eating disorder and on two occasions was hospitalized when suicidal. Karen had indeed only recently begun to open up and talk more intimately about herself in the group. When she is anxious, her speech and thought are disjointed and muddled as they are here. My thought is that her disjointed fragmented state is capturing the whole group's state of mind in response to the news of the new member.

Gladys speaks up and says that she's thinking of leaving the group. Dorothy says that a new member makes her think of how long she has been in the group (she is one of the founder members) and that she still finds the group useful. She still learns a lot. Victor chimes in. "Me too." Victor and Henry review their respective progress in the group, and talk for a few minutes in a disconnected way. Both Victor and Henry are prone to this kind of reverie in the group and can talk in a dissociated way when there is anxiety and turbulence brewing in the room, as if to ward it off and to repair the fragmented group. Both come from families where anger and fear can suddenly erupt in parents or siblings with frightening intensity. While they are talking Gladys's face darkens. I am aware of this and anxiety wells up within me. I am aware of charging my batteries; this is going to be a long night. I ask the group "What's going on?" Karen asks Gladys, "Are you OK?"

Gladys turns to me slowly and malevolently: "I hate you. I was just getting over hating you for moving. I was going to leave the group but then you moved and I couldn't leave because it would seem like I was leaving because of that and I'm busy with work and now this! Now I can't leave because it'll seem like it's because of the new person, not because of my own reasons. I'm just going to leave. I want to go off my meds. I'm sick of it. Isn't that meant to be how it goes; you get better and can cut down, but Dr. B says they are helping so why change. But I'm just going to leave."

I scan the room. Heads are down. The mood is grim.

I address the group. "How are people feeling toward Gladys?"

Victor leans toward her. "I feel supportive. I know what you're going through. You don't have to feel that way."

Henry picks up the thread, once again joining with Victor in the attempt to soothe the rage and fear in the room. He responds to Gladys's comments about her medications and launches into a long disconnected story, all too familiar to the group, about his trials and tribulations with his thyroid medication. It should be mentioned that Henry is an intellectually brilliant man, the son of scientists who seem to relate to people as if they were robots, with little sense of human functioning. He often feels other than human and can only relate in this very split-off, affectless manner. Since being in the group, he has begun to be and to feel more a member of the human race.

I encourage the group to find out what Henry feels at this moment, but it's not so easy to shift Henry from his groove. After a few failed attempts, I ask the group what is Henry feeling toward Gladys that he doesn't know. There is unison. He doesn't want her to leave, they cry. Henry looks pleased. "Yes." He says. "Please don't leave." There is a small ripple of pleasure in the room.

Henry has found a feeling. However, Gladys is still drenched in darkness and everyone knows it.

Gladys ignores the group and Henry. She focuses on me again. "I hate you. I was just getting comfortable with you again. I had been so angry and was just feeling OK with you, and now you're doing this again!" She continues for a time in dark hatred. I ask her to say, if she can, what is it that I am doing to her.

"You're just taking it away from me. I can't leave now. I hate you."

I try to reflect, "I've trapped you," but she is not yet in a state that will permit ingress.

She continues. "I know what it is. You need more money. I know it, once you moved in here. The new office; you'll need new furniture. You gave us a chance to settle in and now this!"

I try again to reach her. "You feel annulled. If I move, I'm annulling you. If I raise fees, I'm annulling you. Like you said when we moved, I'm just dragging you around."

She has heard me, especially the reference to being dragged around, her own words, spoken when the group moved, that resonated with her feeling as a child, but she is still trapped in her familiar chaos. She has responded to the disruptive news of the new patient with a fall back into the repetitive rigid familiar chaos of traumatic neglect and annulment.

She continues: "I can't go on. I just can't do this. I need to leave. I'm not coming back. I'm going back to school in the evenings in September so I'll have to leave anyway. It's just too much. Up to now, everything I've done has been arranged around the group and my therapy schedule. I've organized my vacations around group and my individual sessions. Now you do this!"

The atmosphere in the room is vile, ugly, and hopeless. I am not doing too much better. I can feel the dark pull of Gladys's self-state. I see the rest of the group sucked into her darkness. I am distraught. We have been into and through these passages before with Gladys and it is always slow and painful. It can take weeks until the group comes out the other side. I am deeply upset, and experience a collapse within me into a complementary self-state. I become certain that I have made a grievous error inviting a new member in at this time. I am quickly on the slippery slope of self-denigration. It is all falling apart. How could I have made such an error? How can I possibly think I can run groups, let alone think of writing about and teaching group therapy? I convince myself that there is no alternative but to cancel the new group member. I think of all the repercussions of this; the conversation I will have to have with the patient and the referring clinician and so on. I am now locked in the enactment with Gladys and the group. I feel that I am a terrible persecutory and neglectful object who has no business running groups. In retrospect, in Heinrich Racker's terminology (1968), I imagine that this was a complementary version of Gladys's mother's unmentalized dread that she was not up to the task of having and raising children. Similarly, in a concordant way the group and myself are experiencing the unmentalized, dissociated piece of Gladys's upbringing. We are feeling bullied and tortured by her pain and rage, as she was by her mother. It is a victimized response that leads to an internal collapse that involves self-denigration, helplessness, and disgust.

In the moment of the group, I am, as Donnel Stern would say, "in the grip of the field." I cannot see or feel alternatives at that moment. The group is in the same grip. In such situations I use the multiplicity of the group. I look to see if there is anyone in the group who can access a different self-state that can offer a way out of this grip, and open the path to thinking.

So I ask the group what people are sitting with. Henry says that he's thinking that we shouldn't forget that the group could be of great benefit to the new member too. There is the slightest perceptible shift in the feeling in the room. Henry, perhaps due to his affective disconnection or to his response to the previous moment where the group and I helped him express a deep and simple feeling toward Gladys, is not entirely stuck in the group self-state of horror and helplessness with and in response to Gladys. He is a little more able to stand in a space that allows him a perspective, and allows him to think an empathic thought about the needs of the new member. He is able to feel that the new member is herself a subject, not just an object. In this moment, he is free of the enactment in a way that neither the group nor I can be. Such openings of thought and intersubjectivity in the midst of an enactment are enormously helpful. I am able then to function in a somewhat freer way myself. I notice that Dorothy is looking particularly pained and I become sure that she is responding to Gladys. I ask her what she is feeling toward Gladys.

Dorothy says: "To be honest, and I hate saying this, but Gladys, the first part of what you said made me angry. And I hate saying this because I know that you are in a bad place. But I couldn't help but feel 'oh no, here we go again; now this bad place that Gladys is going into is going to fill up the whole group' and I really can't stand it when you say that you are going to leave. It hurts me so much. In fact what I feel and I hate saying this, is that I think I feel what you say you feel when your sister does what she does to you. It's like it completely takes over and there's no room for anyone else. Then we all have to go along with it and we can't challenge you or even help you."

This is a major shift in the self-state of the group and for Dorothy personally. Dorothy has spent her life being cowed into submission by an officious academic family where the men were valued over her and where no expression of anger was ever tolerated, especially in the only girl. Now a senior administrative professional, she is often presented in her work life with situations that require assertion and confrontation and she struggles mightily. This is why she keeps saying how much she hates saying what she is saying.

Gladys does not look at Dorothy while she talks. She looks away and seems to boil with rage. She turns to me again.

"Well it's your fault. I did nothing. You did it all. You moved! You are bringing new people into the group!" Hatred spills out of her, and I feel for Dorothy who is now being annulled by Gladys.

At this point, my feeling state has changed dramatically. I am not lost in the grip. Henry and Dorothy have helped us to stand in the spaces. We are still in the grip of the field created by this enactment but we are also, in different ways, able to think about and mentalize the experience.

I tell Gladys that I think that she feels very vulnerable, and that she then feels she has only two options: to attack or to run away. I ask her, can she let herself be vulnerable here?

Dorothy says to Gladys: "But I'm not blaming you."

Gladys continues to act as if she's ignoring Dorothy and more hatred toward me comes out, and she insists that she is leaving the group.

Dorothy now erupts in tears of sadness and rage. She says "That's it then. I'm never going to speak in group again. I express my feelings and you see what happens. You just attack."

Gladys responds to her. This is a sign that she is also able, ever so slightly, to step out of the traumatized overwhelming self-state. She says, "I'm just saying what I feel."

Karen says: "I also have to say I felt like oh no, here we go again. This is going to take us over for the next few groups. I also feel like I don't want to deal with a new person. Look Gladys, you are not going anywhere. I've seen you like this before. You're still here."

Henry, Victor, and Karen then talk for a while about how difficult group can be, but they emphasize the virtue in being able to express whatever feelings arise. The effect is a distancing from the heat of the moment, but it is not unwelcome, as it seems to have given Dorothy and Gladys a moment to think. This is an example of the group's self regulating capacity.

Dorothy says to Gladys with more softness in her voice: "Look Gladys, you really hurt me when you say those things."

Gladys, also with more openness says, "But it's not my fault, it's his [Grossmark's] fault."

> Dorothy responds: "But it's no one's fault. That's not what I'm talking about. Not blame. I'm just saying that I felt angry. I didn't want to, but I just felt I needed to express it. No one is being blamed."
>
> I amplify Dorothy's point, sensing that Gladys is now shifting to a self-state of openness and thought. I tell her that this seems to be just how it goes in her family. There is no room for vulnerability and need. It's always about someone being blamed.
>
> Gladys cries. She shakes with anger. "I'm so fucking angry with my sister. You won't believe what's going on. She's pregnant again!"
>
> This has the quality of a bombshell. The group has worked hard over the last year to help Gladys cope with the overwhelming disruption, envy, and isolation she has experienced following her sister's first pregnancy and the birth of her first child.
>
> The group is gripped by this news and the self-state of the group is now utterly vibrant and engaged. Gladys tells a story of family dysfunction. Her sister isn't speaking to her parents and is angry with her. Everyone engages in the conversation that feels full of vitality, empathy, and sharing.

The Group Finds Its Way Out of the Enactment

How did this group release itself from the grip of this painful enactment? Or, in the terms of dynamic systems theory, what facilitated the phase transition out of the attractor state of the enactment? First, Henry introduced the subjectivity of the new member. Then Dorothy tried to express her emotional reaction to Gladys's assault and persevered in her attempt to have her own subjectivity acknowledged. When Dorothy implored Gladys to understand that she was really hurt by her and that no one is to blame, she was implicitly calling to the other potential self-states that Gladys can occupy. She was reaching out to the part of Gladys that can empathize with Dorothy and that can have what Fonagy and his colleagues would call, "reflective function." Finally Karen too was able to step back and in an empathic manner tell Gladys that she was not going anywhere. In that moment Karen and Gladys were standing in a new dialectical space. Karen was saying, in effect: "You are in this awful place and I have been pulled into it with you, but you and I know there are other parts of you, other self-states which still exist even if you cannot reclaim them right now." All of these interactions are the building blocks of emotional meaning and mentalization that allow the group to make a new intersubjective and related experience out of an old repetitive enactment of familiar chaos and dissociation.

Group Leadership, Containment, and Complexity

It is primarily by creating the space within which the group could live through this enactment that meaning and the potential for change emerged. There were many opportunities to intervene with interpretations about what was going on. From the get-go when Karen talked in her fragmented way, I could have commented that this was a reaction to the news of the new member. Certainly later many interpretations were possible when Gladys began her assault. Such attempts to turn these moments into group "material," I believe, would foreclose the enactment and deprive the group of the experience of living through these experiences together and to finding their own meaning and mutual help within the experience. The rush to interpret or give premature closure to such moments is often driven by the analyst's anxiety and can be understood as the analyst's need to dissociate (Reis, 2006). It is hard and disturbing for the analyst to be pulled into such dark places. My work is not to do the group's work for them: to know what is going on before they do. My work is to maintain the frame and contain the intolerable affect and thereby help them to do this work together. This involves allowing my immersion in Gladys's assault, to allow it ingress, to become temporarily stuck in the self-state of self denigration and collapse, and to be available with the other group members when an alternative self-state is evoked that will allow us to stand in a space both within the enactment and outside of it.

The group then is in the presence not only of an object that maintains the frame and is durable in the face of disruption and attack, but also of an object that is affected and moved, along with the group. Alvarez (1992) talks about an "animate object" that facilitates the growth of a human mind by joining with and responding to the needs of the child. She elaborates on Winnicott's (1971) idea of the use of an object that emphasizes the object's survival of the infant's attacks. She paints a picture of an object that facilitates the process of reparation following the envious and hateful attacks of the infant or patient. For Alvarez, the process of reparation is crucial to the development of the child's mind and central to the process of containment. What seems to relate most pertinently to my role in the group is the focus Alvarez places on the changes that the object of reparation undergoes: "A repaired object ... is fundamentally different from an undamaged one" (1992, p. 142). In the group, I believe that one part of me, one self-state, is available to be temporarily damaged and then restored, to be disturbed and then to recover, and to be changed in the process. This facility is the animate and alive version of containment that promotes reparation and the growth of mentalization. Similarly, Bollas (1987) suggests that the analyst must become disturbed by the patient when there is powerful disturbance and distress present.

This is a different conception of the role of the group leader. Such a group leader is effective by being engaged, moved, and changed along with the group. This leader operates within the group and yet is always maintaining the safety and boundary of the experience. This is a conception of leadership that seeks to integrate the idea of complexity in systems and is guided by the position of the relational analyst: mutually yet asymmetrically engaged in the process of emergence and change (Aron, 1996).

In terms of dynamic systems theory, the leader is no more able to stay out of the attractor state—the enactment—than the group. The influence that will perturb the system sufficiently to enable the transition out of the attractor state is most potent when coming from within the group itself, as when this group finds its way to alternate and mentalizing self-states. The leader's role then can be conceptualized as the managing of the phase transition or the period of disequilibrium and instability, and allow for this to emerge from its own process. The leader's role is to live with the group, at the edge of chaos.

Implications for Technique and the Group Analyst's Subjectivity

In terms of group analytic technique, there are a number of considerations that my approach suggests. In order for this work to be possible, it is of primary importance that the frame and boundaries of the group analytic situation be maintained as firmly as possible. Without the experience of a firm, yet responsive frame around the group, the patients cannot enter into the kind of emotional territory and exploration described above. Further, without confidence in the frame and the group members' adherence to all the group agreements (Rutan & Stone, 2001), such as not socializing outside of the group and maintaining confidentiality, the group analyst cannot feel comfortable allowing the development of such enactments and will not be able to tolerate the emotional strain for him or herself.

The maintenance of the frame also involves an appreciation of the group analyst's role as leader of the group and the powerful group dynamics and transferences that leadership evokes (Bion, 1961; Turquet, 1974; Klein et al., 1992). The relational approach has, however, introduced a critical reconsideration of the role of the analyst and the analyst's neutrality (Aron, 1996; Hoffman, 1998; Mitchell, 1993, 1997). As mentioned above, it is no longer considered helpful or even possible for the group analyst to be perched above the dynamics of the group in such a way that objective interpretations of the group process are possible. Such a position asks that we also reconsider the role of disclosure of the group analyst's subjectivity during the group and in particular during enactments such as the one described here.

My guiding principle is to always act according to what will maintain the safety of the group environment such that enactments can unfold as deeply and revealingly as possible. Accordingly, it is important that the group analyst be both comfortable and mindful when bringing his or her own subjectivity into the group. I do so when the heat of the group is milder, which is to say, when there are multiple self-states available in the group such that, first, I can find my own subjectivity (not a given during powerful enactments) and, second, that my subjectivity can be comprehended by the group members. For instance, on another occasion, Karen experienced Victor as bullying her. The group members were in agreement with Karen and talked about their feelings about Victor. I had not experienced Victor in this way and introduced this to the group for consideration. When I introduce my subjectivity in this way, it is in the spirit of inquiry and curiosity, that my perception at this time is one of many possibilities. This, I feel is important in that it not only values the members' many points of view, but also models the open search for meaning and self reflection that I hope will become a part of the group culture. On this occasion I was also mindful that Victor can fall into the role of scapegoat, and that Karen can find injuries where there is the smallest slight. In this instance the atmosphere in the group was one of curiosity and exploration, and my introducing of my subjectivity was stirred into the mix of the discussion in, what seemed to be, a healthy manner and furthered the spirit of inquiry (Lichtenberg et al., 2002) and reflection prevalent at the time.

When the group enters the territory of powerful enactments where self-states become rigid and dissociation predominates as described in this chapter, I am much more focused on maintaining the safety of the enterprise. In a situation such as this, I suspect that revelation and discussion of my sense of fragmentation and despair would have created more terror and trauma in the group members and would have therefore closed down the unfolding of the enactment, rather than allowed it to continue. In situations such as this, the containment of the experience seems to be of the utmost importance. To have injected my own experience at this particular juncture would, I believe, have been an evacuation of the difficult emotions I felt I was being asked to contain. My evaluation was that there was little reflective function available in the group at this point and that all I could do was to hold on to the experience and neither preclude nor evacuate it. It is my ability to hold on under duress, to search for my own reflective self-states, that will be internalized by the group members over time.

In Conclusion

I have illustrated an approach to the theory and practice of group psychoanalysis that utilizes the relational concepts of multiple self-states, the centrality of enactments, and the emergence of meaning and mentalization within them. A theory of healing in group psychoanalysis emerges that emphasizes the analyst's containment of enactments and the value of turbulence in group process. The dynamic systems theory concept that change and growth occur in the moments between order and chaos is applied to the group process, particularly to the moments where the group members stand in the spaces within and between alternative self-states while searching for a way through an enactment.

In the vignette, the group members were not only helpful to Gladys, but as I hope is clear, were also becoming less reliant on dissociation themselves, while growing their own abilities for reflective functioning, mentalization, containment, and intersubjective relatedness.

References

Agazarian, Y.M. (1989) Group-as-a-whole system theory and practice. *Group*, 13: 131–154.
Alvarez, A. (1992) *Live Company: Psychoanalytic Psychotherapy with Autistic, Borderline, Deprived and Abused Children*. Hove: Brunner-Routledge.
Aron, L. (1996) *A Meeting of Minds: Mutuality in Psychoanalysis*. Hillsdale, NJ: Analytic Press.
Bion, W.R. (1961) *Experiences in Groups*. London: Tavistock.
Bion, W.R. (1962) *Learning from Experience*. Northvale, NJ: Aronson.
Bollas, C. (1987) *The Shadow of the Object: Psychoanalysis of the Unthought Known*. New York: Columbia University Press.
Bonnefoy, Y. (1982) *L'Arrière-pays*. Paris: Gallimard.
Bromberg, P. (1998) *Standing in the Spaces*. Hillsdale, NJ: Analytic Press.
Bromberg, P. (2006) *Awakening the Dreamer*. Mahwah, NJ: The Analytic Press.
Durkin, H.E. (1981) The technical implications of general systems theory for group psychotherapy. In J.E. Durkin (ed.) *Living Groups*. New York: Bruner Mazel.
Fonagy, P., Gergely, G., Jurist, E., & Target, M. (2002) *Affect Regulation, Mentalization and the Development of the Self*. New York: Other Press.
Foulkes, S.H. (1975) *Group Analytic Psychotherapy: Method and Principles*. London: Gordon & Breach.
Gadamer, H.-G. (1975) *Truth and Method*. Trans. & ed. G. Barden & J. Cumming. New York: Seabury Press. (Original pub. German 1960).
Gadamer, H.-G. (1976) *Philosophical Hermeneutics*. Ed. D.E. Linge. Berkeley: University of California Press.
Galatzer-Levy, R.M. (2004) Chaotic possibilities: toward a new model of development. *Int. J. Psychoanal.* 85: 419–442.
Ghent, E. (2002) Wish, need, drive: Motive in the light of dynamic systems theory and Edelman's selectionist theory. *Psychoanal. Dial.* 12: 763–808.
Gleick, J. (1987) *Chaos: Making of a New Science*. London: Penguin Books.
Gordon, J. (1994) Bion's post-"Experience in Groups" thinking on groups: A clinical example of –K. In V.L. Schermer & M. Pines (eds.) *Ring of Fire: Primitive Affects and Object Relations in Group Psychotherapy* (pp. 107–127). London: Routledge.
Harris, A. (2005) *Gender as Soft Assembly*. Hillsdale, NJ: Analytic Press.
Hinshelwood, R.D. (1994) Attacks on reflective space: Containing primitive emotional states. In V.L. Schermer & M. Pines (eds.) *Ring of Fire: Primitive Affects and Object Relations in Group Psychotherapy* (pp. 86–106). London: Routledge.
Hoffman, I.Z. (1998) *Ritual and Spontaneity in Psychoanalytic Process: A Dialectical-Constructivist View*. Hillsdale, NJ: Analytic Press.
Joseph, B. (1985) Transference: The total situation. In M. Feldman & E.B. Spillius (eds.) *Psychic Equilibrium and Psychic Change: Selected Papers of Betty Joseph* (pp. 156–167). London: Routledge, 1989.
Kauffman, S. (1995) *At Home in the Universe*. New York: Oxford University Press.
Klein, R.H., Bernard, H.S., & Singer, D.L. (1992) *Handbook of Contemporary Group Psychotherapy: Contributions from Object Relations, Self Psychology and Social Systems Theories*. Madison: International Universities Press.
Lewin, R. (1999) *Complexity: Life at the Edge of Chaos*. 2nd edn. Chicago: University of Chicago Press.

Lichtenberg, J.D. Lachmann, F.M., & Fosshage, J.L. (2002) *The Spirit of Inquiry: Communication in Psychoanalysis*. Hillsdale, NJ: Analytic Press.
Loewald, H.W. (1980) *Papers on Psychoanalysis*. New Haven, CT: Yale University Press.
Mitchell, S. (1993) *Hope and Dread in Psychoanalysis*. New York: Basic Books.
Mitchell, S. (1997) *Influence and Autonomy in Psychoanalysis*. Hillsdale, NJ: Analytic Press.
Orange, D.M. (1995) *Emotional Understanding: Studies in Psychoanalytic Epistemology*. New York: The Guilford Press.
Ormont, L.R. (1992) *The Group Therapy Experience: From Theory to Practice*. New York: St. Martin's Press.
Palombo, S.R. (1999) *The Emergent Ego: Complexity and Coevolution in the Psychoanalytic Process*. Madison, CT: International Universities Press.
Pines, M. (1998) Psychic development and the group analytic situation. In M. Pines (ed.) *Circular Reflections: Selected Papers on Group Analysis and Psychoanalysis*. London: Jessica Kingsley.
Racker, H. (1968) *Transference and Countertransference*. New York: International Universities Press.
Reis, B. (2006) Even better than the real thing. *Contemp. Psychoan.* 42 (2): 177–196.
Rubenfeld, S. (2001) Group therapy and complexity theory. *International Journal of Group Psychotherapy* 51 (4): 449–472.
Rutan, J.S. & Stone, W.N. (2001) *Psychodynamic Group Psychotherapy*. New York: Guilford Press.
Stern, D.B. (1997) *Unformulated Experience: From Dissociation to Imagination in Psychoanalysis*. Hillsdale, NJ: Analytic Press.
Turquet, P.M. (1974) Leadership: The individual and the group. In G.S. Gibbard, J.J. Hartman, & R.D. Mann (eds.) *Analysis of Groups*. Washington, DC: Jossey-Bass.
von Bertalanffy, L. (1966) *General Systems Theory and Psychiatry*. New York: Basic Books.
Waldrop, M.M. (1992) *Complexity: The Emerging Science at the Edge of Order and Chaos*. New York: Simon and Schuster.
Winnicott, D.(1971) *Playing and Reality*. London: Tavistock.
Yalom, I.D. (1975) *The Theory and Practice of Group Psychotherapy*. New York: Basic Books.

Chapter 5

Repairing the Irreparable
The Flow of Enactive Engagement in Group Psychotherapy

Robert Grossmark

Introduction

This chapter will advance the view that dynamic change in group psychotherapy is effected by an enactive form of free association which I term the "flow of enactive engagement" (Grossmark, 2012b). I will build on ideas expressed long ago by Foulkes (1948) and Durkin (1964) that placed group free association at the center of the therapeutic action of group analysis and group therapy. I will then outline the phenomena of trauma, dissociation, and enactment that have been central to the relational conception of psychopathology and therapeutic action drawing in particular on the work of Philip Bromberg (1998, 2006) and D.B. Stern (1997, 2010). I will suggest that the engine of a contemporary group psychotherapy is the group's flow into and out of group enactments of traumatic phenomena and states. This flow can be allowed to move along unimpeded by an engaged and involved yet unobtrusive group analyst just as a more classical analyst might have listened to the flow of a patient's free associations. In the model I will describe the associations as things that *happen* in the group rather than the verbal associations of the members, and the group analyst is embedded in the process rather than abstinent or neutral as in the original Freudian conception. From this flow of enactments emerges the narrative of the unconscious and dissociated life of the group members and the group as a whole. These enactments can often involve the group in painful, disruptive, and distressing affect and experience for group members and group therapist alike (Grossmark, Chapter 4 this volume), and I will offer clinical examples that illustrates the work of group therapy from this perspective.

Group Free Association

Writing at the inception of the practice of group psychotherapy, Foulkes utilized and embellished upon Freud's concept of free association. Freud, you will recall, asked his patients to say whatever came into their minds, to avoid censoring any thoughts according to what they might deem irrelevant or unpleasant. He told his patients to:

act as though, for instance, you were a traveller sitting next to the window of a railway carriage and describing to someone inside the carriage the changing views which you see outside.

(Freud, 1913, p. 135)

For Freud this was the basic rule of psychoanalysis. Foulkes (1948; Foulkes & Anthony, 1957) spelled out the practice of group psychotherapy and amongst his vivid and innovative ideas was the idea of "Free-floating discussion" which was the group equivalent of Freud's free association. Foulkes (1948) described "free-floating discussion" thus:

> The basic rule of Group Analysis, in so far as the patients' verbal communications are concerned, is the group counterpart of free association: talk about anything which comes to your mind without selection.
>
> (p. 71)

Indeed to this day, I believe that many would agree that one of the hallmarks of group analysis or dynamic group psychotherapy is the invitation for the group to talk and interact freely. (This would distinguish the psychodynamic group psychotherapies from those that involve the imposition of structure, manualized exercises or instruction that characterize much CBT and DBT group work.)

Some years after Foulkes we find Helen Durkin (1964), elaborating on the idea that the group members' interactions can be regarded as free associations. She suggested that:

> if the therapist regards the intercommunications as free associations and searches out their latent content, he will have no difficulty in identifying transferences in the group.
>
> (p. 147)

Durkin is suggesting, much like Foulkes, that if the group therapist can allow a certain type of flow amongst the group members, unconscious content and dynamics will be revealed. Her focus, though, is on the verbal "intercommunications" of the group members. Further, like many from the classical tradition, she regards the therapist as situated outside of the group dynamic and able to analyze the latent content of the associations and hence interpret the group transferences (p. 148). While much has changed in our conception of the therapeutic action of both individual and group treatment, I do believe that Foulkes, Durkin, and others laid the groundwork for the value of a therapeutic situation where a flow of interaction can occur. This group interaction is the ground from which something unknown and yet-to-be-registered can emerge. I will return to these valuable ideas in a while.

Trauma and Dissociation in Group Therapy

Much has happened since the days of the abstinent and neutral analyst and the free associating patient in analysis and in group. The concept of free association has been deconstructed (for instance, see Hoffman, 2006) and the contemporary relational environment has emphasized that the therapist is always embedded in the field of the treatment whether it be group or individual. The careful use of the therapist's own experience has been accepted as a useful and transformative element of intervention rather than a failure of technique (for instance, Bromberg, 2006), and psychoanalytic treatment and therapy has been cast as a mutual enterprise (Aron, 1996). As this volume attests, the theories of intersubjectivity (Benjamin, 1995), social construction (Hoffman, 1998) and most importantly dissociation and enactment (Bromberg, 1998, 2006; Stern, 1997, 2010) have replaced the psychoanalytic world of drives and their derivatives, analyst neutrality, and abstinence. Altogether contemporary relational psychoanalysis seems to be a much more accessible and welcoming abode, and would seem to reflect more generally held contemporary authority relations.

I will review here the concepts of dissociation and enactment and rely heavily on the work of Philip Bromberg and D.B. Stern.[1] They and others (such as Howell, 2005) have suggested that dissociation is the primary way that the human mind is structured. From this perspective, dissociation is regarded as both adaptive and maladaptive and is seen as a continuum that embraces normal everyday adaptive dissociation through to profound and pathological dissociation, the kind that one encounters in dissociative identity disorder. From this position the mind is viewed as comprising self-states. The primary motivator in psychological functioning is the maintenance of self continuity. Optimally this is achieved by a flexibility and fluidity among self-states that enable people to live creatively and to adapt to life's challenges. This adaptation is constrained by what is affectively safe. When affect is overwhelming and self continuity is threatened, as in massive or cumulative trauma, the normal process of dissociation is magnified and rigidified and a dissociative structure will predominate the personality.

Dissociation is not in essence a defense, but rather a normal hypnoid capacity of the mind that facilitates the everyday adaptations of life. It is hard to imagine a person without any ability to dissociate. Such a person would not only lack flexibility in adapting from one moment to the next, but also be barely able to organize his or her mind. I am reminded of Funes, the character created by Borges (1941) who has no ability to forget, and is rendered unable to function and live by this condition. Borges describes Funes with the idea of memory in the foreground, but it also seems to me that what is conjured in Borges's sublime tale is the specter of one who cannot dissociate. Funes is not able to access different self-states and alternate registers of human functioning and relating. For him, self-states that enable repose and mirth, for instance, were unavailable. There was no respite from the overwhelming press of stimuli from the world. Living and thinking itself are impossible without dissociation.

Let me distinguish dissociation from repression. In repression, as formulated by Freud, ideas are banished from awareness because of conflict and unpleasure that incompatible ideas would generate. This implies that the experience has already been formulated. It exists or has existed in symbolized form. When repressed, it is put away, but exists in a form that can be retrieved. Wachtel (1977) plays with Freud's archeological metaphor and calls this the "woolly mammoth" hypothesis, which sees the unconscious as containing fully formed bodies, like a fossilized woolly mammoth that exists perfectly frozen in time waiting to be unearthed by the archeologist/psychoanalyst. I grant that this is a greatly oversimplified rendition of an extremely complex and subtle theory of mental functioning, but perhaps it does capture a certain spirit of psychodynamic thinking against which I would like to contrast the dissociation approach.

The idea of dissociation is distinct. The formulation and linguistic coding that creates experience is not taken as a given.[2] The processes that make experience are overwhelmed and impeded in trauma. Events are not pulled together into a coherent experiential or linguistic form. They are unformulated (Stern, 1997). In dissociation, a whole self-state is isolated and sequestered, because to be that self-state is to threaten the self with annihilation: it is unbearable. Accordingly, intrapsychic conflict is neither at the center of this theory nor this approach to treatment. Indeed, from this perspective, intrapsychic conflict is an achievement that follows the integration of dissociated self-states, rather than the primary cause of psychopathology.

D.B. Stern (1997) distinguished between dissociation in the strong and the weak sense. In the face of massive trauma we see dissociation in the strong sense as an adaptive response, a human response to the terror of dissolution of selfhood. We can say that trauma becomes overwhelming when there is an absence of recognition by significant others. The affective destabilization is then overwhelming and the events cannot be experienced and thought about. The hyper-arousal of terror or confusion cannot be managed and transformed by thought. The experience cannot become a part of "me." The person's self continuity is hence protected by dissociation, but at a great price. The normal pathways that allow experience to become recorded linguistically and hence become available for memory, part of one's own narrative, are overwhelmed. There is no recognition or witnessing that can make these events and the emotional pain real and therefore recoverable. The experience, sometimes the actual memories and representations of the experience, and often the affect connected to the experience are dissociated. The point is, they do not go away. They become part of the sub-symbolic (Bucci, 1997) somato-sensory realm that can then come to "haunt" (Bromberg, 2003) the person.

These non-processed psychic events reside in an unformulated (Stern, 1997) yet-to-be-known realm. They are not available for interpretation. Crucially for group therapy, we can say that they can only become known in enactments. That is to say that these unformulated aspects of the person that are not part of the person's sense of "me" are encountered in relation to others. In the treatment situation, and most profoundly in group, it is via enactments between the patient and therapist, between the patient and the other group members, or of the group-as-a-whole that the "not me" becomes manifest.

> Susan, an Italian-American woman in her forties told the group a story of terrible violation and abuse. She had been sexually abused by her male cousins during family summers at a country house. She had never told her parents or anyone at all, up until this moment in group. Up until this moment she had been a friendly and open presence in group, able to offer help to others. She had talked mainly about her problems dating. However, she told of the violation and abuse in a manner devoid of any affect. Group members, many of whom had suffered terrible abuse themselves, reacted with violent intensity. Jenny was enraged that Susan's parents had not noticed or in any way protected Susan. Susan protested that her parents were exemplary. She had never wanted to upset them. Jenny's rage turned to fury and she screamed that she wanted to burn the whole of Susan's family alive for what they had done. George, whose father had been incestuously involved with his younger sisters, wanted to know more details about the actual sexual abuse. Julian, who had been sexually abused by a neighbor as a child, said that he wanted to leave the room because he was feeling nauseous and accused George of being a pervert who was trying to get some kind of stimulation out of Susan's painful story. I myself was overwhelmed and feared for Susan's mental safety. I feared that she could not withstand this onslaught and would be re-traumatized. I told the group that these intense and terrifying emotions were of extreme importance, because we were entering into the actual experience of abuse and violation. In this group enactment, which continued over many sessions (interspersed with other self-states and forms of relatedness) the group came to live through what Susan had yet to experience. The affect—terror, pain, disgust, violence, perversion—that had been dissociated and unthinkable up to this point emerged within and between the group members. Furthermore, each of the other group members entered the fields of dissociated trauma that they had yet to fully experience. George's horror and contempt for his father, Julian's fear and revulsion, Jenny's rage at her abusive parents all became activated in the group enactment. The group indeed felt for a while that it was "on fire" with intense affect and the combustion of previously dissociated affect. Gradually through many sessions the group members were able to talk to each other with more reflective function and to observe the dynamics of trauma and offer support for each other. For instance, George was able to say to Susan that he was sorry for his intrusive questions, but he understood that

> this was a terrible legacy of the incest in his own household. He had, in fact, been a compulsive snoop, at times even stalking women he had developed an interest in. He had never considered himself as anything but respectful of women. This perverse side of him was previously consigned to an alternate dissociated self-state, and regarded as "not me." Jenny asked Susan to understand her rage. Jenny connected to rage that she was previously unable to own. She listened carefully to the group's suggestions that she pushed people away with her burning rage at the whole world. Susan herself had never considered that she was angry with her parents. She gradually filled in a much fuller picture of a complex family system that seemed characterized by denial and dissociation. Most importantly, she began to experience affect as she talked about her family. She also began to reassess how it came to be that no relationship of hers ever lasted beyond a few weeks. She had always regarded this as simply bad luck.

The group had enacted all the parts of the violations and abuses suffered, and even perpetrated (in George's case) by the group members. They came to emotional life within the group sessions. The point here is that until the experience that has been dissociated is actually lived through in an enactment, and is recognized and becomes graspable as lived experience in all its pain and sorrow, it cannot become "really real" and will remain as an invisible force impeding the patient's ability to live fully and meaningfully. All the members I have mentioned here were shocked by the virulence of their own emotions during this period.

Trauma can be manifestly massive, such as that suffered by Susan and the other group members, or it can be subtle and almost everyday, such as the cumulative experiences of a child whose expressions of selfhood are met with controlling or shaming responses, or are disconfirmed by non-recognition. These then become dissociated not-me self-states that can lead to many forms of symptomatology. We see, for example, the hardened concreteness of black and white thinking, disowned hostility, avoidance, and much more. The dissociated experiences become the story that cannot be told. Yet in group the narrative unfolds as enactment and interaction. It is lived through and begins to become real and graspable.

Dissociation also implies a breakdown in the normal and creative process of making experience and making meaning. Here is the weak or everyday dissociation, the consequence of cumulative developmental or relational trauma. This applies to the stories that are prevented from being told, not because they absolutely must be avoided, but because other stories are more dominant. We find a narrative rigidity. This then shapes and constructs attachment patterns which then, to a large degree, govern one's life. Susan was unable to think beyond "bad luck" about her inability to make relationships work. Jenny had lived in quiet and lonely resentment never considering that her own reservoir of rage might keep others from staying close to her.

Enactment in Group Therapy

As I mentioned above, what is dissociated and unformulated and "not me" finds form and expression in enactment. Enactment involves the patient, the therapist, and the other group members in interaction. Meanings and narratives that were unthinkable before emerge in these interactions. The internal pressures and hauntings that have constricted the patient's experience become interpersonal group dynamics that involve everyone including the therapist. As the above example attests, these enactments often involve painful and abrasive interactions and experiences in the group. Rather than being seen as blockages or resistances to the harmonious working of the group, from this perspective, these enactments are the very point of the exercise. The group with Susan may have felt extremely difficult, even disorganizing to me and the members, but I do believe that the work that was done during this enactment was the very reason we were there. Enactments may be regarded, as Bromberg has suggested, as the "royal road" to the unconscious and to change (Bromberg, 2000). Indeed, the affective storm unleashed in the group after Susan's telling of her abuse opened up areas of emotion and experience that had not been available for these group members in this way before. Rather than seeing such a storm as a problem, I would see it as the group enactment equivalent of the "royal road." I will later take up the idea of allowing the enactments to safely unfold, just as Freud would listen to the unfolding free associations of his patients.

But first, a few more words about enactment. For me, the idea of enactment has helped me uncouple myself from the pejorative sense in the concept of "resistance." Rather than a resistance-based idea that would construe group process in terms of what is being avoided and not done, I would rather be curious as to what the group or group member *is* doing. I would rather be curious and open to what is being created, within the enactment, what story is being told, rather than divining what is not happening and what is being "resisted."

From this perspective, treatment takes place through entering, living through and finding some meaning and resolution through the enactments. Sometimes these can feel benign, interesting, even quirky and entertaining, and at other times they can feel like entering an abyss of pain and torture.

A brief—and less traumatic—example from another group. A patient came late to group. I would rather not think about resistances to the task of the group or challenges to the frame of therapy. I would rather let myself not know what is happening and try to see where the flow of the group and my experience will take us, and anticipate the emergence of some as yet undefined meaning. The patient who was late to group was a punctual and impeccably responsible person in his life. It turned out that he had been sleeping and had not woken up on time for the group. He had, however, been dreaming. I held in my mind the idea that one does not have to be physically present in the room to be in treatment, and asked about the dream. The dream was full of dread, loss, and being left. The group picked up on this profound theme in this man's life and gradually put together that they had experienced a painful absence when he had not shown up for group on time. One of the group members talked with emotion about her dread that the late patient had forgotten about or even abandoned the group. I myself had harbored some similar worry. My take on this was that we were involved in an enactment. When the group expressed their feelings, what emerged was the articulation of a previously dissociated agony. The group played the part of the man as a child, dreading that he was emotionally abandoned and forgotten about, and the man himself inhabited the experience of being lost and forgotten as well as the role of the abandoning parent. When not interfered with, with too quick interpretations, the group can find themselves living out what had previously not been formulated. In its behavior, the group had told a story: his story, that he could not have told in words, because it was never formulated in his mind. He had never been attended to in such a way that his experience could be made real. The abandoned little boy was finally getting recognized and did not have to continue life as "not me." He did not have to live forever compelled to be obsessively thoughtful, punctual, reliable, and perfect to the point of psychosomatic anxiety symptoms.

This brief and very simplified example captures the idea that rather than seeing the patient or group as *not* doing something, as resisting, I would rather see what the patient or group is trying to create. I will see the patient as looking for or even forcing the therapist and group into some form of recognition of what the patient has yet to know about themselves. It is a silent scream from a dissociated self-state that the patient has had no access to. Rather than trying to understand or interpret the situation, which might only lead to an intensification of the rigidity of the dissociated, not-thinking state, the therapist can welcome and engage in the enactment with the other group members and the meaning—as yet unformulated, unknown to the patient and group—will emerge in the interaction. It is in what happens and what is about to happen that the action of the group takes place. Only when something feels personally real for the group members and for the therapist can it become truly known and have meaning. Certainly this applies to the first example of Susan's group. She and the group members I mentioned were silently screaming for recognition of their unformulated and unknown pain and trauma.

Groups as Creative and Meaning-Making

It is a truism to say that groups are always interacting. As they do so and group members engage with each other, enactments are unavoidable, just like group interaction. They are inevitable. Enactments are constantly unfolding and involve group members, the therapist, and the group-as-a-whole. There are constant oscillations between rigid, dissociated, and unmentalized states that often cause pain and turbulence for the group and therapist, and more reflective states where the group and the therapist have more space to try to figure out what is going on (see Grossmark, Chapter 4 this volume). It is in interaction and enactment that we find meaning evolving. Here I draw from contemporary psychoanalysts who have emphasized the hermeneutic aspect of treatment (Orange, 2010, 2011; Stern, 1997, 2010). The touchstone here is the philosophical work of Hans-Georg Gadamer (2004). Meaning does not exist such that it can be interpreted, but rather comes into being through enactment itself, through dialogue and intersubjective engagement. Meaning is not regarded as a linguistic formulation, it is an event (Gadamer, 2004). This perspective shifts the nature of the therapeutic action of group and individual treatment. There is a move away from the idea that therapeutic action derives from the interpretation of meaning as a static truth that can be analyzed intellectually from the outside, as it were. (Here we might reference the image I began with, of Freud listening to the patient's free associations and interpreting the meaning from a neutral and abstinent position.) From the hermeneutic perspective, the work of healing involves the creation of meaning in interaction and enactment. The emphasis here is on the engagement and the emergence of what has yet to be known in interaction. I hope that the above examples illustrate that the cognitive and affective meanings for all group members grew out of the enactment. It, the meaning, is not regarded as a static truth that was buried and was waiting to be uncovered (a woolly mammoth). It had to be lived through together to come into being.

From this perspective there is a subtle shift toward a different image of the power of group. Classically, group therapy has been regarded as a way to situate the patient in a regressive situation. The emphasis has been on the regressive pull of the group situation and group dynamics (for example, see Schermer & Pines, 1994). Just as the analytic setting and the analytic couch was regarded as inducing a regressed state such that more primitive emotions could become manifest (Etchegoyen, 1991), group analysts regarded the group setting as similarly regressive. I believe that anyone who has experienced any kind of group, whether small or large, can attest to the evocation of more regressed phenomena. However, I would propose that this is not the *only* aspect of group process that is available for the group and its members. I would suggest that we can fruitfully think of regression as the evocation of different self-states, perhaps more fragmented, less developed, more emotionally charged, and so on. I would foreground the primarily creative potential that these self-states and the group offer. I am not here talking about artistic creative potential, although these self-states may also be the font of actual artistic or scientific creation. Rather, I am talking about the potential to create experience and meaning that had not been realized before. I would say that the groups I mentioned above were engaged in creative work. They found powerful meaning in painful moments. I am proposing that when a group is allowed to flow into and through enactments in a safe way, tremendous creative potential to undo dissociations and make meaning where previously there was emptiness and dull repetition is freed up. Being a part of this creative and vitalizing enterprise is in and of itself a healing experience for many members even when they are not the specific object of the group's work. In other words, when Susan and the group entered the area of trauma in an affectively alive way, what followed was not simply re-traumatization, but a shared experiencing and shared reaching for understanding of and with each other. This shared endeavor is exactly what had been missing from the group members' early developmental lives.

The developmental implications are strong here. There is not space to elaborate on this fully here, but suffice to say that the healing power of this kind of creative group process can be regarded as a version of the growth-promoting qualities of the early mother–child or family–child environment, where meaning is consistently made in interaction between and within the players (for example, Malloch & Trevarthen, 2009; Tronick, 2007). It is the antidote to traumatic non-recognition.

Shame, Repetition, and Witnessing in Group

Shame plays a central role in the formation of dissociative structures and the painful repetitive quality of the lives of patients whose psychology is dominated by trauma and dissociation. Shame is often key to understanding enactments of trauma.

The self-states and needs of the child that are either assaulted or less visibly disconfirmed by the parents create an interminable sense of shame. It is not what one does that is at stake, but an abiding sense of who one *is*. Therefore there is no opportunity for reparation, as there is when one has *done* something wrong and can change one's behavior to right that wrong. When in the grip of shame, there is an inner certainty that there is something terribly wrong and unacceptable about who one *is*. The patient longs for recognition of her pain and this longing itself is felt to be utterly illegitimate and is itself infused with shame and is consequently dissociated. The patient is, as it were, locked in a living nightmare: the only person who can give the acknowledgment that is so desperately needed is the very person who is causing the shame and therefore the least likely to offer it.

This dilemma is at the heart of what we have traditionally called the "repetition compulsion" that drives destructive enactments in treatment and self destructive and masochistic behavior patterns in life. Bromberg (2006) sees these enactments as attempts to "repair the irreparable" (p. 94). But the past cannot be repaired: it is only with the truly felt recognition of that damaged past by an emotionally connected group that the present and future can be freed to be experienced. As with all self-states that are dissociated, shame is not brought into group by being spoken about and announced, but rather is found in the sub-symbolic experiences enacted between patient and group. As the above examples illustrate, the group and the therapist will inevitably fail the patient, and will, in this way, come to know the patient's experience "for what it is" (Bromberg, 2006, p. 94). The lives of all of the patients mentioned in the above examples were suffused with terrible and unbearable shame. None of these people announced this or even were aware that this was so. And as Bromberg suggested, in the case of Susan's group, the group did come to "fail" Susan and the others. The persons causing the shame and pain became personified in the other group members. It is as if the scenes of abuse were replayed in the group with various group members assigned roles in the drama.[3] But unlike the original others who abused and neglected Susan, these group members were able to attempt to own their part in the enactment and thereby offer some recognition and healing to Susan's shame. Via the working through of the enactment, the experiences became known by others for what they were in all their pain and despair.

This process involves an "enactive witnessing" (Reis, 2009). This is a contemporary view of witnessing. D.B. Stern has also emphasized the witnessing element of enactments (Stern, 2010). Much trauma literature has powerfully illuminated the healing power of witnessing (for example, see Feldman and Laub, 1992). The literature is too vast to be addressed in any substance here, but let us note that one of the crucial elements in the formation of traumatic dissociation is the absence of a witness to confirm the reality of the trauma and pain, to recognize the suffering. Much of the trauma literature involves the telling of the trauma to an empathic listener or group. The idea of enactive witnessing shifts the emphasis away from the telling and into the "living through." The anguish of shame and the world of the dissociated, unformulated "not me" does not enter the group through a verbal telling. Rather, as I have shown, it emerges through enactment. When the group connected to and accompanied Susan (and the late patient) into the worlds of trauma and shame and lived within that pain and appreciated it "for what it was," there emerged a new dimension of witnessing. This is a lived and enacted witnessing. The groups mentioned above offered a witnessing of a previously unseen and unrecognized suffering by living through the suffering in real time in the group. Together. Such powerful enactments make the previously shame-inducing shadows of pain "really real" (Bromberg, 2006, p. 66) for the patient and group. This is how one repairs the irreparable. As in the case of Susan, the traumatized group member knows deeply that the other members have actually gotten it. They now know, from their own shared experience and actual participation, the degree and nature of the traumatic suffering.

Repairing the Irreparable Through the Flow of Enactive Engagement in Group Therapy

Working from this perspective raises questions about the group therapist's position and technique. Pertinent questions arise about when to draw attention to what is going on in the group, and when to ask the members to help in understanding the enactments (although one may never use such a word when talking to a group). When do we interpret and when do we offer our own experience of what is happening to the group and to us? My inclination is to respect the power of the enactments and the shared living through that the group offers. As I mentioned above, all the normal rules of boundaries and safety apply, because without a safe and predictable structure, there simply cannot be adequate safety for members to do this work. Within that framework, I am inclined to allow enactments to flow. I trust that the meaning will emerge, and would do well to wait and tolerate whatever difficult experience the group is entering. Unconscious, dissociated affect or traumatic memory is rarely so clear from the outset. I adhere to the idea that when the group can be safely allowed to flow into and through enactments, meaning that is often surprising and potentially reparative will emerge.

This brings us back to Freud's idea of free association. To recap, Freud regarded free association as the key mechanism by which the psychoanalytic cure proceeded (Freud, 1913, 1923) and he recommended that the analyst in no way interfere with this process. Likewise Foulkes and Durkin recommended that the group therapist allow a free-floating group discussion or group free association. My suggestion is that the analyst similarly not impede or obstruct the emergence of the flow of enactive engagement in group.

There are many ways that a group therapist can impede the unfolding of enactments and there were many moments when I could have done so in the enactment involving Susan and the group. Premature interpretation of individual or group dynamics can bring the group out of the world of engagement with each other into a more intellectual realm where the group is asked to "think about" what is happening rather than continue to interact and struggle within the process. Similarly, too quick an exploration of the here-and-now dynamic in the form of questioning what is going on in the moment can bring members into a more removed state of mind. Certainly both interpretation and exploration can offer much needed containment when the group can feel overwhelming and scary. The group therapist's tact and open consideration of each member's needs and vulnerabilities is of utmost importance when enactments of trauma are flowing. Generally I strive for a position that supports the group members as they interact and conveys real curiosity and belief that whatever it is that is happening, it will no doubt ultimately have real meaning for the group. Hence I aim to be both fully engaged and unobtrusive such that the flow of enactive engagement can proceed (Grossmark, 2012a, 2012b). I did support Susan and the group such that they felt held and safe enough in the group, even as they were beset with pain, rage, and overwhelming affect. My encouragement that, even though painful, this challenging time was exactly why they had come to group, and my belief that we would all come through this having achieved some real psychological growth seemed to offer holding and containment even when they felt hopelessness and despair.

I use the term "flow of enactive engagement" to capture the essence of Freud's and Foulkes's initial vision of allowing the flow into unknown psychological territory. A free (and safe) interacting of the group that allows for the emergence of the unformulated. I also seek to evoke the British independent tradition of psychoanalysis where the analyst does not obtrude into the unfolding of the unconscious life of the patient, as captured by Balint's (1968) description of the "unobtrusive analyst." I have adopted this idea to offer a contemporary image of a very much engaged analyst who is also able to be unobtrusive to the unfolding of the patient's inner psychic world in the treatment (Grossmark, 2012a). Further, the "flow of enactive engagement" shifts the therapeutic action away from the mental, spoken, one-person connotation of free association to the enacted and enactive process in which the group and the group therapist are allowed to enter into enactments in a free but safe manner and are not interfered with by interpretations or demands to know what is happening before it has emerged. Patients like Susan, whose lives are dominated by the psychic sediment of dissociated and cumulative trauma, for whom there are no words for their inner life, and who are inhabited by self-states that defy verbal description, tell their lives, their pain, and their psychological make-up in their own idioms of *action* and *engagement*. They are joined by the other group members and therapist who are ready and available to live with and through (Joseph, 1985) these self-states and mutual regressions. It is via the flow of these enactments that the trauma is re-lived. However, rather than a re-traumatization, there is recognition and real-time enactive witnessing of the trauma by the other group members and the therapist who accompany the patient into these areas of previously unbearable pain. The experience becomes really real and the dull pain of ongoing repetition is replaced by a sense of repair via accompaniment, witnessing, and shared survival. The experience becomes real and manageable rather than requiring dissociation to maintain the patient's sense of self and continuity.

I must note, however, that the flow of enactive engagement in group does not imply that the group therapist enters the patient's and the group's world and the emergent group enactment and takes leave of his or her own abilities to think and process the experience. Like the analyst's reverie or evenly hovering attention, it suggests an altered self-state that exists simultaneously with other states. As mentioned above, it also asks that the group therapist be clear and firm around boundaries while allowing for the inevitable boundary ambiguities (such as the late patient mentioned above) and challenges that occur as part of the treatment when one connects with these areas of functioning.

My Dream About Susan

The group therapist is engaged fully in enactments such as those I have described. Feelings, sensations, thoughts, and dreams often flood the group therapist and it is often hard to hold on to one's group therapist self-state (Burton, 2012) amidst these storms. The work is to find a way to "stand in the spaces" (Bromberg, 1998) of many self-states at once, so that even as one is immersed in the traumatic enactment of the group, one can also maintain some hold on one's therapist self.

A few sessions into the enactment presaged by Susan's revelations of abuse, I had a dream. I dreamed that Susan was on fire. I woke up with a clear thought in my mind. Susan, I thought, is a burn victim. And just like severe burn victims, she cannot be touched, because to touch her would cause even more unbearable pain. I thought of the many other possible psychoanalytic interpretations of the dream involving traumatic sexuality and violation of her body, her own aggression and its consuming quality, and so on. I felt all were useful in conceptualizing and understanding Susan. But I did feel, due to the clarity of my waking thought, that the idea of her as untouchable spoke most immediately to the group process and to all the other traumatized members of the group. They could not truly touch each other without unbearable pain. This dream helped me stand in the spaces during these tumultuous group sessions. The group members were trying to really contact each other, with all their trauma and pain. The only way they could do so was in the fiery combustion of these enactments. The pain, aggression, and chaos were inevitable. The group itself was screaming a necessary scream. This knowledge guided me and enabled me to allow this enactment to continue its flow such that the group members themselves found their way to relate to each other from more than one traumatized self-state. This, I believe, is how the repair of what is irreparable can unfold.

Notes

1 While this is familiar territory for those within the community of relational psychoanalysts, it seems to me that it is of value to spell out these ideas for those readers coming from other approaches to group therapy.
2 I have found resonance between these ideas that stress the failure to make experience out of events with Bion's work on alpha function (Bion, 1967; applied to the group situation by Gordon, 1994). Both approaches take an interest in the processes by which experience is made. There are, however, real differences in these theories and their epistemologies. There is no space here to address these.
3 See Davies and Frawley's (1994) work on the psychoanalytic treatment of adult survivors of childhood sexual abuse for a vivid description of the enactment of the myriad constellations of the participants in the original trauma. For instance, the therapist may find herself becoming the denying mother, penetrating abuser, or abused child in relation to the patient.

References

Aron, L. (1996) *A Meeting of Minds: Mutuality in Psychoanalysis*. Hillsdale, NJ: Analytic Press.
Balint, M. (1968) *The Basic Fault*. London: Tavistock.
Benjamin, J. (1995) *Like Subjects, Love Objects, Essays on Recognition and Sexual Difference*. New Haven: Yale University Press.
Bion, W.R.D. (1967) *Second Thoughts*. London: Heinemann.
Borges, J.L. (1941) Funes the memorious. In J. Irby (trans.) and D. Yates and J. Irby (eds.) *Labyrinths: Selected Stories and Other Writings* (pp. 59–66). New York: New Directions, 1962.
Bromberg, P.M. (1998) *Standing in the Spaces: Essays on Clinical Process, Trauma and Dissociation*. Hillsdale, NJ: Analytic Press.
Bromberg, P.M. (2000) Potholes on the royal road: or is it an abyss? *Contemporary Psychoanalysis*, 36: 5–28.
Bromberg, P.M. (2003) One need not be a house to be haunted. *Psychoanalytic Dialogues*, 13: 689–709
Bromberg, P.M. (2006) *Awakening the Dreamer: Clinical Journeys*. Mahwah, NJ: The Analytic Press.

Bucci, W. (1997) *Psychoanalysis and Cognitive Science: A Multiple Code Theory*. New York: Guilford Press.
Burton, N. (2012) Getting personal: Thoughts on therapeutic action through the interplay of intimacy, affect and consciousness. *Psychoanalytic Dialogues*, 22: 662–678.
Davies, J.M. & Frawley, M.G. (1994) *Treating the Adult Survivor of Childhood Sexual Abuse*. New York: Basic Books.
Durkin, H.E. (1964) *The Group in Depth*. New York: International Universities Press.
Etchegoyen, R.H. (1991) *The Fundamentals of Psychoanalytic Technique*. London: Karnac Books.
Feldman, S. & Laub, D. (1992) *Testimony: Crises of Witnessing in Literature, Psychoanalysis and History*. New York: Routledge.
Foulkes, S.H. (1948) *Introduction to Group-Analytic Psychotherapy: Studies in the Social Integration of Individuals and Groups*. London: Maresfield Library.
Foulkes, S.H. & Anthony, E.J. (1957) *Group Psychotherapy: The Psychoanalytic Approach*. Harmondsworth, UK: Penguin.
Freud, S. (1913) On beginning the treatment. *Standard Edition of the Complete Psychological Works of Sigmund Freud* XII (p. 135). London: Hogarth Press.
Freud, S. (1923) Two encyclopedia articles. *Standard Edition*, Vol. 18 (pp. 233–260). London: Hogarth Press.
Gadamer, H.G. (2004) *Truth and Method*. 2nd rev. edn. New York: Continuum.
Gordon, J. (1994) Bion's post-*Experiences in Groups* thinking on groups: A clinical example of –K. In V.L. Schermer & M. Pines (eds.) *Ring of Fire: Primitive Affects and Object Relations in Group Psychotherapy* (pp. 86–106). London: Routledge.
Grossmark, R. (2007) The edge of chaos: Enactment, disruption, and emergence in group psychotherapy. *Psychoanalytic Dialogues*, 17: 479–500.
Grossmark, R. (2012a) The unobtrusive relational analyst. *Psychoanalytic Dialogues*, 22: 629–646.
Grossmark, R. (2012b) The flow of enactive engagement. *Contemporary Psychoanalysis*. 48 (3): 287–300.
Hoffman, I.Z. (1998) *Ritual and Spontaneity in the Psychoanalytic Process: A Dialectical-constructivist View*. Hillsdale, NJ: Analytic Press.
Hoffman, I.Z. (2006) The myths of free association and the potentials of the analytic relationship. *International Journal of Psycho-Analysis*, 87: 43–61.
Howell, E.F. (2005) *The Dissociative Mind*. Hillsdale, NJ: Analytic Press.
Joseph, B. (1985) Transference: The total situation. In M. Feldman & E.B. Spillius (eds.) *Psychic Equilibrium and Psychic Change; Selected Papers of Betty Joseph* (pp. 156–167). London: Routledge, 1989.
Malloch, S. & Trevarthen, C. (eds.) (2009) *Communicative Musicality: Exploring the Basis of Human Companionship*. New York: Oxford University Press.
Orange, D.M. (2010) *Thinking for Clinicians: Philosophical Resources for Contemporary Psychoanalysis and the Humanistic Psychotherapies*. New York: Routledge.
Orange, D.M. (2011) *The Suffering Stranger: Hermeneutics for Everyday Clinical Practice*. New York: Routledge.
Reis, B. (2009) Performative and enactive features of psychoanalytic witnessing: The transference as the scene of address. *International Journal of Psycho-Analysis*, 90: 1359–1372.
Schermer, V.L. & Pines, M. (1994) *Ring of Fire: Primitive Affects and Object relations in Group Psychotherapy*. London: Routledge.

Stern, D.B. (1997) *Unformulated Experience: From Dissociation to Imagination in Psychoanalysis*. Hillsdale, NJ: Analytic Press.
Stern, D.B. (2010) *Partners in Thought: Working with Unformulated Experience, Dissociation and Enactment*. New York: Routledge.
Tronick, E. (2007) *The Neurobehavioral and Social-Emotional Development of Infants and Children*. London: W.W. Norton.
Wachtel, P. (1977) *Psychoanalysis and Behavior Therapy: Toward and Integration*. New York: Basic Books.

Chapter 6

Developing Nuclear Ideas

Richard M. Billow

In the course of leading a group, ideas flow in and out of my consciousness. Some seem to originate from within me, although many emerge from the verbalizations and behaviors of others. Even if the group appears to move on, several ideas linger and begin to impinge. They are now asserting influence on me; unavoidably they affect group process. So I think about why the ideas or set of ideas has captured my attention: what they have to do with the clinical situation—present and past— and to my psychology, to the extent to which I understand it.

I consider how these ideas relate to what others are saying and doing—linking together, if I am able, unfolding intrapsychic, interpersonal, and whole group processes. It is at this point of connection that a *nuclear idea* begins to coalesce, but it must be examined. I try to see if the idea has relevance to others, and is applicable to smaller or larger milieus, or both. This places the idea in intellectual and symbolic contexts, which also have cultural and historical dimensions.

The idea has to feel vital. I can put it aside but not forget about it. Emotional reverberations energize my thoughts, and realizations sometimes occur that surprise me. If I wish to communicate, I must test whether the idea is comprehensible to other group members. Even if they are not having similar experiences, or are having them but do not see things my way, they need still to understand what I am referring to.

This progression, as I reflect, parallels Bion's (1963) notion of the *psychoanalytic object*. Bion left the concept unsaturated, to be built upon, although only a few others have written about it, and briefly (Grotstein, 2007, more extensively). I have found the concept helpful in achieving essential therapeutic goals of containment, cohesion, and coherence. As we shall see, developing nuclear ideas provides a way of thinking and working: shifting interest and discussion from "surface" contents to nonconscious or unexplored psychic processes in the individual and whole group, and thus to draw attention to multiple meanings—to the metapsychology of our interactions.

Bion's theoretical formulations tend to mystify and obscure their broad clinical utility, and also tend to exalt the analyst or group therapist as the "seer" or "exceptional individual" (his terms). Bion (1962) conceptualized the psychoanalytic object as emerging from the "discourse and behaviour of the patient" (Britton, 1998, p. 818) and brought to meaning solely by the analyst, who uses observation, theory, his or her own emotional experience, and intuition. The analyst had to maximize the conditions so as to capture the patient's attention, establish a shared focus, invite symbolic thinking, and eventually, integrate the psychoanalytic object within an interpretation. In thinking about his ideas in terms of my own experience as group leader, member, and observer, I have chosen user-friendly words, and those that I believe more closely approximate what takes place in the group situation.

I will be describing an approach to group that has remained undeveloped in the literature, although, likely, it is as common in your practice as it is in mine. Evolving from the verbalizations and enactments through which the group symbolizes and becomes known, a *nuclear idea* takes shape. The therapist now has an option to test the idea provisionally: to focus attention and redirect group process toward its personal, group, and even societal reverberations.

I conceive of nuclear ideas as emerging from the nucleus of the group process: from intersubjective forces and locations that cannot be fully specified, yet may be possible to observe, name, and utilize clinically. They arise from the indeterminacy of the network of communications and interactions, that is, from within the dynamic matrix (Foulkes, 1964) or "culture" (Whitaker & Lieberman, 1984) of the group, co-created by the therapist's participation and influence, and expressed in the group's "idiom" (Bollas, 1989) and "discourse" (Schlapobersky, 1994), its particular language, symbolization, and enactments.

While Bion provided a starting point, my application is group relational (Billow, 2003a, 2010). As concept and technique, the nuclear idea—with its emphasis on meaning and the development of meaning as transformational (Bion, 1970; Bollas, 1987)—supplements the whole group, interpersonal, and intrapsychic lenses through which the therapist comes to understand group experience and base interventions.

Key Qualities of the Nuclear Idea

A nuclear idea may evolve from any mental phenomenon that captures attention in the group, and thus may be felt, fantasized, and thought about, on conscious and nonconscious levels. It may emerge—singularly or in combination—from a member's verbalizations (including the leader's), a group interchange or series of interchanges and enactments, or the therapist's *reverie*, which become clarified in language. The idea may articulate an observation, a feeling, belief, or memory that takes place in group, and which may be about the group or any group, or a personality, such as a group member or leader.

A nuclear idea entails a process of thinking and developing thoughts. This process may begin and be abandoned early on, developed somewhat or by some individuals, or developed more fully. Thinking is never complete and truths are not absolute, subject to the revisions of time and circumstance, and limited by human limitation in tolerating frustration and mental pain.[1]

When well developed, a nuclear idea possesses *experiential*, *symbolic*, *affective*, and *metapsychological* resonance. The experiential dimension provides empirical and communicable reference. The leader needs to determine if, and to what extent, the group's members are hearing, seeing, and talking about a similar or different experience. The *symbolic* dimension refers to levels of embedded meaning, conveyed in speech (metaphor, verbal imagery, and so on), enactments,[2] and the group's sociopolitical culture. The nuclear idea represents and stirs strong feelings: the *affective* dimension ensures that the idea carries here-and-now emotionally significant weight. Lastly, *metapsychological* significance emerges when thoughts extend to general principles of self, group, and societal organizations. People come to think about how they think (and do not think), and perhaps, when and why.

Anything that takes place in group has potential to inspire and develop into a nuclear idea. Something has transpired—an existential and intersubjective moment or sequence of moments becomes partially articulated in words or behavior. The therapist may take the opportunity to link the idea thematically, to conceptualize further and negotiate meaning with the co-participation of other group members. Let us see how nuclear ideas are introduced and function in the life of four, insight-oriented groups of different types and durations.

Four Clinical Vignettes

1. "Two Groups"

> A Veterans Hospital outpatient psychotherapy group changed leaders, as one psychologist, Lewis, replaced another, Rebecca, who had left the geographical area. The members missed Rebecca, whom they spoke of reverently. Yet the group took to Lewis immediately, perhaps because Rebecca pushed the group to tolerate the painful termination process, which also included praise for her successor.
>
> Lewis supported the members reviewing Rebecca's person and leadership. This continued long after the group evolved with newcomers. Even after several years, the old-timers would reminisce about "Rebecca's group," and how it differed from "Lewis's group." Recounting the dangerous behaviors they had eliminated or modified, this sub-group of self-described "rough guys" (including several females) declared that Rebecca had "saved our lives." Rebecca had put up with "no crap" and was not afraid of them. "We had to clean up our act, watch what we said and how we said it." "Very strict about rules and following them."
>
> Lewis also queried the group about his leadership, which the senior members described as "more hang-back," "relaxed," "not such a rule stickler."

"Rebecca locked the door, while you [Lewis] allow us to come in late." Still, "you can be a ball buster." "If you think someone has an issue that they don't want to talk about, you make us come back to it." "Rebecca did a lot of digging, now we do your fucking work."

One outcome of these discussions surprised the members: they had become and remained "well behaved," even though the style and gender of leadership changed.

Discussion

The core members of Rebecca's group had been through and shared a violent period of adjustment—they were old hands at dealing with their own chaos and that of the new members. Perhaps because of Lewis's inviting and nonauthoritarian style, it became easier for the members to become his investigative allies. And also, perhaps they did not need "tough love"—a phrase used repeatedly in describing Rebecca—not because what Rebecca did was unnecessary, but because the old members were more mature, and modeled (and perhaps enforced) maturity for the new ones.

In terms of enactment and *symbolic* influence, the two leaders—most likely unintentionally—took on parental roles related to earlier and later developmental phases of socialization. Rebecca was a "toilet training" parent. A clear set of behavioral rules and expectations—a reinforced "yes," and a firm "no"—provided a basis for what the members had called "cleaning up our act," a process that was apparently absent or traumatically damaged in these veterans.

Lewis established or reinforced latency ideals of mutuality and cooperation. In doing "his fucking work," the seniors verbally and enactively transmitted behavioral norms and expectations—now internalized—to the new members. While not abrogating authority, and enforcing it when necessary, Lewis democratically shared investigative leadership, and it was the group members themselves who initiated the nuclear idea of the "two groups." Most likely, he encouraged its clarification and elaboration without forethought or conscious awareness. He was both leader and led, augmenting and creatively surrendering (Ghent, 1990) to the force of the idea of the "two groups."

To emphasize this point: Lewis did not make the old group, the ongoing group, or the comparisons between them, an explicit nuclear idea. Here the leader's role was to recognize and enjoy—allowing the members to think for themselves. The members' pungent language captured key qualities of the groups and its impact on the veterans' thinking and behavior.

The nuclear idea of the "two groups" functioned as an unnamed "root metaphor" (Srivastra & Barrett, 1988, p. 37), linked experientially to the sensory-affective features of the therapists but stimulated by and based on their leadership behaviors, both symbolic and real. It operated as a material entity and as a complex "relational image" (Migliorati, 1989, p. 198), utilized in affectively intense exchanges that referenced the group and also extended to extra-group psychological functioning. "Two groups" thus possessed the essential features of a well-developed nuclear idea: *experiential*, *symbolic*, *affective*, and *metapsychological* bearing on and energizing the here-and-now therapeutic process.

2. The "Uncomfortable Role" of Being In Group

I had the unusual opportunity to lead a demonstration group via Skype. The group conference took place in a city outside the United States. In an introductory exchange, the attendees expressed interest in hearing about "truth," "love and hate," "rebellion," and "connection," and I said I would try to address these concepts either in the small group or debriefing.[3]

The room had been set up in preparation for the telecast: I faced a row of participants, with their backs to the large audience of observers. I suggested rearranging the chairs, such that the group of eight was seated in a semi-circle. While this improved the observers' sightlines, my view of several of the members became eclipsed. Further, while I could be clearly seen in close up, the group members, at some distance from the camera lens, were blurry on my computer screen. Since nothing else could be done with the technical arrangements, we began, with 50 minutes allotted.

Not obscured by the electronic compress of our several thousand-mile distance was a familiar jolt of start-up apprehension, which I took as my own magnified by the group's. A woman remarked: "I feel uncomfortable, I can't explain why." Not waiting too long, I asked her if she could try. She repeated herself, and then asked if others could talk. I encouraged her once again to continue. She again appealed to the group, saying indistinctly: "I'm finding it hard to stay in role." Some mumbling among the group members followed, which I could not understand. Then, a man (his back to me) confessed: "We were assigned roles." Another member: "It's difficult not to be yourself."

I responded: "Me too. I was assigned a role and I want to be myself, and I'm uncomfortable too." The room resounded with laughter. "We're all in the same boat," I emphasized. The man tentatively suggested dropping role-assignments, which met exclamations of relief with no dissenters. I referred to the process as a constructive *rebellion*: modifying the rules of engagement seemed appropriate for the brief time we had together and could make it more likely that we could reach some emotional truths.

A woman addressed the group: "I don't like the new arrangement."

"But you went along," another woman responded. "Yes, that's what I do, I go along, then withdraw and sulk until I can't stand it, then protest." The group seemed to enjoy her honesty and began to inquire further about this aspect of her psychology, about which she claimed to know nothing further.

The protesting woman was in my full view, and I said that she seemed to be angry, and with whom? "I don't know … I guess you." Although we were talking about anger, our exchange was amiable and she seemed pleased to be addressed directly. Another woman turned to her: "You could be scary, but I'm glad you spoke up." Said a third woman: "Yes, you made it easier for me."

The man who had revealed the role-playing spoke up: "Maybe I shouldn't have said anything." I said, "Are you apologizing?" "I started it," he reminded us. "You seemed to be intimidated." "No, yes, you're right." He turned enough for me to see the indistinct image of his profile: "I'm the youngest person here."

"And the first man to speak," I emphasized, and then asked him his age, "Twenty nine," and told him that he was old enough to be a full member with equal rights. His thank you seemed emotional, and I felt that our exchange had been intimate, with some special significance for him, possibly related to the theme of being oneself.

And then from the remaining woman, who had been silent: "I'm bored." I said that might be because she had not taken a chance to "connect" (I was referring to the term introduced by an audience member). Another woman interrupted: "I want to connect, but I am distracted by the audience. Several of them are raising their hands [also indicating boredom]."

I said to her that they were envious and that she could tell them to fuck themselves. My remarks drew another round of laughter from the room, and apparently the hands went down. "That feels better," she said. The woman professing boredom then engaged with several others; she said she no longer felt that way.

I asked if anyone else was bored. An older man said he wasn't bored but confused: "Is this supposed to be psychotherapy? Should I talk about my problems?" I said that given our time frame, we wouldn't have time for "problems," and that he should just connect to feelings and to others.

The women who had first spoken in our group addressed him: "You were one of the reasons I was uncomfortable. We know each other from other places and haven't always gotten along. I like that I am in this with you and getting to know you differently." With encouragement, she elaborated on what she had discovered about him.

Everyone in the group had taken opportunity to talk and address others, and after inviting them to do so once again, I closed the session.

Discussion

I heard the opening remarks as speaking for all: "I feel uncomfortable, I can't explain why." This shared and expectable discomfort gave birth to the germ of a nuclear idea that referred to the current state of our group in formation. When a participant revealed that the group volunteers had been given roles to play, as patients, but wanted to be themselves, I heard an opportunity to include myself, and to refine the *nuclear idea* by treating the disclosure metaphorically, metapsychologically, and self-referentially: "Me too. I was assigned a role and I want to be myself, and I'm uncomfortable too."

Although making reference to myself, I was really expanding on the nuclear idea: we were discomforted not only by being put into these roles of demonstration leader and members, but also by being in any group and needing to be ourselves, to think for ourselves, and to make meaning.

The use of the nuclear idea put us on task to reach multiple learning goals: it called attention to the painful quandary of any therapeutic or quasi-therapeutic situation addressing the need and discomfort of being and learning about oneself; it invited the members to share in the discovery process; it lessened the asymmetry between leader-members; it provided an example of the therapist's use of self; it opened the door to metacommunication—symbolic language and thinking; and finally, it modeled risk taking, constructive *rebellion* (Billow, 2010), and the open expression of intense feelings.

When I suggested that the bored audience members could be told to fuck themselves, I was merely extending the nuclear idea in the form of a whole group interpretation. By implication,[4] I was calling attention to a typical and unsurprising dynamic between two types of "uncomfortable roles" in a large group that may impede thinking: envious spectators who cannot actively participate, and the demonstration group members, with specific responsibilities and expectations, assigned or not.

3. "Checkpoints"

> We were several hours into a two-day Institute held in Jerusalem on the topic of "Reconciliation." The members had expressed interest in my writing on "passion" (Billow, 2003a), yet I found myself unable to reveal, stimulate, or feel any. In response to increasing conversational lulls, I suggested that people might be anxious. A woman immediately responded that she was "perfectly relaxed," and suggested that it was I who must be feeling anxiety. My acknowledgment brought no interest or curiosity.
>
> Someone suggested it might be a good idea to return to the theme of the conference. "Everyone here wants peace, yet the process seemed so sad and

difficult," another woman lamented. The Gaza residents talked about their difficulty getting past Israeli checkpoints even to attend a meeting on reconciliation; the Israelis countered with justifications for the barriers. Each side related stories of hardship, loss, and terror.

When attendees from other countries attempted to moderate the rising antagonism, the Arabs and Israelis concurred that these suggestions were unfeasible, given the political climate in the Middle East and the influence of the "military-industrial complex." Intellectualization replaced anger—but no passion.

After a while, I said that, despite obvious ethnic and political tensions, the main barrier in the room appeared to be between everyone else and me. I could not locate, much less get through, a checkpoint and become part of this group. After some denials, reassurances, and hesitations, several members came forth with their doubts: I was an American, a visitor, and outsider; how could I understand their anguish and loss? I acknowledged that I probably understood less than anyone else and would learn and gain more than anyone else during our two days together. I invited the group to deal with me directly when I went "off base."

The nuclear idea, which attended to the group's *refusal* (Billow, 2010) located the impasse in an inhibited need to "check out" the leader. With attention focused on the source of the group's impasse—the distrust of the leader as a sufficiently empathic and knowledgeable container—I achieved a point of entry. Now the group could attend to other barriers—difference and conflict related to ethnicity, citizenry, age, gender, political leanings, and personality. The women came forth to complain that the men—Israeli and Arab—had been doing all the talking. Two young Arab students confessed to being intimidated by their professor, sitting across the room. An Israeli housewife-community organizer confronted what she assumed were bellicose attitudes of the two high-ranking male soldier-psychologists from her country.

"Was reconciliation possible?" remained a question throughout the two days, but now we were checking out each other openly and mutually, painfully learning about the glaring and consequential personal as well as sociopolitical forces and affiliations that are ineliminable aspects of our identities.

Discussion

Supplementing the typical paranoid/depressive dreads and excitements accompanying formation, our group was subject to specific determining influences: fear of and anger toward ethnic and religious difference, and a collective, traumatic disillusionment with leaders, local, national, and international. I had been serving as the personification of the distrusted leader, and a "foreigner" too. Calling attention to the "checkpoint" located the predicament a leader must face with an untrusting and angry group.[5]

The nuclear idea provided a point of entry for the messenger and the message.[6] I shifted from being a shared threat and common target, to a sufficiently safe physical and mental reference that could be confronted and verbally "checked out." The salutary effect was to destabilize the pre-existing ethnic subgroups and prejudices so that members could relate to me, and then to each other, as individuals.

As the common target shifted from me to *a nuclear idea* of "me" (Billow, 2012), group process shifted from a *restrictive solution* (Whitaker & Lieberman, 1964), or static, *basic assumptive fight/flight* (Bion, 1961) stance, to thinking, feeling, and communicating—a self and group reflecting *work group*. Resistances behind the *refusal* unfolded, bringing to the fore intersubjective factors related to age, gender, status, and member-to-member (horizontal) transferences.

4. "Not Being Missed"

> A recent incident occurred in one of my analytic groups, this one of thirty-five years' duration. "I'm just letting everyone know that I'm going to miss the next couple of weeks," said one of our members of four years. He was surprised when people inquired as to his plans. I was surprised by his surprise and asked him: "Why are you surprised?" A woman of many, many more years piped in: "I can understand that, I don't expect people to be interested in me when I'm not here. But I'm interested in you." "I'm not surprised, I feel the same way, I will miss you, but I know I'm not missed," echoed several others.
>
> I found this curious, given that people regularly began with "Where's so and so?" "How's so and so?" Absences were noted and talked about. In individual sessions, group mates often referred to and inquired and worried about other members.
>
> "Everyone seems to miss everyone else, but nobody feels they're missed," I summarized. Several members initially dissented, but they reexamined their feelings in the interlude that followed, which revealed personal narratives: "My father practiced 'children should be seen and not heard'," "I don't know why my parents had children, we seemed to be ignored," "My sister was the pretty one; I was supposed to be smart, and if I wasn't, forget about it, I mean, forget me," "It was about my mother, never about us," "With my father, talk about sports or he disappeared behind a book. I have to concentrate on not being the same."

> When I asked one of the speakers how her feelings affected her group participation, others joined in, so that our discussion extended to our group's culture and process. Members had registered but had not previously talked about the group's greeting and departing rituals: how and if they were addressed in the waiting room and who said goodbye and to whom. Only some of the members anticipated a friendly reception at the start of the session. Group etiquette included monitoring frequency and duration of "talking about oneself," "taking turns," and "attempting to interest others, but never being sure." Post-session introspective preoccupations more than occasionally involved review of possible injury of others and fear of guilt-inducing retribution.
>
> No matter the mutual reassurances and offers of disconfirmatory evidence, members echoed lingering doubts concerning their clarity, perceptiveness, and value to others. One individual's ironic evaluation of our discourse brought appreciative laughter: "What an 'up.' No wonder I love this group!"

Discussion

"Why are you surprised?" I asked the member who was the subject of inquiry, not expecting resonance from so many. I had stumbled upon a group mythos—a belief shared by the majority of members, which was captured by the nuclear idea: "Everyone seems to miss everyone else, but nobody feels they're missed." My intention was not to interpret, direct group process, teach, or confront the members with reality, but to provide an opportunity to assess and publicize the depth of the commitment to an emotional belief that had surprised me. My words were spontaneous and ironic, perhaps obvious, yet they captured an important and unexamined emotional truth located in the member-to-member relationships, and with deep personal resonance. Here was a group where each member testified to the value of the others. Reiterating the sense of not feeling missed in the face of contrary data made vivid the power of trauma and the difficulty of modifying or eradicating its roots and effects on how we think and what we think about.

As therapists, we often do not know where an inquiry will take us. With little therapeutic effort, the nuclear idea segued to throw light on group cultural interactions, which unbeknownst had most likely reinforced pre-existing inhibitory self-stereotypes and strategies of group participation. Thus, a nuclear idea has the potential to serve as a *selected fact* (Bion, 1963, p. 11), to the extent that it clarifies, reorganizes, and brings illuminating depth to prior and ongoing events in the group. From here, as in this vignette, further examination and generation of intersubjective meaning may continue.

Not mentioned in our discussion, and perhaps universal, is the harsh reality of not being missed. Not only Oedipus and those traumatically neglected or used, but the child in all of us deals with the ungraspable fact of not being wanted for *oneself*, or missed. As parents once claimed their sexual relationship, our loved ones claim their privacy. And too, a future looms wherein we—like our long-departed group members—will not be remembered.

Our group left the nuclear idea before such existential elaborations were consciously thought about and explored. A nuclear idea may stimulate an infinite network of associations; we had articulated and interpreted some but not all of its emotional elements. While an exploration of a nuclear idea may be carried out adequately, it cannot be done all at once, and never completely.

Nuclear Ideas as Container/Contained

A productive mind and a productive group are always in the process of growth and transformation, affected by the perspectives supplied by other individuals, ongoing experience, and one's own thinking processes. I contend that every group—to the extent that it is organized as a group—organizes itself by developing relatively stable ideas of itself and of its leader.

Developing the nuclear idea provides a framework for how the therapist—and the group itself—goes about the task of containing.[7] The therapist and group exist as material entities and as representations. Primarily, it is the latter—the individual and group's conceptions (and preconceptions) of its leader and the group—that contain and are contained by the group. Each member is capable of generating particular and even unique nuclear ideas; and the group as a whole develops nuclear ideas. They exist and await discovery and development.

Let us review the four case vignettes.

1. "Two Groups"

The nuclear idea, while arising anecdotally and remaining unnamed, assumed essential holding and transformational containing functions. As the contained, it focused the pungent discussions of "Rebecca's group" and "Lewis's group," serving as an ongoing and fertile source of formulating and clarifying individual and collective meaning. As the container, it "held" the members individually and collectively, stabilizing the transition and the relatively smooth initiation of new cohorts. In its dual function as the container/contained, the nuclear idea spurred cohesion and coherence (Ezquerro, 2010), organizing, expanding, and making known a range of "well-behaved" experiences, interpersonal, emotional, and mental—actual and potential.

2. "Uncomfortable Roles"

As the container of dynamic meaning, the nuclear idea of "uncomfortable roles" revealed and made manageable a locus of anxiety that to some extent defined a core dimension of the group in formation. We were "in the same boat," I had declared, a containing reference to our shared discomfort, which we then addressed realistically as well as psychologically (and metapsychologically). Acknowledging my own discomfort as the leader reduced our emotional distance and fostered empathic bonding (*symbiotic* container/contained interactions, see note 7).

The justifiable *rebellion* against the sponsoring organization's role-playing *instructions*, the benevolent intra-group confrontations, and the leader's playful "tell them [unruly audience members] to fuck themselves"—these were enactments directed to reduce discomfort. They made sense because of the clarity and safety provided by the nuclear idea.

3. "Checkpoints"

Until the introduction of a nuclear idea, group process was marked by the *parasitic* variation of the container/contained. The unproductive intellectualizations, denials of anxiety, and emotional flatness suggested a nuclear idea of the formative stage of our workshop: it was untrustworthy, antagonistic, and unsafe. Thinking and thinkers were avoided or attacked, as in the silent hostility directed toward me, and the failure to challenge a participant's claim of "no anxiety." The "checkpoint" idea encapsulated important sociopolitical aspects of the attendees' experience that were both metaphoric and real, perhaps too real and too dangerous to contain in language without the group leader's active interventions and benevolent presence. I tolerated the participants' projections without retaliating by withdrawing my subjectivity, such as by falling silent, claiming not to be affected by anxiety, or offering lofty interpretations. As a metaphoric extension of a political reality, the nuclear idea invited the attendees to carry out a "checkpoint" in words, rather than surreptitiously halt the process and sabotage the group. Revealed too was the suppressed idea of the leader, an outsider of questionable status as a sufficiently containing figure.

4. "Not Being Missed"

Each member's characteristic defense patterns and anticipatory fantasies relating to not being important, cared about, or missed contributed to the inhibited participation that characterized a dimension of our group. The nuclear idea brought to light but did not resolve a "common tension" (Ezriel, 1950). Nor could it, for "not being missed" and related ideas remain everlasting sources of existential anxiety, common to us all. Still, in being broadcasted, a core nuclear idea of our group sufficiently contained the members, as they went on to explore unresolved historical relationships, revisit trauma, express anger, and mourn.

Connection to Established Group Theory

In his encyclopedic review, Ettin (1999, p. 133) found a unifying thread in the writings of major theorists, who understood group formation and function in terms of "inductive, bottom-up empirical-additive processes." Using different vocabularies and theoretical formulations, these authors described similar communicative patterns of "associative discourses" clustering into recurrent topics and prevalent themes that expressed central and shared psychodynamics. The group occupied itself with dealing with basic struggles, explicit or obscured, configured as "basic assumptions" (Bion, 1961), "common tensions" (Ezriel, 1950), "focal conflicts" and "group themes" (Whitaker, 1989), "barometric events" (Bennis & Shepard, 1956), and/or disruptive subgroups (Agazarian, 2012). The group as a whole, with the therapist's assist, comes to attend to these events and negotiates normative decisions and solutions. Each member "reverberates" (Foulkes & Anthony, 1965, p. 152) with the group, identifying and participating in his or her own way. The cohesive pressure of the group's accumulated affects, ideas, and developments fosters a curative culture (a "work group" [Bion, 1961]), in which the members reduce neurotic tendencies (Bion, 1961; Foulkes, 1964) and restructure their personalities and relationships (Whitaker & Lieberman, 1964).

According to these theorists and others (e.g., Yalom, 1995; Rutan & Stone, 2001), group process is "bottom up," that is, member-inspired and inductive. However, the therapist utilizes techniques that are "deductive, top-down theory-based" (Ettin, 1999, p. 150). Possessing a transcendent vantage point encompassing an overall conception of what will take place, the therapist discerns prototypical patterns in which conflicts are expressed and resolved by the group. The therapist's role is to understand and to help the members understand and deal with conflicts, which the therapist knows about, and "allows" to develop, such that the group resolves on its own.[8]

These modern theoretical formulations present valuable models of disarray, personal and group dysfunctionality, and conflict resolution. Certainly, the therapist possesses special knowledge and technical skills, and maintains a separate and unique role in the group. Nevertheless, relational theory—a "postmodern" theory eschewing reliance on theory and redolence of pre-established ideas—assumes that the defining characteristics of group life are co-created by the members' (including the therapist's) conscious and nonconscious participation, maintained and worked through intersubjectively (Grossmark, 2007; Kieffer, 2007; Poulton, 2013; Schwartz, 2012; Wright, 2004).

The therapist continuously is being challenged by his or her own affectively based mental processes, as well as by pressures emanating from other members. Feelings of persecution and depression are unavoidable. Along with other group members, then, the therapist simultaneously participates from the "top" and from the "bottom," sharing and contributing to tensions and conflicts and participating in efforts to define and resolve them. In effect, the therapist is pulled up from the "bottom" and pulls others along, by developing nuclear ideas and responding to those suggested by others.

I briefly compare the *nuclear idea* to "*focal conflict*," a linear, two vector, tension reduction model of group process. Whitaker and Lieberman (1964, p. 19) conceptualized the events of a therapy session in terms of a slowly emerging shared covert conflict consisting of two elements—a disturbing motive (a wish) and a reactive motive (a fear) ... [that] pervade the group as a whole, and are core issues engaging the energies of the patients ... A group solution represents a compromise between the opposing forces.

When the members find a solution for a *focal conflict*, the group moves on to the next, and so on, such that the successful solutions contribute to the "*group culture,*" expanding the repertoire of possibilities for coping with "*group themes*" (Berk, 2011).

When observed psychoanalytically, *every* thought, affect, or action, is a compromise formation, made up of conflicts among wishes (or drive derivatives), defenses, self-punitive trends, and painful affects (Brenner, 2002). Thinking involves restraint of motor discharge, and consequently, an increase of mental tension (Freud, 1911). Creative mental activity is not characterized solely by the incremental buildup of manageable experience, but also involves intense episodes of emotional turbulence: breaking down existing meaning, confronting what is unknown or confusing, and tolerating upsurges and releases of the irrational. For these reasons (among others), productive group work *always* involves anxiety, and *always* involves compromise between opposing forces: pleasure and unpleasure (Freud, 1911), aggression and reparative love (Segal, 1957), and truth and falsity (Bion, 1965).

To the extent he or she is able to identify them, the group therapist focuses on these compromises as they emerge and play out on intrapsychic, interpersonal, and whole group levels. "Basic assumptions," "focal conflicts," "common tensions," and other theoretical formulations are themselves potential nuclear ideas. Each represents a particular focus: the therapist's opinion of what is going on. How and if the therapist intervenes varies according to personal style and theoretical and technical orientation.

No theory, formulation, or perspective best fits all group situations. For an opinion to be actualized effectively, rather than imposed autocratically on the group, the therapist needs to engage the thinking of other members: to determine if, how, and why they find a specific idea contextually and personally relevant. Group members may have competing ideas that more directly address truth needs—ideas that are more accurate and salient, or simply, a user-friendlier lens to observe how and what the group is thinking about (and not thinking about, and why). And, too, a group may not be ready or just not interested in developing a particular nuclear idea, no matter how luminous, and the idea may have to wait, along with its initiator.

If a nuclear idea is of "genuine psychological use" (Ogden, 2004), its four-dimensional reference points will make themselves known, sooner than later. The "common tension" or "focal conflict," such as involved with the feeling of being a member of "two groups," creating "checkpoints," "being uncomfortable," or "not being missed" will enter *experience* sensorially, and/or be inferred from the group's verbal and nonverbal expressions. *Affects* will be felt and expressed.

Symbolic dimensions of the "common tension" or "focal conflict" will be linked or generalized to other personal, social, and *metapsychological* contexts.

The Nuclear Idea Extends Discourse to the Metapsychological

A nuclear idea may involve a premise, a working hypothesis, a strategy, nonconscious working through, or an exploration and interpretation of group, sub-group, or individual traits, fantasies, and dynamics. But it is more than a conflict, tension, theme, or an interesting process that gets addressed by naming and connecting to individuals, sub-groups, and the whole group. The therapist listens for and seeks to develop a metapsychological mindset and focus of discourse, which at the same time does not get bogged down in intellectualization. Developing a nuclear idea—if it truly represents the four dimensions of *experiential*, *affective*, *symbolic*, and *metapsychological* import—becomes a living event of self/other awareness that changes the psychology in the room.

The nuclear idea vitalizes thinking and being, particularizing the vague or theoretical, and making abstract and universal the concrete. A "common tension"—such as being a part of "two groups," "uncomfortable in role," in need of "checkpoint," or feeling "not missed"—clarifies group process. But presented and treated as a nuclear idea, the formulation extends the scope of thinking. The nuclear idea of "two groups" is far-reaching, condensing the past and providing a forward-directed model of "good behavior." "I feel uncomfortable in taking a role" broadens to the metapsychological (and sociological) question: "What is the nature of being in a group?" Derivatives of "checkpoint" reflect intense internal, interpersonal, and sociopolitical realities, fantasies, and cultural myths that are both ancient and as current as today's newspaper. "I feel I'm not missed," relates not only to group realizations and negotiations, but also to spiritual dimensions that are timeless and irresolvable.

A relational stance, which makes the therapist's subjectivity available for inspection, provides a model of an emotionally reflective self.[9] When incorporated in a nuclear idea, the therapist's subjective experience offers metapsychological reference. For instance, my report of feeling unable to get through a group "checkpoint" also implied that I would not stop thinking for myself, even if my thoughts were unwelcome. Treating the "checkpoint" references metaphorically and metapsychologically involved accessing and publicizing some of my fantasies, anxieties, affects, and thoughts in relation to the group participants' barriers to me and to their own thinking. Perhaps, in revealing a metapsychological dimension of my subjectivity, including allusions to my own helplessness and the group's power, the nuclear idea put the participants in a less dependent (and frightened) position. The members became willing, and able, to observe and understand the rationales behind their own (non)thinking and, in so doing, to think for themselves.

The "uncomfortable role" vignette provides another clinical example of the nuclear idea's extension into the metapsychological. My self-report of how I felt also conveyed a sense of how I thought, and that I would share rather than withhold my thoughts about my thinking. My therapeutic action encouraged other members, who came to report on their thoughts about thinking. One woman spoke of her "going along" with the thinking and action of others; and another woman spoke of her anxiety about broadcasting thoughts in the presence of the first ("you can be scary"). A man spoke of his uneasiness of being the youngest and presenting his ideas. Others acknowledged impaired thinking processes: boredom, distraction, and confusion ("Is this psychotherapy?").

A nuclear idea provokes the curiosity-drive and extends its reach from the personal, interpersonal, and social, to the metapsychological. Without assuming formal leader status, all group members may participate as drivers of this function. They are not leaders of the group, but they may initiate and even lead this discourse (as in the "two groups" and "not being missed" vignettes). The assumption here is that each group member is capable of being a thinking, interpreting subject, capable of doing conscious as well as nonconscious psychological work (Grotstein, 2000).

The nuclear idea is the type of intervention that expands the category of what is thinkable (see Levine, 2012; Ogden, 2011). When effective, it serves as "a point of departure for new meanings and places not yet known" (Levine, 2012, p. 27), for generating new thoughts (Ferro & Basile, 2009, p. 92) and for new ways of thinking. And, since its goals are transformational, and not merely informational, the nuclear idea often stimulates, rather than resolves, tensions and conflict.

Summing Up

The lexical representation of the nuclear idea is often simple in grammatical structure, and straightforward in experiential group reference, but generalizable and complex in symbolic and affective resonance. Something has transpired—an existential and intersubjective moment or sequence of moments that subsequently becomes named and (partially) articulated. It is built on and refined by the group interaction, linked to a shared database of here-and-now verbalizations, nonverbal behavior, and enactments. As a thought or a series of emotional thoughts that are thought about, nuclear ideas are self and group reflective. They offer opportunity for the leader or therapist to focus, refocus, or challenge the group, orienting the members toward the search for meaning, on personal, interactional, group, and metapsychological levels. As we have seen, the nuclear idea can be the organizing principle directing the inquiry, the focus of the inquiry, or the result of the discovery process.

The therapist may choose to develop a nuclear idea thematically, conceptualize further and negotiate meaning with the co-participation of other group members. But a nuclear idea has to catch on, that is, to function in dynamic relationship with thinking, so as to involve the group or some members in an emotional experience associated with learning. It cannot be rushed or imposed on the individual or group; it emerges from the intensity of the clinical experience. Thus, a nuclear idea is provisional, tested in terms of its affective saliency and capacity to generate interest and thought. It can go flat, or be ignored, or applauded. It is not an oracular pronouncement, and should not preclude the potential for competing, and better ideas.

The value of a nuclear idea may seem brief, as the idea becomes absorbed in the individual's and group's development. Or, its influence may be long-lasting, an idea revisited on different levels of awareness and group process and which continues to propel thought, function as a symbolic, affective, and metapsychological narrative, and impact behavior. Relatively stable, core nuclear ideas of the leader and of the group serve containing functions.

The frequency by which nuclear ideas are explicitly made the focus of group investigation varies according to the type, stage, and process of a group, and the membership composition. That which may potentially be treated and developed as a nuclear idea may not seem to interest particular members, or involve all members equally, or be the optimal in significance to the group and its process. Nuclear ideas differ then, in depth, breadth, creativity, and relevance to group and the particular needs and wants of the individual members.

The nuclear idea (a) gives opportunity for new meaning and depth to any experience that has occurred before or is ongoing in intrapsychic and group relations; (b) focuses participants' attention and provides a mode of entry; (c) establishes a shared activity and common goal of understanding; (d) privileges group members as potential sources of transformation; (e) conveys a sense of order to and mutual appreciation of the group; and (f) creates interest in and valorizes attending to other nuclear ideas, such that metapsychologizing becomes part of group culture and process.

It has been my intention to introduce and make accessible a previously undescribed essence of relationally oriented group psychotherapy. As a concept, technique, and description of group process, the nuclear idea does not put the wine of previous theorists in new bottles. Rather, it builds on their excellence, removing the "impurities" of "top down" leadership ideals and remnants of "hegemonic" (Wallerstein, 1988), autocratic psychoanalytic assumptions. In introducing, distilling, and putting into practice key concepts of relational thinking, varietals of nuclear ideas offer a qualitatively different experience for the therapist and the group. Indeed, developing nuclear ideas circumvents (and may even anticipate) the type of meaning deprivation that leads to a profusion of exaggerated *basic assumptions*, *common tensions*, and *focal conflicts*, and which encourages unproductive *rebellions* and *refusals*, and static *resistances*.

All group members of a psychodynamically oriented group share in the invitation to attend to, develop, and harvest nuclear ideas and their quality. I emphasize once again that the therapist's influence remains primary. In offering him or herself as a metapsychologizing subject and relating likewise to other members, the therapist sets up a culture and process in which the group comes to listen for and develop nuclear ideas.

Acknowledgments

I thank Drs. Charles Raps and James Paulson for our productive discussions that helped clarify my thinking and provided editorial feedback. A version of this chapter will appear in the *International Journal of Group Psychotherapy*.

Notes

1. It has been my contention (Billow, 2005, 2010) that the therapist must maintain a dual focus of activity: being supportive yet maintaining a disruptive-creative influence on group process. As a powerful agent of change, the clinician disturbs the very status quo that he or she works to establish. This involves provoking personal and group psychological upheaval, anxiety, and mental pain.
2. The concept of "acting out" is undergoing reevaluation in the contemporary psychoanalytic literature, replaced or supplemented by the concept of enactment (see Ivey, 2008). Enactments are inevitable, providing sources of data not otherwise available for analysis. They form a background for the emergence of new forms of engagement and experience (Aron, 1996; Davies, 1999; Hoffman, 1992; McLaughlin, 1991).
3. These are key concepts from my writings, referring to the individual's and group's need for emotional truth, which involves connecting to basic feelings of curiosity, love, and hate (Bion's [1963] L, H, and K links; see Billow, 2000, 2003a, 2003b). In *Resistance, Rebellion and Refusal in Groups: The 3 Rs* (Billow, 2010), I presented a model of group organization and activity as a series of pathways—each with moves and countermoves—directed to express, redirect, modify, or block the search for emotional truth. The group process may shift from interest in intrapsychic and interpersonal levels of meaning, to strategies of *rebellion*: questioning or challenging the leader, the structures he or she wishes to set up and/or maintain, and the truth-goals and the methods that are pursued.
4. Grice (1989) introduced the technical term *implicate* for indirect speech acts (Searle, 1975), where what is said is distinct from what is meant, implied, or suggested (see also Lakoff, 1977)—for example, by use of figures of speech (metaphor, irony, sarcasm, exaggeration, understatement ("litote"), or intonation and emphasis.
5. A group localizes itself by enacting "*equivalences*" (Hopper, 2003). People bring sociopolitical configurations existing outside the group and enact them in the group. The resulting interactive relationships—intrapsychic, interpersonal, and immediate—are also historic, cultural, and involve the larger sociopolitical setting in which the group (including the therapist) is embedded.
6. That is, the nuclear idea contained and made sense of anxiety and energized bonding and symbolic (*symbiotic* and *commensal*) learning links. See *note 7*.
7. Bion (1962, p. 93 ff.) outlined three prototypes of object relationships that support or interfere with the individual's drive to think, and therefore, to fantasize and to play. The three prototypes are relational models (images and unconscious fantasies) of early caretaker experiences involving containing and being contained. Bion labeled the models, respectively, *symbiotic, commensal,* and *parasitic* (Billow, 2003a). For clarity, I denote these prototypes as *bonding, symbolic,* and *antilinking* mental and social interactions. Reciprocal interaction—a reversible, nesting process—is involved, as the container at one transformational level serves as the contained at another. Being held and also contained at the pre-verbal level of basic trust (*bonding*) stimulates self-reflection—the psychic freedom to think and develop independent thoughts. The group and leader become the *contained*, thought about as collective and individual ideas (*symbolically*). On the level of self, then, the individual comes

to serve as the container of one's mentality, a function provided by a foundation of healthy dependence (*bonding*) on others. On the level of the structure of thought, an idea comes to serves as the container of the individual and group's developing thoughts and emotions, which are the contained (and held *symbolically* by the participants).
8   In Lacanian theory and technique, the therapist, as *Savoir*, informed by knowledge of the unconscious drives (*jouissance*) and desire, and maintainer of the *Symbolic Order*, interprets the metaphoric or metonymic messages contained in the members' communications. Certain members may participate with the therapist in shifting discourse from "in" to "of" the group (Giraldo, 2012, p. 76).
9   Lyon, Berly, and Klassen (2012) apply to the group situation Allen, Fonagy, and Bateman's (2008) concept of the "*mentalizing stance*." They describe how the therapist attempts to hold in mind both the members of the group and the group itself, and simultaneously track one's own shifts in "self-states" as well.

References

Agazarian, Y.M. (2012) Systems-centered® group psychotherapy: Putting theory into practice. *International Journal of Group Psychotherapy*, 62: 171–195.

Allen, J., Fonagy, P., & Bateman, A. (2008) *Mentalizing in Clinical Practice*. Washington, DC: American Psychiatric.

Aron, L. (1996) *A Meeting of Minds: Mutuality in Psychoanalysis*. Hillsdale, NJ: Analytic Press.

Bennis, W.T. & Shepard, H.A. (1956) A theory of group development. *Human Relations*, 9: 415–437.

Benveniste, D. (1998) Play and the metaphors of the body. *The Psychoanalytic Study of the Child*, 53: 65–83.

Berk, T.J.C. (2011) *The Group Focal Conflict Theory Revisited*. Herault, France: Berk Publisher.

Billow, R.M. (2000) Relational levels of the container-contained in group. *Group*, 24: 243–259.

Billow, R.M. (2003a) *Relational Group Psychotherapy: From Basic Assumptions to Passion*. London and Philadelphia: Jessica Kingsley.

Billow, R.M. (2003b) Relational variations of the container-contained. *Contemporary Psychoanalysis*, 39: 27–50.

Billow, R.M. (2005) The two faces of the group therapist. *International Journal of Group Psychotherapy*, 55: 167–187.

Billow, R.M. (2010) *Resistance, Rebellion and Refusal in Groups: The 3 Rs*. London: Karnac.

Billow, R.M. (2012) It's all about me: Introduction to relational group psychotherapy. In J.L. Kleinberg (ed.) *The Wiley-Blackwell Handbook of Group Psychotherapy* (pp. 169–185). Chichester, UK: John Wiley.

Bion, W.R. (1961) *Experiences in Groups*. London: Tavistock.

Bion, W.R. (1962) *Learning From Experience*. London: Heinemann. (Reprinted in: *Seven Servants: Four Works by Wilfred R. Bion*. New York: Aronson, 1977.)

Bion, W.R. (1963) *Elements of Psycho-analysis*. London: Heinemann. (Reprinted in: *Seven*.)

Bion, W.R. (1965) *Transformations*. London: Heinemann. (Reprinted in: *Seven*.)

Bion, W.R. (1970) *Attention and Interpretation*. London: Tavistock. (Reprinted in: *Seven*.)

Bollas, C. (1987) *The Shadow of the Object: Psychoanalysis of the Unthought Known*. London: Free Association Books.
Bollas, C. (1989) *Forces of Destiny. Psychoanalysis and the Human Idiom*. Northvale, NJ: Jason Aronson.
Brenner, C. (2002) Conflict, compromise formation, and structural theory. *Psychoanalytic Quarterly*, 70: 397–417.
Britton, R. (1998) (Book review) *Taming Wild Thoughts* by W. R. Bion. Edited by Francesca Bion. London: Karnac Books. 1997. *International Journal of Psycho-Analysis*, 79: 817–819.
Davies, J. (1999) Dissociation, therapeutic enactment and transference-countertransference process. *Gender and Psychoanalysis*, 2: 241–259.
Ettin, M. (1999) *Foundations and Applications of Group Psychotherapy*. London: Jessica Kingsley Publishers.
Ezquerro, A. (2010) Cohesion and coherency in group analysis. *Group Analysis*, 43: 496–504.
Ezriel, H. (1950) A psycho-analytic approach to the treatment of patients in groups. *British Journal of Psychiatry*, 96: 774–779.
Ferro, A. & Basile, R. (2009) *The Analytic Field: A Clinical Concept*. London: Karnac.
Foulkes, S.H. (1964) *Therapeutic Group Analysis*. London: George Allen & Unwin.
Foulkes, S.H. & Anthony, E. (1965) *Group Psychotherapy: The Psychoanalytic Approach*. Baltimore: Penguin Books.
Freud, S. (1911) *Formulations Regarding the Two Principles in Mental Functioning. S. E. 12*. London: Hogarth.
Ghent, M. (1990) Masochism, submission, surrender—Masochism as a perversion of surrender. *Contemporary Psychoanalysis*, 26: 108–136.
Giraldo, M. (2012) *The Dialogues in and of the Group*. London: Karnac.
Grice, H.P. (1989) *Studies in the Way of Words*. Cambridge, MA: Harvard University Press.
Grossmark, R. (2007) The edge of chaos: Enactment, disruption, and emergence in group psychotherapy. *Psychoanalytic Dialogues*, 17: 479–499.
Grotstein, J. (2000) *Who is the Dreamer Who Dreams the Dream: A Study of Psychic Presences*. Hillsdale, NJ: Analytic Press.
Grotstein, J. (2007) *A Beam of Intense Darkness*. London: Karnac.
Ivey, G. (2008) Enactment controversies: A critical review of current debates. *International Journal of Psychoanalysis*, 89: 19–38.
Hoffman, I.Z. (1992) Expressive participation and psychoanalytic discipline. *Contemporary Psychoanalysis*, 2: 1–14.
Hopper, E. (2003) *The Social Unconscious: Selected Papers*. London and Philadelphia: Jessica Kingsley.
Kieffer, C. (2007) Emergence and the analytic third: Working at the edge of chaos. *Psychoanalytic Dialogues*, 17: 683–703.
Lakoff, R. (1977) What you can do with words: Politeness, pragmatics and performatives. In R. Rogers, R. Wall, & J. Murphy (eds.) *Proceedings of the Texas Conference on Performatives, Presuppositions and Implicatures* (pp. 79–106). Arlington, VA: Center for Applied Linguistics.
Levine, H. (2012) The analyst's theory in the analyst's mind. *Psychoanalytic Inquiry*, 32: 18–32.
Lyon, K.B., Berley, R., & Klassen, K. (2012) Unbearable states of mind in group psychotherapy: Dissociation, mentalization, and the clinician's stance. *Group*, 36 (4): 267–282.

McLaughlin, J. (1991) Clinical and theoretical aspects of enactment. *Journal of the American Psychoanalytic Association*, 29: 595–614.

Migliorati, P. (1989) The image in group relationships. *Group Analysis*, 22: 189–199.

Ogden, T. (2004) The analytic third: Implications for psychoanalytic theory and technique. *The Psychoanalytic Quarterly*, 73: 167–195.

Ogden, T. (2011) Reading Susan Isaacs: Toward a radically revised theory of thinking. *International Journal of Psychoanalysis*, 92: 925–942.

Poulton, J.L. (2013) *Object Relations and Relationality in Couple Therapy*. Lanham, MD: Jason Aronson.

Rutan, J.S. & Stone, W. (2001) *Psychodynamic Group Therapy*. 3rd edn. New York: Guilford Press.

Schlapobersky, J. (1994) The language of the group: Monologue, dialogue and discourse in group analysis. In D. Brown & L. Zinkin (eds.) *The Psyche and the Social World*. London: Jessica Kingsley.

Schwartz, H. (2012) Intersubjectivity and dialecticism. *International Journal of Psychoanalysis*, 93: 401–425.

Searle, J. (1975) Indirect speech acts. In P. Cole & J.L. Morgan (eds.), *Syntax and Semantics, 3: Speech Acts* (pp. 59–82). New York: Academic Press. (Reprinted in S. Davis (ed.), *Pragmatics: A Reader*, pp. 265–277. Oxford: Oxford University Press, 1991.)

Segal, H. (1957) Notes on symbol formation. *International Journal of Psychoanalysis*, 78: 43–52.

Srivastva, S. & Barrett, F. (1988) The transforming nature of metaphors in group development: A study in group theory. *Human Relations*, 4: 31–64.

Wallerstein, R. (1988) One psychoanalysis or many? *International Journal of Psychoanalysis*, 12: 60–70.

Whitaker, D. (1989) Group focal conflict theory: Description, illustration and evaluation. *Group*, 13: 225–251.

Whitaker, D. & Lieberman, M. (1964) *Psychotherapy Through the Group Process*. Chicago: Aldine.

Wright, F. (2004) Being seen, moved, disrupted and reconfigured: Group leadership from a relational perspective. *International Journal of Group Psychotherapy*, 54: 235–250.

Yalom, I. (1995) *The Theory and Practice of Group Psychotherapy*. 4th edn. New York: Basic Books.

Chapter 7

Progressing while Regressing in Relationships

Ronnie Levine

Regression and relapses to more primitive interpersonal interactions and behaviors, such as addictions, can torment both therapist and patient alike, often generating despair and hopelessness. Friends and loved ones also suffer in relationships when living through these destructive interactions. Yet, regressions can sometimes provide opportunities for the development both of a more integrated self and of a more mature relating. Looking through the lens of current psychoanalytic thinking, this chapter offers a model of emotional development arising from understanding regression as a cyclical back and forth process between regressive and progressive states. I present a case that serves as an example of this model and illustrates the transformative effects of group treatment.

Many of the current psychoanalytic perspectives (object relations, relational, modern, intersubjectivity, attachment, self-states, interpersonal neuropsychoanalytic) now converge on the theoretical importance of emotional communication between patients and therapists and the practical need to develop interventions beyond interpretations. From these perspectives, the key for working with regressive experience lies within the therapeutic relationship, including the unformulated and preverbal engagements within the relationship.

For many of us in the group field, studying the interactions and relationships between the therapist and the patient and among patients has been our bread and butter. Group therapists regularly witness the profound effects that nutrient relationships and interactions have in the development of resilience and mature relating. Louis Ormont, from his unique modern psychoanalytic perspective, was particularly innovative in how to use the group to approach the regressed and/or preverbal patient and how to move the member and the group to more mature relating and functioning. Ormont was one of the pioneer group therapists who did not rely on the exclusive use of interpretation, but instead focused on the emotional interchanges—what was communicated consciously and unconsciously about the self and self/object relationships—among group members and the therapist. In his interactional approach, he developed interventions born from his understanding of his and the patient's experience. He was innovative in how he utilized bridging and joining to "hold" a member (providing maturational engagements, emotional education, and ego support) and to create a group attitude (transitional space) for exploration and interest in another. Ormont was convinced group therapy could provide through a modern relational approach to the contract, the exploration of a range of reactions, thoughts and feelings, and maturational interactions that engage internal self/object experiences, an experience that promoted a sturdier self and more mature relationships. In this chapter, I will bridge some of the current psychoanalytic thinking with Ormont's approach to group therapy.

Regression in Relationships

It is the difficulties in relating to others that drive people to our therapy offices and fill our group therapy practices. These people, or those they are involved with, have difficulty sustaining good, cooperative, mutually gratifying relationships. Along the way, their interactions become plagued with destructive, regressive tendencies. Relapses to destructive infantile behaviors such as primitive self-soothing behaviors, primitive expressions of need, and feelings or addictions may emerge, causing pain and unhappiness to all. The wish to be able to maintain a mature way of relating is often undermined.

There is, of course, nothing new with the observation that relationships inevitably have troubles—troubled relationships are as old as the Bible. The Bible is replete with relationships that have gone awry. From the very beginning, when man and woman are created, there are difficulties with commitment and cooperation in the relationship with God. God sets the frame, provides a contract, and then there is perpetual backsliding.

Adam and Eve cannot keep their hands off the forbidden fruit. And next is Cain, depicted as a selfish man—who perverts his love for God for a love of himself. Envious of God's preference for his brother Abel, Cain kills his brother, who had gained a generous capacity to have and express his gratitude to God. Following the murder, Cain's response to God, "Am I my brother's keeper?," has resonated throughout the ages as an expression of the triumph of a ruthless narcissism over responsibility and concern for the other.

Genesis continues to describe a treacherous, ruthless social world. Corruption and lawlessness are a way of life: this group cannot keep to the group contract! God, the ultimate group leader, decides at last to terminate this dangerous narcissistic group, reconstituting it for a new group (doing what many group leaders wish when finding themselves with a destructive, uncooperative bunch). He asks Noah to help him in this task. Noah, it is said, is a bit better than anyone else in his sinful generation. While following God's requests, he fails to shows any sign of concern or desire to save his extended family, let alone the world's population. Yet, his compliance is at least a development of an evolving interest in another. Unlike his neighbors, Noah seems willing to forego some narcissistic gratification for a relationship that goes beyond himself. He is a transitional figure. God's relationship with man also evolves—he terminates the group but revises the contract—he will not destroy the group again, at least by flood.

It is left to Abraham, imperfect but dedicated, to become the first person presented in Genesis to form a committed, cooperative relationship with God. He is willing to enter into a relationship that allows for commitment, active negotiation, and concern for others. He has found in himself a capacity to love beyond self. It is Abraham who becomes the patriarch.

Genesis can be seen as both a story and a teaching concerning the development of man's relationship to God—the progression from Adam through Abraham reflecting a shift from a narcissistic state to a more mature and cooperative relationship. Western civilization has utilized these revered figures or mythic heroes as guiding models for our interpersonal relationships. Yet, in the depiction of these models developed in Genesis, even with the ones who had achieved more cooperative mature ways of relating, there are often portrayals of regression—a slip up to a self-involved or destructive way of relating. Why do the relationships in the Bible continue to emphasize destructive, regressive tendencies, even in the revered personalities? The Bible seems to be telling us that regressions in relationships are unavoidable.

Perhaps the ubiquity of the difficulties in sustaining responsibility and concern in relationships can provide some consolation to therapists, their patients, and the patients' families who struggle with the challenges of relapses to addictions and to primitive narcissistic states of relating. The journey to mature relating does not follow a linear path; such an expectation or belief will likely cause discouragement when inevitable regressive self-states occur. Regressive pulls emerge at vulnerable moments, especially in intimate relationships. Life's transitions and disturbing interactions—perceived or real—can be disruptive and destabilizing, causing regression to earlier narcissistic states in a search for the fulfillment of desire and comfort.

The movement back and forth from narcissistic states to mature, cooperative, concerned states continues throughout life, and appears to be part of the normal processes for both self and relational development. These regressions to narcissistic self-states and progressions to mature relating may be the way human beings—through this delicate and dialectic balance—allow for the development of a vital self and mature loving relationships. It is a process of maturation and integration. These cycles of regressive and progressive pushes and pulls on self and relationship may serve to either generate or regenerate each other, potentially becoming either a source for creative emotional expansion and/or a destructive force for the self and the relationship.

From Self-Involvement to a Capacity for Concern and Reflection

Many object-relations, relational, and modern psychoanalytic clinical theorists write about the development of self/object differentiation, beginning with an omnipotent/narcissistic stage, moving through an intermediary stage, and evolving to a more differentiated state: an Adam to Noah to Abraham progression. As one progresses to a more differentiated self/object state, there is a higher level of emotional integration, with increased capacity for reflection and for recognition of the other's subjectivity. This is marked by a capacity to tolerate contradictory, frustrating, disappointing, and ambivalent experiences—love and hate—for another with the concomitant capacity to tolerate the same from the other. There is an increasing tolerance for the flaws within one's self and for the limitations of the other. This stage, what Klein and Winnicott refer to as the depressive position, is an achievement of integration, but it is not a static or stable achievement.

Why do We have these Cycles of Regressions and Progression?

While there are many factors—constitution, level of ego integration, quality of internal objects, and the consolidation of the self—that determine quality, frequency, and extent of regression, all regressions are essential ways of processing experience. No self can fully metabolize the totality of experience. Regression may be a necessary means of accessing and addressing the inaccessible parts of the self. Regressions move to different emotionally vulnerable and unformulated points of trauma, developmental and structural weakness, and unresolved conflict. Regressive states may hold an unfiltered, raw, immediate way of experiencing that could be a source for creative, inspired experience, a sense of aliveness—a regression in service of the ego.

For the purposes of this chapter, I would like to underscore these attributes: regression is an intrapsychic and relational phenomenon (Balint, 1968). The back and forth movement may be necessary to form, develop, and internalize a good internal object. Current relationships provide the context for accessing and reworking internal object relations. Contemporary neuropsychoanalytic, attachment, trauma, and relational self-state theorists (akin to the object relations and modern psychoanalytic idea of internalized self/object relationship) discuss a concept of an embedded interpersonal imprint that is out of awareness, and can only be surfaced in primitive modes of interacting in intimate relationships (Lyons-Ruth, 1999). Regressions are conceptualized as unavoidable forms of communicating in relationships and relationships are the necessary context for manifesting and addressing internal relational regression. In varying degrees, we will have periods of turbulence in our relationships that will stir up earlier self/objects imprints and return us to primitive modes of functioning.

Regression to narcissistic forms of relating within a relationship can allow for a maturational process in a relationship, or can be damaging to the relationship, and many times is both damaging and an impetus for maturation for the relationship. During regressive periods, the sense of the other is undermined. In severe regressive narcissistic states, the capacities to recognize the other, to realize the impact of one's communications on the other, and to experience the other's subjectivity are completely lost. For regressions to be useful and adaptive in a relationship, the regression cannot be so severe as to be destructively malignant for the relationship and the individuals. There has to be some eventual recovery to an awareness of the other. This is facilitated by a relationship having the capacity to contain the regression and provide maturational experiences.

Real relationships exert external demands and induce internal pressures, generating anxiety, frustration, and humiliation that deplete the ego/self resources from sustaining a higher level of integration and concern. The painful interactions in a current relationship may be too much to bear without having had a sturdy good internalized object relationship to help with enduring the pain. These interactions can arouse defective self feeling and toxic and persecutory internal objects that disrupt a sense of self cohesion and stability. Lacking sufficient self-soothing and self-affirming functions to sustain a stable self, one regresses to a former self-state, in search of a good object/feeling, desperate to restore a sense of wellbeing.

Each self-state has an imprinted corresponding internal relationship with an object that defines the way a person perceives and reacts to his/her object. The regression may lead to a self-state of a more nourishing time, where a younger self had (or imagined) some kind of loving self object to provide some sense of cohesion and stability. In this state, there may be a clinging to earlier ways of repair and self soothing as a way of evoking sustenance.

Most often, the trigger in the present (such as destabilizing experiences of abandonment, fear/terror, humiliation) returns the self to the vulnerabilities of the past: an insufficient object and an immature, incapable self. There is a pull to the familiar early inadequate or damaging self/object attachment, an imprint of interactions, which incorporated the early bad/vulnerable feelings one had about oneself and for the other as well as the experience of not having received sufficient self-soothing and self-affirming responsiveness to help protect or regulate these terrible feelings. In this self-state is a reliving of terrible reactions (internal objects) formed from the interactions of the past. There can be a reawakening of intense historic longing for the insufficient object of the past, which now experienced in the present relationship will come to its senses, become a good object, fully recognize the self, and restore one's wellbeing, or one will be rescued from the bad object, or that somehow one will be more effective this time in making a reparative outcome. Sometimes, there is also a reawakening for the desire for retribution for earlier grievances. The current relationship is now cast with the early primitive lens of that self-state, and one reacts and manages one's feelings and organizes one's life in the same earlier ineffectual ways to the accompanying object relationship. It is going home, with the present relationship, to an original disappointing object relationship frozen with the same expectations, longings, hurts, and mode of relating.

These regressions to the early attachment cause relapses from a more integrated depressive position self to more narcissistic modes of relating to the other. The self can retreat to primitive preverbal thoughts and omnipotent fantasy that dictate ways of engaging or disengaging the other. These regressive self-states can take the form of a self sacrificed to protect the other from one's hate and disappointments manifested in self attack, self doubting or a self sacrifice that makes inauthentic, compliant adaptations. There can also be a grandiose solution that restores the self by sacrificing the other. In this position, one lives in an omnipotent illusion of self sufficiency designed to eradicate the vulnerability of dependency and desire by either dispensing with the need for another or by having the fantasy (or experience) of possessing and ruthlessly controlling or destroying the other.

For individuals, relationships, and groups, stagnation in this omnipotent narcissistic period can be a disaster. In relationships, each partner's more primitive behavior can evoke in the other earlier out-of-control and out-of-awareness states and interactions. Where there had been collaboration, there are now omnipotent solutions. There is no recognition of the other as separate and as having a separate experience: no concern, no listening, and no acknowledgment of the effect one has on the other. Communications tend to be primitive forms of managing distressing and uncontainable emotions—requiring the other to have certain feelings and discharging of feelings. There are retreats to self-destructive and destructive addictive forms of self soothing; withdrawal to an illusion of an invincible form of self sufficiency (there is only me, and my way); a flight into self-absorbed grandiose fantasies (I am special: powerful, desired, loved which permits infantile demands to be cared for and have one's mind read, and allows for self-indulgent, destructive, and addictive behaviors); and abusive sadistic–masochistic, entrenched victimizer–victim forms of relating (I am in charge of you, it is your fault, I want to hurt you—I can't live with or without you, you are causing me to fall apart)—all of which can cause destructive controlling of or losing control with the other, with oneself, and disengagement. The milestone achievements and integration of the depressive position—stability born from a cohesive self, self reflection, a self awareness of consequence, and a self/other differentiation—seem to have receded. In their place a younger primitive self is surviving. The enduring, more primitive self-state carries both compelling creative and pathological self/object experiences that have not been metabolized and integrated in the mature functional self.

Relationships are complicated and the relapse or regressive self-states in one partner can evoke and provoke a destructive cycle of primitive modes of relating in and with the other. The attraction to each other may be driven by unconscious matching of relational self/object imprints. The relationship tie may be drawn from partners carrying unconscious identifications with relational imprints. A partner may be carrying healthy and destructively desired or unwanted disavowed self objects. (For more on the draw to unhealthy identifications to others, Aledort's (2009) Bad Fit concept describes the binding excitement of early imprints for partners involved in a self-destructive relationship.) A relationship can trigger core conflicts between partners such as the way aggression, control, desire, intimacy, vulnerability, and affect are self and mutually regulated and self/object representations are expressed. All of these can be the fuel for painful interactions in which the sense of the other is overshadowed by the narcissistic needs for the other.

Toxic regressions can be damaging disruptions and cause rupture to a relationship. However, when there is commitment to valuing and maintaining rather than destroying the relationship, these regressive experiences provide the relationship reparative opportunities for dissociated parts of the self to be introduced and integrated into the relationship. These regressions can be opportunities for dialogue. Reflection replaces venting and manipulation as communication is enriched with awareness and tolerance for feeling. If these regressive, narcissistic states can be endured, the emotional give and take in the relationship can move its partners to developing an awareness of one's impact on the other and an awareness of the other's experience. With this new consciousness of self and other, these emotional interchanges produce mutual reparative emotional communications. The mutual weathering/containing of primitive self/object experiences generates, for the relationship and self, a sense of continuity and a feeling of aliveness. This integration allows for a deepening of intimacy and gratitude. These regressions are the gateways for progressive intrapsychic and relational experiences.

The integrative processes of progression, regression, and progression continue as long as the relationship is committed to having vulnerabilities and self-defeating interactive patterns understood. This requires courage for both partners to move beyond a status quo acceptance of the secure and familiar destructive or stale forms of engagement to an unfamiliar cooperative terrain of relating and interacting. It also requires an allowance or an acceptance of each other to move in and out of mature relating, without an acceptance of being treated badly.

The psychotherapy relationship provides opportunities to explore regression and relational imprints, experiencing the earlier experienced self/object painful interactions as they are manifested in the present therapeutic relationship. Though these states can be sometimes difficult to live through for the therapist and the patient, psychotherapy can be a transformative experience—the relational process with regressive states can lead to a more integrated self with resiliency and fluidity for both the therapist and the patient. To be effective, the therapy has to be versatile in providing a range of maturational emotional reactions and interactions that can address the unfolding of differing subjective and relational development states (from narcissistic to a mature self/object state), a holding and containing environment, emotional education, and ongoing experiences of interacting relationships living through and surviving regressive experiences. When this is experienced within the context of a secure therapeutic relationship, there is potential for maturation, integration, and intimacy. The achievements of the depressive position are renewed and enriched. But the regressive experiences never end in one's life. These journeys, progressions, and regressions continue throughout life; however, through increased re-integration and experiences of reliability, life can become more stable and resilient, as regressions become easier to progress from. We therapists are there to help people withstand, recover, and relate.

Group as a Transformative Agent

How can group be helpful in transforming regressive experiences to progressive, integrative ones? Group—and not just the traditional psychotherapy group—has much to contribute in addressing problematic shifts to narcissistic states and in facilitating fluidity and resilience, which can lead to a more self/object, differentiated state. One kind of group, the twelve-step program, has brilliantly distilled the hallmarks of the depressive position, providing a process for a person to move from an omnipotent state by learning his or her limits, taking responsibility, making reparations, and then connecting to something beyond one's self. This group, in providing a structure and a sponsor to educate, support, and focus, is attempting to support externally what has never been internalized. The group's acceptance of relapses without shaming permits members to move forward without withdrawing from the group. In a similar fashion, the Al-Anon model can also help to facilitate self/object differentiation from the partner.

The therapy group offers something unique. It provides ongoing committed relationships with a leader and its members, and their interactions in the here and now can address varying narcissistic states and facilitate maturational development. These interactions, which are held, and limited within the confines of a group contract, create essential ingredients—reliability, stability, and a continuity of connections—which allow for a therapeutic working and re-working of regressive self/object experiences. In the group, relational ties can develop to the group as a whole and its members. The paths of these relationships can be explored, interactions can be investigated, and alternative ways of relating and understanding can develop. Supportive as well as difficult, uncomfortable, and injurious interactions can be examined. Group can be very good (and sometimes too good) at triggering terrible feelings. Interactions can trigger multiple members' unconscious reactions, and the enactment of relational imprints. Rather than just being a hopeless cycle of repetition and enactment, however, the therapy group provides opportunities for these experiences to be understood as well as providing, through interactions, the maturational emotional nutrients (mirroring or joining, recognition, regulation of emotional stimulation, titrated aggression, emotional education) required for the development of resilience, differentiation, and new ways of relating and coping. Because it features sustained multiple relationships, group therapy can have the capacity to hold and engage. There develops a harmonic movement back and forth from self need to an interest in the effect of his/her relational interactions.

Regression can Occur or be Triggered in Many Ways in Group Treatment

A group member may enter the group in a vulnerable state due to disappointment, loss, crisis, or frustration. Or, in the course of the group's interactions, a member can experience an injury: a criticism, a slight, an attack from another member. Or maybe it is the experience of being excluded from a conversation that leads to feelings of envy, neglect, shame, and defectiveness. Perhaps, having revealed the depth of one's vulnerability and the rawness of need, a member may not have received the longed-for response from the group that would sufficiently insulate self from the impending experience of humiliation and abandonment. Possibly, another member's conscious and unconscious communications have aroused intolerable feelings or have evoked unconscious unacceptable parts of self in a member. The group's here-and-now interaction can produce an array of painful injuries or threats that can induce the retreat to another self-state: a more vulnerable one that is ill-equipped to deal with the feelings that are evoked and is no longer effectively able to communicate to one's tormentor. Perhaps a member may never have attained an ability to manage overwhelming feelings effectively, or alternatively, there may have been some acquired capacity to not take things too personally and some ability to advocate for self. Either way, a member has suddenly slipped back to a different historic self-state, an old familiar one that has rendered a sense of helplessness. Responses and perceptions are now governed by this developmentally younger state, but now we have a group to witness, react to, and work with this young self.

Case Presentation

A seasoned group member, Vicki, who has developed in group an ability to articulate her feelings, keep people in mind, and understand others, suddenly upon receiving a hostile criticism from an explosive member, experiences herself as falling apart. She falls into an internal state of self doubt and self attack—her emotional insulation, which had been working well, is suddenly not protecting her stability. She has now lost a sense of integration as she has slid back to an earlier self-state in which she experienced herself as a frightened, defective person tied to a highly devaluing internal mother. She has now fallen into a tearful and helpless state.

This painful self-state that is now presenting itself was her predominant self for the first few years of Vicki's group life. At that time, Vicki was easily wounded, could not articulate her feelings, and craved attention, but pushed people away by the demands for desired attention that she placed on others, based on a sense of deserved entitlement for her long suffering and deprivation.

The group had helped Vicki develop an ability to identify her feelings and articulate them to others. The group had the understanding that the ability to communicate and understand thoughts and feelings helps its members define and consolidate themselves and allows for movement from narcissistic to more mature relating. All expressions—verbal and nonverbal even when manifested as behavior, attitudes, self or bodily feelings—were understood as communications. Expression now as communications builds relationships, allowing for the development of a defined self and a relationship that takes into account the other as a separate person.

When Vicki began group, she had a limited ability to communicate her feelings. In the group, she chiefly expressed herself by crying and having headaches. The first order of business for the group was to help put her thoughts and feelings into words. The group, already trained by me that all nonverbal and verbal behaviors and attitudes were communications that needed to be translated, asked, "What are the headaches saying?" and "What are the tears expressing?" Eventually, she began to speak. She was sad, had felt left out, and did not believe anyone cared about her. She had been afraid to tell anyone for fear of reprisal. The group was beginning to understand her. The next time she complained of being sick, the members, developing the relationship link, asked, "What did the group do to make you sick?" or "How did we cause you to cry?"

Gradually, Vicki spoke. She was now blaming everyone for neglecting her, not preferring her, and not considering her. She was the one that trudged long distances to get here. Some members began wondering whether it was such a good idea to help her to speak. They did not like her criticism of the group and her desire to control them and they told her so. Vicki asserted that they were not being fair. An empathetic member was able to translate her communication: "Vicki, you want to be appreciated for the effort, and I really do appreciate the effort you made." Another member admired her ability to defend herself. This perked her up. With increased support and interest from additional members, Vicki began to relate to others, but in a self-referential manner. One member talked about the struggles she was having with a successful career, and Vicki said that she was jealous. Another member talked about a painful relationship, and Vicki would recall her own painful relationships.

Vicki began to learn the difference between the feelings that concerned her self, and feelings toward another member. She began to put her toe in the water toward relating to another: "I feel warmly toward you." She was also beginning to listen.

Vicki was slowly evolving from a narcissistic position, to communicating her feelings in a more relational and defined way. She began to recognize her anger and aggression, and the way they were affecting others, and became more effective in communicating these experiences. As she was getting more comfortable with articulating her feelings, Vicki began to distinguish between how she felt about others and how she felt about herself. Vicki was developing another internal imprint of herself in relation to others. She was moving from experiencing herself entirely as a passive victim (while, at the same time, unconsciously operating in preverbal ways to maintain control of others) to having increased experiences of herself as an active subject based on self-definition with an awareness of another. During the week, Vicki was keeping the good relationships of the group in her mind, and this provided some comfort.

This is the point where written case studies often end. There is some development of a case, new gains have been achieved, and the patient, the group, and the therapist have proven to be effective. However, life does not usually develop in such a linear fashion. Imprints of the self in relation to a destructive internal object can continue to erupt and disrupt stability. Emotional insulation needs to be repeatedly strengthened, and new imprints with benign internal objects have to be reinforced. Despite her gains, Vicki was still sensitive and a slight could send her back to an earlier self-state.

This brings us to the current setback. Vicki was in a more vulnerable state. An outside relationship was not doing well, causing her to withdraw. In her withdrawal was a hidden hope that someone would recognize her and attend to her in a way in which her mother never did. Sally, however, took her withdrawal as a personal betrayal and criticized her for her absenting herself. This triggered Vicki's regressive reactions associated with a self-state that was attached to an imprint of a hypercritical mother. Vicki lost her bearing and self-confidence. She became speechless, which held another hidden hope that she would be finally rescued from this cruel woman. The good internal objects formed from the group, that at other times had soothed, provided insulation, and helped build her confidence, could not, at this time, mitigate this earlier destructive internal object.

I asked the group what was going on with Vicki. The group responded, each member attempting to provide words for her experience. Some validated Vicki's perceptions or joined her feeling: "Sally spoke terribly to you" or "Of course she should feel upset. It was insensitive of Sally to be so critical."

Then I asked, "What was Vicki's silence saying?" A member attempted to translate Vicki's tears, "I think you are hurt that your silence was so misunderstood. You wanted someone to reach out to you and instead you got clobbered." "Vicki, I feel bad for you," offered another. "I think you are hurt and angry. You can have both feelings." Another observed, "This is what you were like when you first came to group, remember? You did not know how to ask for what you needed or tell the group how you felt." Reacting to this a member said, "It was too much pressure on everyone to get it right. I would be relieved if you let Sally have it and say what you want." "Yes," offered a shy member, "but it's hard to ask when you are feeling bad and afraid of getting clobbered. She just may not be able to do that right now." These communications seemed to help Vicki restore some composure.

Meanwhile, Sally was becoming alarmed that she was being ganged up on; she did not think she had done anything wrong. She did not like Vicki's apparent disinterest when she was talking. It made her feel unimportant. She, too, had a right to talk. I asked a member what he thought. "That is true," he said, "but it was mean. You might have just told her how you felt, rather than attack her for being a self-centered snob. Or you may have asked what was going on with her." "And why did you assume her silence was an indictment of you?" The group continued to work with each member, providing their reactions and insights on Vicki's and Sally's communications and the historic imprints, shame, hurts, and expectations that were triggered by each other and reproduced in the group.

Eventually, Vicki was able to tell Sally that she did not like the way Sally spoke to her, but would have been interested to know that Sally was hurt by her pre-occupation. Sally, feeling reassured by this response, remarked that she somewhat regretted her hostile jab. They both moved to having more of an ability to hear each other's experience, while still retaining their feelings. The regression to an unfilled hope for a maternal presence that would rescue her from terribly dangerous interactions was partially attended to by Vicki developing supportive relationships with the group, and her increasing ability to say what was on her mind. It was further addressed when Vicki could express her anger and disappointment in me for failing her and then feel understood by me. I will elaborate on this in a later section of this chapter.

Building Resilience in Group

The group was helpful in working with each member's regressive states and transforming them into a progressive process. The whole process works to strengthen each member's resilience. Living through this back-and-forth process becomes the foundation for building resilience—with the group providing a reliable safety net, and a confidence in all its members that emotional maturity can be restored. The repeated experience of the group and its members surviving regressions promotes the development of a reliable good object in the group and in its members. The group, internalized as a good reliable object, allows for a faster recovery from the regressive experiences. The group learns to be less fearful of regressive states and more available to address them therapeutically. This process generates good feelings and deepens connections for the members of the group.

The group interest in each other allows for members' gradual development of emotional insulation that allows for stable functioning, engaging, and resilence. Emotional insulation is derived from internalizing good object feelings arising from the group, an observing ego developed from internalizing the group's integrative function of reflection, and a memory held by the group that supports and reminds members of their strengths during painful regressive moments. The group memory also contains the repertoire of the members' self/object states which creates an experience of cohesion for its members ("We knew you when. ... We lived through it with you. We are still here for you."). The group continues to work toward integration and builds resilience by helping each of its members develop an ability to listen and communicate feelings effectively. Each member brings his or her own creative talent and regression which when expressed and understood deepens the emotional experience of the group and expands the holding capacity for the group and its members.

This group was functioning in a progressive way, but groups—both small and large—can have cycles of progression and regressions. Individual members, subgroups, and groups can operate in narcissistic destructive ways to impede therapeutic progress. Rather than communicate their thoughts and feelings directly, members may avoid, block, exclude, excite, arouse, dismiss, attack, scapegoat, monopolize/dominate, direct/instruct, judge, withdraw, isolate, caretake, and collude with others to keep themselves from addressing and containing uncomfortable feelings. Members can be intolerant of the intensity and of the experience of primitive feelings. An inability to hold and contain feelings leads to an unbearable experience of helplessness. Internal self/object relationships are triggered and life histories are manifested in group re-enactments. In a progressive or an adaptive regressive phase, the group is fluid and effective in bringing emotional material to the surface and integrating it into the group's experience. Malignant regressions due to overwhelming fear, hate, or desire can compromise the therapeutic functions of the group and are destructive to its members' capacity to contain and effectively communicate feelings to each other. Emotional communication among members can be stiflingly rigid, polarized, unsafe, and preverbal. The leader's function is to help the group hold divergent unacceptable emotions and thoughts and to put these experiences into words. Obstacles to feelings are explored and recognized. The focus is to convert the action into language and have limits and contract boundaries enforced.

Vicki developed in a progressive way with regressive bumps to a more mature way of relating. For some, the journey is more difficult and painful to endure. The entrenched isolation, the staving off of vulnerable traumatic experience, and the grandiose primitive behaviors (e.g., duplicity, denial, impulsivity, manipulation) employed to preserve self sufficiency make for a long and tortuous process for the member and the group. Just being able to show up in the group is a move toward accepting a reliable other to begin the process of regressing and progressing within a relationship. This consistency and the relationship may be too much for a person to bear, so relapses and dropouts happen. The member's inconsistency, destructive behaviors, and group demands also may be too much of a drain on a group. There may be joining and rejoining until there is some acceptance for withstanding the process or at least until the therapeutic process of regressing within relationships has proven less toxic than the painful process of regressing in life without helpful relationships.

The Group Leader's Experience with Progressing while Regressing

Finally, there is the leader. The leader has periods of regressions and progression regularly triggered by the emotions and defensive styles of the group or the challenges of life. There are times I am better insulated and my thinking is crisper than other times. These regressive lapses can be a source of emotional confusion, but they can also be a rich source of emotional information. The group leader's regressions are the essential means where we become in contact with the emotional life of the group, its members, and ourselves. These regressions can be therapeutic, if the leader can sort out the countertransferential feeling, the self/object relationships, and resolve his or her own narcissistic barriers that interfere with his or her curiosity, self reflection, and emotional availability. We leaders have a few things going for us to help us be effective. First, we have the insulation of the role and the contract which helps us become object directed, assists with bearing the group's aggression and other uncomfortable feelings, and provides us time to study our own feelings and vulnerabilities. Then, we have our feelings—our rich source of information—to help us understand and address emotional communication. Most important, we have the group to consult—if we are available to listen fully to what the members are saying about our performance and the group dynamics. If we give the group the idea that they can say what is on their minds, including their thoughts about the leader, we can learn. We can have our interventions and enactments all included as part of the process.

I found the group to be very helpful with my work with Vicki. Her longing for love along with her dissatisfaction and mistrust of what she received pervaded her early relationships in the group and was most prominent in her relationship with me. Her hidden hope, then demand, that I could rescue her from her painful interpersonal experiences in the group led to a persistent dissatisfaction of me for failing her. As the group treatment progressed, Vicki was able to bring her dissatisfaction directly to me. She would often complain about my style and her disappointments in me, sometimes setting off my critical internal objects. Vicki was both the vulnerable child, in her need to be found lovable, and a controlling mother, distancing others by her judgmental or self-referential remarks. While feeling vulnerable, she often behaved in the group as the critical controlling mother, and her communications expressed both the vulnerability and the criticality. I had the dilemma of not wanting to be controlled, yet wanting to support her.

It was helpful for Vicki to replay her maternal interactions with me and have us both survive and remain interested in having and understanding our relationship. This was a better version from what she had received in the past. Nevertheless, the induced relational interaction triggered my own internal self/object relationship, which further constricted my responsiveness. I became aware of my impatience, a wish for her to grow up quickly—something that might have been said to me in my past and that also dovetailed with Vicki's critical internal object relationship. I found Ormont's approach to the group and his interventions, particularly bridging and joining, useful as a way to approach these engagements. The multiple voices of the group helped train me to listen and respond to Vicki's need as well as her criticism. Sometimes, I relied on the group to provide what I could not give or what Vicki could not receive from me. I could count on the multiple reactions and relationships to provide Vicki with the necessary emotional support and limits from the confrontation of unfair demands and the group could count on me for emotional availability, understanding, and strength (in the holding and protecting). Together, our mutual reliance formed a safer, more reliable environment for the group members, Vicki, and me. The group provided the transitional space, or the analytic third as Ogden (1994) calls it, to help transform my relationship with Vicki, and the regressive experiences in it, into something new.

Two interactions advanced Vicki's relational connections, which had been developing in the group. In one group, a member brilliantly described, in an empathetic manner, that Vicki's presentation in the group was endearingly vulnerable but was hard to reach because of a distancing prickly protective coat. Vicki began to glow. She said she felt fully recognized. She returned to the next group reporting a good group dream. She was really now a member of the group. This new connection engendered warmth and more interest in the others and a new receptivity to me.

Following this session, we had another interaction that was helpful. While I had been developing increased warmth for Vicki, she still retained some residue of suspicion toward me. I was caught off guard when she had interpreted what I genuinely felt to be a warm bridge linking a supportive member to her as undermining her. "You don't want me to speak" she shot out. I was stunned. I thought I had been a kind of cheerleader to her at that moment by bringing a supportive ally to her. Usually, I would explore with Vicki what she found objectionable in what I said, and she would freely tell me how terrible and thoughtless I was—just as bad as her mother. If she had been available in the group for exploration, I would explore why I would not want her to speak or what I would not want to hear. Perhaps, I may have explored why my failings were so hurtful to her. The group would also work with her to understand and support her reactions as well as supervising me on my comments. There would be a coming together in the discussion. But this time was different. She appeared frozen in an angry, isolated position. One member ventured to say that maybe Vicki was so hurt because she had been letting down her guard and was enjoying Dr. Levine and the group. This was met with a cold rejection, accusing the member and the entire group of only having an interest in protecting the leader.

It did seem that her increased good group feeling had put her in an unsafe position with me and with the group. The good feeling between us also seemed to have caused me to become more inflexible with Vicki's feelings. I wanted to hold on to these good feelings between us at the expense of being attuned to what Vicki was actually feeling in the moment. In being caught up with my aspirations for Vicki, I had lost emotional contact with her. She was in a different developmental self/object state from the one of the previous warm engagement. Vicki was right when she had said to me, "You do not want me to speak." I did not want to hear that she had moved away from me or regressed to a different relational self-state.

She was too injured now to allow any further exploration of our interaction. The group, feeling helpless by Vicki's polarization, wanted to know how I felt. The relationship called for flexibility. There had been times she (and I) needed me to withstand, investigate, and set limits to her attacks. At this moment, she needed me to acknowledge my empathic failures, and join her experience. I told them I was at first surprised and hurt. However, I realized now that I was not sufficiently keeping Vicki's mistrust of me in mind, and I was not sufficiently listening to what she needed. I had not been attuned to her. I was operating from the growing positive feelings in our relationship, but in a way, taking them for granted. I was working to connect Vicki with others, when Vicki just wanted to talk. Vicki should have the room in this group to express herself and relate at her pace. My comments had interrupted her.

Vicki was reassured by hearing that she had affected me (and that I was interested in recognizing different needs derived from her multiple self/object states). She reported in subsequent sessions that I did care for her and became slightly more tolerant of me. It seemed that acknowledging my errors, sharing the burden of badness, blame, and shame relieved Vicki of experiencing herself alone in her badness (imprisoned in her internal bad self/object relationship). It was also a relief for me to freely accept and acknowledge my flaws, which had the effect of making the bad feelings bearable by disconnecting my present shame in the moment (bad/defective group analyst) from my historic shame (bad/defective person) derived from my bad self/critical object imprint. Our failures (and a particular self-state) were not our totality. We were both good and bad to each other. For each of us, our relationship was providing acceptance and integration of a wider range of self/object experiences. She and I had more room to explore our relationship, receive from each other, and to go through the ongoing process of progressing while regressing with each other. Meanwhile, the group enjoyed feeling effective with its ability to successfully contain experience.

These early, more primitive, regressive self-state imprints do not go away. The right trigger may cause them to emerge again, but the right emotional experiences of the group can help them recede and can provide new interactional imprints—new ways of relating. The maturation process—progressing while regressing—facilitates resiliency and strengthens a wider repertoire of responses. The multidimensional emotional interactions lead to maturation for both the patients and the therapist. The group is a therapeutic process for all.

Acknowledgments

This chapter is based on a lecture titled "Progressing while Regressing in Relationships" presented as the second Louis Ormont Lecture at the annual meeting of the American Group Psychotherapy Association, Chicago, 2009.

References

Aledort, S.L. (2009) Excitement: A crucial marker for group therapy. *Group*, 33: 45–62.
Balint, M. (1968) *The Basic Fault: Therapeutic Aspects of Regression*. London: Tavistock.
Lyons-Ruth, K. (1999) The two person unconscious: Intersubjective dialogue, enactive relational representation and emergence of new forms of relational organization. *Psychoanalytic Inquiry*, 19: 576–617.
Ogden, T. (1994) *Subjects of Analysis*. Northvale, NJ: Jason Aronson.

Chapter 8

Use and Impact of Empathic, Other-Centered, and Self Listening/Experiencing Perspectives in Analytic Group Psychotherapy

James L. Fosshage

Before I begin to discuss my topic, the use and impact of listening/experiencing perspectives in analytic group psychotherapy, I wish to tell you how I came to value group therapy. When I began analytic training at the Postgraduate Center for Mental Health, New York City, at the age of twenty-eight, I looked for a training analyst who ran groups. Dyads were comparatively easy for me. Groups were more difficult. I had several consultations with Helen E. Durkin, PhD, the author of *The Group in Depth*, one of the first major books on analytic group therapy published in 1964. I read her book and was quite impressed with it. For those of you who knew her, the story I am about to tell will come as no surprise.

Unfortunately my parents had died when I was relatively young. A former analyst of mine had also died just as I was transitioning to another analyst. At the time of my consultation, Helen was in her mid-seventies. At one point I openly expressed my anxiety about her age, "Helen, I'm afraid that you will die on me before I finish my analysis." She retorted, "Well, Jim, it is true that I am getting up there in years, but I am in good health and very well might outlive a lot of those young whipper snappers." With vitality, authenticity, and directness of that order (most unusual in the heyday of ego psychology), I knew she was my gal. And, fortunately, she was right, for she remained spry and healthy for my analysis and for sometime thereafter. It is most fitting and meaningful to me to dedicate this chapter, as I did my keynote address, to Dr. Helen Durkin.

For almost two decades I (1995, 1997b, 2003, 2011a) have focused on the listening perspectives of analysts, drawing on Kohut's (1959, 1982) conceptualization of the *empathic mode of observation* and adding my conceptualizations of the *other-centered and analyst's self listening/experiencing perspectives*. In my view, analysts, knowingly or not, variably oscillate between these three perspectives as they attempt to understand and respond to their analysands. In addition, I have posited that these three listening/experiencing perspectives are central in human relations, especially in our personal experience of and communication with one another. Thus, patients, as analysts, use these three listening/experiencing perspectives in relating to their analysts, that is, how they experience, feel toward, and communicate with their analysts.

In this chapter, I, now for the first time, apply the use of these listening/experiencing perspectives to the members and therapist of analytic group therapy. As I delineate the evolution of listening perspectives within psychoanalysis, I will address the emergence of the conceptualization of the empathic listening mode of perception within its historical context and the major questions, misunderstandings, and issues surrounding it. I will then present the subsequent conceptualizations of other-centered and self listening perspectives and describe in detail the valuable information these perspectives provide that is, in my view, necessary to achieve a more comprehensive understanding of the protagonists and their interaction whether in an individual or group analytic process. I will close with a clinical vignette of a group therapy process to illustrate the oscillation and conscious use of these listening perspectives.

Evolution of Listening/Experiencing Perspectives

While Freud (1915) was well aware that "our perceptions are subjectively conditioned and must not be regarded as identical with that which is perceived" (p. 171), his observations and theories were embedded in the positivistic science of his day and emphasized the analyst's objectivity and the patient's transference distortions of reality. Heisenberg's formulation of the Uncertainty Principle in 1927 initiated a revolutionary change in paradigms from positivistic to relativistic science, making it unquestionably clear that the observer affects the observed, both perceptually and interactively.

This paradigm change in epistemology from positivistic to relativistic science, now called objectivism to constructivism, significantly contributed to a second paradigm change from intrapsychic to relational field theory. With the observer affecting the observed, it was recognized that the analytic dyad creates an intersubjective (Atwood & Stolorow, 1984; Stolorow, Brandchaft, & Atwood, 1987) or relational (Greenberg & Mitchell, 1983; Mitchell, 1988) field that involves "the intersection of two subjectivities" (Atwood & Stolorow, 1984), a term that accentuates the subjectivity, in contrast to objectivity, of each participant and their bi-directional interactive influence on one another.

In response to the first, and still ongoing, paradigm change from positivistic to relativistic science, Kohut, beginning in 1959, updated psychoanalytic epistemology in re-conceptualizing its method of observation. Kohut (1982) recognized "the relativity of our perceptions of reality," "the framework of ordering concepts that shape our observations and explanations" (p. 400), and that "the field that is observed, of necessity, includes the observer" (1984, p. 41). Deeming the patient's subjectivity as the principal focus of the analytic endeavor, Kohut (1959, 1982) delineated how our method of observation relies on empathy and vicarious introspection, what he called the "empathic mode of observation," and designated it as the method by which the field of psychoanalysis itself is defined (1977, p. 302).

The epistemological transition from objectivism to constructivism understandably has not been an easy task for psychoanalysis at large (Schwaber,

1981, 1997, 1998; Lichtenberg, 1981; Hoffman, 1983, 1998; Stolorow & Lachmann, 1984/85; Fosshage, 1994, 1995, 2003; Stern, 1997). It has not been easy clinically to relinquish the security of an objectivist position with its degree of certitude and elevation of the analyst as the "knower," especially during those most difficult periods of analytic entanglements, whether in individual or group psychoanalytic settings. It has not been easy to embrace, instead, the potentially insecurity-producing ambiguity of a constructivist position that tends to level the playing field as the analytic protagonists attempt collaboratively to understand "who is contributing what to each other's experience" (Fosshage, 1994, 2003), a fundamental question for individual and group analytic therapy.

Thus, the two paradigm changes in psychoanalysis—objectivism to constructivism and intrapsychic to relational field or systems models—have profoundly affected our conceptualization, use, and impact of different listening/experiencing perspectives. *Whether within the individual or group setting, listening perspectives affect the protagonists' experience, inquiries, and impact on one another.*

In his conceptualization of "the empathic mode of observing," Kohut (1959, 1982) delineated, in my view, the psychoanalyst's principal listening perspective, that is, to attempt to understand from within the patient's perspective. While I believe that the empathic mode is the central, overriding listening perspective within an individual, and now group, analytic process, I, subsequently, have conceptualized two additional listening/experiencing perspectives, what I (1995, 1997b, 2003) have termed the other-centered listening and the analyst's self perspectives. These listening perspectives offer invaluable information about our patients, ourselves as analysts, and the analytic interaction to be delineated. I have proposed that human beings naturally oscillate between these three central listening/experiencing perspectives in all realms of human relatedness, including the therapeutic process. While I initially focused on analysts' listening perspectives in keeping with the asymmetrical focus on understanding the patient, I have now broadened these perspectives to all persons so that I have renamed the "analyst's self perspective" as one's "self perspective." Apart from the impact of the asymmetrical focus on patients in analytic therapy, patients, whether in individual or group therapy settings, also make use of these listening perspectives in attempting to understand and communicate with their therapists and with one another. In analytic group therapy, analyst and group members variably use empathic, other-centered, and self listening perspectives when focusing on one another and the group process itself.

The principal context for this chapter is the use and impact of these three listening/experiencing perspectives within analytic group therapy. When I write of the analysand and analyst, I view it as also directly applicable to the group setting. I use analysand, patient, and group member interchangeably, and the same for analyst and therapist.

Empathic Listening/Experiencing Perspective

The empathic mode of observation, to reiterate, refers to a listening perspective designed to understand as best as one can, through affect resonance and vicarious introspection, the analysand's experience from within the frame of reference of the analysand. In other words, through resonating with the analysand's affective experience and using analogues of our experience (Stolorow, Atwood, & Orange, 2002), we attempt to infer (Lichtenberg, Lachmann, & Fosshage, 2010) our way into the analysand's experiential world. In formulating the empathic listening stance, Kohut attempted to bring the patient's subjective experience more immediately into focus, a focus that had previously been too commandeered by the analyst's "objective" point of view.

All analysts variably use empathic listening in efforts to understand the analysand's "experiential world" (Stolorow et al., 2002), the fundamental analytic task. When we ask such questions as "What were you feeling at that moment?" we are asking from an empathic perspective. Self psychologists (Kohut, 1982; Ornstein & Ornstein, 1985, among many others) and Schwaber (1981) have emphasized its *consistent usage* as the basis of analytic inquiry and understanding.

Controversy over the empathic listening perspective, however, mushroomed from, if you will, the left and the right, coalescing around four interrelated issues:

1 Does the empathic listening stance, in focusing exclusively on the analysand's experiential world, attempt to eliminate the analyst's subjectivity? If so, does it inadvertently reveal an implicit objectivist underpinning?
2 When using the empathic stance, does the analyst solely reflect back the analysand's experience, again attempting to eliminate the use of, and certainly the disclosure of, the analyst's perspective and subjectivity?
3 Does responding empathically simply result in being "compassionate" or, even worse, being "nice" to the analysand, avoiding needed confrontations?
4 Does empathic inquiry focus exclusively on conscious experience and, thereby, neglect unconscious factors?

I will address these issues conceptually and historically.

Does the empathic listening stance attempt to eliminate the analyst's subjectivity? In contrast to eliminating the analyst's subjectivity, Kohut emphasized the *use of the analyst's subjectivity* during empathic inquiry, comprised specifically by the analyst's empathic capacity, vicarious introspection, and theoretical concepts. Yet, he also subscribed to Freud's and then current (in the United States) ego psychological pathological model of *countertransference* that focused on recognizing and ejecting the problematic aspects of the analyst's subjectivity from the analytic encounter. This stood in contrast to the interpersonal, object relational, Kleinian, and, subsequently, relational authors increasingly using the term "countertransference," following Heimann (1950), much more broadly to refer to normative reactions to the transference that are informative of internal patterns of organization and interpersonal interaction.[1] A number of these authors who redefined and made use of the analyst's countertransference, in contrast to Kohut, tended to view the empathic perspective, with its sole focus on the analysand's experience, as eliminating rather than making use of the analyst's subjectivity.

The differences were, in part, definitional, that is, the definition of countertransference, and, in part, emphasis, that is, referring to the use of different aspects of the analyst's subjectivity. For example, if we expand the definition of countertransference to refer to the analyst's experience of the patient, what Kernberg (1965) termed the "totalist perspective," it follows that all analysts use their countertransference or subjectivities in listening, regardless of listening perspective—for what else is there (Fosshage, 1995)? *All analytic listening is filtered through our subjectivities.* Kohut featured the analyst's empathic capacity, vicarious introspection, and theoretical models as well as the non-pathological countertransference reactions to and partial designators of selfobject transferences (Kohut, 1971). A broad range of relational authors have subsequently extended the use of those aspects of the analyst's subjective experience (or countertransference) that illuminate the analysand's patterns of relational interaction, what I refer to as making use of data from the other-centered listening perspective.[2]

There were a few remnants of objectivism in Kohut's writings and, perhaps more importantly, an initial enthusiasm amongst the earliest advocates of the empathic perspective (emanating from a welcomed freedom from the imposition of objectivism) that sounded almost as if it provided a "sure way" to the analysand's world. Subsequently, relational self psychologists and intersubjectivists—for example, Lichtenberg (1981), Fosshage, (1994, 1995), Orange (1995), Stolorow, Atwood, and Orange (1999, 2002), among others, and Schwaber (1997, 1998)—have taken strides to emphasize that the process of empathic listening is necessarily filtered through the analyst's subjective experience, highlighting the underlying constructivist, in contrast to objectivist, epistemology. I have coined the term "empathic listening/experiencing perspective" to accent the use of the analyst's subjectivity. And, while I am delineating these listening perspectives from the analyst's perspective, patients in individual and group treatment variably use the same listening perspectives.

Analysts process information implicitly and explicitly to inform a direction of inquiry, that is, to sense what is important, what needs elaboration, what needs clarification, and what needs inquiry for illuminating intentions, affects, and meanings. While the empathic stance "is designed 'to hear' as well as possible from within the vantage point of the analysand, this is clearly a relative matter, for what is heard is *always variably shaped* by the analyst" (Fosshage, 1992, p. 22). The extent of the analyst's or group member's shaping and how closely it resonates with and captures the patient's experience contributes substantially to whether or not the group member being focused on feels heard and understood. In the extremely complex multi-directional influences within a group system, an analyst's or a group member's contribution can range from a disruption of another group member's direction and sense of being heard and understood to an expansion of a group member's reflective awareness and articulation of both conscious and unconscious intentions, meanings, interpersonal impact, and other experience.

When using the empathic listening stance, does the analyst solely reflect back the analysand's experience, again attempting to eliminate the use of, and certainly the disclosure of, the analyst's perspective and subjectivity? Kohut (1977) assessed that an analyst could not remain anonymous, neutral, and a blank screen, interacting, if you will, like an interpreting computer, but must be sufficiently responsive to enable the analysand to make use of the analyst as a selfobject. He designated this as "empathic responsiveness," that is, the analyst is responsive on the basis of his empathic understanding of the analysand. Empathic responsiveness brought the analyst's subjectivity and responses more fully into play, directly countering the notion, once again, that the empathic stance aimed to eliminate the analyst's subjectivity from the interaction. Subsequently relational self psychologists have expanded the range of responsiveness or interactions markedly (e.g., Bacal, 1985, 1998; Bacal & Carlton, 2010; Fosshage, 1995, 1997b, 2007; Shane, Shane, & Gales, 1998; among many others).

Does responding empathically simply result in being "compassionate" or, even worse, being "nice" to the analysand, avoiding needed confrontations?[3] As described, Kohut came to use the term "empathic" confusingly in two ways—first, to refer to a listening perspective and, second, to a type of response. Critics frequently have conflated these two meanings. For example, Bromberg (1989) wrote: "the defining element of [the empathic] stance is its dedication to full empathic responsiveness to the patient's subjective experience" (p. 282). This conflation implied that the self psychologically informed analyst withheld aspects of his or her subjectivity from the playing field, contributing to the notion that these analysts were attempting "only" to be compassionate or, in the vernacular, "to be nice" to their analysands. To confound the matter even more, while the explicit objective of empathic listening is not compassion, empathic listening and understanding from within the analysand's frame of reference does tend to foster a mutual compassionate resonance and a sense of feeling heard and understood. This stands in contrast to the more experience distant interpretations based on "outside" perspectives and interpretive "leaps" that can be more easily experienced as "confrontational," missing the mark, or simply "not getting it." This compassionate resonance, involving recognition and understanding of the analysand and the analysand's experience, is certainly a major "healing" factor.

Bromberg (1989) asserted that an analyst, thus oriented (referring to the self psychologist's empathic perspective), becomes focused on "how it feels to be the subject *rather* than the target of the patient's needs and demands" (p. 286). I believe that Bromberg here makes an important distinction between two experiential perspectives: identification with the subjective experience of the patient verses identification with the other as "target" of the patient's actions. In my view, an analysand will variably need to experience the analyst as identified with and understanding the analysand's experiential world and, at other times, needs to hear what it is like for an other to be in the interactive field with the analysand in order to understand better his or her internal organizing and behavioral contributions to interpersonal experience. To assess what will be facilitative for an analysand at any given moment, I believe, requires an overriding empathic perspective—for example, attempting to understand the meanings that an intervention might have for an analysand. To respond fully as the target of the analysand's needs, affects, and interactions, however, requires additional listening perspectives, to be delineated.

Does empathic inquiry focus exclusively on conscious experience and, thereby, neglect unconscious factors? Perhaps emphasizing a singular focus on the analysand's consciously articulated experiential world in empathic listening contributed to a misperception that the analyst does not deviate from or expand the analysand's reflective awareness and conscious articulations either in inquiry or interpretive formulations and, thereby, forfeits consideration of unconscious processes and meanings. In addition, the close focus on the analysand's subjective experience implicitly, if not explicitly, challenged the validity of "objective" interpretive leaps to presumed unconscious meanings. It would be easy for those who interpret in that matter to assume that, when focused on empathic inquiry, unconscious meanings are neglected.

Fundamental to psychoanalysis is the postulation of unconscious mental activity, first Freud's dynamic unconscious involving intrapsychic structural conflict and, more recently, the inclusion of implicit (unconscious or non-conscious) learning and memory that has expanded exponentially the domain of unconscious processing (Clyman, 1991; Grigsby & Hartlaub, 1994; Stern et al., 1998; Boston Change Process Study Group, 2008; Fosshage, 2005, 2011b; among many others). Unconscious and conscious processing—that includes perceiving, categorizing, consolidating memory and learning, regulating shifting priorities in motivation (intentions) and affect, and conflict resolution—is always occurring simultaneously during our waking hours. Research evidence makes clear that during sleep unconscious processing of the same order continues in REM and non-REM dreaming (Fosshage, 1997a).

How do we gain access to unconscious processing? Freud, of course, developed the free association method and found dreams to be "the royal road to the unconscious." Ego psychologists subsequently accented the unconscious components of conflict and defenses that emerged latently in conscious articulations. More recently we have expanded the range for listening not only for conflict but also for explicit and implicit non-verbal and verbal communications of intentions, affects, meanings, and procedural knowledge. Empathic listening is "simply" focused on hearing and understanding these communications from within the patient's frame of reference. "Empathy and judgment" interpenetrate (Goldberg, 1999), yet the attempt is *to be* in the analysand's experience and to make our inferences and assessments, as best we can, from within the analysand's experiential world.

The use of empathic listening does not minimize the importance of unconscious processing. To the contrary, clinical experience indicates that a sense of safety is enhanced through the analyst's intently listening from an empathic perspective, for it militates against (does not, of course, eliminate) the disruptive influence of an analyst's imposition of his or her vantage point. Diminishing the need for protection against the analyst's interpretive judgments that are not close to the patient's experience increases a sense of safety and reflective space and facilitates the emergence of unconscious conflicting and non-conflicting intentions, affects, memories, meanings, and processing, including unvalidated (Stolorow & Atwood, 1992) and unformulated (Stern, 1997) experience, and implicit patterns of organization (implicit knowledge) into reflective conscious awareness. In other words, empathic understanding tends to make the boundaries between conscious and unconscious, explicit and implicit, more permeable and fluid and increases conscious access to previously unconscious feelings, intentions, thoughts, and connections.

Additional Listening/Experiencing Perspectives

Empathic listening and responsiveness unquestionably utilize the analyst's subjectivity in listening and responding to analysands. Yet, when a clinical moment requires focus on the analyst's experience of the analysand in their relational interaction (what Bromberg referred to as being the "target" of the patient's responses) or on the analyst's experience of himself or herself during an interaction, the inclusion of additional listening/experiencing perspectives and data is needed, broadening the range and use of the analyst's subjectivity. The conceptualization of additional perspectives clarifies alternatives from which we can draw upon in a clinical moment and, in addition, contributes to understanding the differences in what analysts hear.

What other listening/experiencing vantage points are there? Surprisingly, relatively few authors have focused on alternative listening perspectives. I (2011a) have reviewed the perspectives offered by Lichtenberg (1981), Gabbard (1997), Goldberg (1999), and Smith (1999). Here I will delineate my conceptualizations of two additional listening/experiencing perspectives.

I have proposed that *analysts experientially oscillate between the empathic, other-centered and analyst's self listening perspectives* (Fosshage, 1995, 1997b, 2003, 2011a). The *other-centered perspective* refers to an analyst's experience of the analysand as "an other" in a relationship with the patient—what it feels like to be the other person in the interaction. When we experience an analysand as hostile, controlling, loving, or manipulative, we are experiencing the analysand primarily from the vantage point of an other in a relationship with the analysand. This information about the analysand and the interaction potentially informs us about how the analysand impacts others, about the analysand's patterns of relating and about change in those interaction patterns. These interaction patterns, in addition, provide an entrée to an analysand's internal patterns of organization that have been established on the basis of lived experience, for patterns of organization and interaction are intricately interrelated. For example, a person entering an interaction with a set of expectancies tends to create a confirming relational interaction. Racker's (1968) concordant and complementary countertransferences can be viewed as corresponding with analysts' experiences emanating from empathic and other-centered perspectives respectively.

The empathic perspective advantageously positions the analyst to attend closely to how the analysand experiences his or her world, a process that implicitly acknowledges and validates the "reality" of the analysand's experience, contributing to a deep, self-enhancing sense of being "heard" and to a co-creation of reflective space. Empathic listening, however, is quite complex, for an analyst in listening to an analysand's explicit and implicit verbal and non-verbal expressions must hear and infer the message (content) and the music (process). An analyst must differentiate between foreground and background features of an analysand's articulated experience. And an analyst must sense into and facilitate the emergence of the implicit, as of yet unarticulated, intentions and meanings.

The other-centered perspective provides information about how others may experience the analysand and the analysand's patterns of interaction, facilitating understanding of what happens in the analysand's relationships. Other-centered experience also provides clues for underlying patterns of organization (e.g., an analysand's expectancies in the interaction) as well as information about an analysand's breaking out of old patterns and establishing footholds for new ways of relating.

The disadvantage of using the empathic perspective exclusively for interpretive focus is to deprive an analysand of direct feedback on how the analyst experiences the analysand in the interaction, useful in illuminating interaction patterns and how the analysand impacts his or her relationships. The disadvantage of other-centered listening/experiencing data is that the analyst's other-centered experience, when communicated, may be too distant from the analysand's experience for the analysand to be able meaningfully to appropriate.

Moreover, analysts have traditionally used what I am calling other-centered experience to assess underlying (unconscious) motivations that have all too often superseded the analysand's expressed intentional experience. To assess intention or motivation on the basis of the interpersonal consequences of an analysand's actions (the analyst's other-centered experience) warrants considerable caution, for the interpersonal consequences might or might not reflect the analysand's intent. For example, hostile humor interpersonally feels aggressive and triggers aversion; yet, a person might be totally unaware of the aversiveness for the primary motivation may be to connect and the procedure for connecting (a learned familial attachment pattern) is through hostile jibing. While other-centered experience can reveal how the analysand impacts others, and invaluable information about interaction patterns and relationships as well as evidence for related organizing patterns, empathic inquiry is required to assess what the primary conscious and unconscious motivations are from within the analysand's experiential world in order to weave together a complex picture of the analysand's "internal" and "external" experiential world.

While the empathic and other-centered perspectives both focus on the analysand, an analyst during an interaction also needs to be aware of his or her own subjective experience of feelings, reactions, and assessments, what I call the *analyst's self perspective*. For example, if an analysand experiences and inquires if her analyst felt disapproving or angry, the analyst must assess his or her own subjective experience, in this instance judgment and affect, in order to make sense, as best as one can, of who is contributing what to the analysand's experience.

In my view, the timely use of experience derived from each listening/experiencing perspective facilitates and deepens inquiry of both conscious and unconscious processing and provides a more comprehensive understanding of both analysand and analyst and their interaction. While we can, within limits, consciously choose a particular listening/experiencing perspective, many factors from the analyst, analysand, and interaction contribute to a triggering or activation of a particular perspective, a rapid oscillation between the perspectives, or a simultaneous occurrence of several perspectives. For example, whenever an analysand expresses strong affect directed to the analyst, be it anger or love, it immediately triggers an other-centered perspective, what it feels like to be the other in a relationship with the analysand. It could also trigger simultaneously the analyst's self perspective—for example, feeling defensive in reaction to the analysand's anger or feeling enjoyment or anxiety in reaction to the analysand's love.

Apart from these problematic reactions, an overriding use of the empathic perspective, whether foreground or background, helps us assess how and when to use information from these respective perspectives therapeutically. As a general principle, to unravel a poignant difficult analysand/analyst interaction, whether in individual or group treatment, I believe that, if we start within an analysand's perspective (e.g., intentions, affects, and expectancies), including relevant historical resonances, and work our way utilizing the analyst's other-centered data to the analysand's contribution to the interpersonal interaction, we can sustain reflective processing for both analysand and analyst and arrive at the most comprehensive understanding of the analysand's internal organizations and contribution to relational experience that is palatable and digestible. In especially difficult entanglements, however, the analyst must begin with the analyst's self perspective, acknowledging his or her contribution to the problematic interaction before it is possible to inquire into the analysand's experience. This is especially true, of course, when the analysand has had a history of parental blaming and refusal to acknowledge their contribution.

I now propose that individual patients and group members, not just analysts, oscillate between these three listening/experiencing perspectives as well, for they are an inherent component of human relatedness. Recognizing that all of us utilize these perspectives has led me to rename the third listening perspective from the analyst's self to one's *self listening perspective*. One's self listening/experiencing perspective might include either of the other listening perspectives along with additional personal meanings, affects, resonances, and thoughts.

While the oscillation between listening perspectives is based on a complex of conscious and unconscious factors, including internal and external triggers, I believe that a conscious awareness of different listening perspectives can increase therapists' understanding of the clinical content and process as well as facilitate the analytic exploratory process. In addition, patients' awareness of different listening perspectives can enhance their reflective awareness as well as understanding of self, other, and self-with-other. To be able to enter into the experiential worlds of other people increases group members' empathic capability, non-judgmental understanding of and compassion for other persons, and enriches the complexity of their relational and organizing experience. Moreover, a group member's experience of empathic understanding, feedback of other-centered experience, and self perspective experience from other group members facilitates a process of detoxifying shame and promoting compassionate understanding of previously problematic, at times dissociated, aspects of oneself—a process of personal integration. Awareness of these oscillating perspectives can help all the protagonists of the individual and group analytic settings increase awareness and complexity of understanding "who's contributing what" in a relational moment.

Clinical Vignette

The following clinical vignette illustrates the natural (unconscious/conscious) activation and oscillation and conscious selective use of the three listening perspectives that facilitate exploration, understanding, and explanation of a group interaction that, in this instance, entailed intense threat, denigration, and aggression. I have condensed and followed this thematic interaction within a therapeutic group process that occurred approximately over a ten-week period.

> Having been in individual psychoanalytic treatment with me for approximately six years, John, a man in his late twenties, had recently joined my analytic group. Quite anxious about the group's acceptance of him (information empathically acquired from his individual sessions), he entered the group with a superior, disdainful attitude and seriously challenged me in our individual sessions if the group was up to his analytic level. John's superior, denigrating attitude intensely provoked the other-centered perspective and thematic issues in another man in the group, in his mid-thirties, we'll call him Tony. John and Tony sparred. John was not at all sure that this group was a "fit" for him. In turn, Tony exclaimed: "I can't stand your superior attitude. It makes the

group feel unsafe." And finally, Tony in exasperation forcefully said, "One of us has to leave. If you stay, I'm leaving." John retorted, "I'm not sure that this is the group for me. The group doesn't talk about what is going on in the group."

Other group members tried to inquire empathically (empathic listening perspective) into John's experience of the group as well as his past experience in groups. I remember supporting these questions non-verbally and augmented the ongoing empathic inquiry with reflecting emotional resonance with John's experience of coming into a new group, not knowing what to expect. Feeling a bit safer, John was able to say that from the very beginning the group did not feel welcoming to him, for they had not inquired about him for almost the entirety of the first session. Several group members were able to self reflect (their self perspectives) and take responsibility for their lack of inquiry, remembering that it was not out of lack of interest but out of concern about John's anxiety and a sense that it would put him on the spot. The group members had first attempted to understand from an empathic perspective, but had assumed (most likely picking up on John's non-verbal communication of aversion to the group) that John did not desire their inquiry. They then felt that, when they had inquired, John was monosyllabic, aversive, and even disdainful. Subsequently, a number of them shared how they had experienced him (from their other-centered perspective), referring to his superior and disdainful attitude (validating Tony's experience). With a little, what I like to call "an analytic nudge," noting that they had not said anything, they acknowledged that they had not talked about it. These group members had listened empathically and then pulled back, acknowledging their responsibility for not having inquired for fear of provoking John.

When one or more members in a dyad or group (in therapeutic or other relationships) is able to take responsibility for his/her/their contribution to the problematic interaction, in this instance a shut down of the process of getting to know one another, it creates momentarily a safe place for the other to acknowledge his or her responsibility without shame. In this instance, the group members' acknowledgment created momentarily a safe enough place for John to reflect on his experience (his self perspective), enabling him to share his hurt and anxiety about the group's unwelcoming response and to begin to see and acknowledge his protective, disdainful attitude that pushed people away and, as I added, created a painful negative feedback loop, that is, anticipating based on past experience that he would not be welcomed, protectively pushing people away, and then feeling isolated and unwanted. We were able to talk about how both John and some of the other group members were feeling initially anxious and protective and how their individual anxieties

> were co-created by specific expectations formed out of past experience and the cues of the current situation.
>
> I was then able to inquire empathically into Tony's intense reactions to John. Encouraged and feeling safer with John's openness about his vulnerability and critical attitude, Tony began to talk about how John was like his judgmental, humiliating father that threatened him and got him angry. I helped to make clear (from an empathic perspective) the experienced threat mobilized a powerful aversive reaction in him that was aimed to repel a potentially harmful replication of a humiliating experience (aggression bolstering assertion for purposes of preventing self injury) (Fosshage, 1998). Whereas John and Tony were on the verge of leaving the group, after approximately ten weeks of work they were both able to understand far better each other's inner experience from an empathic perspective and their interpersonal impact from each other's sharing of their other-centered and self experience. Both John and Tony were surprised and impressed with how their understandings alleviated their intense negative reactions to one another, increasing their positive evaluation of and emotional commitment to the group process.

Conclusion

I have proposed that in human relationships we oscillate naturally between three listening/experiencing perspectives—the empathic, other-centered, and self perspectives—in our efforts to relate personally and communicate our experience of and with one another. Thus, I have argued that patients and therapists in individual and group analytic therapy all utilize these three listening perspectives to understand one's own and the other's experience and who is contributing what in an interaction moment.

In my view, all analysts *variably* use empathic listening in efforts to understand the analysand's experiential world, the fundamental analytic task. Evidence strongly indicates that empathic listening, through creating a safe reflective space, actually reduces protective barriers and increases the fluidity between unconscious and conscious processing. While the empathic listening/experiencing perspective, in my view, is the fulcrum for analytic work, additional listening/experiencing perspectives are required to provide the range of data necessary for a comprehensive understanding of the patient within individual and group analytic therapy.

I have proposed that therapists in individual and group analytic therapy need consciously to use the ongoing experiential oscillation between three listening/experiencing perspectives—the *empathic, other-centered, and self listening perspectives*—to understand the patient's experience from "within," the patient's problematic interaction and organizing patterns that encumber relationships, changes within those patterns, and who is contributing what in the moment-to-moment analytic interplay. To assess what interventions will be facilitative for a patient at any given moment, in my view, requires an overriding empathic perspective in that we attempt to anticipate and understand the meanings that an intervention might have for a patient. I have also argued that analysts' use of an overriding empathic perspective, combined with the frequent use of other-centered and analyst's self listening perspectives, enhances the use of the analyst's subjectivity, increasing the range of listening and responding to facilitate the psychoanalytic process and development of patients in individual and group analytic therapy.

In addition, patients' awareness and conscious use of different listening perspectives within analytic group therapy enhances their reflective awareness as well as understanding of self, other, and self-with-other. To be able to enter into the experiential worlds of other people increases group members' empathic capability, non-judgmental, compassionate understanding of other persons and enriches the complexity of their relational and organizing experience. In addition, a group member's experience of empathic understanding, feedback of other-centered experience, and self perspective experience from other group members facilitates an understanding and integration of various aspects of one self and self/other differentiation.

Awareness of these oscillating perspectives can help all the protagonists of the individual and group analytic settings increase awareness and complexity of understanding "who's contributing what" in a relational moment, integrating and deepening one's self and one's relational experience.

Acknowledgments

This chapter is based on my "Conference Opening Plenary Address" presented at the 69th Annual Conference of the American Group Psychotherapy Association in New York, March 8, 2012. Portions of the address and this chapter are borrowed from my paper "The Use and Impact of the Analyst's Subjectivity with Empathic and Other Listening/Experiencing Perspectives" (2011a).

Notes

1 I am using the term "relational" with a small "r" to cover a range of psychoanalytic approaches that are anchored in relational or intersubjective field theory, including interpersonal, American Relational (capital "R"), and the more contemporary object relational and self psychological perspectives (see Fosshage, 2003).
2 Internal patterns of organization have been variously described with the terms, internal objects or introjects (Klein, 1975), internal working models (Bowlby, 1973), internal representations (Sandler & Rosenblatt, 1962), principles or patterns of organization (Wachtel, 1980; Stolorow & Lachmann, 1984/85; Fosshage, 1994; Sander, 1997), RIGs (Stern, 1985), pathogenic beliefs (Weiss & Sampson, 1986), mental representations (Fonagy, 1993), expectancies (Lichtenberg, Lachmann, & Fosshage, 1996), and implicit relational knowing (Stern et al., 1998).

3 Self psychologists in the use of the empathic mode have been criticized for attempting to be "nice" to the patient, whereas that empathic inquiry can feel closer to and more understanding of the patient's experience, not an unfortunate occurrence. We, of course, do not want to avoid needed confrontations, understanding that the term "confrontation," of course, is a complicated and tricky word in terms of meanings.

References

Atwood, G. & Stolorow, R. (1984) *Structures of Subjectivity*. Hillsdale, NJ: Analytic Press.

Bacal, H. (1985) Optimal responsiveness and the therapeutic process. *Progress in Self Psychology*, 1: 202–227.

Bacal, H. (1998) *Optimal Responsiveness: How People Heal Their Patients*. New York: Jason Aronson.

Bacal, H. & Carlton, L. (2010) *The Power of Specificity: When Therapy Works and When It Doesn't*. New York: Jason Aronson.

Boston Change Process Study Group (2008) Forms of relational meaning: Issues in the relations between the implicit and reflective-verbal domains. *Psychoanalytic Dialogues*, 18 (2): 125–148.

Bowlby, J. (1973) *Attachment and Loss. Vol. II Separation*. New York: Basic Books.

Bromberg, P. (1989) Interpersonal psychoanalysis and self psychology: A clinical comparison. In D. Detrick and S. Detrick (eds.) *Self Psychology: Comparisons and Contrasts*. Hillsdale, NJ: Analytic Press.

Clyman, R.B. (1991) The procedural organization of emotions: A contribution of cognitive science to the psychoanalytic theory of therapeutic action. *Journal of the American Psychoanalytic Association*, 39 (Supplement): 349–382.

Durkin, H. (1964) *The Group in Depth*. New York: International Universities Press.

Fonagy, P. (1993) The roles of mental representations and mental processes in therapeutic action. *Psychoanalytic Study of the Child*, 48: 9–48.

Fosshage, J. (1992) Self psychology: The self and its vicissitudes within a relational matrix. In N. Skolnick & S. Warshaw (eds.) *Relational Perspectives in Psychoanalysis* (pp. 21–42). Hillsdale, NJ: Analytic Press.

Fosshage, J. (1994) Toward reconceptualizing transference: Theoretical and clinical considerations. *International Journal of Psycho-Analysis*, 75 (2): 265–280.

Fosshage, J. (1995) Countertransference as the analyst's experience of the analysand: Influence of listening perspectives. *Psychoanalytic Psychology*, 12 (3): 375–391.

Fosshage, J. (1997a) The organizing functions of dreams. *Contemporary Psychoanalysis*, 33 (3): 429–458.

Fosshage, J. (1997b) Listening/Experiencing perspectives and the quest for a Facilitative responsiveness. In A. Goldberg (ed.) *Conversations in Self Psycholgy, Progress in Self Psychology, Vol. 13* (pp. 33–55). Hillsdale, NJ: Analytic Press.

Fosshage, J. (1998) On aggression: Its forms and functions. *Psychoanalytic Inquiry*, 18 (1): 45–54.

Fosshage, J. (2003) Contextualizing self psychology and relational psychoanalysis: Bi-directional influence and proposed syntheses. *Contemporary Psychoanalysis*, 39 (3): 411–448.

Fosshage, J. (2005) The explicit and implicit domains in psychoanalytic change. *Psychoanalytic Inquiry*, 25 (4): 516–539.

Fosshage, J. (2007) Searching for love and expecting rejection: Implicit and explicit dimensions in co-creating analytic change. *Psychoanalytic Inquiry*, 7 (3): 326–347.

Fosshage, J. (2011a) The use and impact of the analyst's subjectivity with empathic and other listening/experiencing perspectives. *Psychoanalytic Quarterly*, LXXX (1): 139–160.

Fosshage, J. (2011b) How do we "know" what we "know"? And change what we "know"? *Psychonanalytic Dialogues*, 2 (1): 55–74.

Freud, S. (1915) The unconscious. *Standard Edition*, 12: 159–171.

Gabbard, G.O. (1997) A reconsideration of objectivity in the analyst. *International Journal of Psycho-Analysis*, 78: 15–26.

Greenberg, J. & Mitchell, S. (1983) *Object Relations in Psychoanalytic Theory*. Cambridge, MA: Harvard University Press.

Goldberg. A. (1999) Between empathy and judgment. *Journal of the American Psychoanalytic Association*, 47: 351–365.

Grigsby, J. & Hartlaub, G. (1994) Procedural learning and the development and stability of character. *Perceptual Motor Skills*, 79: 355–370.

Heimann, P. (1950) On counter-transference. *International Journal of Psycho-Analysis*, 31: 61–84.

Heisenberg, W. (1927) Über den anschaulichen Inhalt der quantentheoretischen Kinematik und Mechanik. *Zeitschrift für Physik*, 43: 172–198 (English translation: J.A. Wheeler and H. Zurek, *Quantum Theory and Measurement*. Princeton: Princeton University Press, 1983, pp. 62–84).

Hoffman, I. (1983) The patient as interpreter of the analyst's experience. *Contemporary Psychoanalysis*, 19: 389–422.

Hoffman, I. (1998) *Ritual and Spontaneity in the Psychoanalytic Process*. Hillsdale, NJ: Analytic Press.

Kernberg, O. (1965) Notes on countertransference. *Journal of the American Psychoanalytic Association*, 13: 38–56.

Klein, M. (1975) *Envy and Gratitude, and Other Works, 1946–1963*. London: Hogarth and the Instiute of Psycho-Analysis.

Kohut, H. (1959) Introspection, empathy, and psychoanalysis. *Journal of the American Psychoanalytic Association*, 7: 459–483.

Kohut, H. (1971) *The Analysis of the Self*. New York: International Universities Press.

Kohut, H. (1977) *The Restoration of the Self*. New York: International Universities Press.

Kohut, H. (1982) Introspection, empathy, and the semicircle of mental health. *International Journal of Psycho-Analysis*, 63: 395–408.

Kohut, H. (1984) *How Does Analysis Cure?* Hillsdale, NJ: Analytic Press.

Lichtenberg, J. (1981) The empathic mode of perception and alternative vantage points for psychoanalytic work. *Psychoanalytic Inquiry*, 3: 329–356.

Lichtenberg, J., Lachmann, F., & Fosshage, J. (1996) *The Clinical Exchange: Technique from the Standpoint of Self and Motivational Systems*. Hillsdale, NJ: Analytic Press.

Lichtenberg, J., Lachmann, F., & Fosshage, J. (2010) *Psychoananlysis and Motivational Systems: A New Look*. New York: Analytic Press.

Mitchell, S. (1988) *Relational Concepts in Psychoanalysis*. Cambridge, MA: Harvard University Press.

Orange, D.M. (1995) *Emotional Understanding*. New York: Guilford Press.

Ornstein, P. & Ornstein, A. (1985) Clinical understanding and explaining: the empathic vantage point. In A. Goldberg (ed.) *Progress in Self Psychology, Vol. I* (pp. 43–61). New York: Guilford Press.

Racker, H. (1968) *Transference and Countertransference.* New York: International Universities Press.

Sander, L. (1997) Paradox and resolution. In J. Osofsky (ed.) *Handbook of Child and Adolescent Psychiatry* (pp. 153–160). New York: John Wiley.

Sandler, J. & Rosenblatt, B. (1962) The concept of the representational world. *Psychoanalytic Study of the Child,* 17: 128–145.

Schwaber, E. (1981) Empathy, a mode of analytic listening. *Psychoanalytic Inquiry,* 7: 261–275.

Schwaber, E. (1997) A reconsideration of objectivity in the analyst. *International Journal of Psycho-Analysis,* 78: 1219–1221.

Schwaber, E.A. (1998) From whose point of view? The neglected question in analytic listening. *Psychoanalytic Quarterly,* 67: 645–661.

Shane, M., Shane, E., & Gales, M. (1998) *Intimate Attachments: Toward a New Self Psychology.* New York: Guilford Press.

Smith, H.F. (1999) Subjectivity and objectivity in analytic listening. *Journal of the American Psychoanalytic Association,* 47: 465–484.

Stern, D.B. (1997) *Unformulated Experience.* Hillsdale, NJ: Analytic Press.

Stern, D.N. (1985) *The Interpersonal World of the Infant.* New York: Basic Books.

Stern, D.N., Sander, L., Nahum, J., Harrison, A., Lyons-Ruth, K., Morgan, A., Bruschweiler-Stern, N., & Tronick, E. (1998) Non-interpretive mechanisms in psychoanalytic therapy: The "something more" than interpretation. *International Journal of Psycho-Analysis,* 79: 903–921.

Stolorow, R. & Atwood, G. (1992) *Contexts of Being: The Intersubjective Foundations of Psychological Life.* Hillsdale, NJ: Analytic Press.

Stolorow, R. & Lachmann, F. (1984/85) Transference: the future of an illusion. *The Annual of Psychoanalysis,* 12/13: 19–37.

Stolorow, R., Atwood, G., & Orange, D.M. (1999) Kohut and contextualism: Toward a post-Cartesian psychanalytic theory. *Psychoanalytic Psychology,* 16 (3): 380–388.

Stolorow, R., Atwood, G., & Orange, D.M. (2002) *Worlds of Experience.* New York: Basic Books.

Stolorow, R., Brandchaft, B., & Atwood, G. (1987) *Psychoanalvtic Treatment: An Intersubjective Approach.* Hillsdale, NJ: Analytic Press.

Wachtel, P.F. (1980) Transference, schema and assimilation: The relevance of Piaget to the psychoanalytic theory of transference. *The Annual of Psychoanalysis,* 8: 59–76.

Weiss, J. & Sampson, H. (1986) *The Psychoanalytic Process.* New York: Guilford.

Chapter 9

Interventions at an Impasse

Vulnerability, the Group Leader's Use of Self, and Sustained Empathic Focus as a Bridge Between Theory and Practice

Marty Livingston

Group therapists are often concerned with the question of what goes into a seasoned leader's choices of how and when to intervene in a group's process. My own belief is that specific interventions at moments of impasse or other dramatic moments are not as central to therapeutic process as the leader's attitudes and beliefs that are conveyed through a day-in/day-out stance. It is in this day-in/day-out, bread-and-butter stance that we need to seek an understanding of the relationship between theory and practice.

The Relationship Between Theory and Practice: A Bread-and-Butter Stance

My quest for an understanding of the relationship between theory and clinical actuality goes back to my training in the 1960s. At this point, I would like to share a story about my early days as a patient in a group that will shed some light on what I was being taught in the 1960s about the relationship between theory and practice. Mannie Schwartz, my group leader and analyst, was a very prominent proponent of "Psychoanalysis in Groups" (Wolf & Schwartz, 1962). Often, when there was a panel comparing theories, he was chosen as the representative of the Classical position.

One day, an attractive young woman of whom I was very fond came into group very upset. As she talked, it became clear she was feeling out of control and afraid that she was crazy. Mannie listened intently and said very little. The group was supportive. At the end of the session, Mannie got up to leave, looked across the room, paused for a moment and then blew her a kiss. She was visibly relieved. I was upset.

The next day, as I walked in for my individual session, I was livid: "You teach me not to act out with a patient, to stay a blank, and here you go clearly expressing a love for her. How do you explain that according to all the theory you've taught me?"

Mannie shrugged and, with a warm smile, replied, "It was what she needed."

I learned two lessons about theory and practice. First was that, sometimes, a spontaneous response to a patient's need is more important than rigid theory.

Second, the theory of the day had to be momentarily abandoned, since it could not incorporate this responsiveness. I was never happy with that and searched over the years for a theory that could accommodate more human relatedness and emotional availability.

An experience of the analyst's emotional availability and understanding within his or her day-in/day-out stance is essential to understanding curative process and mutative change. Questions about the interactions of insight, relationship, and affect are relevant in all three major modalities of psychotherapy—individual, couple, and group. However, as I have pointed out previously (Livingston, 2004), the relational aspects of the analytic process and the issues of emotional availability and shared affective experience are especially central in group therapy, where multiple subjective interactions are the main vehicle of treatment.

I prefer not to dwell on specific technical recommendations. Instead, I will discuss the attitudes and understandings that serve as a foundation for the therapist's interventions. These attitudes, based on an understanding of therapeutic process, and the group leader's theoretical orientation, are conveyed by his or her bread-and-butter stance. They underlie the stable and consistent, moment to moment, and session after session responsiveness that patients come to count on. It is these attitudes that function in the background, creating safety and allowing the therapeutic process to deepen and unfold. It is these underlying attitudes that I want to focus upon first. They are important day by day and even more essential during experiences of impasse. These attitudes determine, consciously or unconsciously, the interventions a leader chooses. In the next section I will present a more detailed look at the choice of foreground interventions this background leads to, an approach I will refer to as a sustained empathic focus.

I will also discuss impasses and the concept of focus as a bridge between theory and practice, but first I want to introduce the bread-and-butter attitude that underlies my interventions. This central attitude toward deepening the therapeutic process and its relationship to the concept of "Vulnerable Moments" was introduced in book form (Livingston, 2001). Later, Louisa Livingston and I (Livingston & Livingston, 2006) clarified the concept further and began to refer to the interventions stemming from this attitude as a "sustained empathic focus." The concept of focus is key to understanding the relationship between theory and practice. It is very useful in helping group leaders at all levels in choosing interventions to deepen the therapeutic process.

Within my bread-and-butter attitude as a group psychotherapist, informed by a self-psychological approach, my focus is upon each patient's subjective/affective experiences and on emerging vulnerability in the here-and-now of the group experience. I will now expand upon two main points in the subsections below. The first is that a clinical focus on affect and narcissistic vulnerability, and with it the facilitation of what I call "vulnerable moments," can greatly enable the deepening of the therapeutic process in group psychotherapy. The second is that the vulnerable involvement of the group leader in the therapeutic relationship also plays a key role in promoting change.

The Background of my Bread-and-Butter Stance: A Clinical Focus on Affect and Narcissistic Vulnerability and the Facilitation of "Vulnerable Moments"

Integration and regulation of affect are central in any psychoanalytic understanding of development and of the analytic process itself. This centrality of affective experience is particularly crucial to what self-psychologists refer to as the development of a cohesive and vitalized sense of self. In fact, Stolorow, Brandchaft, and Atwood (1987, p. 66) point out that "selfobject functions pertain fundamentally to the integration of affect into the organization of self-experience, and ... the need for selfobject ties pertains most centrally to the need for attuned responsiveness to affect states in all stages of the life cycle." My intense interest within this endeavor lies in the self-state of vulnerability—emotional openness to affective experience—which I consider an underused concept in group psychotherapy.

Vulnerability is commonly viewed as a danger and a burden, and so it is—but it is more than that. Kohut's (1977) "tragic man" has a precarious sense of self that is vulnerable to depletion, even fragmentation, when necessary developmentally supportive experiences are not sufficiently available. The effort of protecting a vulnerable self, and of maintaining needed ties to early caretakers, leads to fixed relational patterns and a brittle sense of identity. This in turn imposes limitations on an individual's "striving to express the basic pattern of his self" (Kohut, 1977, p. 133). Any move toward change may be experienced as a threat to such a rigidly established identity.

The word "vulnerable" means susceptible to being wounded. People who relinquish their usual characterological defenses open themselves to wounds of many sorts, from peripheral encounters with shame and rejection to direct personal attacks and potentially devastating losses. Any of these can evoke memories of early traumas, and resulting fears of the dissolution of the existing sense of the self and its attachments. It is thus no wonder that the protective shields people raise become so deeply a part of their characters. Still, at various times and for various reasons they are lowered briefly, although seldom without an accompanying sense of confusion and, above all, danger. These occasions, when rigid barriers are softened and people open themselves to new experience, are the "vulnerable moments" to which I am referring.

These often fleeting moments when a person risks exposing and experiencing parts of the self that are habitually hidden from others are potentially pivotal moments of change. What is most often experienced in these moments are developmental longings and the feelings related to them. Often these are painful feelings of exposure and tenderness, and acute awareness of the danger of possible shame and rejection. The experience of vulnerability lies in the subjective sense of newness and risk, however, and in the sense of being "seen," rather than in the specific content of any particular situation. Vulnerability is the subjective experience of relinquishing habitual patterns of self-protectiveness.

It is because of the subjective sense of these dangers that everyone has a tendency both to be drawn to and to avoid vulnerable moments, and also why they are central to a self-psychological approach to therapeutic process. The safety created by the development of a confident expectation of the self psychologist's empathic immersion in the patient's subjective experience (and attention to breaks in this empathic bond) is central to the promotion of change, *precisely because it allows the unfolding, and thus the exploration, of long-suppressed longings and vulnerabilities* along with the previously warded off painful affects connected to the fate which these yearnings met in early experiences.

The creation of safety and empathic bonds within the group invites the patient to share, to process, and thus to integrate the associated painful affective states that previously, without containment and support, had been experienced as unbearable. It is not, as self psychology has been criticized in the past, a palliative treatment or coddling. Rather, it takes into consideration where the patient is at the moment developmentally, regarding how much affect can be tolerated without retraumatization or a resort to more primitive protective devices that could interfere with the usefulness of the group and the leader. Deepening the therapeutic process means deepening these painful affect states within the affect-regulating and containing environment of a cohesive group and empathic leader to the extent the patient is developmentally able to do so.

The aim of the process is essentially the development of increased capacity for affect regulation, at first within an empathic bond and eventually, for brief times, even when on one's own. Increased capacity for what is initially mutual affect regulation with a caretaker or caretaking group, and then becomes a more independent regulation, allows the patient to resort less to self defeating and self limiting protective measures.

Everyone possesses an underlying awareness of their own vulnerability, although protective patterns sometimes limit our conscious experience or expression of these feelings. Kohut said, "Narcissistic vulnerability is a ubiquitous burden of man, a part of the human condition from which no one is exempt" (1977, p. 292). Depending on a person's psychological flexibility or defensiveness, self-experience can range from an open and fluid state to a crystallized, fixed, and desperately protected one. Sometimes an individual is able to communicate and describe clearly his experiences of vulnerability; this is the open—the visibly vulnerable—end of the continuum.

At other times, though, a person may fear his sense of self to be in such jeopardy, in such imminent danger of fragmentation, as to require rigid protective maneuvers that preclude reflection, exploration, or even open communication. This is the defended and relatively closed end of the continuum. Still, when someone else (such as a therapist) can really understand such precarious self-experience, the sufferer may be able to open up to that understanding, and this opening too may lead to a vulnerable moment in the potentially curative sense that I am describing.

I want to make clear that vulnerability is an inner experience, not a kind of "behavior." The development of a relationship in which it is safe enough to risk communicating and sharing these experiences is central to curative process, because, despite the risks involved, the increase of vulnerability is an inherent aspect of psychotherapy. It is precisely in these brief moments of vulnerability that there is an openness to new experience and mutative change. It then becomes possible to process previously intolerable affect, or perhaps risk experimentation with previously foreclosed options and to let go of rigid and limiting protective patterns.

It is understandable that patients and therapists alike tend to avoid vulnerable situations. Yet moments of vulnerability are both an inevitable concomitant of new openness and a sign that it is occurring. These moments in treatment must be welcomed as meaningful, as well as feared as dangerous, and a good therapeutic relationship must be able to contain their threatening aspects.

The therapist's recognition of and attitude toward the emergence of vulnerable moments is crucial to the analytic process. Their importance is often overlooked, and therapists sometimes fail to focus on them when they occur. In groups particularly, where there are always other subjectivities present to obscure or distract from the anxiety of the moment, these valuable opportunities may be allowed to dissipate. Yet unless they are sustained and protected, their potential to deepen a healing intensity and intimacy will be lost. These losses of potential deepening and facilitation of the analytic process must be diminished. Vulnerable moments are vital to therapeutic change.

Once a vulnerable moment arrives, however, or when one seems to be emerging, the question arises of how to intervene. This is a compelling issue for all therapists. For group therapists, surrounded as they are by multiple and diverse subjectivities, the question of how and when to intervene in a group's process is especially complex. As I have stated above, my belief is that specific interventions at dramatic moments are not as central to therapeutic process as are the attitudes and beliefs that the leader conveys through a consistent day-in/day-out stance. That is what I have been referring to as my bread-and-butter stance. At this point, I will elaborate on some of the attitudes and understandings that serve as a foundation for a therapist's useful interventions. These are the attitudes that underlie the stable, moment-to-moment, session-after-session responsiveness that patients come to count on.

As a group therapist working from a self-psychological point of view, "deepening of the therapeutic process" means that, through the analyst's empathic immersion in the patient's subjective world view, earlier and earlier forms of selfobject, developmental longings (along with associated fears of retraumatization and related affective experiences) are uncovered, legitimized, and accepted. As these patterns are experienced and illuminated, they become available for processing and interpretation.

A sensitivity to, and an intense empathic interest in, vulnerability—and the inherent selfobject longings that it encompasses—tend to elicit an openness to the very experiences that further the therapeutic work. An analyst who values these moments, and is alert to opportunities to create them, will find that they occur more frequently. The leader must develop a sensitivity to the subtle signs of emerging vulnerability; these may be verbal, or they may be as nonverbal as tone of voice, quality of posture, or simply a softening in the eyes.

The leader's appreciation of vulnerability, and the creation of safety for it, can manifest itself (and be implemented clinically) in several ways. One is by slowing down process to focus upon emerging material related to the patient's affective experience in the moment and to the current self-state (e.g., the patient's sense of cohesion, or danger, or fear of falling apart, or a feeling of vitality or depletion). Staying a moment longer than is usual or comfortable with the patient's subjective state frequently allows this affective experience to deepen. Simply encouraging patients to "experience what they experience" or to "stay with the feeling" (Levitsky & Perls, 1970) can lead to surprising moments of openness. The group leader's prolonged empathic immersion in each member's emotional (subjective) life creates, in itself, an intensity and a support for these moments. Vulnerability versus self-protectiveness is itself one of these dimensions of the state of the self, and an important aspect of self-experience. Empathic inquiry into underlying self-states encourages a shift from the defended toward the vulnerable end of this dimension. Such inquiry into moment-to-moment fluctuations in self-experience can take the form of questions like, "What is it like to be you right now?" or "What were you experiencing just then?" Looking for the triggers that evoke affective fluctuations is also often helpful to many patients.

The Conceptual Background of my Bread-and-Butter Stance, Part Two: The Importance of the Group Leader's Emotional Availability and Involvement

The factor that most contributes to the sharing of vulnerable moments in a group is the formation of the relationships that develop between the members and the leader, and among the members themselves. These bonds are built over time, in the context of the group leader's consistent attitudes and interventions as they manifest themselves session after session. These attitudes, and these bonds, are essential in creating the expectation of safety and an emotionally responsive surround in a group. It is this confident expectation of emotional availability and responsiveness, both from the leader and from the other group members, that encourages vulnerability and forms the foundation for meaningful interpretations that allow each individual to risk and to grow.

The expectation and experience of good-enough relationships, then, contribute to the development of an internalized capacity to tolerate loss and painful affect—in other words, to build structure.

Integration and regulation of affect are central in any psychoanalytic understanding of development and in the analytic process itself. This centrality of affective experience is particularly crucial to what self-psychologists refer to as the development of a cohesive and vitalized sense of self. Stolorow et al. (1987, p. 66) point out "the need for selfobject ties pertains most centrally to the need for attuned responsiveness to affect states in all stages of the life cycle."

A self-psychological approach to curative process stresses the patient's developmental needs, particularly the need for empathic responsiveness and at times for an emphasis on their own subjectivity. At these times, the introduction of the leader's subjectivity can become a break in the empathic bond. However, self-psychology also recognizes the legitimacy, at times, for a bond that includes the analyst's own vulnerability and responsiveness.

When I did my training, the analytic world was based on the leader as a blank screen. The goal was to bring transferential distortions to the fore so they could be relinquished and mourned. They were seen as immature, unrealistic demands for libidinal gratification. The blank screen made sense with that model. Self-disclosure was seen as muddying the waters and blocking the analysis.

So, both classical psychoanalytic theory and classical 1970s self-psychological theory stress the patient's unfolding transference to the disadvantage of the here-and-now, "real" relationship that is a central part of the clinical work, if not always the theory. However, most, more modern, approaches, especially within the group therapy world, and many self-psychologists, have moved to a model that views many of the patient's needs for nurturance as legitimate. Relationship, both here-and-now and transferential, is key to the process. We talk about affect regulation and corrective experience. The patient's difficulties are seen as originating from unmet needs for help in affect regulation. So, curative process is not all about mourning unrealistic and distorted wishes. Yet the dictum that the leader be a blank screen still hangs on.

We no longer believe that all the patient's expression of desire is inappropriate and from the past. Most recent theory sees some of the patient's demands as legitimate reaching out for help. The blank screen is no longer necessary in order to maintain the clarity of the transferential distortions as the vehicle of curative process.

The question is now, how do we address the legitimacy of many of these demands? What form does this take? What is nurturing? Does it have to do with a leader who is seen as human and vulnerable? Each group and each therapeutic dyad is unique. Some groups will do best with a leader who stays in the background providing understanding and safety. Others thrive with a leader who is an active participant who shares his or her own experience and feeling.

What facilitates safety and the unfolding of a curative process? As Stolorow often says at conferences, "It depends." There are no rigid technique answers. It depends on the subjective and personal meaning to each participant.

Another question is, "What is the role of the leader's desire to connect and to reconnect after a rupture?" Ana-Marie Rizzuto (2004) points out:

> The analyst's voice must signal the intention, not only to convey something meaningful for the moment, but also, most specifically, to convey the wish to establish emotional contact with the patient. This is the indispensible affective component of speech without which language is not communication from one person to another, but, as one of [her] patients said repeatedly, "only words."
>
> (p. 208)

Looking back at my early experience as a patient in a group, my group leader Mannie's response to his patient was intuitively grounded and clinically very meaningful. As he said, "It was what she needed." With decades of experience, he could call on, and trust, his own responsiveness. He did not need theory at that moment. However, in approaching his novice student, he was not helpful, unless we consider the fortuitous encouragement to search for my own answers outside of Freudian theory to be ultimately very meaningful. At that moment though, the interaction left me feeling that human responsiveness and availability were parameters, deviations from standard technique, that needed to be regarded with caution.

With hindsight, I look on his intervention as founded on years of an empathic bond with his patient, years of listening to and validating her subjective experiences. With all the differences between how he led his day-in/day-out groups and the relational experience that I longed for both as patient and as group leader, I do remember Mannie as a wonderful listener (when he was not providing theory-based interpretations). It must have been that quality of listening that enabled him to sense his patient's vulnerable self-state and her developmental level. His response was totally "empathically informed." What he could not do was to reflect on it later in a teaching manner. He was, perhaps, less able to be empathic with my need for integration than he had been with his responsiveness to the woman in the group. I felt dismissed and on my own.

The Foreground of my Bread-and-Butter Stance and Selection of Interventions: Sustained Empathic Focus

For clinical theory to be useful, it must be grounded upon an alternation between experience-near immersion in clinical data, on the one hand, and a more experience-distant process of organizing and making sense of the experience of immersion, on the other. Organization and conceptualization can then guide the clinician in a return to an experience-near empathically informed responsiveness and engagement. Focused experience-near attention is not only clinically effective but also provides data for further theorizing.

In this alternating and interweaving process, it is the concept of "focus" that provides the bridge. For theory to be clinically useful, it should provide a sense of focus and organization for the clinical work. Within self-psychology and modern relational theory, my wife Louisa Livingston and I have tried to make a contribution to the understanding of the interplay between theory and practice. In the previously mentioned article on sustained empathic focus (Livingston & Livingston, 2006), we wrote that one important bridge between theory and practice is the concept of "focus." For theory to be clinically useful, it should provide a sense of focus and organization for the clinical work. A self-psychological/intersubjective model leads to a particular emphasis in my clinical work that guides both listening and intervention.

All psychoanalytic theories suggest a focus on depth, process, and underlying dynamics, as opposed to surface content. Within that focus, each school of analytic thought prioritizes, that is, suggests, a focus upon particular underlying content. My stress is upon each group member's subjective, affective experience in the here-and-now of the group, and particularly on the experience of vulnerability. This leads to a very different focus from, for example, a more classical emphasis on making the unconscious conscious and on derivatives of sexual and aggressive drives. Louisa and I refer to the central foreground attitude in our self-psychological/intersubjective viewpoint as a "sustained empathic focus."

Interventions at Moments of Impasse

Essentially, an intervention is anything a leader does or does not do with the intention of facilitating the therapeutic process. When we speak of interventions, hopefully, we are talking about the relationship between theory and practice. A clinician, with varying degrees of awareness, must make choices. In any analytic process, even in the one-to-one setting in which most therapists began their clinical life, the amount of data to be grasped is immense and confusing. It is no wonder that, when faced with an impasse, leaders often feel lost and wonder what they should be doing. However, at moments of impasse, the real question is often not, "What do I do?" The more meaningful underlying question is, "How do I go about choosing what to focus upon?" The key is to develop increasing clarity and awareness of this process of choosing what to focus upon in understanding and intervening in times of impasse as well as most other times.

Thus, in listening to an unfolding group process from a self-psychological view, the therapist chooses to focus upon each group member's inner experience. In a sustained empathic focus, we prioritize the emergence of developmental needs and the affective and personal meanings that an event in the group has for each patient. The leader tries to understand events from within the subjective experience of each member and to amplify and clarify early tendrils of yearnings and disappointments. The emphasis is on a sustained empathic attention to these affective experiences. The aim is the creation of safety to allow the working through of these often-painful feelings. This is not any different, or less important, when the leader has a sense of impasse or panic.

This approach is founded on the work of Stolorow and Atwood (1992) who relate the therapeutic action of the analytic process to a model of developmental trauma, emphasizing the fate of the child's painful affect states: an original developmental need is met with rebuff or disappointment, producing an intense and painful affective experience that the child can not manage on his own. Then, in the second phase, the child experiences a secondary longing for an attuned response. He looks for a caretaker's empathy and understanding of the original disruption in order to modulate, contain, and ameliorate his painful reactive affect state (p. 53). Unfortunately, parents whose misattunement creates such primary failures are unlikely to provide the longed-for modulating empathic responsiveness. It is this secondary failure to provide affect regulating support for the processing of painful affect that leads to "walled-off painful feelings [that] become a source of lifelong inner conflict and vulnerability" (p. 54).

Successful group treatment provides the safety and nurturing experience that allows a re-engagement with this developmental failure. In particular, an empathically attuned clinical focus on emerging vulnerability provides the longed-for and necessary support for these walled-off painful affects, and so invites their processing. Structure building is essentially the development of capacity for affect regulation, and of sufficient self-cohesion to allow for the processing of painful states without resorting to defensive, and self-limiting, patterns.

Focusing on Affect and Vulnerability: An Illustration

The following group session illustrates how the leader's steady emphasis on shifts in affect and self-states can facilitate the emergence of vulnerability and deepen the therapeutic process. Deeper and often painful affect states that have been avoided through repetitive, often self-destructive, protective patterns then become available for exploration. The capacity for affect regulation develops slowly as a consequence of experiences like these. The development of this capacity is an essential aspect of structure building and therapeutic process.

The ongoing analytic group in this example consists of five women and three men. All but one of them have been together for several years, and they work well together. In this segment the action centers on Maria, a businesswoman in her mid-forties, who has been going through a very busy and difficult period of expansion in the company she owns and heads. The past month's pre-Christmas season has been particularly stressful. Her response to this stress has been to return to a pattern of addictive eating and an obsessive focus on trying to prevent errors. In group, she has been quiet much of the time or, as in this session, involved in a pressured relating of the details of her work situation. The transcript begins about fifteen minutes into the session. Maria is visibly worn down and upset. She has been going over and over the details of an incident in which one employee made several mistakes. She is clearly stuck and so is the group.

Maria:	Now, on top of being busy, so much is going wrong. What can I say? I just keep going over and over it in my head. I try to be professional in dealing with this guy, but what I really want to say is, "How can you do this? What the hell happened? How can you get this so wrong?" I didn't. I handled it. So what do I want now in group? I know I chose this. This is what I wanted. I'm going to bill a fortune. Nobody is forcing me to do this. I'm not a victim.
Marty:	So, as you expand the business you can expect more problems?
Maria:	Yes. Bigger accounts—bigger problems.
Marty:	So, you are responding to each one and doing what you can to repair the damage?
Maria:	Right.
Marty:	The other thing you need to do is to step back after a while and look over things to see what to learn for next year.
Maria:	Right. If I want this scale, this is what comes with it, and I have to be able to ... [Maria pauses momentarily, slowing her obsessional presentation a bit in response to my slower pace and tentative tone. I sense this as the softening of her pressured barrier and an emerging self-state change. I try to focus on the affect involved.]
Marty:	What are you feeling at this point?
Maria:	I'm terrified that I really sold myself and I'm scared that I'm going to look bad. I'm afraid I've taken on more than I can do. I'm wearing down. That's what I don't want to feel. I'm not giving up. That's why I wanted to come here tonight. I wouldn't even have to say anything. I just needed to be with my family. I was thinking of my father when I was walking here. He'd say, "You'll be okay," and that would just somehow make me feel better. Just knowing that.
Marty:	[Again focusing on the affect and encouraging her to slow down and tolerate a bit more of her feelings, I persist.] So, what feelings are you afraid of? What are you trying not to feel? It sounds from what you are telling us that there are some feelings when a client is disappointed. Something is triggered that you need to avoid.
Maria:	[Slowing down thoughtfully] That's a good question. It doesn't seem real. It seems too horrible.
Natalie:	It is real. It feels horrible that you are letting somebody down and you are responsible. It's very horrible.
Roz:	[to Natalie] You can certainly identify with that from your job.
Natalie:	It's horrible.

Maria:	It feels like I will be ousted … that I'll go out of business. I'll be blackballed. I'll be wiped out. There's no room for a mistake. It's like with my mother. I couldn't make a mistake … and I did make mistakes and everything got ruined forever … and I can't disappoint people. They count on me. They really believe that I can do this. That's why they chose me, because they really, really believed in me. Other companies are different than mine. They know that they would be disappointed with them. With me, there's a connection, so they really trust me.
Roz:	You never talked about your mother before.
Maria:	My mother was just very … she would yell, tell me I was bad. [Maria shrugs. She seems stuck again.] I don't know what I feel.
Marty:	You are having a hard time touching these feelings that come up when somebody is disappointed.
Maria:	Yes, and even when you just started to say that, I felt I don't want you to be disappointed in me now. I don't want to have to feel that here. I try really hard. I want to please you too. I tried my best. I did. I did. I tried my hardest. Even with this one client who kept changing what she wanted. It didn't come out of the blue. It wasn't all my fault. She kept changing it, but she won't care. That won't matter. She is just going to say, "You fucked up! It was your people and you are the boss." She's not going to own her piece in it. And then what am I going to say? She's going to say, "You're bad!" I made a mistake and what am I going to say? What am I going to do? [Questions like these about actions are part of Maria's obsessional protective system. They lead the process away from her emerging vulnerability. At the same time, however, they alert the sensitive listener to the very feelings they are frantically trying to avoid.]
Marty:	[Persisting gently but firmly, and focusing on the experience of affect rather than on the choice of an action.] And what are you going to feel when she yells at you about the mistake?
Maria:	That she picked the wrong person … unworthy. [Then after a long pause] I keep thinking that I'm going to feel that she's right. That's why I'm scared. Then I try to prove that she's not. It's really hard. [I add a strongly empathic grunt here and she continues.] I'm operating as if she is right and I have to prove she's wrong. [A focus on affect and emerging vulnerability often leads, as it does here, to the exploration and softening of poisonous underlying organizing beliefs. As Orange, Atwood, and Stolorow (1997, p. 66) have pointed out,

it is often the desperate quest for an antidote to crushing organizing principles adopted early in life that forms the motivational basis for obsessive and addictive patterns like the ones we see in Maria.]

Marty: You need to prove things because you are carrying around these painful feelings ... feeling that you are bad, that you are a disappointment.

Maria: Yes, I am. [And then, after a long pause and in a different, somewhat childlike voice] I can't please my mommy. I can't please her no matter how hard I try. If I'm grown up, if I'm a little girl. I can't please her. It's impossible!

Marty: And that feels awful.

Maria: [Crying softly without speaking and then after several minutes] It's hard. If I stay with her [the client], she's going to keep going on with it. How disappointed she is in me. How the job is not good. How can I do this to her? [Then, after a long pause] So, I guess what I need to do now is to stay with my feelings. I can do that here. It feels like an attack. It feels like I'm going to explode. The shame I'm going to feel is beyond what I can deal with. [Sobbing] It will hurt too much ... and I'm going to want to die. I feel like I can't do this. I can't have my feelings. Just give me chocolate. I can't have my feelings. I'm not big enough. Like, give me a pacifier. [Then after a long peaceful pause shared by the whole group] Everything feels a little less intense now.

Marty: So, if you feel people with you, you might be able to tolerate those feelings.

Maria: Yes, if somebody called me while I'm here and I was in the room with all of you ... I could probably ... I would be scared, my heart would be pounding in my chest, but I would feel enough of an anchor. But in my office, in the middle of all this work, I might not be able to take it. It's too much. [Crying again] I really feel upset, call on somebody else.

Marty: It's okay. Feel upset. Stay with your feeling. [Maria continues to cry softly and I ask:] What does it feel like?

Maria: It feels big, really big. I don't want to remember. It's what I felt when I was a little kid and she was doing that and I just got really scared. I would hide under the table. You can't stop it. You can't turn that off. I couldn't make her stop criticizing, criticizing. The only solace was to get away ... to go in some closet or under some furniture. [Then after another long pause:] I'm okay. I never felt it so "bigly." [Maria laughs and the whole group laughs warmly with her. Then she continues:] No wonder I hated that dark house.

[later in the session]

Maria: That's where I am. It's okay for other people but not for me because I'm dealing with this mother. I flinch all the time ... not always physically, but I flinch when someone might be disappointed.

Marty: You are scared that they are disappointed and that they are going to rub your nose in it. It's not just a fear that they will go away. It's more that they're not going to go away. They are going to stay and humiliate you.

Maria: Right. They're not going to say, "Okay fine, bye." No, they are going to stay and they're going to complain and also tell people and I'll lose all the business.

Marty: That's the humiliation that they are going to trigger.

Maria: Yes, that they are going to set off.

Marty: They are going to trigger the old humiliation ... like when your mother felt you were bad.

Maria: Right. I see how strong my reaction is.

Marty: And how strong your urge is to prevent that feeling ... as if you could prevent it.

Maria: I can prevent it ... if I just eat chocolate all day. [The group laughs with her.]

Marty: If you eat chocolate or if you get all the accounts just right, or if ...

Maria: And if nothing goes wrong. If I can just prevent that feeling.

Marty: If everything is right, then you won't have all that devastating feeling, then all the criticism and abuse won't have happened.

Maria: Well really, what I'm saying here is ... I'm thinking that I'm not strong enough to have all these feelings. That's what this is really about.

Marty: *That's what this is really about.*

Maria: It's just a feeling, another batch of feelings that I'm protecting myself from.

Marty: And when you don't feel strong enough to have them, then you need someone to be with you. You weren't strong enough when you were little. You haven't been strong enough by yourself to have these feelings.

Maria: I really felt that so many times this week. I just wanted to be with you guys. I really did.

Marty: You get confused whether to have the chocolate and take the feeling away or whether you want to take the risk of exploring the feelings and looking for support.

Roz:	I was thinking before that if you got one of those calls here, you could be strong enough to face the feelings. [Notice, we keep coming back to the focus on affect and affect regulation. At each turn Maria is gaining strength from the group support and the working through process. Each time we return to the theme she experiences and explores a deeper sense of the affective and personal meaning in her responses to people being disappointed and succeeds in opening an increasing vulnerability. This vulnerability to criticism and shame is related to the softening of her organizing principles and her openness to new experience and change. She and several other members of the group are slowly building the capacity to explore and regulate these painful (shame-related) feelings. This repetitive process within the session is actually a microcosm of an aspect of the working through that needs to take place over time in order to build enduring structure.]
Maria:	Yeah. I'm afraid that I'm not strong enough. I'm going to get all flushed. Like, "Oh my God, do I have to feel that physical shame reaction?" I'll get all red and my heart will beat out of my chest. On the business level I have to not defend myself ... to stand there and take it and try to understand how disappointed they are with me. I was thinking about that. I have to play that role in the business. I can't just say, "Screw you!" But I just feel like crying. I'm going to feel overwhelmed and angry and put down ... And then I want to die ... to throw myself off a roof.
Marty:	You feel like you did when your mother thought you were horrible and you were alone.
Maria:	Sometimes my father helped, but he'd say, "Oh, you know how your mother is." Like don't feel so bad. Then I felt more confused. What was he saying? Deny what I feel?
Natalie:	That's not really protecting you.
Daniel:	No, because your feeling was, "I don't give a fuck how she is. Save me from this loony woman! Do something to make it right."
Maria:	Yeah. That didn't feel like taking care of me, that felt like he was snookering me into something with him.
Marty:	It certainly sounds like the opposite of an invitation to share feelings.
Natalie:	Yes, it sounds like a message that you have to live with it.
Maria:	Yeah. Yeah. I was sloughed off.
Marty:	So you couldn't go to him with the feeling and expect any help.

> [Towards the end of the session.]
>
> *Marty:* So, you feel stronger, supported, here, and you can touch the feeling and even then it's like a hot radiator. The urge to get away is so strong that you can only touch the feelings for a few moments at a time.
>
> *Maria:* And then I get lost. It is real hard to stay with the feelings in the room. It's like I'm allergic to my own feelings. I can't tolerate it. It's like needing to practice, to get used to the feeling so I don't have to make sure that no one is disappointed.
>
> *Marty:* It would be such a relief if you didn't have to do all those things to run from your feelings. You wouldn't have to be perfect all the time.
>
> *Maria:* I'm running all the time.

Discussion

This session illustrates the role of the therapist in "deepening" therapeutic process through a persistent focus on inner experience, affect, and emerging vulnerability. It also illustrates an important aspect of the deepening process: the development of the capacity to tolerate painful affect. Maria's addictive quest (for antidotes to the crushing organizing principles that prove to her that she is worthless and unlovable) is driven by her belief that the affect triggered by these principles is intolerable. She feels threatened by the horrible and heretofore unbearable sense of shame and fragmentation she anticipates if anyone is disappointed in her. Her inability to deal with this affect on her own has led her to develop self-limiting protective patterns.

Second Illustration: An Impasse

The second clinical illustration presented next is one that highlights the leader's focus during a period he senses, at first, as an impasse. Impasse has been defined, half jokingly, as when a group is not doing what the leader thinks it should be doing. When everything is going smoothly, I experience myself as attuned to what is happening in the room. As I get older, after many years of experience, I usually feel that the group is doing what it needs to do. My job is to understand, sometimes reflect, and to provide a focus. This is all related to supporting affect regulation and creating safety. When I am viewing events from this empathic stance, I generally do not experience the stuckness, powerless, or even panic, often referred to as an impasse.

My focus during times of impasse, as it always does, remains on the subjective, affective experience of each group member. It is also helpful to reflect underlying themes during an impasse. These comments reassure the group that there is a process unfolding and that the leader is capable of moving toward understanding it. In addition, searching for a theme enables the leader to feel more involved and active rather than stuck and powerless.

Impasse itself is a subjective experience, sometimes shared and sometimes individually experienced. The experience often includes a sense of helplessness and even hopelessness. When a group seems to be at an impasse it usually means that my own subjectivity and desire is interfering with my attunement. So, my use of my own feelings often centers on returning to an empathic involved position. Often what I am sensing is the need, in myself or in a group member, for the repairing of a rupture. Am I picking up a narcissistic wounding or an empathic break that has been missed?

In this instance, Tony wants to talk about "real" things in his life and the leader wants the group more in the room dealing with underlying process. That sort of process can easily lead to an empathic rupture and the experience of impasse in the group. The role a leader's attitudes, basic stance, and sustained empathic focus on the patient's subjective/affective experience can play here in facilitating vulnerability and the deepening of therapeutic process is clearly illustrated. The interventions described are an expression of the attitude involved in a sustained empathic focus, particularly, in this case, on emerging vulnerability.

> Tony begins the group. He feels frustrated. He reports that since he no longer has the need to come in with emergencies, he doesn't have any "stuff" to bring in. "I have a lot of stuff going on in my life that I would like to talk about, but instead, we get into something that is in the moment. It's meaningful, but it's not about what's going on in my life. I can't figure out how to bring it in. So I don't." I reflect, "What I hear is that there is something valuable in being involved in what goes on, but at the same time there is something that is important that …" Tony, feeling heard, continues. "All the stuff in my life." Now, more on target I add, "that you want to bring in; that you want us to know about, to know what is going on in your life." Tony responds excitedly, "Yeah, yeah! That! And I can't organize it well enough to deliver it in a simple fashion."
>
> Roz adds a resounding "Yeah!" and Alice, a sensitive and often supportive expectant mother, elaborates, "I think that I really understand what you are saying. Several of us have talked about that before. It's like having some uneasiness or restlessness … or a lot of things … and if you can't frame it neatly … you feel like you are going to take a lot of time with it." Tony now inserts still another "Yeah, that's right!" Alice continues with a more serious tone, "Because you need a lot of time and it feels awkward to bring it in. You feel like, 'How long are people going to be able to stay with you on this?'" Tony

nods a strong assent and adds, "It's like being on stage and I don't have my material." Alice continues the active sharing of these experiences, "No music, the lights are not on properly, it's really hard. It's torture to have to perform, to compete for what you need."

Roz is an active third in the interaction, "It really is tough. It's like having to improv. That's really hard in group. I can do it in individual, but not in here." Tony, still excited with the sense of being understood and not alone with his struggle, takes it a step farther. "It's very hard to get the space to improvise in group. Individual, you can go on and on if you need to, but in group, it's totally different. It's very scary." Alice agrees soundly, "Very scary."

"What is it that is very scary about it?" I ask gently. Tony responds softly as the affect deepens, "You'll lose people. I felt it even then, when I was speaking earlier. I felt that I started talking about something and then I felt, 'I'm losing it. I'm not sure exactly what I'm talking about.' Then I found something and everybody came back again. That's the scary feeling. I'm losing it. I have nothing to say … like I don't know where I'm going with this …" Alice completes his thought, "but I know that I need something. I really do want something." Tony picks up the thought, "Right, a meaningful need." Then turning toward me, "It's your job to help me figure out what it is that I'm trying to do or to say … I mean … it's not like you don't do it. You do. It's just …" Alice, again right on Tony's wavelength, joins in. "He does it when you …" Tony picks it back up enthusiastically. "He does it when it looks like you are really dying. Then he says, 'This is what is going on or what I hear you feeling is …'" Seeing an opening to touch the emerging vulnerability, and also really beginning to feel deeply attuned to Tony's affect and need, as well as to the empathic break produced by my wanting him to be more in the room and pursuing process on my terms, I underline, "So there are times when I respond in the way you need … [and then after a brief pause] but there are other times …" Tony smiles softly and finishes my sentence playfully in his own words, "when you let him hang out there. 'Let him hang for a while; see what he comes up with.'"

The group is silent for a moment. Then Alice thoughtfully comments, "I think that's a universal group feeling … that feeling about hanging in the wind." The group seems to drift for a while and then I try to bring them back to an exploration of the affective experience of unmet needs. "So, when you say that it's my job, that I do something sometimes and not often enough, what is it that I do? And what is it like for you when I don't?" Tony reflects inwardly for a moment and then offers some clarification. "Well … you get to the bottom of the situation and you go, okay, this is what is going on … this is what it seems like you need.' And then I go, 'Yeah!, Yeah' … and then the whole thing takes on a different clarity and I start to have feelings about it." Getting a clear sense of Tony's vulnerability and what is wanted, I feel close to Tony. I reflect, "So, sometimes you need some help in getting a sense of what it is you really need and kind of organizing the disturbing feelings." Tony continues, "Like where am I going. You help me to organize and to say what I feel. There are times when I have very little tolerance for you not doing that right away. I feel impatient … like, 'Get to the bottom of this thing,' especially when it's someone else going on and on."

Several members talk about wishing that I would do more organizing. Tony agrees that that might feel good, that he would like more direction. Then he turns to me and adds, "That's not your style. You aren't that directive." "No, I guess I'm not," I respond with a warm laugh. I feel that we are on the same wavelength and continue. "Your wishes are very important to explore along with what it's like when I don't fulfill them. That's more important than a lot of content. What seems important to me right now is getting a clear sense of what you miss." Then turning to the group, "Tony is pretty clear that he wants me to get a sense of what he missed … what needs weren't met or aren't being met right now here in the group … and to spell it out." Then, turning back to Tony and gently probing the vulnerability, "Sometimes I can do that. More important is our really understanding your experience of really missing a coach."

"That's something that I've missed my entire life," Tony responds, full of thought. "That feeling of wanting a parental person to know. People would go, 'What's wrong?' And I couldn't say." Leaning a bit forward, I relate back to him, "Sometimes you need someone to recognize from your facial expression or just looking at you … to recognize what you're feeling and to help you put it into words." He continues softly, "I remember … there was a point in my life … like when I was eleven or twelve … I pouted for two days, three days, to see if anybody fucking noticed. I'm not talking! For three days! What's going on? Then I went overt to my aunt's house. I never thought of her as taking care of me, but she's real down to earth. So, she looked at me and right away she goes, 'What's bothering you?' I was so stunned right then. I couldn't tell her 'Like three days ago someone hurt my feelings.' I couldn't do that. I felt stupid … so I said 'nothing' and then there was nothing to say."

"At least she asked," Alice said in a caring tone. "Yes, and I couldn't tell her," Tony repeated. Seeking further elaboration, I tentatively reflect, "It still felt good that she asked … that was like a first step." Tony helps me to fine-tune my understanding and in doing so moves us deeper into his affective experience. "Yes … but the sadness is stronger than any good feeling. The

> sadness is that I really wanted my parent ... it was too far removed already ... it was family, but it was removed. I couldn't feel the same connection to her even though she was someone I could have connected to." Now more on target, I respond, "You really needed your mother to know." Tony relaxes and confirms my understanding with a simple, but meaningful, "Yeah."

This fragment of a group session is a good illustration of the role of the therapist and a focus on emerging vulnerability and affect in the process "deepening." What is deepened in the therapeutic process, from a self-psychological perspective, is the emotional exploration of underlying developmental needs and the intense affect aroused when they are not met. This process is clear in Tony's exploration of his need for help from the leader. At first, both Tony and the leader have a sense of stuckness and impasse as he focuses on a surface wish for coaching and assistance in bringing his outside life into the group when he does not have a crisis to work on. Through a sustained focus on affect, the leader is able to facilitate a more vulnerable amplification of Tony's yearnings for mirroring, for his mother to know his hurt, and for help in the regulation of walled off painful affect.

The Leader's Use of Self

A good leader is always using his or her self-experiences. It is often a quiet inner experience and process. This is very different from self-disclosure. The leader's use of self-experience, and particularly self-disclosure, at times of impasse, has to be allowed to emerge spontaneously. It can never be rigidified as a "technique." It becomes part of an attitude, a willingness to be vulnerable, to be seen. Incidentally, please note that I am considering self-disclosure as only one option in the leader's use of his or her own experiences. I think that all good leaders use their own inner experiences constantly, with or without awareness. We talk about disclosure when group members are aware of these aspects of the leader's experiences (sometimes intentionally, sometimes inadvertently).

Let's look now at an example of a group leader's use of his or her own experience. The group is proceeding smoothly. Everyone seems satisfied. Yet, I'm having trouble paying attention. My impulse is to treat it all as superficial and try to get them to go deeper, to find something to focus on actively. I contain this impulse (often an important step). I can then slow down and listen for a theme. They are all talking about being afraid that even if they are more open and reach out in the group, they will still be "typecast" by their defenses and not seen as the whole person they are. One woman voiced it as, "I don't want to be seen as uptight. That's not who I am. That's my protection." I reflected that as an underlying theme and the group seems to progress, but I still feel helpless and stuck, at an impasse.

Then I find myself preoccupied with an administrative decision I have to make at an upcoming conference. I have to choose between two deserving colleagues, both friends. They both very much want to lead a group at the conference and will be hurt if not chosen. Then I realize that one group member had talked about feeling "stale" last week and wondered if he was "done with group." The group didn't pick it up. Now, this week he is quiet and withdrawn. I realize that I want the group to address his experience and they were not doing it. I have to choose between my concern about the quiet member, on the one hand, and staying attuned to the people involved in the present discussion which seemed to be important to them, on the other.

I choose to interrupt and express my concern about the quiet member. He sighs and begins to talk about having called another group member during the summer break. He was hurt when he didn't get a call back. This leads to an intimate exchange between the two men that touches several group members who share some vulnerable feelings about being terrified of risking rejection, of still feeling seen as their protection and not being taken in. Then one of the women in the group suggests that perhaps when the quiet patient felt "stale," that was his protection talking. Maybe he feels abandoned in the group. That brings a teary silence in the room. The impasse is broken and I feel fine from there.

Before we leave the topic of impasse and the interplay between theory and practice, I want to say a few words about an inherent paradox in what I am proposing. Kohut, the originator of a self-psychological approach (1971), often suggested that we hold our theory lightly and not let it become rigid technique. If sustained empathic focus, and the leader's desire to deepen the process, becomes rigid technique, it may end up invalidating some patients' need to stay with content at times. Sometimes patients need room to justify and prove what they are trying to express. Content becomes a demonstration, a primitive expression of affect. At these times, an unrelenting focus on subjective, affective meaning, and underlying process, becomes a threat and can become part of co-creating an impasse. It is a good example of an impasse occurring when the therapist wants something the patient isn't providing. Once we really understand an issue, technique, and most ruptures, are often a question of timing.

I'll close with a brief anecdotal example about an impasse:

> One day, long ago, a young group leader taking his group on an exploration of the Shawanga mountains, leads them into a fascinating cave. They go deeper and find themselves in total darkness. After a while, they begin to fear being lost in the depths of this cave forever. A sense of uneasiness bordering on panic sets in. They look to their leader for help, but he's feeling helpless and afraid too. The young leader hears a quiet sound coming from deep in the cave. It sounds like an old Native American chant. Then the voice suggests that the group sit together. They sit down in a circle and hold hands. Time passes.

> Our hero begins to see a tiny opening about a football field away from where they are sitting. He soon realizes that he can lead the group out. The impasse has lifted.
>
> He turns to thank the old man who senses his wonderment. The old man says quite simply, "Eyes get used to the dark."

Concluding Remarks

The concept of vulnerable moments and a self-psychological/intersubjective emphasis on the processing of previously walled-off, painful affect provide a background understanding of what needs to be deepened in the therapeutic process and what leads to mutative change and the capacity for affect regulation and containment. Sustained empathic focus is meant to provide a more active, foreground, guide to the choice of interventions in furthering this deepening process. It suggests a focus based on a particular theory. A different theory might point to a different focus. It is a choice of focus that provides the bridge between theory and practice. That is how theory informs practice.

In this manner, there is no need to jettison theory at moments of impasse or at any point. The leader's bread-and-butter stance eventually becomes an integral part of who they are and how they function. In key moments, intuition and responsiveness can be trusted and perhaps reflected upon later. It is when intuition does not flow or does not feel trustworthy that a more conscious choice of focus becomes crucial.

References

Kohut, H. (1971) *The Analysis of the Self*. New York: International University Press.
Kohut, H. (1977) *The Restoration of the Self*. Madison, CT: International Universities Press.
Levitsky, A. & Perls, F. (1970) The rules and games of gestalt therapy. In J. Fagan & I. Shepherd (eds.) *Gestalt Therapy Now* (pp. 140–149). Palo Alto: Science and Behavior.
Livingston, M. (2001) *Vulnerable Moments: Deepening the Therapeutic Process*. New York: Jason Aronson.
Livingston, M. (2004) Vulnerability, affect and depth in group psychotherapy. *Psychoanalytic Inquiry* (issue on group therapy), 23 (5): 646–677.
Livingston, M. & Livingston, L. (2006) Sustained empathic focus and the clinical application of self-psychological theory in group psychotherapy. *International Journal of Group Psychotherapy*, 56 (1): 2006.
Orange, D., Atwood, G., & Stolorow, R. (1997) *Working Intersubjectively: Contextualism in Psychoanalytic Practice*. Hillsdale, NJ: Analytic Press.
Rizzuto, A.-M. (2004) Paradoxical words and hope in psychoanalysis. *Psychoanalytic Psychology*, 21 (2): 203–213.
Stolorow, R. & Atwood, G. (1992) *Contexts of Being*. Hillsdale, NJ: Analytic Press.

Stolorow, R., Brandchaft, B., & Atwood, G. (1987) *Psychoanalytic Treatment: An Intersubjective Position*. Hillsdale, NJ: Analytic Press.
Wolf, A. & Schwartz, E. (1962) *Psychoanalysis in Groups*. New York: Grune & Stratton.

Chapter 10

Group Psychotherapy and Neuro-Plasticity

An Attachment Theory Perspective

Philip J. Flores

Introduction

Brain mapping studies (Braun et al., 2000), electrostimulation studies (Rizzolatti & Sinigalia, 2006), studies of brain receptors (Insel & Quirion, 2005), and recent advances in modern technology have provided researchers with state-of-the-art neuroimaging techniques that have made it actually possible to record and visualize changes in brain function, neuro-chemistry, synaptic strengthening, neuronal connectivity, and synaptogenesis. Terms like "cortical re-routing," "neurogenesis," "intensive operant shaping," and "brain neuronal reorganization" are reflective of the mounting evidence of the brain's plasticity throughout the lifespan and dislodge the pre-1980 notion that the brain is hardwired at birth and not subject to alteration in adulthood (Taub & Uswatte, 2000; Morris et al., 2001; Weis et al., 2000). New discoveries like these are providing tantalizing evidence that the brain, like the rest of the body, can be altered intentionally. Just as aerobics sculpt the muscles, so psychotherapy sculpts the gray matter in ways group psychotherapists are only beginning to fathom.

These advancing techniques have provided attachment theory with concrete evidence that helps explain not only how the brain operates, but also how it responds to psychological interventions. For instance, a number of comparative studies have demonstrated regional metabolic changes (Saxena et al., 2003), normalization of ventricle and dorsal brain structures in basal ganglia, amygdala, and hippocampus (Goldapple et al., 2004; Furmark et al., 2002), and increased RBF in the limbic system as a result of psychological interventions. Kay's (2008) review of numerous fMRI studies, comparing subjects with similar diagnosis and age, have found that those subjects receiving psychotherapy for a year showed marked changes in structural and neurobiological markers while control subjects receiving no treatment did not. Other studies, utilizing pre-treatment SPET imaging on depressed subjects revealed reduced serotonin uptake in the medial forebrain bundle compared with healthy non-depressed individuals. After a year of therapy, the treated individual's single photon emission tomography (SPET) patterns had returned to normal. Untreated patients stayed the same (Lehto et al., 2008).

Neurobiology and Attachment Theory

Attachment theory is part of the newer relational models within psychodynamic theory. It has not only synthesized the best ideas of psychoanalysis, cognitive sciences, and neurobiology, but also provided a useful model for conducting group therapy (Flores, 2004; Mikulincer & Shaver, 2007b). The magnitude of accumulated evidence from developmental neurobiology (Siegel, 1999), the neurosciences (Schore, 2003a; Sroufe, 1996), and developmental psychoanalysis (Stern, 1985) garnered attention within the psychoanalytic community for Bowlby's work and moved attachment theory beyond the fringes of psychoanalytical theory. As Cortina and Marrone (2003) describe it, "attachment theory proposes a completely new framework from which to understand clinical and developmental phenomena" (p. 14).

While classical developmental theory has always recognized the importance of early childhood experiences on adult psychopathology, it took attachment theory to place the significance of these early attachments in their proper perspective. Intimate long-lasting relationships are an integral part of human nature and the inability to establish long-lasting gratifying relationships is directly related to the quality of early attachment experiences. The mechanisms by which we become and stay attached to others have a biological basis and are increasingly discernible in the basic structure of the brain, and these attachments have far-reaching implications for optimal health, social functioning, and even survival. Lannon (1996) captures these sentiments perfectly when he says, "Attachment is not just a good idea; it is the law."

The Mandate for Attachment: Why Interpersonal Relations are Essential for Optimal Brain Functioning

Clinical experience and research findings from treatment outcome studies, child development, animal studies, and evidence gathered from the neurosciences with both adults and children confirm the importance of attachments (Schore, 2003a; Stern, 2004; Lewis et al., 2000; Norcross, 2002). An integrative analysis of these findings has important implications for a group therapy format that emphasizes a relational or interpersonal approach to group treatment. The research evidence is robust and impressive. The integration of the recent discoveries of the neurosciences with attachment theory reveals five basic tenets.

1 Attachment cannot be reduced to a secondary drive (Diamond & Marrone, 2003).
2 The central nervous systems of all social mammals is an open feedback loop requiring stabilization (Lewis et al., 2000) and ongoing external regulation by attachment relationships (Schore, 2003a).
3 This requirement for external regulation and stabilization is a biological necessity and is not age or phase specific (Bowlby, 1980; Siegel, 1999).

4   The establishment of attachment and secure base in therapy predicts successful treatment outcome (Safran & Muran, 2000; Norcross, 2002).
5   One's ability to establish healthy regulatory relationships outside of the therapeutic milieu is synonymous with mental health and is indicative that psychotherapy treatment has been successful (Kohut, 1984).

1. Attachment is a Fundamental Motivation in its Own Right and Cannot be Reduced to a Secondary Drive

Attachment theory, like self psychology, can be considered an offspring of object relations theory. While these three theories share important similarities, they hold different allegiances from classical drive theory. The most decisive factor that differentiates attachment theory from the other two theories is the degree to which it differs from classical drive theory on the importance of attachment. Attachment theory holds firmly to the position that the pains, joys, and meaning of attachment cannot be reduced to a secondary drive. Attachment is recognized as a primary motivational force with its own dynamics, and these dynamics have far-reaching and complex consequences (Bowlby, 1973).

It is also important to remember that attachment theory is not so much a psychological theory as it is a biological theory. Companionship and community are woven deeply into our DNA. Natural selection favors mechanisms that promoted parent–offspring proximity in an environment of evolutionary adaptation. Attachment is not just psychologically driven, but is also adaptive and propelled by powerful biological needs for interpersonal closeness. A primary biological function is to secure assistance and survival in the case of adversity. This is true for all social mammals and applies to parent–offspring relationships in other species, not just human beings.

2. The CNS of all Social Mammals is an Open Feedback Loop Requiring Stabilization and Ongoing External Regulation by Attachment Relationships

Attachment theory holds the position that our central nervous system is an open feedback loop, which requires input and external regulation from other social mammals or "attachment figures." Secure attachment creates stable neurophysiological homeostasis and the lack of it produces disruptions in neurophysiological systems. Furthermore, strong attachment bonds relentlessly shape developmental phenomena including the physiological and neurobiological maturation of the brain (Cozolino, 2002; Siegel, 1999), the capacity for affect regulation (Fonagy et al., 2002), and the internalized self-object representations (Internal Working Model) that organize and influence a person's behavior in relation to others (Diamond & Marrone, 2003), as well as self-esteem, cognitive appraisal capacities (Mikulincer & Shaver, 2007a), and self-image (Lewis, J., 2000). All social mammals regulate each other's physiology and modify the internal structure of each other's nervous system through the synchronous exchange of emotions. The nature and impact of this interactive regulatory relationship is the basis for attachment and the memory of it is recorded in the change that takes place.

3. This Requirement for External Regulation and Stabilization is a Biological Necessity and is Not Age or Phase Specific

Attachment theorists recognize that both one-to-one and group or network attachments are necessary because originally they serve a biological function to insure survival. During early development, attachment helped secure assistance for the infant during times of threat or danger. However, as the individual grows older, "affiliative relationships" with peers and groups became more important because they involve greater reciprocity and a semantic order (Lichtenberg et al., 1992). Affiliative relationships are not based purely on physical proximity, but are mediated by a complex set of meanings and representatives.

While infants and their parents are biologically hard-wired to forge close emotional bonds with each other, the need for regulatory attachment relationships is a lifelong process and not phase specific. Attachments serve important emotional regulatory functions for adults as well, and existing neuro-pathways can be strengthened or weakened all through adult life. Emphasizing that attachment was necessary from the "cradle to the grave," Bowlby criticized the position of classic psychoanalytic theory of orality—which viewed adult attachment needs as indicative either of pathology or regression to immature behavior—because these conceptualizations were derived from outdated theories that are not supported by subsequent research evidence. The sacrificing of normal healthy needs for support and emotional regulation is reflective of a cultural bias that overemphasizes self reliance and individuation to the point that dependency and biologically determined requirements for CNS stabilization have become an identified pathology.

4. The Establishment of Attachment and Secure Base in Therapy Predicts Successful Treatment Outcome

Because the strength and quality of the therapeutic alliance (attachment) accounts for the greatest variance in successful treatment outcome, it is crucial that group therapists recognize the power of attachment bonds and use this information wisely. One of the primary advantages and benefits of group psychotherapy is the shared opinion that a properly constructed group environment not only provides a neurobiological organizing function, but also extends opportunities for understanding and correcting dysfunctional interpersonal patterns (Ormont, 2001; Rutan & Stone, 2001; Yalom & Leszcz, 2005; Gans & Alonso, 1998; Buchele, 1995). Interactions in group are not just overt behaviors or even primarily psychological functions, but are neurobiological in nature. Advances in the neurosciences (Schore, 2003a; Siegel, 1999) have taught us that alterations in external interpersonal interactions are registered as concurrent changes in the person's neurophysiology and emotional states. These changes are reflective of alterations or modifications of what is commonly referred to as self and object representations. Such an approach takes on added significance when one considers that all psychopathology manifests itself interpersonally and, as some (Tronick & Gianino, 1986) propose, all psychopathology may be the outcome of repeated unsuccessful efforts to repair misattunements and empathic failures. New attachment experiences that challenge the validity of early working models is what makes personal development and successful psychotherapy possible.

Schore's (2003b) review of hundreds of neuroimaging studies supports this assertion and has demonstrated the importance of the implicit, body-based nonverbal affective communication that occurs within the critical component of the inter-subjective field of the therapeutic alliance; and it is this critical process which accounts for the greatest structural changes in the brain during effective therapy. The neurosciences are leading the way to an understanding of human behavior which is moving beyond the limits of the mind–body dualism which has dominated the health sciences for the last three hundred years. It is emerging evidence like this that has prompted Lewis and colleagues (2000, p. 167) to write, "Dividing the mind into 'biological' and 'psychological' is as fallacious as classifying light as a particle or a wave."

5. One's Ability to Establish Healthy Regulatory Relationships Outside of the Therapeutic Milieu is Synonymous with Mental Health and is Indicative That Psychotherapy Treatment has Been Successful

Successful treatment outcome from an attachment theory perspective holds one basic and simple premise: until group members are able to develop the capacity to establish mutually satisfying relationships, they will forever remain vulnerable to stress, dysregulation, and a host of physical and mental aliments (Anderson, 2003). Successful treatment from this perspective is accomplished when the individual is able to establish and maintain healthy regulatory relationships outside of the therapeutic milieu (Kohut, 1984). While this overly simplistic portrayal of attachment theory gets to the heart of the matter, it does not do justice to the intricate complexity of accomplishing such a modest maneuver. To keep the significance of attachment theory's primary premise in perspective, we are biologically determined to form close emotional attachments to other social mammals in order to keep our CNS stabilized and operating at optimal efficiency.

Attachment Styles: Contributions for Clinical Applications and Limitations

Attachment is an instinctual, primary behavioral system which evolved to enhance infant survival, but "continues from the cradle to the grave" (Bowlby, 1979a, p. 129). The attachment system has three primary functions: 1) regulation of proximity to a caregiver in time of stress; 2) provision of comfort and security (safe haven); and 3) development of a secure base which makes exploration possible. More recent evidence reveals a fourth function in that secure attachment primes the brain for the capacity for mentalization, an absolutely necessary process that equips the individual for collaborative and cooperative existence with others, a task for which the brain was evolutionarily designed (Fonagy et al., 2002). Research has identified four clear individual differences in attachment styles: 1) secure; 2) insecure-avoidant; 3) insecure-ambivalent; and 4) insecure-disorganized. These styles predict a range of psychological and interpersonal variables across the lifespan (Ainsworth, 1991; Main & Hesse, 1990). As Bowlby (1979b) and Ainsworth (1989) remind us, insecure attachments are primarily defensive strategies designed to maintain contact with rejecting, unavailable, or inconsistent caregivers. These patterns of relating are reciprocally influenced and, once imprinted into the limbic system, are difficult to extinguish, becoming self perpetuating across a person's life span.

Limitations of attachment paradigm: Despite robust research evidence supporting the consistency of attachment styles across one's life span, there is an absence of strong evidence to support that insecure attachment styles (with the notable exception of disorganized attachment), in themselves, directly produce psychopathology or the development of specific diagnostic mental disorders (Mikulincer & Shaver, 2007a). As Fonagy and colleagues (2002, p. 98) suggest, "Moving from a model where the early relationships was seen as a template for later relationships—a model that appears naive in light of more recent evidence—we argue that it is the quality of depth processing of psychosocial environment that can be set by early experience." The depth processing that Fonagy is identifying is not a given, but a hard won developmental acquisition that is called mentalization. From this perspective, attachment is not an end in itself, but exists in order to allow a representational system to develop that aids human survival by equipping an individual for the collaborative and cooperative existence with others for which the human brain was designed. The evolutionary function of attachment is to equip the person with the kind of environment necessary which allows the understanding of mental states of self and other to fully develop. Mentalization—the ability to recognize that the internal world is separate from, but related to, external reality—is essential for functioning in a stressful social world. A developing brain is put at an extreme disadvantage when a child has to direct its efforts toward monitoring the attachment figure's mind rather than having help in discovering its own mind.

Mentalization, narratives, and self-reflective function: Talking intimately with another about oneself is a developmental function that not all adults achieve. Mentalization captures the essence of this developmental achievement. It involves both a self-reflective and an interpersonal component, which ideally provides a capacity to have an experiential understanding of feelings or mental states in self and others. Mentalization is not just a cognitive process because it extends beyond an intellectual understanding and represents the ability to *link thinking to feeling*, thus helping the person "connect to the meaning of one's emotions."

Knowing oneself and sharing that knowledge with another requires the capacity of putting one's feelings into words, a developmental task that requires the acquisition of inner speech or what Meares (1993) refers to as self-narrative. Attachment theory, especially because of the work of Margaret Main (1995) and her development of the Adult Attachment Interview (AAI), has shown a connection between attachment status in childhood and narrative styles in adulthood. Fonagy and colleagues (1994) describe this reflexive self function (RSF) as the ability to think about oneself in relation to another which is a necessity for intimacy.

A clinical example will help illustrate this principle.

> Andrew was referred to group by his individual therapist because of his difficulties maintaining relationships. After a number of weeks into the group, Andrew's style of relating became painfully obvious to the group leader and the other group members. He had great difficulty relating to others interpersonally about the emotional material stirred up in the here-and-now of the present relationships in the group. Andrew could be supportive and compassionate of others' painful experiences or stories, but he could not stay engaged with others once the interpersonal exchange required that people relate beyond the historic content of their experience. When Andrew spoke about himself, he could not keep others engaged. Group members would become distracted or drift off because his exchanges became bogged down in the minute details of his painful past history. People in group could feel sorry for Andrew, but they could not feel drawn in by him. It wasn't that it was unusual for new group members to feel compelled to tell their story when they first joined the group; that wasn't the problem. Everyone usually enters a group having to spend some time letting other group members know their history. Andrew's problem was that he remained trapped in his narratives. His stories became rote and stereotyped. It took a concerted effort by the group leader to steer the group away from their eventual indifference or boredom and their stereotyped responses to Andrew (e.g., "Oh, that's horrible, you had a terrible childhood, I can't believe they did that to you"), and guide them to deal directly with the feelings that Andrew evoked in them. Using his knowledge of Margaret Main's work on narrative styles and attachment, the therapist was able to cut across the dichotomy between historical truth and narrative truth. By focusing on the form of Andrew's narratives, rather than their content, the group leader was able to help the group and Andrew see that Andrew's preoccupation with his history was a way for him to stay attached to his past pain and hurt in the hope of evoking protective attachment behavior in potential caregivers. The group leader's actions in this example are an important reminder that therapists are more helpful when they attend as much to the way their patients talk as to what they talk about.

The Confluence of Attachment Theory and the Neurosciences: Implications for Informing the Application of Group Psychotherapy

If group psychotherapy is to become more grounded in empirical scientific theory, group therapists must pay closer attention to the vast amount of research evidence and information that the neurosciences are generating about the human brain. Our task, as group theorists, is to integrate this information and translate these discoveries into meaningful and practical clinical applications to help inform more effective group treatment. One of the important contributions generated by this domain of study is the recognition that neurogenesis and brain plasticity are amplified by certain experiences and optimally enriched environments. Not all environments provide the types of activities and experiences that enhance brain plasticity, learning, and change. First and foremost, the proper environment must be established to ensure that the brain will be primed for exploration and discovery, without which positive brain change, learning, and retention of that learning is impeded. The group environment that best delivers these crucial elements is one that functions as a secure base. The strength of a secure base captures one of the important paradoxes of attachment theory: secure attachment liberates!

Just as a securely attached child will take more risks exploring a strange room, while in the presence of a secure attachment to its mother, a securely attached group member will take more risks in exploring his/her internal world and the relationships with other members in the group if the group environment serves as a secure base. As group leaders, we want our group members to explore themselves, which many have not done previously because it has been too perplexing or frightening to do alone. However, a secure base does not mean a rigidity controlled environment that sacrifices spontaneity, complexity, and diversity for an unrealistically imposed fantasy that relationships are always predictable and never messy or challenging. Attachment-oriented group therapy with its emphasis on cohesion or secure base does not mean an unrealistically supportive, safe environment. Rather, it pertains to creating an environment where personal agency and differences can be safely explored, which allows the inevitable conflict that arises in any authentic relationship to be addressed. The group is secure when it is predictable and members can protest, disagree, and challenge each other and the group leader without fear of abandonment or violence. As Siegel (2006) and Cozolino (2006) remind us, the human mind emerges from patterns embedded within the flow of energy and information contained inside the brain as well as between and among brains. The group leader's task from this perspective is to promote and integrate the diverse pieces of energy and information within the group into a coherent whole that allows the group to move between the shores of rigidity and chaos. The group leader's aim is to foster a process of shared reflection that generates multiple perspectives on experience, helping group members from getting trapped in the "reality" of one view.

Six Factors for Promoting Brain Plasticity and Change in Group

1. Few things prime the brain for change more than strong attachment bonds.
2. Enriched environments, emotional arousal, and optimal levels of stress are required for brain change.
3. A non-linear relational theory of therapeutic action is required to enhance learning and brain plasticity.
4. Experience over explanation: procedural memory and the importance of working in the implicit domain.
5. The brain is profoundly social and hard-wired for cooperation, caring, and fairness.
6. Initial changes in the brain are just temporary: the advantages of long-term therapy.

1. Few Things Prime the Brain for Change More Than Strong Attachment Bonds

Examining all the possible implications attachment theory has for guiding group treatment suggests that therapy works because of one basic simple principle: exposure to people changes people—or more correctly, a powerful attachment experience alters a person's central nervous system. When group members become attached in group, not only are their central nervous systems engaged, but they also engage the biological mechanisms that permit their brains to be modified. If the therapeutic relationship is powerfully established, group members will eventually begin to extract the new rules that govern the relationship with the group leader and other group members and the modification of their nervous system has begun. From a neurobiological standpoint, group psychotherapy is a delicate establishment of regulatory attachment relationships aimed at stabilizing physiology and revising implicit emotional memory of attachment patterns.

Attachment is not just an abstract concept, but also a complex physiological process. The brain is profoundly social and highly plastic, malleable, and pliable throughout one's lifespan. The evidence about the way our brains function and are wired explains why we are biologically determined to form strong attachment bonds with others and how these relationships relentlessly shape and sculpt our neurophysiology and neurobiology. However, our experience-dependent brain is not a passive recipient to either internal or external environmental influences. It is not an inanimate vessel that we fill. Rather, the brain is more like a complex, dynamic eco-system constantly adapting to its ongoing experiences. We cannot expose our brain to toxic relationships any more than we can selectively introduce drugs into the system and expect the entire brain to not be profoundly impacted.

2. Enriched Environments, Emotional Arousal, and Optimal Levels of Stress are Required for Brain Change

The brain is driven to pursue novelty and challenge (Berns, 2008), and some of the greatest sources of novelty, challenge, and satisfaction come from the necessity of negotiating the demands of ongoing intimate relationships. The brain's drive for the novelty experienced in relationships is as strong as any other primary drive because the pleasure experienced as the result of the dopamine release when a relationship is successfully managed is highly rewarding. Because relationships are also challenging and emotionally arousing, they are highly effective in inducing high enough levels of optimal stress to stimulate cortisol, which primes the brain and body for action. All authentic relationships are unpredictable and require constant ongoing cooperation and attention. Becoming locked into rigid styles of relating not only dooms a relationship, but also does little for priming the brain for novelty and exploration—two crucial components for brain plasticity.

Just "belonging to a group" can create central nervous system homeostasis and stabilization which reduces cortisol to more manageable levels, thus combating the debilitating effects of chronic stress which interferes with learning and memory. There are few things as stressful as isolation. This is a fact so well recognized that when researchers are conducting animal studies on stress, isolation is the primary method for inducing stress in their subjects. While optimal levels of stress enhance learning and memory, chronic stress and too much anxiety interfere with learning and memory. Stress engraves memories important to survival, but too much of it cannibalizes the very structure that does the engraving. This is why it is crucial that group therapists put great effort in creating the correct therapeutic environment that balances security with emotional arousal.

3. A Non-Linear Relational Theory of Therapeutic Action is Required to Enhance Learning and Brain Plasticity

Because all specific diagnostic categories result from or are caused or exacerbated by current or past relational difficulties, therapeutic interventions that enhance the capacity for establishing, maintaining, and, when necessary, repairing attachment bonds need to be applied continually and repetitively during the course of treatment. It is important to remember that learning is a non-linear process. This is why continual practice and repeated exposure is required. Learning is not a gradual incremental increase achieved over linear time, produced by sequential events. After a period of repeated stimulus, a "potentiation threshold" is finally reached within the brain, triggering a neurochemical event, and the system is bombarded with glutamate and calcium resulting in an "ah ha" experience. The light bulb turns on and the person finally "gets it." Since the new discoveries in the neurosciences are helping us to understand that both learning and behavioral change are non-linear processes, a non-linear theory of how open systems work is required to better capture the dynamics inherent in all group processes and group therapies.

Non-Linear Systems: Non-Linear Relational Systems Theory (NLRST; Lyons-Ruth, 2005) attempts to capture how people in relationships sense and negotiate how or where they can go together ("fittedness") in their attempts to enlarge the breadth and depth of the dialogue between them. Interpersonal strategies take shape as members of the group sense what they are able to do and what they are not able to do together. A properly run group expands the possibilities within the group. The recognition process is not a reflective one, but a specific acknowledgment by all parties that a certain fitting together has occurred in the service of progressing together in working toward mutually held goals. The change that occurs as a result of this process is not the result of the group leader acting as the therapeutic agent directing the change, as is often suggested by most linear models of change. Rather, whatever change occurs does so as a result of the relationships and the alteration of the implicit rules of relatedness that naturally unfold because of the negotiation that occurs among the parties pursuing their common goals.

One tool for fashioning a non-linear and active theory of psychotherapeutic change comes from the essential insight of attachment theory which identifies how strategies for engagement with others in a relational dialogue are represented implicitly or actively without reliance on language and verbal symbols. Non-Linear Relational System Theory (NLRST) of therapeutic action and change describes more accurately how increased energy input into any self-organizing system (increased interactions between people in the group putting more energy into their relationships) leads to small incremental change which contributes to increased articulation in the constituents of the system. This increased articulation can lead to sudden emergence of new forms of organization.

4. Experience Over Explanation: Procedural Memory and the Importance of Working in the Implicit Domain

There has been a growing recognition (i.e., Stern et al., 1998) within psychology for the last few years that new conceptual tools are required to explain how change occurs as the result of psychotherapy, both in individual and in group psychotherapy. It has long been recognized that "something more" other than interpretation, explanation, or insight is required in successful treatment. Attachment theory has helped provide a different theoretical perspective that has resulted in a shift from an emphasis on the symbolic, verbal, declarative realm to a greater emphasis on the procedural, implicit, relational realm. Learning and change are recognized as occurring through the relationship and intersubjective moments ("moments of meeting") between or among the participants that create new neurological organizations, thus altering procedural knowledge and the implicit unspoken rules of being with others.

Writing about the advantages of an attachment perspective, Fonagy and colleagues (2002) suggest that an alteration of treatment technique needs to be carefully considered since many psychoanalytic propositions about development have turned out to be naïve and inadequate. For instance, the focus on memory and the retrieval of forgotten or repressed experience is now generally discarded in favor of an approach that examines the interpersonal and interactional aspects of relationships that have been retained as procedures or patterns of actions that come to organize later behaviors (Fonagy et al., 2002). Memory is no longer conceived of as a caldron of recorded, stored formative experiences, waiting to be retrieved by uncovering analytic work (Diamond & Marrone, 2003). Rather, formative experiences emerge as analogous procedures representing an intricately interlinked sequence of events that become organized as mental models (Cortina & Marrone, 2003). These internal working models (Bowlby, 1980) exist, encoded at the limbic level and are readily observable through an individual's style or manner of relating. Once a rule is learned and becomes a basic property of the brain and implicit memory, the rules are difficult to unlearn because this information is not readily available for conscious recall. The goal of group therapy, from this perspective, is the observation of rules of behavior or patterns of interaction, the identification of maladaptive models, and the subsequent strengthening, and establishment of more adaptive rules of engagement.

The world Grand Master chess player Gary Kasparov (2007), in his book aptly titled *How Life Imitates Chess*, captures these sentiments perfectly when he writes:

> Rote memory is far less important than the ability to recognize meaningful patterns. When we tackle a problem, we never start from scratch, we instinctively look for past parallels. We work out the authenticity of the parallels to see if we can work out a similar receipt from these slightly different ingredients ... We depend on these patterns the way we depend on our autonomic nervous systems to keep us breathing. A champion chess player can spot a simple checkmate in three moves without hesitation even if he has never seen that exact position before in his life.
>
> (pp. 54 and 120, 2007)

Limbic resonance and the implicit domain: When group members become emotionally attached in group therapy, not only is their implicit memory engaged, but also the biological mechanisms that permit implicit memory to be modified are engaged. The link between memory and emotions is crucial for learning and plasticity to be maximized. Since all emotional learning takes place at the limbic level, and the limbic system is anatomically interconnected with memory, emotionally charged information is stored and encoded here, functioning as a motivational map. The amygdala, as a central arousing component of the limbic system, flags significant events, as if to say, "Remember this. This is important." From a psychobiological standpoint, group psychotherapy is a delicate establishment of regulatory attachment relationships aimed at stabilizing physiology and emotions, and revising the emotional memory of attachment patterns. If relationships are powerfully established, group members will eventually began to extract the new rules that govern their relationships with others and the modification of their nervous system has begun. The attachment model emphasizes experience over insight—implicit learning over explicit learning. This is the reason why explanations and self-help books rarely change anything. Experience over time is what produces change in therapy. Insight has little effect as an agent of change. In fact, insight is usually the result of change.

Our emotional brain, as often as not, resonates with that of other social mammals, frequently without words or cognition. A wordless communication that we often ignore or take for granted reflects a process that Lewis and colleagues (2000, p. 63) call *limbic resonance*, which involves "a symphony of mutual exchange and internal adaptation whereby two mammals become attuned to each other's inner states." This is one reason why in-authenticity, emotional contrivance, and neutrality do not work in therapy. Emotions come from phylogenic, ancient times and the ability to read and display them is an inborn given—honed by millions of years of evolution. Because of this, contrived feelings, mimicking emotional states, and pretense on the therapist's part, no matter how well intended, are worst than useless. The patient's inborn ability to read emotions correctly far exceeds the therapist's ability to deceive the patient.

A clinical example will help illustrate the power of limbic resonance and wordless emotional communication.

> Mark, an extremely bright thirty-five-year-old MBA, had been in an outpatient therapy group for about six months when he began describing a series of difficulties in what had been, until recently, a promising career. He had been on a fast track for a VP position at a Fortune 500 company when two job changes were made necessary because of his recurrent difficulties with both of his bosses at two different blue-chip companies.
>
> After describing a particularly troublesome encounter with his new CEO at work, Mark gave the group a troubled look and stated, "I wish I knew what the hell was bugging my boss."
>
> "Think it has anything to do with your authority conflicts?" One group member asked.
>
> "Authority conflicts?" Mark asked. "What are you talking about?"
>
> Another group member promptly offered, "Maybe you do the same thing with your boss that you do with our group leader."
>
> "What?" Mark looked befuddled.
>
> "Yeah," another member nodded in agreement. "It isn't so much what you say, but what you do. You're always rolling your eyes and smirking at the group leader whenever he speaks."
>
> A fourth group member chimed in. "You have this weird grin on your face whenever you respond to Dr. Aronson. Because I've gotten to know you in the group over the last few months, I now understand that you get that silly

smile whenever you're nervous. But, I could see how someone could interpret it the wrong way, like you were mocking them or making fun of them."

Mark was shocked to learn that his behavior was so transparent. He had no idea that he was communicating a message he didn't even consciously know he was sending. With the group's continual monitoring and challenging of him, Mark's "acting out" with the group leader diminished dramatically over the next few weeks. As his awareness of his implicit communication increased within the group, he was able to translate this change outside of the group with his boss as he attempted to salvage his once promising career.

One night he entered the group gushing with excitement as he described how he had taken the group's feedback and applied it successfully in response to an especially challenging encounter with his new boss. Because Mark's struggle was a universal theme that the entire group could identify with and because he delivered his experience with such heart-felt sincerity, his story galvanized the entire group with the richness of its authenticity and raw emotional honesty. Mark's struggle and his reported success was no longer just Mark's success: it had morphed into a shared group triumph. Mark had changed. Gone was his usual bravado or self-righteous indignation. Instead, Mark spoke with humility and honesty about his fears as he struggled to overcome his sense of crippling entitlement and destructive indifference.

The group, as well as the group leader, felt impacted by the enormity of Mark's achievement. An emotional contagion hung rich and heavy in the room as the entire group bathed in the shared elation of his victory. It was a tender and moving moment for everyone.

Tears welled up in the group leader's eyes. As he beamed at Mark, a single tear trickled down the corner of his eye.

Mark caught a glimpse of the group leader out of the corner of his eye. He turned and gawked at him.

"Is that a tear?" Mark asked, astonished at what he saw.

The group leader nodded yes.

Mark burst into tears. "You really get it, don't you? It matters to you that I was able to accomplish this, doesn't it?"

The group leader smiled warmly and nodded again, choosing not to hide or disown what was obvious to everyone in the group. It was also a feeling that the entire group shared with him at this second.

Mark put his head in his hands and sobbed for a few moments. Gasping for breath, he looked around at the group and shook his head. "My father never noticed my successes."

> He clenched his fist. "He would usually just stare at me with such indifference. If he even bothered to speak, it was usually something critical. How I could have done it better. Don't get a big head."
>
> Mark looked up at the group leader. "The only way I could get any kind of reaction from my father was when I screwed up. Then he would notice."
>
> Even though the group leader hadn't uttered a single word, his communication was unmistakably obvious and had a profound emotional impact on Mark as well as the rest of the group. The discourse at that moment in group did not call for emotional neutrality, contrivance, or even interpretation. Instead, it required transparency and authenticity equal to the demands of the genuine human encounter that had just unfolded in the group. The remainder of the session was spent with the rest of the group joining in a rich and poignant exploration around the simple power inherent in a person's non-verbal emotional response to another. It was an important reminder to the entire group of the potency of authentic engagement in the reparative process and the basic human need to be noticed and truly seen by another. Words, in such authentic encounters, are usually incidental.

5. The Brain is Profoundly Social and Hard-Wired for Cooperation, Caring, and Fairness: Mirror Neurons—Learning by Observation and Imitation

The brain is a dynamic and adaptive system with a built-in capacity for fairness, cooperation, and care-giving (Denninger & Witte, 2007) and it is the mirror neuron system that allows for this capacity for empathy, imitation, and learning through observation and understanding the intention of others because these inherent social, interpersonal features enhance survival of the species. The instantaneous understanding of the emotions of others, rendered possible by the emotional mirror neuron system, is a necessary condition for empathy which lies at the root of most of our more complex interpersonal relationships (Rizzolatti & Sinigalia, 2006).

Constructing environments that ignore or do not promote the need for care-giving, care-seeking, mutuality, and reciprocity interferes with the genetically programmed brain's need for attachment. When care-seeking behavior is met by effective care-giving behavior (attunement, empathy) or the opportunity to repair ruptures, all parties feel regulated and satisfied. This satisfaction reflects a need that all developmentally mature adults have in their drive to give and receive in relationships. In contrast, if care-giving is ineffective (poor attunement, the care-giver distracts the care-seeker from fully exploring his/her experience), no secure base is established and exploration is inhibited. Unmet care-seeking and all the behavior associated with it (acting out, clinging, manipulation) remains active; old defensive rules for survival in a hostile, un-empathic environment get activated (McClusky, 2002).

Attachment is tied to biological motivations other than mere survival or reproduction. Caring does good things to the brain, whether the person is receiving it or providing it. Research evidence points to the importance of intrinsic motivations in most mammals for pleasure and positive affect (i.e., caring, cooperation, love, and bonding). Cooperation with others activates the pleasure centers of the brain, the same parts that are stimulated by rewards like food and money (Berns, 2005). Caring and cooperation produce pleasure in all but the most seriously damaged individuals. This satisfaction reflects the need that all developmentally mature adults have: the need to give and receive in relationships. Evidence accrued from studies with both animals and human subjects confirms that all social mammals' brains are hard-wired for cooperation and trust; at least until they gather evidence that it either costs them too much or that they are being taken advantage of by another. In short, the brain is hardwired to recognize when it is giving more than it receives. It is essential therefore that the group leader construct an environment that not only promotes cooperation and caring, but also allows for the repair of the inevitable ruptures and betrayals that occur in any authentic ongoing relationship.

6. Initial Changes in the Brain are Just Temporary

Familiarity, intensity, and extended duration in time are all required for an attachment relationship to be able to provide the kind of stabilization and modification of the central nervous system that translates into long-lasting brain change. Attachment and practice over an extended period of time is required to produce long-lasting changes in the brain. Repetitive attachment potentiates the synapses and they work better through increased experience which strengthens the neural connections. In a process called long-term potentiation (LTP), excitation is prolonged allowing synapses to become synchronized in their firing patterns and organized into neural networks (neurons that fire together, wire together). Information is not contained in single neurons or single synapses. Rather, information is contained in patterns of excitation, in networks of excitation, where the same neurons can overlap in different networks and be used in different settings (Sapolsky, 2004). The more a neural pathway is utilized, the more it is etched into the brain. The neuronal circuits that do not get activated or are under-utilized experience loss of synaptic strength or pruning. Short-term treatment does not allow for enough practice for extinguishing negative plasticity and "rewiring" the new implicit rules of relatedness.

Conclusion

A model of group treatment that integrates the new discoveries of the neurosciences is needed in order to offer a better translation of the implications that these research findings have for informing the clinical application of group therapy. Bowlby (1979a) and Kohut (1984) suggested years ago that the origins of the specific pathogenesis in an individual's early development is not so much related to the particular rearing practices of the parents as it is to the emotional climate of the home. In a similar fashion, it is not so much the specific techniques or approach of the group leader that influences successful treatment outcome, as it is the creation of the proper therapeutic climate that allows for the conditions that optimize brain plasticity and neurogenesis. This is why rotating therapists work against the requirements that secure attachment demands. Medicine and psychotherapy have lost sight of the importance of *specificity* in treatment—especially as far as specificity applies to the attachment relationship. The members of a therapy relationship are not interchangeable. Therapy, like any other attachment relationship, derives its power to persuade and change from the specific people involved in the relationship. After a duck has been imprinted to Konrad Lorenz, it cannot be told to follow another ethnologist. Therapy that works is not interchangeable. The patient becomes healthier within the specific context of the relationship with the attachment figure. The outcome of therapy is generally determined by who does it.

An equally important contribution from the neurosciences is that their discoveries do not lead to the need for the development of another new model of group treatment, but actually validate many current methods already being utilized. Instead attachment theory offers a trans-theoretical formula that identifies and substantiates what all effective therapeutic models and treatments already do. The field of "interpersonal neurobiology" has validated the venerable notion that talking with someone—especially if the encounter is meaningful and occurs within the context of emotional arousal, attunement, and a strong emotional bond—will alter neural pathways and synaptic strength. All forms of group psychotherapy, from psychodynamic, interpersonal, and Systems-Centered Theory (SCT) to Cognitive Behavioral Therapy (CBT), are successful to the degree to which they accomplish this task and enhance growth in relevant neuron-circuitry.

References

Ainsworth, M.D.S. (1989) Attachment beyond infancy, *American Psychologist*, 44: 709–716.

Ainsworth, M.D.S. (1991) Attachments and other affectional bonds across the life cycle. In C. Parkes, J. Stevenson-Hinde, & P. Marris (eds.), *Attachment Across the Life Cycle* (pp. 33–51). London: Routledge.

Anderson, N.B. (2003) *Emotional Longevity: What Really Determines How Long You Live*. New York: Viking Press.

Berns, G. (2005) *Satisfaction: Sensation Seeking, Novelty, and the Science of Finding True Fulfillment*. New York: Henry Holt.
Berns, G. (2008) *Iconoclast: A Neuroscientist Reveals How to Think Differently*. Boston: Harvard Business Press.
Bowlby, J. (1973) *Attachment and Loss. Vol. 2: Separation: Anxiety and Anger*. New York: Basic Books.
Bowlby, J. (1979a) *The Making and Breaking of Affectional Bonds*. London & New York: Routledge.
Bowlby, J. (1979b) On knowing what you are not suppose to know and feeling what you are not suppose to feel. *Canadian Journal of Psychiatry*, 24: 403–408.
Bowlby, J. (1980) *Attachment and Loss. Vol. III: Loss*. New York: Basic Books.
Braun, C., Schweizer, R., Elbert, T., Birbaumer, N., & Taub, E. (2000) Differential reorganization in somatosensory cortex for different discrimination tasks. *The Journal of Neuroscience*, 20: 446–450.
Buchele, B.J. (1995) Etiology and management of anger in groups: A psychodynamic view. *The International Journal of Group Psychotherapy*, 45: 275–286.
Cortina, M. & Marrone, M. (2003) *Attachment Theory and the Psychoanalytic Process*. London: Whurr Publishers.
Cozolino, L. (2002) *The Neuroscience of Psychotherapy*. New York: W.W. Norton.
Cozolino, L. (2006) *The Neuroscience of Human Relationships: Attachment and the Developing Brain*. New York: W.W. Norton.
Denninger, J.W. & Witte, J.M. (2007) *The Neurobiology of Group Psychotherapy*. Presentation at the Annual AGPA Conference. Austin, TX, February.
Diamond, N. & Marrone, M. (2003) *Attachment and Intersubjectivity*. London: Whurr Publishers.
Flores, P.J. (2004) *Addiction as an Attachment Disorder*. Northvale, NJ: Jason Aronson.
Fonagy, P., Gergely, G., Jurist, E.L., & Target, M. (2002) *Affect Regulation, Mentalization and the Development of the Self*. New York: Other Press.
Fonagy, P., Steele, M., Stele, H., et al. (1994) The theory and practice of resilience. *Journal of Child Psychology and Psychiatry*, 35: 231–257.
Furmark, T., Tillfors, M., Marteinsdottir, I., Fischer, H., Oossiota, A., Langstrom, B., & Fredrikson, M. (2002) Common changes in cerbral blood flow in patients with social phobia treated with citalopram or cognitive-behavioral therapy. *Archives of General Psychiatry*, 59 (5): 425–433.
Gans, J.S. & Alonso, A. (1998) Difficult patients: Their construction in group therapy, *The International Journal of Group Psychotherapy*, 48: 311–326.
Goldapple, K., Zindel, S., Garson, C., Lau, M., Bieling, P., Kennedy, S., & Mayberg, H. (2004) Modulation of cortical-limbic pathways in major depression. *Archives of General Psychiatry*, 61 (1): 34–41.
Insel, T.R. & Quirion, R. (2005) Psychiatry as a clinical neuroscience discipline. *JAMA*, 294 (17): 2221–2224.
Kasparov, G. (2007) *How Life Imitates Chess*. New York: Bloomsbury.
Kay, J. (2008) *Neurobiology of Psychotherapy*. Grand Rounds. Department of Psychiatry & Behavioral Sciences. Emory University School of Medicine, Atlanta, GA, June.
Kohut, H. (1984) *How Does Analysis Cure?* Chicago: University of Chicago Press.
Lannon, R. (1996) *Attachment Theory & Group Psychotherapy*. AGPA 35th Annual Conference, February 23, San Francisco, CA.

Lehto, S.M., Hintikka, J., Niskanen, L., Valkonen-Korhonen, J.M., Saarinen, P.I., Vanninen, R., Ahola, P., Tihonen, J., & Letonen, J. (2008) Midbrain serotonin and striatum transporter binding in double depression: A one-year follow up study. *Neuroscience Letters*, 441: 291–295.

Lewis, J.M. (2000) Repairing the bond in important relationships: A dynamic for personality maturation. *American Journal of Psychiatry*, 157: 1375–1378.

Lewis, T., Amini, F., & Landon, R. (2000) *A General Theory of Love*. New York: Random House.

Lichtenberg, J.D., Lachmann, F.M., & Fosshage, J.L. (1992) *Self and Motivational Systems*. Hillsdale, NJ: Analytic Press.

Lyons-Ruth, K. (2005) *The Development of Conflict and Defenses in Implicit Relational Processes*. Presentation at the How Psychodynamic Psychotherapies Change the Mind & the Brain Conference, LA.

Main, M. (1995) *Clinical Aspects of Attachment: The Work of Mary Main*. Lecture given at conference, University College, London.

Main, M. & Hesse, E. (1990) Parents' unresolved traumatic experiences are related to infant disorganized attachment status: Is frightened and/or frightening parental behavior the lining mechanism? In M. Greenberg, D. Cicchetti, & E.M. Cummings (eds.) *Attachment in the Preschool Years* (pp. 161–182). Chicago: University of Chicago Press.

McCluskey, U. (2002) The dynamics of attachment and systems-centered group psychotherapy. *Group Dynamics: Theory, Research, & Practice*, 6 (2): 131–142.

Meares, R. (1993) *The Metaphor of Play*. Northvale, NJ: Jason Aronson.

Mikulincer, M. & Shaver, P.R. (2007a) *Attachment in Adulthood: Structure, Dynamics, & Change*. New York: Guilford Press.

Mikulincer, M. & Shaver, P.R. (2007b) Attachment, group-related process, and psychotherapy. *International Journal of Group Psychotherapy*, 57 (2): 233–245.

Morris, D., Crago, J., Uswatte, G., Wolf, S., Cook, E.W. III, & Taub, E. (2001) The reliability of the Wolf Motor Function test for assessing upper extremity function following stroke. *Archives of Physical Medicine and Rehabilitation*, 82: 750–755.

Norcross, J.C. (2002) *Psychotherapy Relationships That Work: Therapist Contributions & Responsiveness to Patients*. Oxford and New York: Oxford University Press.

Ormont, L. (2001) Meeting maturational needs in the group setting. *International Journal of Group Psychotherapy*, 51: 343–360.

Rizzolatti, G. & Sinigalia, C. (2006) *Mirrors in the Brain—How Our Minds Share Actions & Emotions*. Oxford and New York: Oxford University Press.

Rutan, J.S. & Stone, W.N. (2001) *Psychodynamic Group Psychotherapy*. 3rd edn. New York: Guilford Press.

Safran, J.D. & Muran, J.C. (2000) *Negotiating the Therapeutic Alliance: A Relational Treatment Guide*. New York: Guilford Press.

Sapolsky, R.M. (2004) *Why Zebras Don't Get Ulcers*. 3rd edn. New York: Henry Holt.

Saxena, S., Brody, A.L., Ho, B.S., Zohrabi, B.S., Maidment, R.N., & Baxter, L.R. (2003) Differential brain metabolic predictors of response to paroxetine in obsessive-compulsive disorder versus major depression. *American Journal of Psychiatry*, 160: 552–532.

Schore, A.N. (2003a) *Affect Dysregulation and Disorders of the Self*. New York: W.W. Norton.

Schore, A.N. (2003b) *Affect Regulation and the Repair of the Self.* New York: W.W. Norton.
Siegel, D.L. (1999) *The Developing Mind: Toward a Neurobiology of Interpersonal Experience.* New York: Guilford.
Siegel, D.L. (2006) *The Social Brain in Human Relationships: Insights from Interpersonal Neurobiology.* AGPA Conference, March 1, San Francisco, CA.
Stern, D.N. (1985) *The Interpersonal World of the Infant.* New York: Basic Books.
Stern, D.N. (2004) *The Present Moment in Psychotherapy and Everyday Life (Norton Series on Interpersonal Neurobiology).* London: W.W. Norton.
Stern, D.N., Sander, L.W., Nuhum, J.P., Harrison, A.M., Lyons-Ruth, K., Morgan, A.C., Bruschweilerstern, N., & Tronick, E.Z. (1998) Non-interpretive mechanisms in psychoanalytic therapy: The something more than interpretation. *International Journal of Psycho-Analysis*, 79: 903–921.
Sroufe, L.A. (1996) *Emotional Development. The Organization of Emotional Development in the Early Years.* New York: Cambridge University Press.
Taub, E., & Uswatte, G. (2000) Constraint-Induced Movement therapy based on behavioral neuroscience. In R.G. Frank and T.R. Elliott (eds.) *Handbook of Rehabilitation Psychology* (pp. 475–496). Washington, DC: American Psychological Association.
Tronick, E.Z. & Gianino, A. (1986) Zero to three. *Bulletin of the National Center for Clinical Infant Programs*, 6 (3): 1–6.
Weis, T., Miltner., W.H., Huonker, R., Friedel, R., Schmidt, L., & Taub, E. (2000) Rapid functional plasticity of the somatosensory cortex after finger amputation. *Experimental Brain Research*, 134 (2): 100–203.
Yalom, I.D. & Leszcz, M. (2005) *The Theory and Practice of Group Psychotherapy.* 5th edn. New York: Basic Books.

Chapter 11

Using a Systems Lens to Illuminate the Intersubjective Field in Group

Barbara R. Cohn

Introduction

With the advent of intersubjective theory, psychoanalytic technique has undergone profound changes (Stolorow & Atwood, 1992).[1] Group theorists have re-evaluated treasured concepts such as resistance (Billow, 2010), therapeutic focus (Livingston, 2012), and acting in and out (Wright, 2004). Therapist subjectivity is front and center in the leader/group relationship and interest in a "co-created third" leads naturally to a re-evaluation of and re-investment in self disclosure (Cohen & Schermer, 2001).

In this chapter I am going to discuss what I term "classical" systems theory and its relevance to contemporary psychoanalytic group thought. I believe that including a systems lens in an intersubjective or relational view augments our understanding of group events and adds importantly to our repertoire of group interventions.[2] I will emphasize two different applications of the theory: the elucidation of enduring self/group organization within the small group and the location of meaning in the social surround.

The presence of social context in individual and group life as represented by a "social unconscious" has been written about extensively by Earl Hopper who states, "Ultimately the meaning of human affairs always requires that we contextualize them in time and social space in appreciation of open living systems" (Hopper & Weinberg, 2011 p. xviii). Hopper has developed the concept of social unconscious, as theory and descriptor. I will show how systems theory can highlight the presence of social meaning as it enters and impacts group process and thus, the intersubjective field of the group (Hopper, 2003; Hopper & Weinberg, 2011).

Many group therapists already use a general understanding of systems theory as part of an eclectic approach to group work. To some, systems thinking may be such an automatic aspect of their understanding of group events that they may question why the theory needs special emphasis here.[3] In turn, there has also been recent interest in open systems theory in the relational field (Grossmark, 2007). Donnel Stern (2003) in a paper entitled "The fusion of horizons: Dissociation, enactment, and understanding" says, "All understanding is context dependent, and one of the most significant contexts for clinical purposes is the self-state" (p. 843). I would add that in addition to the self-system, the group system as well as the social context or supra-system can be mined for meanings. By describing various systems terms below I hope to provide clinicians with a language they can use to potentiate their awareness of systems configurations, and in concert with relational thought, add to standard reductionist methods. As my title suggests, by expanding clinician consciousness in this way I hope to further illuminate the relational field.

Systems theory is a construct I have used widely and deeply in many aspects of my professional life: as a training director in a large hospital organization, as a supervisor, and as a clinician. I am not certain whether I chose the theory or whether the theory chose me.[4] What I can say is that whenever I am confronted by a series of complex organizational or clinical events, it is a systems understanding that comes readily to mind. Because I spent so many years working in a hospital system, there were many times when I became caught in organizational enactments that evoked a host of intense, disturbing feelings. Systems thinking came to my rescue in that as I analyzed dysfunction in various areas of the organization, I was better able to understand the forces that impinged upon me, co-creating my experience.

The impact of systems realities on small groups in hospitals was widely written about in the 1970s and 1980s during a period where inpatient wards were set up as therapeutic milieus (Kernberg, 1973; Klein & Kugal, 1981). By the time I became training director in 1986, inpatient units were no longer regarded as therapeutic settings and systems thinking was not considered relevant. Despite the fact that "the system" was ignored by others, I discovered that systems events operated in powerful and perhaps even more insidious ways upon my experience (Cohn, 1988).

Discovering a systems pattern is initially a right-brain experience in which complex data and hierarchical levels of data are connected meaningfully and rapidly by metaphor (often visual) as in a dream. In this regard I can say that a systems view originates as a highly subjective construction and can be understood as a relational event that occurs between a clinician and the particular system in focus as "the other."

Shapiro and Carr (1991), who advocate a systems lens to understand organizational dynamics, assert that the view of one individual in a system should be regarded as partial truth, a piece of a complex mosaic that can be fully fleshed out only by a collaboration among other people in the system who add to the picture. They suggest a meeting of the minds they call "the interpretive stance" (p. 75). The interpretive stance is a dialogue between system members that entails communication and reconciliation of views of the system, its impact upon individuals, and their respective system roles. Such dialogue continues until a consensus is reached about the most relevant system meanings.

Discoveries of systems configurations are, I believe, comparable on a wider scale to the constructivist view described by Stern as the emergence of "truth" in the interpersonal locus between analyst and analysand (Stern, 1997). Stern describes how new meaning can appear when analyst and analysand remain open to views outside of their established and reciprocal "prejudices" (transference/countertransference dynamics) of one another. I believe that systems theory is a tool that allows clinicians to extricate themselves from systems enactments which "prejudice" them in similar ways.

Using a Systems View as Part of a Relevant Focus

Livingston (2012) in a recent paper discusses the importance of focus in group work. Group therapists have an array of choices in what they think about and comment upon and Livingston states that to be effective in our work we need to choose a focus. Livingston suggests an experience-near, affective focus in the here-and-now as most valuable for a group leader. Indeed, many contemporary group theorists privilege more "right brain" affective experience as the pathway to lasting change (Dluhy & Rubenfeld, 2004; Kahn & Feldman, 2012).

While I very much agree that too much commenting on too many factors is not an effective strategy for therapeutic intervention, I hope to illustrate that as group process is always an affective and regressive experience, systems ideas can be brought into the group in highly impactful ways. In fact, I have found that even in a dyadic context, a systems analysis can introduce valuable new meanings (Cohn, 2007).

Classical Systems Theory[5]

Contemporary systems theory was devised by a theoretical biologist, Ludwig von Bertalanffy, after World War II (von Bertalanffy, 1950). Von Bertalanffy was concerned that the various sciences were becoming more and more specialized, each with its own language, and thus increasingly unable to communicate with one another. Systems theory was devised as a metatheory, one with principles and concepts that could apply to all specialties and facilitate dialogue between them. I do not see evidence that von Bertalanffy's desire to foster communication between the sciences ever came to pass, however, systems concepts have been put to good use, particularly in organizational analysis and in the field of group psychotherapy. The fact that a systems view is a meta view means that it does not contradict other understandings of events, rather, it simply adds additional meaning:

> In the early meetings of a beginning group, Dan, a dentist, was chronically late. His lateness was understood as an unconscious expression of ambivalence about joining the group, related to genetic factors in his individual history, as well as representing an interpersonal event between group members. In fact several of the other members were encouraged by the leader, an interpersonal group therapist, to express their here-and-now reactions to Dan's lateness.
>
> (AGPA open session, 1992)

Dan's lateness is also a systems event. Systems theory considers Dan's ambivalence about joining to be a feeling that is shared by all group members; in fact, such ambivalence is considered to be a normative experience in early group formation. Thus, systems theory sees Dan, an individual member, as expressing something for the whole group. The group leader has a choice to focus on Dan as sole repository of this ambivalence, a scapegoating configuration that is itself a form of system organization, or to encourage group members to identify with Dan and speak about their own mixed feelings about joining.

From a systems perspective, understanding the ambivalence as a characteristic of the whole group rather than isolating it in only one member promotes development of the group as a system where more complex feelings can be expressed by all. Thus, a focus on the systems meaning of Dan's lateness moves the small group in the direction of greater complexity and differentiation.

Systems thinking is non-linear and Dan's lateness is not caused by any one factor. From a systems perspective, Dan's lateness is a manifestation of the complex interactions of many variables in the group system and levels in the system hierarchy, interacting in complex ways to create a system pattern. In this case we might term (and visualize) this system configuration as, "one foot in the door, one foot out the door."

Systems Theory and the Group Field

In 1981 James Durkin published *Living Groups*, a compilation of papers that applied General Systems Theory to small group work and the culmination of the meetings of the General Systems Theory (GST) Committee of the American Group Psychotherapy Association mentioned in note 4. *Living Groups* is a treasure trove of systems ideas that has unfortunately disappeared from most contemporary group study. Chapters in this book discuss subjects such as the mechanisms of applying systems theory to groups, energy transformation, and developmental characteristics of the system-forming process. At the end of the volume, Durkin presents a glossary of terms—some quite technical, all fascinating—that describe various applications of the theory.

In my study of the subject I highlight several of these terms that I will discuss below. My list of terms is not comprehensive and I recommend that those who are interested reference the glossary themselves.[6] Systems are by definition hierarchical in that any particular system under study is always embedded in a larger, supra-system and itself contains sub-systems. It is the "observer" who determines what level of hierarchical organization is chosen as a focus and considered "the system" of study. Thus a human being is a system made up of sub-systems like the endocrine system and the digestive system. For current purposes the small group is considered "the system" with individual members being the sub-systems and the context in which the group occurs being the supra-system.

Systems are in part defined by their boundaries (Cohn, 2005). Boundaries alternate between relative permeability, during which time they allow new matter/

energy/information to enter the system, and relative impermeability, during which time new information is prevented from entering by thickening or closing of boundaries. In his glossary of terms, Durkin presents the verb "boundarying." Boundarying is defined as "The complementary processes whereby living structure opens/closes its own boundaries ... Opening leads to structural transformation and growth. Closing leads to structural consolidation and protection" (Durkin, 1981, p. 340).

Homeostasis/heterostasis is a second complementary process that typifies systems functioning:

> Homeostasis is a function of living structure in which it maintains physiological, psychological or other structural equilibrium in the face of external disturbance. Heterostasis is a complementary function in living structure in which it transforms its physiological, psychological or other structural state in the direction of greater adaptiveness.
>
> (p. 342)

As will be discussed below, systems organize to maintain themselves and alternating homeostasis/heterostasis allows for expansion or elaboration of a system—for example, continuation.

An important term in Durkin's glossary is "isomorphy." Isomorphy is the idea that a pattern that occurs in one level of a system is often echoed or replicated in a different form in other levels of the system hierarchy.[7] Durkin defines isomorphy as, "An identity of structure lying beneath a diversity of content in the comparison between individual living structure" (p. 343).

> In a group session four weeks before the end of the training year and concomitant changeover of co-leaders, a patient who served as mainstay for commitment to group and who often gave testimonials about the therapeutic benefits of long-term membership, dropped a bombshell. This motherly woman reported that the new clinic director had announced that all patients who had benefitted from individual treatment in the past year would no longer be offered new individual therapists in the upcoming training cycle. She added, almost as an afterthought that her work schedule was changing and thus she would have to leave the group as well.
>
> Following this announcement the group engaged in a spontaneous go-around in which each group member gave a reason why he or she needed to leave the group when the current leaders departed.
>
> The group leaders were stunned. They had carefully prepared the group for their leave-taking with a thoughtful and gradual termination process during which group members were given ample opportunities to air their feelings

> about the impending loss. All the careful termination work seemed to be coming undone by forces beyond group leaders' control. The leaders were thrown into a panic.

What happened? The director of the clinic in which the group was housed seems to have made an untimely, thus destructive decision. In precipitously announcing the end of the expected individual treatment for patients, he failed to model a more gradual termination process that allowed sufficient time to process these endings. In fact his sudden announcement enacted a sudden, traumatic abandonment similar to the multiple losses that characterized the histories of many of the patients. We can speculate that the clinic director (isomorphically) may have been given a sudden (abandoning) directive from his supervisor who may himself (isomorphically) have been in a panic in reaction to anticipated budget cuts in the larger hospital spurred by prospective entitlement cuts by the US Congress.

The motherly patient retaliated by an announced sudden abandonment of the group which represented an identification with the aggressor/abandoner and an isomorphic enactment. This non-reflective and punitive defense, "needing to leave group," spread like wildfire in a group contagion.

> Leaders were counseled by their supervisor to reinforce the group boundary by differentiating their own more constructive model of termination from the thoughtless model of the clinic director (statements that needed to be made tactfully and that required courage from a professional and political point of view). Leaders disclosed that they had been blindsided by the announcement of the directive and encouraged group members to share similar feelings. Leaders also presented what would have been a more thoughtful model on the director's part—making the announced change at the beginning of the treatment cycle so that patients had ample time to process anticipated endings of individual treatment.
>
> Leaders thus re-established a more gradual and nuanced model of termination inside the group that allowed for individual internalization of this model. Leader interventions were not experienced as dry, intellectual concepts, but rather much needed psychic windows that opened space in the group for the energy of multilayered inquiry and thus, psychic growth.

Related to continuation is the system term "negentropy." Entropy is the process by which all living systems (inevitably) degrade over time. Negentropy is a process that moves against entropy. Citing Durkin, "Entropy … the inherent tendency to descend from organized to unorganized states" (Durkin, 1981, p. 341). "Negentropy ... inherent self-organizing activity of living structure moving actively to counter the force of entropy" (p. 345). Systems once formed operate to maintain themselves and there are multiple examples in organizations and society where systems are no longer useful but continue simply because they can.

> A group of clinical supervisors met to evaluate psychology interns at their facility. A discussion ensued about a particular intern, Joyce. One senior supervisor commented that although Joyce had some clinical talent, she also had many areas of weakness such as a sense of entitlement, unwillingness to consider use of behavioral treatments in combination with more traditional techniques, a tendency to be late to supervision and non-compliance with paperwork. A few minutes later another senior supervisor who had not heard the first supervisor speak, joined the meeting by conference call and talked enthusiastically about Joyce, whom she described as a "star" in every way. Instead of acknowledging and welcoming these different views, the group ignored them and moved on to list the failings of a second student.

There is covert but palpable competition between members of this meeting/group due in part to normative professional jockeying but intensified by system-wide anxieties about possible lay-offs at the clinic where they work. The stated purpose or goal of this meeting, however, is to share experiences and to come to a consensus about the psychology interns, a supposed cooperative endeavor. Prior to the second supervisor's joining the meeting, the meeting/group was denying competing views by bonding around affectively charged criticisms (there were jokes and thinly disguised distain) of the intern under discussion.

To become more functional, the group would have needed to delineate a thicker boundary between the outside climate of denied competition and an inside spirit of cooperation. Yet because the boundary was overly permeable, a genuine spirit of collaboration could not be achieved. Instead, there was an enactment of denied competition inside the group isomorphic to the outside clinic supra-system and a false bonding represented by the scapegoating of the interns with a focus on their weaknesses. Such scapegoating represented a failure to stay on task because any evaluation of the interns needed to include a discussion of their strengths as well as their failings. Also interns in this particular placement were excellent clinicians in training so it was simply inaccurate to focus exclusively on intern weakness.

A more functional group would have recognized the conflict between supervisors when it appeared in the small group and worked with it in a more constructive fashion. Instead, negentropy prevailed in that the meeting/group continued in a non-functional form. The fact that this meeting was no longer able to accomplish its task rendered it a "false" group comparable to a false self.

The above two examples illustrate the systems concepts of isomorphy and negentropy. Using these concepts to highlight systems patterns provides information to those who are part of the system. Amelioration in system functioning can often be achieved by a combination of increased knowledge which is the result of a system analysis and a re-assertion of system boundaries. Reinforcing the boundary around the small group system allows for integration of new information which can lead to greater differentiation and more relevant functioning.[8]

Holding the System in Mind

The view of the small group as a system is a template that is held in the group leader's mind. In this regard it represents a constructivist approach. Donnel Stern describes the emergence of meaning in the relation between analyst and analysand in the following way:

> Once one is able to supply a suitable context, a meaning emerges; one has understood. But the advent of new meaning not only marks the union of conduct with a fitting context; new meaning actually constitutes this union ... The explicit new meaning that arises in the fusion is only one of the possibilities that might have come into being. It did not exist previously in the mind, at least not in finished form, but was given its shape in the moment of the fusion.
>
> (Stern, 2003, p. 844)

The group leader can be central in organizing what seem at first to be hopelessly chaotic, even extra-group data into meaningful system patterns. Patient understanding of seeming random or discrete events as interconnected system events paves the way for further engagement and investment in the group.

> A psychodynamic process group for women met weekly in a psychiatric outpatient clinic of an inner-city hospital. Women in the group were middle aged, with dysthymia and personality issues. With one or two exceptions group members were Black or Hispanic and had chronic socioeconomic problems as well.
>
> Female leaders of the group were psychology interns and psychiatric residents, Caucasian, East Asian, or Asian. Their tenure of leadership was for one or at most, two years. An ongoing challenge for leadership was the persistent push by group members to emphasize supportive and social connections and to avoid therapeutic inquiry. A second challenge for the leaders was to become relevant despite their significant age, socioeconomic, and ethnic differences from the patients.

> A session took place in mid-May about six weeks before the leadership turnover. Attendance had been good throughout the year but for the first half-hour of this hour-long session only one member of the eight-person group showed up. This particular patient was usually silent during sessions to the point where she often fell asleep. Her behavior earned her the nickname, "Dor Mouse at the Mad Hatter's Tea Party," a private joke shared by leaders and their supervisor. In this particular session the "Dor Mouse" spoke cogently about the impending loss of the two leaders and expressed genuine regret that they were leaving. Such feelings had been vehemently denied by group members up to this point.
>
> After forty minutes another group member, Mickie, entered the room and spoke excitedly about a third member, Sandra, who was in crisis. Mickie detailed with growing alarm a list of Sandra's problems. These included impending eviction, cut off of entitlements, and possible heart failure. In fact Sandra had recently been in the ICU for a chronic and worsening heart condition. Suddenly Mickie's cell phone rang and it was Sandra on the line. Mickie rose from her chair, walked over to one of the leaders and thrust the cell phone in her face. She insisted that this leader speak to Sandra due to the "life and death" nature of the crisis.

A more traditional psychoanalytic view would find rampant resistance and acting out in the group; the absence of 70 percent of the members, the lateness of the second member, and the insistence by Mickie that a leader take a phone call in the middle of a session are just three of the most obvious examples.

If we apply an intersubjective approach, we can look at the actions of the three members who attend the session (the Dor Mouse, Mickie, and Sandra, by phone call) as well as the members who do not attend, as enactments. The group by its absences may be working unconsciously to induce feelings in the leaders that they do not matter and this is likely something the patients feel in response to the yearly changeover of leadership. Also leader attempts to analyze and deepen patient understanding can seem irrelevant in the face of "real-life" problems like eviction and heart disease. Thus, leaders might also feel discouraged and skeptical about the effectiveness of psychotherapeutic inquiry with this group. Such doubts are a problem not just for the leaders, but also for their supervisor (a part of the hierarchical treatment system) because she wants to demonstrate that psychoanalytic theory can be relevant here.

What can a systems lens add to our understanding of the situation beyond the above ideas? If we consider everything that happened both inside and outside the group boundary including the absences as meaningful parts of a whole system configuration, we can advance our understanding and find new meanings.

First, we can speculate that the group has split itself into two parts or sub-groups and that these sub-groups are essential to maintaining the integrity of the whole group system at this juncture. (Object relations theory views such primitive splitting as a developmental stage in the life of the infant.) One sub-group, members who do not attend the session, can be understood as guardians of the idea that while patients mean a great deal to one another (there is extensive telephone contact among members between sessions), leaders don't really matter. Such a group split advances the idea that the group system will endure through its extra session contact despite leadership change. The other half of the split makes room for an opposite set of feelings embodied in the words of the "Dor Mouse," who may have been unconsciously selected by the group members to communicate that the leaders *will indeed* be missed.

The enactment of Mickie and Sandra, the "phoning home," can also be understood as a powerful communication of need and dependence on leadership with the expectation that leaders will contain and soothe panic around the possibility of catastrophe. Although such an urgent and primitive desire for soothing does not represent advanced group work, with the impending loss of leadership, it makes sense that the leaders are needed in this way. We can understand this behavior as an attempt to maintain the integrity and endurance of the system as a whole. It is as if the "present sub-group" is coming to the mother/leaders with a symbolic "boo boo" so that they can kiss it and make it well.

Thus, despite the lack of verbal expression and the splitting of the group members, we can understand these seemingly chaotic group events as self-organizing and meaningful components of the whole group system. One can visualize the system as two, oval-shaped circles, one larger than the other delineated by thick lines, surrounded by a larger circle with a more faint line. Essential to understanding the above events as parts of a whole system pattern is the ability of the leaders and their supervisor to maintain a template of whole group system in their minds.

Role Specialization in Systems

Another important aspect of system organization is that of enduring patient roles. Over time, individual group members exhibit consistent patterns of behavior that can be characterized as roles. Roles serve as organizers of individual identities and as important building blocks to whole group system organization. K. Roy MacKenzie says, "The idea of social role connects the interactional style of the individual with the functional needs of the group" (1990, p. 61). The overarching goal for an individual who assumes a role in the group is to grow in complexity and differentiation over time. Such development is true for the whole group system isomorphically, "the group developmental task of increasing complexity of interactional opportunities fits the individual agenda of learning role flexibility" (p. 62). Growth on an individual level is both facilitated and/or constrained by the development of the whole group system.

Individual roles have both identifying and defensive meaning to the individual. At times roles can be limiting to individual growth—for example, repetitive, stereotyped, and oppositional—yet remain relevant to whole group organization. A classic example of group role that appears problematic while continuing to provide meaning to the whole group system is the "difficult" patient. Over time certain patients emerge in groups as "difficult" either in their tendency to monopolize, express primitive affect, or to adopt certain stances such as assistant leader to the exclusion of working on their own problems. Understanding "difficult" patient behavior from the point of view of psychoanalytic concepts may include a genetic understanding of the patient's stubborn, uncooperative, or impulsive behavior and a consideration of these behaviors as deeply embedded defenses (Bernard, 1994). Such ideas while accurate can lead to a therapeutic impasse in that interpretations and confrontations do not often penetrate such encrusted defenses.

A systems perspective of the ongoing (homeostatic) usefulness of "difficult" role/behavior to group system functioning has been written about by Jerry Gans and Anne Alanso (1998), who describe the "difficult patient" as a co-construction between patient, group, and leaders, and more recently and entertainingly by Scott Rutan (2005), who makes a distinction between "difficult" patient behavior and "difficult patients." Thus, we can understand the development of group roles such as that of difficult patient both as a form of resistance to change *and* as elements of system organization:

> Miriam was a sixtyish, chronic schizophrenic woman [in a group of similarly compromised patients] who presented herself as the most obviously fragmented group member. She frequently made such stereotyped and unrelated statements as "The thought came to me yesterday, you (referring to herself) don't have long to live" or "I was sitting in a coffee shop and the number ten, ten days left on this earth, came to me." ... [The leader] began to refer to Miriam as "the-keeper-of-the-group-gate," as someone who launched and terminated each session predictably, thus maintaining the illusion that nothing new had happened within a session ... As "gatekeeper" Miriam assured all in the group that they were in the same place every week with the same cast of characters and, most importantly, that no disturbing changes had taken place.
>
> (Cohn, 1988, p. 326)

When leaders deem that roles are serving a primary resistance function, traditional interpretation or confrontation can be attempted, but at times emphasizing their *system meaning* is a more effective way to bring about change:

> The first evidence of the relaxing of the [role] resistance occurred in a session where Miriam expressed some genuine new anger at another group member for criticizing her and then reverted to her ritual of repetitive fears. The

[leader] commented on how "it was a good thing that Miriam was helping the group forget about her anger, which had been unsettling [exaggerating relief that Miriam was reverting to her accustomed role]." Miriam took offense at the [leader] for the latter's suggestion that the "gatekeeper role" was more important that her newfound anger. She then proceeded to get angry at the [leader] (a new and relevant behavior).

(Cohn, 1988, p. 326)

Applying Systems Concepts Without Animating the System

It is natural when undertaking a system analysis to animate the system—for example, to conceive of a system as having motivations, even a mind. Von Bertalanffy warned that such animating represented an incorrect application of the theory (von Bertalanffy, 1968). In *Living Groups*, McKenzie (Durkin, 1981) speaks to this issue and expands the discussion:

> The study of the group as a social system, that is, as an organizational entity, has been hampered by the language generally chosen to describe group-as-a-whole phenomena. A group is not an individual, and terms used to describe it must be appropriate to a group level in the organizational hierarchy ... a group has no-cerebral cortex and cannot think. What happens in a group may cause each of the members to think and indeed, their thinking may at times have some commonalities, but it is the individuals, not the group, who are managing information in a symbolic fashion.
>
> (Durkin, 1981, p. 114)

In my work with systems theory, I have found the following distinction to be useful: the essence of a "living system" is that it does not have a mind, yet an effective way to understand and work with systems is to develop *metaphors* that describe various system states and the most effective metaphors are often made up of animating properties. Despite the use of such metaphors, one must return again and again to a fundamental view of a system as having invariant principles and properties rather than a mind and feelings.

> A psychology intern was placed in a day-program to perform a six-month rotation of clinical work. Over the next several weeks her rotational supervisor failed to assign the usual patients and groups to her. At first, the intern blamed herself; perhaps she was too old looking, perhaps she had been uncooperative.
>
> In analyzing the nature of the day-program system, it was discovered that a long time and cherished clinician had recently retired and the system had not sufficiently mourned this loss to make room for new blood, the intern.

> In developing the above system analysis, the training director and intern group devised the following visual metaphor; a staff of day program clinicians with deadened faces and dry eyes standing in a closed circle facing outward, caught in a state of rigid, impacted grief.

While the above image was valuable in understanding the dysfunction of the day program system, it was understood as a metaphor that illustrated shared unconscious states of mind of the day program staff rather than an animate system. By creating a metaphor that provided a systems analysis outside of the day program boundaries and bringing that image into the day program system, the intern crossed those system boundaries making them more permeable and bringing new knowledge that resulted in increased functionality of the day program.

An understanding of the above system terms gives group leaders a language/pictorial template to apprehend systems. I suggest that therapists who utilize such whole group concepts as Foulkes's "group matrix" and the self-psychological concept of "group as self/object" can employ systems metaphors to elaborate and operationalize whole group understanding (Foulkes, 1949; Kieffer, 2001).

A Systems Analysis Helps to Ground Clinical Meaning in (Enduring) Contextual Truth

The relational field emphasizes that there are always multiple truths in any given clinical moment. The idea that there is one salient "truth" or that the analyst is the one who can know this truth and deliver it to the patient has been replaced by the concept that meaning is found/constructed in each clinical encounter. For the last ten years there has been vigorous debate in the analytic field about whether such constructed meaning can qualify as "truth" (Eagle et al., 2001; Altman & Davies, 2003; Eagle, 2003; Orange, 2009).

Critics of the relational approach argue that if clinical meaning is dependent on the specifics of each analytic encounter or as Stern says, "a fusion of horizons," enduring patient self-experience becomes elusive:

> In the excessive swing of the pendulum that characterizes the position of the new view theorists—specifically, in maintaining that one constitutes the patient's mind through "interpretive construction"; that there is no preorganized structure of the patient's mind, independent of the interaction with the analyst; that in trying to understand another, one is only addressing one's own subjectivity—In all this, there is the danger that the very existence of the patient's mind structured independently of the analyst is called into question, and that one is in the business of creating, not understanding, the patient.
>
> (Eagle et al., 2001, p. 485)

Although I am not aware of similar critiques in the group field, Schermer touches on the matter in a recent review of Richard Billow's book *Resistance, Rebellion, and Refusal in Groups: The Three R's* (Schermer, 2012). After praising the work as original, indeed courageous, Schermer goes on to question the place of (patient) truth in a relational exchange that focuses on a constantly evolving here-and-now experience: "Billow is really speaking of an evolving truth (with lower case "t") that emerges in dialogue ... Billow gets backed into a solipsistic corner of subjectivity when it comes to 'truth'" (pp. 162–163).

Although most relational writers in the group field do not go so far as to claim that the only patient self is one co-constructed in the moment, the current emphasis by many of our top theorists on "here-and-now" experience as the most valuable therapeutic focus can lead to studied exclusion of enduring self-experience that exists beyond the group boundary (Yalom & Leszcz, 2005; Agazarian, 2004)[9] While these respected group theorists assert that whatever is experienced/learned within the group can be taken home in the form of a more well-informed and elaborated self (and brain), I do believe the almost exclusive emphasis on the here-and-now can leave a patient scratching her head about what just happened and its relevance to life outside of the group.

A systems view includes the effects of the larger, supra-system/context on the group and thus the individual as sub-system within. While such an understanding is valuable as only one piece of learning and is optimized by an affectively charged group experience, it can ground the patient self in a valuable system framework and expand the self descriptively. Thus, I believe that a systems view is both consistent with the relational concept of constructed self or self-states, yet it also provides patients with a more enduring self-definition ("truth") by emphasizing the self in context.

> Lila and Oscar came to couple therapy to work with me on their long-standing somewhat traditional marriage. Now that their children were well launched Lila had returned to the work place while Oscar retired to his home and his computer. Lila was chronically furious at a bewildered Oscar whom she insisted was unwilling to modify his long time role as breadwinner to take on some of the household chores. While I thought many of Lila's beefs were justified, I began to feel frustrated and helpless with Lila's unwillingness to give Oscar airtime in the sessions as well as her insistence that Oscar would "never change."
>
> Lila began a particular session with an escalating diatribe about her overwhelmingly busy day and then launched into a series of "always" and "never" criticisms of how Oscar didn't "get" her. She cited Oscar's insistence on a half hour of her time to discuss plans for an upcoming trip even though "he should realize she didn't have a moment to spare."

> I did my best to empathize with Lila's frustration, noting my growing alliance with Oscar, and then I presented the systems idea that Lila might be carrying the banner for individual needs in the relationship while Oscar was acting in concert with interdependent longings. I went on to say that both states of being were necessary in their marriage.
>
> Ignoring my comments, Lila's voice suddenly softened as she engaged in a seeming digression to bemoan the incompetency of bureaucracies in contemporary life. Her point was that because "everything takes four times as long as it should due to the 'stupidity' of people on the other end of the (phone) line," she could not find time to confer with Oscar and respond to his desires for collaborative decision making.[10]

Some might see Lila's focus on the "here and there" (Hopper, 2003) as a diversion and a retreat from my comment about their marital system. Others might focus on a more experience-near view of possible transference meaning of Lila's comments; perhaps it is I, the therapist, whom Lila finds incompetent and impossible to reach.

I decided however, to take Lila's words more literally and reasoned that by expanding her view of the marriage as a system that was embedded in what many, myself included, see as an increasingly incompetent bureaucratic culture, Lila was freeing herself to view her marriage from a new, more benign perspective, and to consider that bureaucratic inefficiencies rather than Oscar's demands were the true culprits in her state of overwhelm. Being able to view Oscar as a fellow victim of a cultural configuration freed Lila to see her husband as potentially responsive unlike "the person on the other end of the phone line."

Together with this couple new meaning was constructed: the idea that they were dealing with normative tensions between independent and interdependent longings. The articulation of this new meaning allowed some opening of the system and loosening of their previously rigidly perceived roles. Developing a view of the problem as a systems issue led to a new understanding of the marriage in context and helped to break the log jam of projections and unending relativism.

The Place of Systems Thinking in the Intersubjective World

As described above, many relational theorists consider open systems thinking central to understanding the patient/analyst encounter. Grossmark (2007) discusses "dynamic systems theory" as essential to group. His emphasis and that of other writers is on the fluid or ever-changing aspect of the group system. Rubenfeld (2001) pointed out that unlike earlier notions of general systems theory (von Bertalanffy, 1966; Durkin, 1981, Agazarian, 1989) that conceptualized a group, like all living systems, as drawn toward equilibrium and homeostasis, complex systems—and a psychotherapy group is a superb living example—must maintain disequilibrium and instability to adapt to changes in the internal and external environment. Rather than seeing a group as always engaged in maintaining homeostasis, this view sees groups as always engaged in adapting to new and changing circumstances. In particular, perturbations to an open system cause destabilization and turbulence that then open up the opportunity for change (Grossmark, 2007, p. 484).

Such an emphasis on disequilibrium and heterostasis, I believe, represents an incomplete view of how systems function. As detailed above, homeostasis/heterostasis is a complementary process made up of alternating states of balance and disequilibrium. A state of flux or change represented by heterostasis is natural and necessary for a system to remain relevant. Yet, periods of homeostasis are also necessary to integrate new knowledge into existing structures and to elaborate the (self/group) system. Translating such a process into the group, new experience while essential, vitalizing, perhaps even a greater truth, needs to be absorbed by recognizable, enduring self-systems and group dynamics in an analytic endeavor. If there were no state of homeostasis to balance disequilibrium, the constant flow of ever-changing experience would be overwhelming to growth, representing total fragmentation, discontinuity and dissociation—a form of group insanity.

It is true as Grossmark notes, that family, organizational, and self-systems (healthfully and defensively) exhibit a predilection for maintaining existing structures and balance—for example, homeostasis—and that there is great value in a postmodern approach that challenges the enduring "truth" of existing structures and concepts that otherwise can be oppressive. Roger Frie (2009), in the introduction to a book that takes psychoanalytic theory beyond a postmodern emphasis, says:

> For many postmodern psychoanalysts, especially those in the American relational school, postmodernism provides the means to distinguish themselves from classical Freudians and other analytic approaches ... Yet the uncritical adoption of postmodern thinking, and its implementation in psychoanalytic practice, necessarily gives rise to a series of questions: ... how does this play out in a clinical theory that seeks to restore a measure of hope and basic continuity of experience in the individual ... How does the radical decentering of human subjectivity mesh with the reflective capacities of the person upon which therapeutic dialogue and understanding depends?
>
> (p. 15)

The Value of Hermeneutic Thinking

Stern (1997) described the constructivist approach and the hermeneutic philosophy of Gadamer as one that elucidated the construction of meaning. More recently, Donna Orange, psychoanalyst, philosopher, and major contributor to postmodern analytic theory, suggests that "hermeneutic analysis can place the self-experience in (social) and historical context" and that such placement is necessary to analytic work (Orange, 2009).[11] In comparing the philosophies of Derrida and Gadamer, Orange asserts that both philosophical traditions replace "more authoritarian attitudes with a more open and egalitarian relational psychoanalysis, but the tradition of hermeneutics tempers "constructivist skepticism" with "a strong dose of hermeneutic passion for understanding based on an epistemology of perspectival realism," in systems terms, context (Orange, 2009, p. 130). Thus, relational philosophy and systems theory have in common an emphasis on context as a necessary therapeutic focus. Orange adds:

> Another concern ... is that the emphasis on coconstruction in contemporary relational psychoanalysis tends to privilege the here-and-now or the momentary ... The hermeneutic attitude, to which I am more inclined, may not meet Eagle's concern for the loss of the real and enduring in "new view" psychoanalysis (Eagle et al., 2001), but it does emphasize understanding the patient and the analytic pair in multiple historical contexts. Continuity and fluidity are equally important to a psychoanalytic hermeneutics.
>
> (p. 131)

The Systems Lens in Private Practice

It is natural that in the safety and security of a private office, group leaders tend to let the larger context slip out of mind. Whereas in an institution, such as a hospital, interdependence between systems is more salient and thus harder to ignore, in private practice the illusion of independence from the social context is easier to maintain. In fact, in order for a small group to gel and begin to flourish it is necessary that the group frame support the view that events outside the group cannot penetrate the sanctity of the group boundary. Yet, I believe it is a mistake for small group leaders to exclude context from their (potential) awareness. A leader's imagination needs to be able to expand to the larger social surround and to use this view to more fully understand events in the group. Social realities such as insurance companies and managed care and even such positive social events as the American Psychological Association's recent endorsement of group psychotherapy have an impact on small group function.

Managed care engineering can enter group process in direct and destructive ways such as in instances where "assignment" is accepted and patient care is reviewed every few sessions to determine whether or not the patient's treatment "warrants" continued reimbursement. In such cases patients are put into self-defeating postures where financial support of treatment is dependent on the maintenance of severity of illness rather than improved functioning. Such intrusions not only interfere with patient progress but also include a concept of the "provider" as someone whose "greed" needs to be "managed" and whose clinical judgment needs to be questioned and monitored. If private groups are run under such conditions, leaders are better off making patients aware of the above attitudes rather than denying that they have an effect on the ongoing work.

In private groups where therapists "do not accept assignment," other social forces frame and influence ongoing process. Following is an example in which economic/social events operated isomophically to create a whole group resistance.[12]

> Art was a long-time member of a private practice therapy group, one of two men in the six-member group. He was divorced and from time to time discussed problems with dating but his main topic of discussion was his fast-paced job as a commodities trader on Wall Street. Art had a predilection for making and then losing large sums of money within a day or a week, and over time he became convinced that this pattern indicated his deep-seated need to destroy any success he achieved. The group listened to Art's descriptions of sums made and then lost with fascination that turned to horror when Art described losing tens of thousands of dollars in one false move. Women in the group found Art generally sympathetic and likable, alternating mothering then flirting with him. Art's ongoing disasters often took center stage and eventually several members gently asked for more air time. One female member expressed anger at the therapist for letting Art dominate the discourse, chiding the male therapist for "playing favorites." Despite these dissatisfactions there was general sympathy, even protectiveness of Art, who appeared to all as an attractive but deeply troubled man.
>
> Several years passed in this long-term group and Art began to show improvement in that his money losing episodes occurred less frequently. Then, a new group member, Charlie, was introduced into the mix. After a get acquainted period, Charlie, a musician, began to challenge many of Art's statements, seeming to ache for a fight every time Art opened his mouth.
>
> Charlie questioned Art's values and chided him for "always needing to make the next million bucks," and for "crying in his beer, oh sorry, I mean your Barons de Rothschild champagne," when he would "lose enough money to feed a mid-size third world country." Charlie expanded his critique to the entire psychoanalytic enterprise, wondering aloud if he should continue in a group "so focused on building up our egos no matter how perverted our values."
>
> Art appeared defenseless against Charlie's clever critiques and over time Charlie emerged as the clear winner. Instead of defending Art and challenging Charlie's aggressive forays, the group sat back to watch the show. Both men resisted therapist and group attempts to understand their disagreements on a deeper level, either as displaced attacks on the therapist and/or manifestations

> of obsessive competition with other men, but, in truth, these attempts were half-hearted.
>
> Where were the several women who up until now had been defenders of Art? More importantly, where was the group leader and why did he not intervene more forcefully in what clearly emerged as a long, drawn-out scapegoating process? In retrospect it seems like the whole group including the leader became caught in an enactment, co-creating Art as a symbol of reprehensible and thoughtless greed. It was only after the leader associated to and then commented on current economic realities outside the group, that the idea of Art as a symbol for the Wall Street firms, whose policies had brought the US economy to a state of near collapse, was clarified. After identifying Art as the group symbol/scapegoat for an insecure economic climate, the leader remarked that Art as a whole person had been forgotten. He suggested that this "temporary amnesia" about Art might have something to do with current societal panic about the economy and that these fears had penetrated the group. He invited members to talk more directly about their individual economic insecurities as well as their general fears for future stability of the economy. After an extended discussion about these contextual matters, the leader invited the group to close the group boundary indicating that although they couldn't solve national economic problems, they could profitably resume their psychoanalytic work. After group members were able to acknowledge economic fears rather than projecting them onto Art in a scapegoating process, the conflicts between Charlie and Art became much more manageable as "garden variety" competition between two interesting group members.

The above is an example of social context operating to co-create a group resistance within a small group as well as a demonstration of how such a resistance can be commented upon to open up a group system to more internal work. Following is an example of social "difference" replicating itself in a group. Here, the idea is presented that difference as it is defined by social convention needs to be acknowledged and grappled with as social reality before such difference can be metabolized into the ongoing group process.

> Kathy, a thirty-five-year-old from the Mid-West, joined a long-standing group well versed in here-and-now work. She spoke vaguely of marital difficulties and problems with her appearance (she had had two face lifts) and gave incomplete answers to group member questions about various aspects of her life. She appeared as a pretty though aging cheerleader-type whose happy-go-lucky

façade failed to mask a refusal to delve beneath the surface. After numerous attempts to get to know Kathy better, the group gave up and focused on more available members.

A male patient, Dan, spoke of feeling "emasculated" by his boss and his wife and then associated to a lawsuit current in the news in which the plaintiff, a Caucasian male, claimed he was not admitted to a law school because of equal opportunity admission policies. Dan cited this as an example of how "people in the majority" such as he, "are being brought to their knees by this political correctness." He concluded by stating that life was becoming impossible for "your typical white male."

Kathy erupted triumphantly saying, "ah ha, I knew I wouldn't have to wait long to find racial prejudice in this group." The group was taken aback by Kathy's outburst although some members agreed that those who opposed equal opportunity measures betrayed prejudice. Another contingent of the group disagreed, saying that the group and Kathy in particular were failing to understand Dan's feelings of helplessness and his experience that the "deck was stacked against him." All agreed that Dan was externalizing his problems by blaming others and failing to examine his own intrapsychic and interpersonal issues that led to his chronic feelings of powerlessness in the world.

No one, however, was prepared for what happened next. A group member expressed curiosity about the intensity of Kathy's reaction to Dan. Kathy in turn explained that although she appeared Caucasian, both her biological parents were African Americans who had nurtured her ability to "pass" in white society. In fact during her childhood, Kathy's parents did not allow her to play with other Black kids in the neighborhood. Instead, they dressed her up "like a doll in frilly dresses" and made her "sit quietly on a chair" each and every day. Kathy went on to marry a Caucasian corporate executive and to frequent "high society" parties where she often witnessed surprisingly blatant racial prejudice, "at the highest levels of business and culture."

The group was stunned. Many felt guilty of getting caught in racial prejudice but they also felt tricked by Kathy's silence about her racial origins. By creating the illusion that the group was all white, it can be argued that Kathy succeeded in ferreting out racial bias. Yet, Kathy's withholding of information was also an enactment as "passing for white" was an automatic aspect of Kathy's identity presentation. By "passing" Kathy co-created the experience where once her true identity was known others felt the same emotional charge about race that Kathy harbored. (The group leader who had been aware of Kathy's racial origins, was startlingly caught in the enactment in that Kathy's true racial identity "slipped out" of her mind.)

The group leader had a number of choices of focus. She might have commented on Kathy's behavior as a defense, emphasizing how by keeping her racial identity a secret, Kathy had managed to offend or alienate others in the context of getting to know them. The leader could also have commented on the interpersonal locus, asking group members to speak about their feelings regarding Kathy's withholding of information in order to give Kathy feedback about the effect of her self-presentation on others.

Instead, the leader chose to underline the social or contextual reality inherent in Kathy's complex identity and self-experience. She invited the entire group to reflect upon how racial and ethnic differences affect all of us in unfamiliar social settings. She suggested that it is a fact of our social lives that placed into unfamiliar situations we tend to search for people like us and have initial suspicions about those we perceive as "other."

Kathy treats herself as a stereotype, presenting her person as a lightning rod and drawing out hidden prejudice, sleuthing secretly for bias not far below the surface. Kathy functions in a society that reinforces her false self-presentation, what clinicians might term her narcissistic defenses. The group leader chose to comment on the above contextual reality hoping to find a common ground of experience for the group and for Kathy. By commenting on the racially conflicted culture in which we all live, she encouraged Kathy to connect with others in the group.

Eventually Kathy would need to look inward to achieve greater understanding of how she acted out her inner world, but first it was necessary for her and the group to acknowledge the ways the culture promotes, even locks in, Kathy's deeply held and denied self-hate. In focusing on cultural realities, the group leader not only accessed a common experience for all group members, but also began to build a whole group boundary where the culture inside the group could develop a level of sensitivity and understanding that differentiated it from its social context.

Combining an Intersubjective and Systems View to Prioritize Therapist Interventions

> An LGBT group had been meeting for two years in a counseling center. Patients were graduate students with various areas of concentration and for the last year the group had comprised eight male patients and two female leaders, one of whom was lesbian and the other heterosexual. The heterosexual leader took a two-month leave of absence during the first part of the second year to give birth. The lesbian leader was also pregnant at the time of this particular session and planned to leave the group permanently during the upcoming summer break.

> One man began the session by speaking at length about his relationship with his father whom he did not know for the first twenty-five years of his life. As an adult, this patient who was raised in another country "found" his father in the United States and had several meetings with the man. He had just heard that his father, who lived on the opposite coast, had been hospitalized for "seizures" with an uncertain prognosis.
>
> The patient spoke movingly about the possibility that just as he had "found" his father he might lose him again. He recounted a fatherless childhood where he created a "pretend or fantasy father." He described the fantasy father in detail and spoke about how comforting it was to have this imagined father always with him. He stated that even if his real father died, he could continue to be comforted by the presence of this "first (fantasy) Dad."
>
> The group including the leadership was touched by the man's story and several members let him know how much they were saddened by what he recounted. Next, a second man spoke hesitantly about an experience he had had during the previous week: in the course of waking from a nap, he had "imagined or remembered" something important. He was hesitant to recount the experience in detail for fear that the group would think he was "crazy." He added that what he was going to tell them would be both "a lie but also a truth." He went on to describe an image of himself as a child who was raped from behind by an adult, most likely his father. He added that the memory was terrifying; and he was not certain it actually happened although it had the ring of truth. A theme of "real and imagined" seemed to be forming with ambivalence about whether it was important to distinguish between the two forms of experience.
>
> At the end of the session as patients left the room, a third group member came up to the lesbian leader and asked to speak to her in private. They went into another room where this patient stated forcefully that he had decided that the group was not for him. He said that he was very different from the other patients, much healthier, and that he intended to leave the group for good. The leader encouraged this patient to bring these plans into the next session adding that there were most likely others who shared his thoughts and feelings.

What can an intersubjective focus highlight in this group session? This case was reported to me as an outside consultant and I listened to the recounted group process with growing emotion. All of the wrenching loss I have ever experienced or ever will experience seemed to be condensed in an intense, momentary feeling state as my eyes filled with tears in reaction to the story of the fantasy father. I felt as if I were about to lose something precious and that such a loss was too much to bear. I was spilling over with loss and dread.

Such feelings helped me consider the depth of feeling about the impending loss of the lesbian leader and a possible unconscious belief that the group could not go on without her. I also considered that the group leaders might share these unconscious beliefs and might have signaled to the group that such feelings were too frightening to discuss openly.

I also considered that group members experienced the group as a refuge, a place where instead of being marginalized as a minority, they represent the majority. In connection with this, having a homosexual leader, even if she was of another gender, may have added to deep feelings that this particular group was precious and unique. When the heterosexual leader was absent for two months on maternity leave, group members indulged in criticisms of her and her supposed stereotypic heterosexuality, referring to her as a "breeder." However, some discussed opposite feelings: how difficult it is for gay people to have children, implying longings to parent.

When the lesbian leader started to "show" her own pregnancy, members most likely felt betrayed, but there was probably also delight that their homosexual leader could create life. We can speculate there were desires to protect her from feelings of envy and aggression (common patient reactions to therapist pregnancy) as well as whole group (unconscious) sentiments that acknowledging the impending loss of this "bearer of life" was too painful.

Using a systems lens, I looked to the extra group context for additional understanding and considered that the patient who pulled the leader aside after the session stating urgently that he needed to leave the group, signaled that the group system was not containing all of the elements that had to be processed. A systems approach would understand the words of this patient as important elements to bring into the system boundaries. The group might be attempting to create a homeostasis by leaving an important reality (the leader's plans to leave) outside the session and by insisting that "fantasy is preferable to reality." The communication from the patient after the group was over brought up the brutal fact that people can leave "for real." Systems thinking would suggest that this harsh reality was critical information to bring into the group system at this time.

I decided that the words of this third member represented a mandate that the group must deal with "real departures" as a first priority. I therefore suggested to the leaders that they needed to remind the group of the lesbian leader's departure and to help the group bear such difficult processing. I added that leaders needed to foster a group system that could expand and contain a host of new feelings, deep grief, hot anger, feeling used and abused, and a conviction that something precious and irreplaceable was being lost.

Conclusion

In this chapter I have reviewed systems theory to provide group analysts with a language to expand the field of intersubjective understanding. Systems theory by definition concerns itself with systems and hierarchical levels of a system and therefore can be utilized to find new meanings in patterns within a small group as well in as in the larger context. My goal has been to show that adding a systems view to the repertoire of group leader/patient understandings can provide patients with a self-experience that is more enduring yet one that remains responsive to an ever-changing relational field.

What happens to our ideas of intersubjectivity and even subjectivity when we see people in groups moved by pressures and configurations that they are not only unconscious of but are also not fairly located in their individual selves? The one-person idea of the unconscious may say something about this, but it does not come close to an adequate description. How then do we integrate ideas of intersubjectivity when we think of systems? This chapter represents an attempt to begin to answer such questions.

Notes

1 In fact, it questionable whether the word "technique" still applies to what is now conceptualized as a mutual encounter.
2 For purposes of the current discussion I will use the terms "intersubjective," "constructivist," and "relational" interchangeably. Schermer in a recent review describes self-psychology, relational psychology, and intersubjectivity as "cousins," implying overlapping DNA (meaning) but also significant differences (Schermer, 2012). Group theorists who refer to themselves as "relational" emphasize the centrality of therapist subjectivity in the therapeutic endeavor in contrast to a search for "objective" patient truth and describe a therapeutic relationship that is to my mind essentially intersubjective (Dluhy & Rubenfeld, 2004).
3 An informal count of the percentage of group experts who gave "how to" advice in a recently published book, *Complex Dilemmas in Group Therapy*, edited by Motherwell and Shay (2005), indicated that at least 50 percent of these experts used a systems approach as part of their solutions to group leader dilemmas.
4 In the early 1970s I attended my first American Group Psychotherapy Conference. The man who brought me to the conference suggested that I accompany him to a meeting, chaired by Helen Durkin, where the application of General Systems Theory to small groups was discussed, debated, and developed. I did not realize at the time that I was witnessing history and that many of the AGPA members who participated in this "think tank," which continued to meet for many years, would become pivotal figures in the group therapy field. I want to thank my husband, Bernard Frankel, for taking me to this historic meeting.
5 I use the term "classical" systems theory to distinguish the theory from Systems Centered Therapy developed by Yvonne Agazarian and implemented by others (Agazarian, 2004). SCT is a well-known body of organized theory and technique that is derived from the tradition of systems thinking but represents a unique approach to group that diverges in theoretical detail and application from the present discussion.
6 The book is out of print but can be found in most libraries or purchased online.
7 Many psychoanalysts liken isomorphy to the analytic concept of parallel process and such a comparison is enlightening to a point. Parallel process, however, describes an unconscious process between individuals; isomorphy identifies similarities of system meaning or organization between system levels.
8 When change occurs on one level of the system in the direction of greater functionality, such change can "trickle up or down" into other levels of the system hierarchy. Change can be manifested by new behavior or simply be represented by an increase in

knowledge. A more thorough discussion of such hierarchical system change is beyond the scope of the current discussion.

9 Robert Grossmark says, "I agree that the concept of the here-and-now needs to be re-evaluated and unpacked" (personal communication). He thinks, however, that this represents a somewhat divergent issue from the criticisms of Eagle et al. who refer to "objective truth." I believe including a system context in a search for meaning does include a level of "truth" that endures for the patient beyond what is usually referred to as (subjective), relational truth.

10 The triad of couple plus therapist has many systems dynamics similar to those of a small group and thus illustrates well the value of contextualizing clinical work.

11 I would like to express gratitude to psychoanalyst Jennifer Leighton who introduced me to the work of Donna Orange in the course of writing this chapter.

12 Previous clinical examples have been generally representative of occurring group processes. The following two examples represent a compilation of several different groups combined to highlight the clinical issues under discussion.

References

Agazarian, Y.M. (1989) Group-as-a-whole systems theory and practice. *Group*, 13 (3/4): 131–155.

Agazarian, Y.M. (2004) *Systems Centered Therapy For Groups*. New York and London: Karnac.

Altman, N. and Davies, J.M. (2003) A plea for constructive dialogue, *Journal of the American Psychoanalytic Association*, 51S: 145–161.

American Group Psychotherapy Conference Open Session. (1992) *Contrasting Views of Representative Group Events*. Audiotape.

Bertalanffy, L. von (1950) The theory of open systems in physics and biology. *Science*, III: 23–29.

Bertalanffy, L. von (1966) *General Systems Theory: Foundation, Development, Applications*. New York: Brazilier.

Bernard, H.S. (1994) Difficult patients and challenging situations. In H.S. Bernard and K.R. MacKenzie (eds.) *Basics of Group Psychotherapy* (pp. 123–156). New York: Guilford Press.

Billow, R.M. (2010) *Resistance, Rebellion and Refusal in Groups: The 3 R's*. New International Library of Group Analysis. New York and London: Karnac.

Cohn, B.R. (1988) Keeping the group alive: Dealing with resistance in a long-term group of psychotic patients. *International Journal of Group Psychotherapy*, 38: 319–335.

Cohn, B.R. (1994) Recycling Yalom: Using a systems analysis to facilitate work in inpatient groups. *Group Analysis*, 27: 407–418.

Cohn, B.R. (2005) Boundary issues: Creating the group envelope. In L. Motherwell & J. Shay, J. (eds.) *Complex Dilemmas in Group Psychotherapy: Pathways to Resolution* (pp. 3–12). New York and London: Brunner-Routledge.

Cohn, B.R. (2007) Reader's forum, contextualizing the self: Integrating a systems perspective into psychoanalytic therapy. *International Journal of Group Psychotherapy*, 57: 387–395.

Cohen, B.D. & Schermer, V.L. (2001) Therapist self-disclosure in group psychotherapy from an intersubjective and self-psychological standpoint. *Group*, 25: 41–57.

Dluhy, M. & Rubenfeld, S. (2004) Self-psychological and relational advances in group therapy. *Group*, 28: 245–258.

Durkin, J.E. (ed.) (1981) *Living Groups: Group Psychotherapy and General Systems Theory*. New York: Brunner/Mazel.

Eagle, M. (2003) The postmodern turn in psychoanalysis: a critique. *Psychoanalytic Psychology*, 20: 411–424.

Eagle, M.N., Wakefield, J.C., & Wolitsky, D.L. (2003) Interpreting Mitchell's constructivism: Reply to Altman and Davies. *Journal of the American Psychoanalytic Association*, 51S: 163–178.

Eagle, M.N., Wolitsky, D.L., & Wakefield, J.C. (2001) The analyst's knowledge and authority: Critique of the "new view" in psychoanalysis. *Journal of the American Psychoanalytic Association*, 49: 457–488.

Foulkes, S.H. (1949) *Introduction to Group-Analytic Psychotherapy*. New York: Grune & Stratton.

Frie, R. (2009) Introduction: Coherence or fragmentation? Modernism, postmodernism, and the search for continuity. In R. Frie & D. Orange (eds.) *Beyond Postmodernism: New Dimensions in Clinical Theory and Practice* (pp. 1–23). London and New York: Routledge.

Frie, R. & Orange, D. (eds.) (2009) *Beyond Postmodernism: New Dimensions in Clinical Theory and Practice*. London and New York: Routledge.

Gans, J.S. & Alonso, A. (1998) Difficult patients: Their construction in group therapy. *International Journal of Group Psychotherapy*, 48: 311–326.

Grossmark, R. (2007) The edge of chaos: Enactment, disruption, and emergence in group psychotherapy. *Psychoanalytic. Dialogues*, 17: 479–499.

Hopper, E. (2003) *The Social Unconscious: Selected Papers*. International Library of Group Analysis 22. London: Jessica Kingsley.

Hopper, E. & Weinberg, H. (eds.) (2011) *The Social Unconscious in Persons, Groups, and Societies, Mainly Theory*. New International Library of Group Analysis: London: Karnac.

Kahn, G. & Feldman, D. (2012) Relationship focused group therapy to improve neuropsychological regulation in couples and individuals. In I. Harwood, W. Stone, & M. Pines (eds.) *Self-Experiences in Group Revisited* (pp. 72–87). New York: Routledge.

Kernberg, O.F. (1973) Psychoanalytic object relations theory, group processes and administration. *Annals of Psychoanalysis*, 1: 363–386.

Kieffer, C.C. (2001) Phases of group development: a view from self-psychology. *Group*, 25 (1/2): 91–105.

Klein, R.H. & Kugal, B. (1981) Inpatient group psychotherapy from a systems perspective: Reflections through a glass darkly. *International Journal of Group Psychotherapy*, 31: 311–328.

Livingston, M. (2012) Sustained empathic focus: Intersubjectivity and intimacy in the treatment of couples. In I. Harwood, W. Stone, & M. Pines (eds.) *Self-Experiences in Group Revisited* (pp. 57–71). New York: Routledge.

MacKenzie, K.R. (1990) *Time-Limited Group Psychotherapy*. Washington DC: American Psychiatric Press.

Motherwell, L. & Shay, J.J. (2005) *Complex Dilemmas in Group Therapy: Pathways to Resolution*. New York: Brunner-Routledge.

Orange, D. (2009) Toward the art of living dialogue: between constructivism and hermeneutics in psychoananalytic thinking. In R. Frie & D. Orange (eds.) *Beyond Postmodernism: New Dimensions in Clinical Theory and Practice* (pp. 117–142). New York: Routledge.

Rubenfeld, S. (2001) Group therapy and complexity theory. *International Journal of Group Psychotherapy*, 51 (4): 449–472.

Rutan, J.S. (2005) Treating the difficult patient in groups. In L. Motherwell & J. Shay (eds.) *Complex Dilemmas in Group Psychotherapy: Pathways to Resolution* (pp. 41–49). New York: Brunner-Routledge.

Schermer, V.L. (2012) [Book review] Resistance, rebellion, and refusal in groups: The 3 R's. By Richard M. Billow, *International Journal of Group Psychotherapy*, 62: 161–164.

Shapiro, E.R. & Carr, A.W. (1991) *Lost In Familiar Places*. New Haven and London: Yale University Press.

Stern, D.B. (1997) *Unformulated Experience: From Dissociation to Imagination*. Hillsdale, NJ: Analytic Press.

Stern, D.B. (2003) The fusion of horizons: Dissociation, enactment, and understanding. *Psychoanalytic Dialogues*, 13: 843–873.

Stolorow, R.D. (1997) Dynamic, dyadic, intersubjective systems: An evolving paradigm for psychoanalysis. *Psychoanalytic Psychology*, 14: 337–346.

Stolorow, R.D. & Atwood, G.E. (1992) *Contexts of Being: The Intersubjective Foundations of Psychological Life*. Hillsdale, NJ: Analytic Press.

Wright, F. (2004) Being seen, moved, disrupted, and reconfigured: Group leadership from a relational perspective. *International Journal of Group Psychotherapy*, 54: 235–250.

Yalom, I.D. & Leszcz, M. (2005) *Theory and Practice of Group Psychotherapy*. 5th edn. New York: Basic Books.

Chapter 12

Rethinking Tavistock
Enactment, the Analytic Third, and the Implications for Group Relations

Gregory S. Rizzolo

The past two decades have seen a growing interest among psychoanalysts, psychologists, and neuroscientists of various theoretical orientations in what has become known as the concept of intersubjectivity (Gallese, Eagle, & Migone, 2007; Coelho & Figueiredo, 2003; Benjamin, 1995). Although theorists from different fields and schools of thought have used the term differently, one interesting and increasingly popular usage pertains to the kind of relationship that can develop between mutual subjects, rather than between a subject and the object of his drive or developmental need (Benjamin, 1995). This version of intersubjectivity refers to the realm of experience in which the other is seen neither as an intrapsychic object, nor as an external object that can be used as a vehicle for drive discharge, but rather as a separate subject with a distinct set of mental experiences. With the growing interest in this area of experience, writers have revised a number of familiar concepts, such as projective identification and enactment, and introduced new ones, such as the analytic third (Ogden, 1994, 2004a; Benjamin, 1995, 2004; Aron, 2003).

However, the Tavistock model of group relations seems to have had trouble responding to this way of thinking. It continues to depict the mind in terms of reified mental items or things that can be passed around, as if from one isolated-mind-container to the next. Furthermore, its characterization of the group consultant as a detached leader with inscrutable, or immaculate, perception into the group's unconscious seems to render it incompatible with the intersubjective emphasis on the co-creation of meaning (Gertler & Izod, 2004). Largely as a result of these issues, it has been difficult to make use of the Tavistock model in extending intersubjective thinking to the study and practice of group relations.

In this chapter, I would like to revisit some of the central concepts of the Tavistock model. Through a critical discussion of these ideas, I shall try to initiate a dialogue about intersubjectivity and its implications for our understanding of group relations. I propose that an intersubjective approach requires us to look not at how reified mental contents are being moved around within a given group, but rather at how intersubjective experiences can be co-created by the group members and their conference consultants. I shall focus on how enactments between the participants in a group can lead to a transformation of self and other through the experience of mutual subjugation and the realization of a shared third space. In addition, I shall introduce the concept of the alien group self. I argue that if the consultant cannot hold the group in mind, that is, if he cannot cultivate and maintain an empathic recognition of the group's subjective experience, without pressuring the group to conform to his own experience or theoretical presuppositions, then the group can form a group self in accommodation with his subjective experience of it.

I believe that this shift in perspective has several implications for the theory and practice of group relations. It suggests that the consultant is not a neutral, rational observer of the group life, but is inevitably an unconscious participant in co-creating the phenomena that he observes. Moreover, it implies that experiences in groups belong authentically to those who experience them. That is to say: members do not "contain" projections for the group in some impersonal way, such that they can return the projections and disown responsibility for what they have done or experienced while serving as a "container." From this vantage point, by contrast, the group can facilitate the emergence of authentic and previously dissociated aspects of self-experience for each of its members.

To understand the Tavistock model, one must first understand the concept of projective identification, particularly the way in which Bion adapted it from Kleinian theory to make sense of group dynamics. In the Schreber case, Freud (1911) described projection as a process in which the individual suppresses an internal perception, which undergoes a process of distortion and ultimately re-enters consciousness in the form of an external perception. It differs from projective identification in that it involves the projection of discrete perceptions, and not entire ego structures (Greenberg & Mitchell, 1983).

Projective identification, by contrast, describes a process in which intrapsychic conflict does lead the individual to split off entire ego segments and project them into an object (Klein, 1946, 1959). Klein introduced the concept in her discussion of the schizoid position. The newborn infant forms a libidinal cathexis with the mother's breast. At the same time, however, he protects himself from internal persecution by projecting the death instinct into the breast. He then experiences the breast as both a "good" and a "bad" object. He introjects the good breast, which becomes a focal point of cohesion in his nascent ego. At the same time, however, he introjects the bad breast in an unconscious attempt to gain control over it. Now ridden with internal conflict between his good and bad parts, he is forced to project one of these parts out into the world.

Projective identification originally described an intrapsychic process involving just one person and his intrapsychic fantasies about evacuating parts of himself into another person (Mitchell & Black, 1995; Meissner, 2009). However, a footnote in Klein's "Notes on some schizoid mechanisms" (1946) emphasizes that the projector projects parts of himself not just onto, but also "into" his object (p. 8). This note has been a source of inspiration for those who prefer to think of projective identification as having an interpersonal component, in which the projected material leaves the mind of the projector and takes up residence within the mind of a recipient.

Bion (1959, 1962) was among the first theorists to rework the idea of projective identification in a way that bridged the gap between the intrapsychic and the interpersonal. He believed that psychotic anxiety could lead an individual to split off parts of himself and project them into a recipient, who would cooperate by introjecting them. To become the projector's container, Bion felt that the recipient needed to have a certain valence—a sort of magnetic attraction that could draw the projected material to him. In the role of container, the recipient's personality was thought to be "obliterated" (Bion, 1961, p. 178). He became an "automaton" in the other's fantasy, until he could give the projection back. This way of thinking turned the process from a fantasy that existed just in the mind of the projector into an interpersonal interaction that involved the unconscious participation of at least two people.

In "Experiences in groups" (1961), Bion applied the idea of projective identification as an intrapsychic–interpersonal process to the study of irrational group phenomena. He began by assuming that the group was greater than the sum of its parts. Therefore, it made sense to speak about the behavior and mental life of the group-as-a-whole, without making reference to any of the group's individual members. On a conscious level, a group charged with a particular job, or task, might show "work group activity," mental functioning designed to further the task that it has been organized to accomplish (p. 188). Unconsciously, however, psychotic anxiety—the fear of annihilation by the death instinct—would typically cause the group to regress to the schizoid defenses of splitting and projective identification. The group would unconsciously split off the seemingly dangerous parts of itself and project them into a member or external object with the right valence. This recipient would then contain the unwanted parts. Thus the group would act "as if" it had convened for the purpose of defending against its anxiety (p. 94).[1]

Theorists in the Tavistock tradition draw on Bion's idea of projective identification in order to understand irrational experiences in groups and social systems in a variety of different contexts (Hayden & Molenkamp, 2004). The Tavistock conference model, however, is primarily focused on increasing awareness of group dynamics through experiential learning in the context of day and residential conferences. These conferences are staffed by teams of consultants with varying levels of didactic and experiential training in the model, with a conference director in the highest position of authority. The membership, by contrast, typically consists of students, mental health professionals, legal and business professionals, and others who are interested in group dynamics. The design of a Tavistock conference typically includes a variety of events, each of which provides a different context for examining the psychodynamics of the group itself.

Whereas some events focus on the real-time unfolding of group processes, other events are geared toward the reflective examination of events that have already occurred within the conference. Hayden and Molenkamp (2004) provide a useful description of typical events that one might expect to encounter on the conference schedule. I quote it at length in order to give unfamiliar readers a sense of what a typical conference might involve:

> **Conference Opening:** In this initial event, the staff and members meet each other as groups. The Conference Director states the task of the conference [e.g., to provide a context for the study of group dynamics], gives some background information, and outlines the structure of the events. Lately some Directors have transformed the opening into a joining event in which the members and staff are invited to state their reasons for being at the conference. This approach is controversial because it implies to some a warming up of the relations between staff and members that may weaken the transferential qualities of the relations and thereby deprive members of potential learning.
>
> **Small Study Group:** Eight to twelve members are assigned to a group, usually mixed and balanced for maximum heterogeneity. A particular consultant works with the study group to facilitate its task of examining its own behavior in the here and now.
>
> **Large Study Group:** All members of the conference (anywhere from 20–90 participants) meet together with the task of studying their own behavior in a situation in which face-to-face interaction is problematic or impossible. Two to four consultants, depending on the number of members, are assigned by the Conference Director to provide consultation to the Large Group's task, which, like the Small Study Group, is to examine its own behavior in the here-and-now.
>
> **Intergroup Event:** After the Director's opening description of the task and the format of the event, members are free to form groups of their own choosing. The task of the event is to study relations as they happen between and among groups. In order to provide consultation for the intergroup task, staff members are assigned to specific sectors, or rooms, where members may choose to meet and receive consultation of their work.
>
> **Institutional Event:** This event also begins with a description of the event by the Director. Members are again free to form groups as they wish. The staff, however, are not assigned to specific member workspaces; instead, the staff members meet as a group themselves, in public, so that group members can observe their functioning if they wish. If consultation is desired, staff members are available on request to consult single groups and intergroup meetings, and representatives of groups are invited to interact with the staff group.

Role Analysis Group: The Role Analysis Group is a non-experientially based session that offers members an opportunity to reflect, with the assistance of one or more consultants, on the role(s) each has taken so far in the conference. It generally allows them an opportunity to think about how they would like to apply what they have learned in the conference to their continuing participation.

Conference Discussion: This event, which occurs toward the end of the conference, provides an opportunity for all members and staff to discuss the events of the conference and to begin making meaning out of their experiences together. One focus often held by the staff is to understand the system of the conference as a whole; there is no attempt, however, to provide closure or summary.

(pp. 147–149)

As a preliminary look at the above descriptions indicates, the conference events vary between those with a "here and now," experiential focus (e.g., the large and small study groups), and those with a reflective function (e.g., the role analysis group) where prior conference events are examined. In addition, each event manipulates the boundaries and frame of the setting (e.g., small v. large groups; open v. closed groups; one group v. many groups), exploring the impact of these perturbations on the functioning of the group as a whole.

One might attempt to define psychoanalysis in terms of what Gill (1984) has termed intrinsic criteria (e.g., the induction of a regressive transference neurosis, the centrality of the analysis of the transference) and extrinsic criteria (e.g., a trained analyst, session frequency, the use of a couch, an "analyzable" patient). However, beyond the enumeration of these generic criteria, it can be difficult or impossible to predict with any certainty how a given session will unfold or what the analysis will look like within a particular dyad. Similarly, beyond a description of the conference frame, the guiding theoretical framework, and the central focus on the group's psychodynamics as they occur during the conference itself, it would be difficult to give the reader a more concrete or specific idea of what might transpire within a group in the context of a Tavistock conference. The uncertainty inherent in surrendering oneself to such a process, and the anxieties that are implicitly evoked, become a central part of the groups experience in the conference.

The anxiety that members often experience on entering a Tavistock conference can relate in part to the relatively open and unrestricted role that they are given within the group. At the conference opening, members are typically invited to do whatever will enhance their learning (Hayden & Molenkamp, 2004, p. 151). Members often forget this invitation, however, and begin to comply with their fantasies of what the staff wants or expects them to do. The group's efforts to cope with its anxiety by complying with the staff become grist for the mill, as the consultants work interpretively to bring the implicit group processes into reflective awareness. A tension tends to develop between the group's reflective functioning and its tendency to become submerged in projective processes and collective action to cope with anxiety. Different group members are thought to take on different roles as they become recipients, or containers, for different aspects of the group's unconscious. The group then struggles to understand how it is using various different members to contain the disavowed parts of itself that it is too anxious to hold.

The consultant's task, as defined by Hayden and Molenkamp (2004), is to fulfill a carefully defined role, which depends on "strict adherence" to the objective of facilitating the group's learning to the exclusion of all other concerns. To this end, the consultant "consults only to the group, not to individual members of the group, and only within the time boundaries prescribed" (p. 150). Furthermore, because it is seen as inconsistent with their primary objective, the consultants "do not engage in social niceties, advice-giving, nurturance, or direction." Although the authors do not articulate the logic behind this abstinent stance, it appears to reflect the Tavistock model's origins in object relations theories grounded in drive metapsychology. From this perspective, to engage in supportive behavior must, beneath the surface, represent the gratification of a libidinal wish or the collusion with groups' defense against a hostile feeling toward the consultants or other members. Gratification and collusion stand in contrast to the objective of harnessing neutralized drive energies for the purposes of thinking about the group.

Rather than engaging in gratification or collusion with the group, consultants are trained to maintain a neutral position with respect to the group's collective fantasy life and their own subjective experiences of the group. Although "consultants may not always be fully conscious of what is happening in the group," they are instructed to focus consistently on the group's processes and to present observations and interpretations in a way that will increase the group's awareness of its own psychodynamics (Hayden & Molenkamp, 2004, p. 150). Hayden and Molenkamp describe four specific kinds of intervention:

> **Description:** The consultant may simply describe what is seen; for example, no male members have spoken for the last ten minutes, the female members are seated opposite the male consultant, or certain words or phrases have become part of the group's language. Such descriptions, unalloyed feedback, call attention to the dynamic configurations of the group or to other observable data about the group.
>
> **Process Observation:** In this type of intervention, the consultant may comment on participation patterns of activity, the development of norms, emotional expression, and other aspects of how the group is pursuing its work task and/or engaging in the survival task.
>
> **Thematic Development:** Consultants who are attuned to the mythic, archetypal dynamics of the group may cast their interventions in terms of

primitive aggression or sexuality that threatens to disrupt the group's work task. At times, the group may be re-creating or re-experiencing the primal horde dynamics of incest or parricide or other symbolic events chronicled in mythology and fairytales.

Mondo: In Zen practice, the teacher often responds to questions with abrupt, pithy remarks designed to produce instant enlightenment, or *satori*, by calling attention to the obviousness or the absurdity of the question. Some consultants offer similar interventions, designed to shock the group into an immediate awareness of what is happening.

(pp. 150–151)

The prescribed role of the consultant, including the interventions available to him, locate him in a position that is similar to that of the classically trained analyst, with respect to his own countertransference and his privileged perception into the unconscious of his object of study. He is entrusted with the task of simultaneously being a part of the group and maintaining reflective distance, controlling his own mental life sufficiently to maintain analytic objectivity. He then uses observations and interpretations in order to cultivate a benign split in the group between an experiential and reflective position, reflecting the split that he must work to maintain within his own psyche in order to serve his analytic function.

Having discussed Bion's expansion of the concept of projective identification and its role in the Tavistock model, I would like to address three ways in which this concept makes it difficult for us to integrate the model with an intersubjective approach.[2] To begin, this way of thinking about projective identification presupposes an epistemological difference with the intersubjective approach. The model assumes that there is an objective reality that can be accessed through neutral observation from a position outside of the group life. It consists of good and bad introjects that can be detected and tracked as they move from one container to the next. An intersubjective approach would suggest, by contrast, that psychic reality is the product of interaction between all of the people in a group. From this perspective, insight is co-created in the context of a particular field or system. Mental life is not discovered, but created through interactions between self and other.

In addition, these approaches differ in their understanding of what motivates psychological life. In the Tavistock model, psychic life is motivated by the libido and the death instinct. These drives power the ego. The ego is composed, in turn, of drive-cathected introjects from infancy (e.g., the good and bad breast). Irrational group phenomena result when conflict between members' introjects leads to splitting and projective identification. From an intersubjective viewpoint, by contrast, the main tendency of the mind is to establish subject and object relations (Benjamin, 1995; Stern, 2005). The dialectic between subject/object relations is seen as central to establishing a creative life in relation to others. As I shall attempt to demonstrate later in this chapter, group life looks different when viewed through this lens instead of the lens of an instinct model.

These models differ, finally, in their understanding of causality and the nature of change. The Tavistock model takes a linear approach. It assumes that psychological experiences can be explained by tracing them back through a series of proportional, cause-and-effect links that already exist in the minds of the relevant people (Galatzer-Levy, 2004; Stern, 2005). For example, let us suppose that a group member experiences an emotion that seems stronger than what he claims he "really" feels. This model assumes that there must be a proportional cause for the intense feeling. It finds no such cause for the affect within the individual's psyche. Accordingly, it suggests that the individual is containing something for the group. It appears, therefore, that the individual's affect resulted linearly from a proportional cause: the group's powerful projection.

Intersubjective thinking, by contrast, implies a non-linear approach. From this perspective, subjective experience is seen as the product of chaotic interactions between subjects, rather than as the result of a linear series of proportional causes and effects (Galatzer-Levy, 2004, 2009; Kieffer, 2007). The mind can be thought of as a subsystem within a larger environment. Small changes in the environment can create pathways for disproportionately large reorganizations in the system. The environment thus facilitates rather than causes the reorganization of subjective experience. Returning to my example, someone experiences an emotion that seems stronger than what he "really" feels. From this viewpoint, his feeling of unreality indicates that the group has created an atmosphere in which a significant reorganization of his self has become possible. The affect feels "unreal" because it reflects a novel and unexpected dimension of self-experience. The complex interaction between multiple systemic variables may be seen as contributing to the development of an environment in which unexpected forms of experience became possible.

By adhering to Bion's model of projective identification, and to the notion of the consultant as a neutral observer of the group's projections, the Tavistock model seems to render itself incompatible with these aspects of an intersubjective approach.[3] I shall now turn to examine how experiences in groups can be thought of as the product of interaction between mutual participants in intersubjective relationships. As Litowitz suggests, intersubjectivity appears to be a concept that can be integrated into a number of different approaches (personal communication, November 12, 2009). It is often associated with the work of Orange, Atwood, and Stolorow (2001). However, it also plays an important role in the work of relational Winnicottians (e.g., Benjamin, 1995, 2004) and neo-Kleinians (e.g., Ogden 1994, 2004a). In addition, it plays a role in the developmental theories of Stern (1985) and Fonagy et al. (2002), and it appears in Chodorow's (2004) essay on the American Independent tradition. While many of these theorists use this term, there is little consensus about what it is or what it might mean for psychoanalytic theory and practice.

Some approaches emphasize the central importance of an intersubjective field in shaping our subjective experiences of ourselves and others (e.g. Stolorow & Atwood, 1992). The unconscious is thought to consist not only of repressed thoughts, feelings, and wishes, but also of potential mental activity that has been unvalidated and remains unformulated in the context of one's relationships (Stolorow & Atwood, 1992; Stern, 2003). Thus, we need the other's recognition to experience potential aspects of our own subjectivity. What we can and cannot know about ourselves and others depends on what is permitted and what is prohibited in the matrix of our intersecting subjectivities (Gerson, 2004).

Although I too find it useful to think in terms of an intersubjective field, it is important to note that this approach has been met with criticism on two significant accounts. First of all, it does not distinguish adequately between relationships in which the other is perceived as an internal object, and those in which he is perceived as a separate subject (Benjamin, 1999). Second, it tends to emphasize how one's self is influenced by what the other can or cannot recognize in one's experience. That is, the self is typically the recipient of empathic attunement. It neglects how the experience of empathizing, that is, being the one who recognizes the other, can also be essential for self-development. To experience our subjectivity in relation to the other, I believe that one must not only be recognized by the other but also be able to recognize him as a separate subject.

For these reasons, it seems necessary to think more specifically about the dialectic between our relationship to the other as an object and our relationship to him as a subject. Winnicott (1969) first articulated this dialectic in his paper on object relating and the development of object usage. In his terminology, object-relating describes a way of engaging with the other in which the individual seeks to assert his omnipotence, relating to him primarily through projective mechanisms and internalization. These modes of contact serve to bring the other into the realm of his psychic reality. The individual thus gains a sense of omnipotent control over the other-as-object. Given a good-enough environment, a healthy individual will also develop the capacity to *use* objects. This entails the creation of a transitional space in which the individual can perceive the other as a separate center of experience. As Winnicott writes: "a world of shared reality is created which the subject can use and which can feed back other-than-me substance into the subject" (p. 94).[4]

I contend that psychological growth is enhanced by the capacity to sustain a tension between these two modes of relating (Benjamin, 1995; Ogden, 2004a). However, breakdowns in recognition seem to be an inevitable part of relationships. The loss of mutual recognition frequently gives way to enactments in which those involved engage unconsciously in attempts to negate one another as independent subjects. Benjamin (2004) refers to these kinds of interactions in terms of the interplay between "doer" and "done-to." The "doer" turns the other into an object in his psychic reality, while negating him as a subject in the world outside of his omnipotent control. By contrast, the "done-to" submits to the "doer" in an attempt to control him by taking up a role in his fantasy life and manipulating it to his own advantage. Each is unable to gain the other's recognition. It is as if that there were only two modes of engagement: submission or resistance to the other.

An example might help to illustrate what this can look like in a group relations conference. Let us suppose that there is a large group event. A consultant, whom many members experience as lacking in emotional warmth, offers an interpretation. Consciously or unconsciously, the members feel rejected by this emotionally withholding authority figure. However, they rightly sense that one way to please him would be to act as if they are thinking hard about his comment. They pretend to make use of his comment, in the hopes that the icy consultant will begin to treat them with more compassion.[5] Not about to be seduced, the consultant recognizes their good behavior as an attempt to manipulate him into abandoning his strictly interpretive position. He responds to their coercion in kind by making interpretation about the group's hostility, using his transference-based authority and the weight of established theory to coerce the group into accepting his perspective on what it is doing. Rather than facilitating self-reflection, he is experienced by the members as engaging in a form of intellectual retaliation against their immature or needy selves in an expression of his own will to power.

Benjamin (2004) describes this kind of enactment in terms of a "twoness," in the sense that both participants are negating the other and defending against a mutual engagement. However, while there is certainly a defensive aspect of this mode of relating, it appears that this kind of enactment can also serve as a vehicle of self transformation. To explain this process, we must supplement our understanding of doer/done to relations with Ogden's (2004a) novel approach to the process of projective identification.

As I discuss above, Bion (1961) held that the recipient's personality is obliterated in a projective identification. The recipient's personality matters only in so far as it predisposes him to lose it. For Ogden, by contrast, nobody's personality is obliterated in a projective identification. Instead, Ogden conceptualizes a projective identification as a mutual enactment in which both the projector (i.e., the doer) and recipient (i.e., the done-to) join together in a momentary state of merger with each other, leading to new forms of self experience for both parties. Personality is not obliterated, but rather elicited. The projector imagines that the recipient contains a part of his self. By imagining that a part of his self is being contained in this other, that is, in the "not-I," the projector can experience this aspect of himself in a way that was previously unavailable to him. The recipient colludes in the process to elicit aspects of self that could only be reached through this temporary merger state.[6] He is the co-author of his experience, in so far as he uses this relationship to elicit aspects of his own self-experience that feel new, strange, or other to him.

Ogden (1994, 2004a) refers to the intersubjective bond between the projector and the recipient as the subjugating analytic third.[7] This can be thought of as a process or relationship in which both participants experience a merger between the "I" and the "not-I," negating themselves as distinct individuals in order to become "other" and thereby make possible a transformation of their separate subjectivities. Their separateness is destroyed momentarily so that they can be re-created. The idea is reminiscent of Ghent's (1990) claim that submission to the other may express the wish to surrender to a relational process in which new and potentially more authentic forms of self-experience can emerge.[8] From a contemporary interpersonal-relational perspective one might develop this idea further in terms of an enactment of dissociated, unformulated self-states in a dyad or group (Bromberg, 1996; Stern, 2003). The relational configuration in a dyad or group at any moment reflects one of many potential relationships between participants' multiple selves. Each participant elicits, validates, and opposes emergent self-states in the other/s, while likewise being the object of such treatment. A cyclical process of confrontation, submission, surrender, and recognition emerges, with the potential of bringing unrecognized self-states into relation within each person's experience of "me-ness."

In the context of group relations work, the implication of Ogden's argument is that the members and consultants within a conference do not contain split off and projected mental contents for one another; rather, they enter into a particular kind of relationship in which novel dimensions of self experience are elicited through mutual experiences of merger. In practice, this position requires a change in how we think about projection, containment, valence, and role assignment in groups. Rather than approach a group with the questions, "Who is containing what?" and/or "What am I containing for you?" consultants might approach a group with curiosity about how system is functioning to elicit emergent dimensions of self experience in themselves and in the group-as-a-whole. Interpretations might address transference–countertransference themes in the group, without denying or disavowing the authenticity of the consultant's experience. This means a departure from interpretations that imply that any consultant or participant within the group is "just a container" for its split off good/bad objects, and not a mutual actor in the co-creation of his subjective experience and that of the group as a whole.

To illustrate this dimension of group experience, I will return to my last example. Despite their guardedness with the emotionally unavailable consultant, the group members might begin to experience a new aspect of their subjectivities through an enactment with him. Let us suppose that they pretend to work with his interpretation in a coercive manner, motivated by the desire for his positive regard. As the group members fight to gain control over this frustrating consultant, some might begin to form an internal representation of him and, watching themselves through his eyes, experience themselves as simultaneously "I" and "not-I." On the one hand, they might feel like mature adults who have chosen to attend an experiential learning conference; on the other, they might feel like little children acting out against a real grown-up. In this way they retain some sense of who they are as adults, while identifying with the consultant's implicit view of them.

Meanwhile, the consultant may be similarly impacted by the minds of the group members. In an attempt to gain control over the manipulative and highly defended group members, he might build up a representation of the group in his own mind, where he can more easily manage it. He might then experience a split in his self between what he sees as his real, or authentic, self and what he imagines to be the group's idea of him. Thus, he might experience a split between his sense of self as a competent and/or talented group consultant on the one hand, and a sense of himself as a sadistic and neglectful voyeur on the other. He retains some sense of himself as an effective group leader, while also identifying with the way in which the members of the group see him at this point in the conference. His interplay with the group members' minds thus opens new realms of self-experience for him, such that he can feel both like his familiar self and like a different person.

For both the group members and the consultant, then, the merger between the "I" and the "not-I" amounts to a sense of being "other than me." Thus the intersubjective merger, or bond, produces new forms of self-experience for all those involved. One must then ask, however, how the participants can begin to reclaim their transformed subjectivities and to re-engage with one another as distinct individuals. While a number of theorists agree that this is an essential part of the process, it remains unclear how it can be reached or negotiated by the participants involved. Ogden (2004a) suggests that, one the one hand, a state of mutual recognition and self/other differentiation result when the analyst, or consultant, becomes able to interpret the transference–countertransference in the group, while, on the other hand, the analysand becomes able to make "genuine psychological use" of the insight. "Genuine psychological use," in this context, means a deepening of the group process in the form of new associations and insights in the ensuing moments or later in the conference. It is often difficult, however, to achieve a state in which genuine psychological use is possible. Unless some change has already occurred in the group, the group might feel "done-to," or further impinged upon, by the consultant's interpretation, rather than understood by him (Benjamin, 2004). The consultant might then confuse the member's submission with the development of insight and the attainment of a depressive position.

Benjamin (2004) claims, by contrast, that the analyst, or in our case the consultant, must first surrender to the inevitability of his own participation in the enactment. She suggests that this process might require more than self-analysis on the consultant's part. It might require him to reflect with the group about how he has participated in the breakdown. Through sensitive self-disclosure, he lays the foundation for a safe relationship in which acceptance is possible and interpretation no longer feels like an assault. The members can then begin to accept their own contribution to the enactment and to recognize one another, including the consultant, as separate centers of self-experience.

I agree with Benjamin that mutual recognition is often on the way toward being restored when an analyst or consultant can accept his participation in the co-created experience. It has not been thoroughly explored, however, how the intersubjective field can be altered to enable the consultant, or any member, to step outside of an enactment and to make the first move toward restoring mutual recognition. Kieffer (2007) refers to this process as an "emergent" phenomenon. This implies that some systemic variable has undergone a qualitative or quantitative change, such that the subjugating system is destabilized. A re-organization can then occur in the group, enabling a new kind of intersubjectivity to appear spontaneously.[9] Grossmark (2007) similarly conceptualizes this process in terms of a non-linear dynamic system.[10] Enactments temporarily leave the group mired in a position where reflective functioning becomes impossible, coercive, and even a means of dissociating from anxiety or despair at the prospect of losing oneself in affect. The role of the group therapist or consultant entails allowing oneself to become temporarily immersed in enactments, while remaining available to respond when alternative self-states[11] become available in the group, signaling the possibility of a phase transition and the emergence of a shared reflective space or, in the language above, a shared third. It seems to me that more conceptual and empirical research is required before we can begin to speculate about the particular conditions that facilitate this form of emergence.

If the group does regain some capacity for shared reflection, the members might begin to experience a different kind of intersubjective relationship: a shared or usable third (Benjamin, 2004). This form of thirdness can be thought of as an elaboration on the idea of a transitional space (Winnicott, 1959). The participants have survived one another's attacks and are now better able to use, or recognize, one another. They can now begin to reclaim their altered subjectivities and to put themselves back together in a new way through dialogue with the other as an independent subject. This shared third realm of experience does not necessarily replace the subjugating third. Instead a creative tension can develop between these two modes. This can lead to an optimal degree of disorganization (Galatzer-Levy, 2004). In this case, the wish to be negated and transformed as a subject is balanced by a capacity to sustain mutual recognition, a sense of differentiation between self and other, and an ability to work through the subjugating bond.

In a group relations conference, the emergence of a usable third might be marked by a sense among the participants that personal subjectivity can exist in a dialectic with the intersubjective matrix within the group, without unbearable dread of losing oneself to the group or pressure to negate one's dependency on the group through narcissistic or schizoid defenses. Characteristic affects might include guilt and concern for the other as a separate entity, as well as gratitude for new self-experiences that have emerged through the merger. Moreover, the group atmosphere might shift such that members and consultants feel less preoccupied with doer/done-to dynamics, as outlined by Benjamin, and can afford to take greater responsibility for and to be more curious about their role in the group. Although for the sake of argument I have deliberately emphasized the differences between the approach I advocate and that of a more traditional Kleinian–Bionian sensibility, there is also an important degree of continuity between the two perspectives. This continuity seems most apparent in the parallel between what a Kleinian might describe as the dialectic between the paranoid–schizoid and depressive positions and what I describe here as the dialectic between a subjugating and a shared third.

I contend, furthermore, that when the subjugating third is not balanced by mutual recognition between the group participants, an alien group self can begin to take shape. The concept of an alien self derives from Fonagy et al.'s (2002) interpretation of Winnicott (1967). Fonagy et al. demonstrate that otherwise healthy infants tend to accommodate their self-experiences to match the mental state of a poorly attuned caregiver. Failing to find himself represented in the caregiver's mind, the child instead finds her in himself. As he continues to mature, he might gradually internalize a representation of her mental state as a core part of his self. This internal object is thought to remain alienated from what he imagines to be his "true" or authentic self. As a result, the person might lack a sense of self-cohesion, encounter difficulty in interpreting his own and others' mental states, and experience chaotic episodes of dysregulated and unmentalized affect. His only way of obtaining relief from the "alien self" might be to externalize it through projective identification, replacing a fragmented internal state with the relatively organizing experience of being at odds with a hostile entity in the external world.

As Terman (2009) notes, "the group is not the individual writ large." It would be a categorical error to argue that a trauma in its "infancy" had led to pathology in its "adulthood." However, I believe that it can still be useful to borrow this term in an attempt to understand the group's sense of who or what it is in relation to the authorities charged with leading it. The alien group self can be thought of as a collective identity that is formed in an act of over-accommodation to a consultant's mind. The members maintain their connection to him, while subjugating the group to his thoughts, wishes, theories, etc. It is possible for a tension to develop between multiple alien group selves or between an alien group self and an authentic group self. The authentic group self reflects the group's idea of what it could be with a leader who was better able to hold its members in mind in a state of shared recognition. This tension can lead to defensive group processes that serve to prevent fragmentation and to restore a sense of cohesion in the group self.

To illustrate the idea of the alien group self, let us consider what it might look like in a group relations conference. Suppose that a consultant conducts himself in accordance with the belief that he should be "strictly adherent" to his neutral, interpretive position. The members seek his guidance as the authority in this unusual setting. He responds with silence, or with Delphic interpretations of the group's unconscious impulses and fantasy life. It begins to seem to the members that the only way to obtain his support will be to locate themselves somewhere within the framework of what he can "observe." They begin to accommodate their experience to match his. The result is a collective vision of the group self that is formed in an over-identification with how the consultant sees it.

The group might try to cope with an alien group self in a number of different ways. For example, it might project this self onto a particular member or sub-group in an effort to minimize the impingement and restore the group's sense of self-cohesion. The designated member or sub-group might then begin to act as if they were consultants. They might keep their eyes on the floor, or gaze pensively into the space beyond the group. In addition, they might try to withhold expectable human responsiveness from one another in imitation of the pokerfaced consultant. They might also make comments that sound like "consultations," or speak in a way that seems to be patterned on a consultant's real speech habits. They are often experienced as rude, haughty, and standoffish by the other members.

If the group fails to project this alien self onto a scapegoat, it can suffer self-fragmentation, that is, an inability to reconcile this self with the other aspects of his self-organization. This, in turn, can result in dysregulated affect. The members can lose the ability to mentalize their experience, that is, they become unable to process or symbolize it. From a traditional viewpoint, the group's intense feeling states may seem to confirm the existence of the drives—leading the consultant to conclude that he has discovered what the group is really like beneath all of the social niceties, at the level of primitive aggression and sexuality. I am suggesting, however, that what has been "discovered" is not a fundamental truth about the group's unconscious, but rather the product of a failed meeting of minds—a result, that is, of the consultant's failure to hold the members in mind.

At other points, the alien group self might find expression in a sub-group of regular conference goers with prior experience in the model, who implicitly identify themselves with what they imagine to be the consultant's model of the mind. These members might try to embody the death instinct by making wildly aggressive comments or gestures. Alternatively, some of these members might make overt sexual comments or advances toward other members in what seems like a somewhat forced celebration of their libidinal impulses. They might further idealize themselves as being in touch with human nature, while devaluing those who are reluctant to join with them in their carnal utopia.

Finally, the alien group self might appear in the form of a "work group." This group devotes itself to the task of deconstructing its experience in accordance with the terms and categories offered by the consultant. It appears to be "using" the consultant's interpretations to gain a deeper understanding of its unconscious instinctual life and object relations. This is not object-usage, however, which implies a transitional space between subjects. Rather, it is the group's way of giving itself over to the consultant in a self-negating act of accommodation to his theoretical mythology, which is felt in this case as an impingement. The so-called "work" of self-reflection thus becomes an act of self-alienation. By thinking in his terms, the group begins to feel more like him and less like itself.

Up to this point in my argument, I have attempted to show how subjective and intersubjective experiences can be thought of as co-created by group participants through mutual experiences of subjugation, merger with the other, and the restoration of a third characterized by mutual recognition. In the following section, I shall attempt to illustrate some of these ideas through a critical discussion of a case study reported by the director of a recent group relations conference at New York University (McRae, 2004). I shall focus my critique on a staff meeting in which I argue that a subjugating third emerges between the director and her staff. I contend that this subjugating relationship plays a central role in helping the director to integrate what she views as the split parts of her self; namely, the part of herself that she experiences as a "professional" and an "expert" in group relations and the part of herself that she identifies with working-class African Americans. In addition to an experience of subjugation in the director–staff member relationship, her report evidences the emergence of a shared third space, in which she becomes able to relate her staff members as separate subjects and to reclaim a more integrated sense of her own subjectivity, transformed by the temporary merger with the other.

Case Illustration

McRae (2004), the conference director and the author of the case study in question, opens her report with a statement about the social factors that led her to organize a group relations conference. She describes her motivation in the language of an objective consultant, or social scientist, who is somewhat detached from the events at hand:

> In the past few decades we have seen some transitions: women and those from minority groups moving into positions of power and authority in organizations that are predominantly white. Making this transition in authority, role and task need to be examined from the perspective of those who are new to authority roles and the social identity groups to which they belong, as well as by those who have traditionally been in positions of authority.
>
> (p. 226)

Having only read this passage, we cannot know what her level of personal investment is in the social issues that she describes. We know only that she sees them as worthy of further study. Presumably, if we were conference attendees, we would have had access to a similar statement of purpose in the conference brochure or at the conference opening, without any explicit reference to the director's personal investment in the conference theme.

It later appears, however, that McRae did have a more personal investment in this particular subject. Her professional interest in the issues not withstanding, a part of her seems to have sought this experience as a way to work through a split or dissociation between two selves that she was struggling to integrate within her experience of "I" or "me." The split between these two aspects of her I-experience came into focus as she was grieving the death of her brother, a barber in a working-class inner-city neighborhood, who was fatally wounded by a stray bullet during a conflict outside of his barbershop:

> The loss of my brother highlighted my connection to the working class and to African Americans and what it meant to be the other, the outsider, and a container of what society deems as negative. The loss also made me want to claim the other parts of myself: for example, the professional, the expert ... It was time to integrate the various parts of myself more completely ... They

are all a part of me, and each brings strength to me and informs me of different lifestyles, ways of being, and ways of knowing.

(p. 228)

As she writes, dealing with her brother's murder stirred up her sense of identification with her black working-class background—her brother was a barber, and their parents had been sharecroppers. Yet she knew that another part of her identified with her role as an "expert" and "professional" in psychology at a predominantly white university. It is important to note that, at this point, her tone shifts from that of a scientific investigator to that of a person in mourning seeking an experience of personal transformation. The group becomes what Bollas (1979) describes as a "transformational object." More than an opportunity to study race, class, and authority in the abstract, the group was also invested with the implicit function of helping to integrate the dissociated selves of a director in mourning.

Given her theoretical background in the traditional Tavistock model, with its emphasis on the notion of the consultant as a neutral container/observer, McRae seems unlikely to make much of how the split within herself impacted the events that occurred in the group. However, I posit that her divided sense of self and her hope for the group to be a transformational object did have an impact on the experience of the group-as-a-whole. To substantiate this argument, I shall focus on a meeting between McRae and her staff members, in which the opening statement to be given to the conference members was discussed. The description of the meeting suggests that McRae became both a projector and a recipient in a network of projective identifications and introjections, leading to a disorienting sense of merger with different parts of the white women on her staff:

> In the first staff meeting, it was impossible to get the staff to join in my opening statement to the conference membership on the issues of oppression, privilege, and disenfranchisement as they related to race and ethnic identity ... With a high level of anxiety, I began to question my own decisions, and this set the tone for the entire conference ... The projections of incompetence, weakness, and passivity are attributes that are not a part of how I am usually experienced. In fact, I tend to pull for the opposite stereotypes ascribed to black women. There was one white woman colleague on the staff with whom I have worked who claimed that she and I had an out-of-body experience, we switched roles, and she became the assertive black woman and I, the stereotypic passive white woman ... I felt like I lost my voice and my mind ... I split off my strong parts into the white women, while identifying more with the weakness and passivity ascribed to white women ... I became the sharecropper's daughter again.

(p. 233)

She writes that, in response to an uncooperative staff, she became anxious and began to question her competence. It felt to her as if she had lost her assertive black self. She found herself identifying with a form of weakness and passivity that she associates with white women. At the same time, the identification with white women elicited a part of her self identified with a particular view of her family of origin: herself as the daughter of disempowered working-class parents. Meanwhile, she felt that her strength was contained within the white women, one of whom now seemed more like an assertive black woman.

McRae attributes the experience to her staff's projections onto her as a person of color and working-class origins, and to her valence, which predisposed her to be obliterated. Her conclusions may be accurate. However, from my perspective, she neglects the question of how she too may have contributed actively to what occurred in the group.

The concept of the subjugating third provides a useful framework from which to begin trying to make sense of McRae's own contribution. In this staff meeting, she becomes both the recipient and the projector in an experience of mutual subjugation. The dual experience enables her to become simultaneously "I" and "not-I," and therefore "Other-than me" (Ogden, 2004a). She is enabled, as a recipient, to experience herself as weak, disempowered; her sharecropper self ("I") is elicited in connection with feeling like a passive white woman ("not-I"). She also experiences the assertive parts of her black self ("I") as contained within the dominant white women ("not-I"). The result is a disorienting episode in which two dissociated aspects of self-experience are elicited through a sense of merger with the "not-I," enabling an integration of disparate selves within a broader sense of self, with room for co-existing (if conflictual) modes of experience.

Looking further into the case material, it seems plausible that McRae's way of relating with her staff was influenced by a desire to identify with an idealized mentor, a black female consultant who seemed to integrate seamlessly her racial and professional selves. McRae writes admiringly of the self-cohesion that her mentor had achieved in her eyes:

> What I could not be was Kathy White. While very much alike in several ways, we are also quite different. In my eyes, she is the essence of sophistication, elegance, and what she calls the professional class. On the other hand, I am from a working class background, and it often shows in some of my behaviors and values: my hair is locked; I often accent my attire with Afrocentric objects; I am an activist from the late sixties and seventies who is outspoken about racial injustices and oppression; I have challenged the organization on its work around racial issues. Some might say that I carry my race boldly and defiantly, while Kathy has learned to weave hers into the fabric of her being, choosing carefully when to show her colors.
>
> (p. 230)

The passage draws our attention to Kathy's smooth integration of her racial identity into her identity as an elegant, sophisticated member of the professional class. By contrast, McRae describes herself as a bold, defiant, Afrocentric activist—an identity of which she seems proud—and yet one that seems, in her mind, to clash with the part of her that aspires to membership in the professional class that Kathy embodies for her. Later in the narrative, McRae proceeds to describe Kathy as a kind of ideal hybrid between black and white.[12] Building on this theme of dualities that can be reconciled within McRae's image of Kathy, McRae describes Kathy as both a strong and a passive woman. Kathy is depicted as having an uncanny ability to get what she wants from the institute that sponsors the conference.[13] At the same time, she is described as gentle, politic, retiring, and graceful. McRae needs Kathy to be an idealized object, with the potential to integrate irreconcilable tensions between white–black, passive–assertive, professional–working class. To some extent, then, one might read her immersion in a process of subjugation with the white female staff in terms of a displaced desire to merge with an idealized mentor, with the possibility of finding some way to reconcile the tensions within her.

At an unexpected point in the conference, the subjugating enactment between McRae and her staff gave way to an emergent experience of what one might refer to as a shared third. Just prior, McRae was caught in an enactment in which her consultants seem to feel over-authorized, while she herself felt de-authorized. The staff was bombarding her with questions and reminders. She writes: "I was continuously asked or reminded that I needed to consider certain tasks if I had not already, or I was asked to make a decision that someone thought needed to be made immediately" (p. 234). She interpreted the staff's incessant questions and demands as an attempt to prove that she was neglectful and incompetent. She began to feel as if her staff knew better than her how to run the conference and that she was failing abysmally to fulfill her role as director.

Then suddenly a shift occurred in the group. An unexpected question from the staff, which could have been felt as another attack, authorized McRae to reclaim her role as director:

> "Unfreezing" for me occurred during a staff meeting when it became clear that my staff and mentor expected me to do my job. It came in the form of a simple question from one of the consultants, "Mary, as Director, what do you think we should do?" This question, at that particular time, acted as a reminder of the role I had taken. It challenged me to get in touch with past experiences of being an effective leader, and it highlighted the reality of my role and competence. I had organized this conference. I was also able to hear the voice of my mentor telling me that in the role of Director, one takes in projections and holds them without internalizing them, using them as data to understand the life of the organization.
>
> (p. 235)

The question—"As Director, what do you think we should do?"—could have been heard in many different ways, depending on the tone, the style of delivery, and the context in which it occurred. Given the enactment between McRae and her staff, one could imagine it coming across with a note of condescension, conveying an implicit criticism of her lack of confidence as captain at the helm of this conference ("What do *you* think we should do?"). One could also imagine it coming across as a pressured insistence that the staff make use of its leader, a desperate plea for leadership, or simply a gentle invitation to take control. In any case, this comment—which does not seem remarkable in and of itself—either enabled or reflected a phase transition in which McRae moved from a passive mode of self-negation to a reflective mode of experiencing herself and the staff members.

For the first time in the account, we witness what appears to be the emergence of a shared third. McRae begins to reflect on the subjective experiences of her staff members, describing them to us as dynamic subjects, rather than static aggressors/doers in a stereotyped battle between passive white professional woman and a working-class black female activist. In the following passage, for example, McRae begins to reflect on the mental state of one particular consultant, attributing an affect and motivational state to her:

> The working class "girl" in me has difficulty getting in touch with the fact that middle-class women and men from any racial group would envy her, the sharecroppers' daughter. [At one point] a consultant who had a long-standing relationship with my mentor told me that she thought that requiring students in my group dynamics class to attend the weekend conference was unethical. Of course, this comment was made during the Institutional Event when the staff was doing their work publicly and one of my students was in the room. I experienced her comment as an angry attack, not envy. I saw her as a privileged White woman with a sharp mind and one of the most skilled consultants I have known. Why would she be envious of me? It was later when I realized that I held a highly prized role, was performing well, and had developed an envious relationship with someone who was a powerhouse of experience and charisma.
>
> (p. 234)

Here McRae describes an episode in which a privileged white female consultant challenged her for requiring students to attend the conference. She initially heard this challenge as another assault from one of the white female consultants, an assault that was intended to humiliate her in front of a student and presumably de-authorize her even further. Her mode of listening indicated her enmeshment within doer/done-to dynamics, a position from which she did not (or could not) consider the possibility that this woman had a separate subjective experience that motivated her participation in the exchange. Feeling more confident and better able to contemplate both her own subjective experience and the mental state of her staff members, she is now able to wonder if perhaps this consultant, an accomplished person in her own right, felt envious of her role as the director. This line of thinking indicates a qualitative shift in the narrative. The other is no longer just a static pawn in a battle around race and class, but also a subject with separate affects and intentional mental states to which McRae did not have access in the moment.

As McRae transitions into a position from which she can reflect on the other's mental state, she also begins to reclaim her own subjectivity from the experience of merger. She expresses a novel sense of empowerment and pride in her unique contribution to the role of director, while distinguishing it from her mentor's leadership style:

> Taking up the role of Director requires tremendous authority and responsibility ... Directors each have different qualities that make them special in the role. It is important to take what the mentor has that feels like a fit and to step out with one's own interests with which the mentor may or may not agree.
> (p. 235)

Her statement conveys a sense of herself as a separate center of experience and initiative, differentiated from Kathy, with a unique contribution to make to the role of director. Moreover, the tone conveys a sense of self-authorization, as if she is giving advice to future conference directors, which in itself marks a departure from the confused, at times self-depreciating tone at previous points in the study. Her experience of self-authorization seems enhanced, rather than threatened or diminished, by her contrasting experience of herself as the black daughter of a working-class family. One gets the impression that she has gained an expanded sense of I-experience and begun to locate herself in a reflective mental space from which she can feel, as she writes in the opening of this study, that "[These multiple selves] are all a part of me, and each brings strength to me and informs me of different lifestyles, ways of being, and ways of knowing" (p. 228).

Ogden (1982) emphasizes the point that "the projector exerts pressure on the recipient to experience himself and behaves in a way congruent with the unconscious projective fantasy" (p. 14). In concluding this discussion, I am left wondering how McRae might have contributed to the experience of subjugation in the group. Perhaps because of her investment in a more traditional understanding of the Tavistock model, she does not explore this issue. From an intersubjective perspective, however, one must consider how the director's countertransference needs, desires, and fantasies might have contributed to the group's experience. In addition, I am left wondering about the extent to which the women on McRae's staff experienced their behavior in the conference as an alien accommodation to McRae's fantasy of what they would do. To what extent did these white women need to behave like racists and/or classists in order to provide her with the experience of self-transformation that she sought and to find their own place in her mind? Finally, one might speculate about the impact that McRae might have had on the conference, had she chosen to reflect more openly on her countertransference with the group. It is my hope that an intersubjective approach to group relations will provide a theoretical framework within which consultants can begin to explore these questions in their work.

Conclusion

I have attempted to show that an intersubjective approach to group relations requires us to shift our focus from how reified mental items are projected and contained to how mutual participants collude unconsciously to co-create subjective and intersubjective experiences in the group. I focused, in particular, on the dialectic between the wish to negate the other and the need for mutual recognition. It appears that enactments in which the participants are negated as subjects can paradoxically become vehicles of self-transformation. For this to occur, it is essential to balance these enactments in the subjugating third with the eventual emergence of a shared or usable third space. Without it, mutual subjugation can lead to the development of an alien group self, in which the group reorganizes its identity in an accommodation to its consultant's mind. Through an extended clinical vignette, I have tried to illustrate the kinds of case material and the types of questions that one might find interesting from the perspective that I outline.

An important implication of this perspective is that the consultant inevitably plays a more central role than has previously been given to him in determining what transpires during the conference. As I argued in my critique of McRae (2004), the consultant's unconscious fantasies about the group inevitably impact what she is attempting to observe in ways that she cannot prevent, anticipate, or totally regulate in the manner of a neutral container/observer. Rather than being seen as a criticism or devaluation of the consulting role, this way of thinking opens up new ways of conceptualizing group relations, with an emphasis on the co-constructed nature of both subjugation and recognition.

An additional implication has to do with authenticity and responsibility. The approach that I am advocating suggests that the "recipient's" personality is not *obliterated* in a projective identification, but rather that his personality is *elicited* in new forms. He is the co-author of his self-experience, and not the passive container of projected contents. In other words, his experience is authentically him, and not just what the group "put into" him. As I have discussed above, his feeling of being unlike himself in the conference can be explained by the fact that he is experiencing new aspects of his personality that existed only as latent potential within him up until this projective identification. He may feel unlike himself, but he is still himself; accordingly, he must take partial responsibility for his experience in the group. It would not make sense, in this paradigm, to argue that the group used him without adding that he was also using the group. Unfortunately, "the group made me do it" is a fairly common thing to hear, both from group members and from consultants who prefer to disavow their own role in their behavior.

Although this chapter makes an initial attempt to think intersubjectively about experiences in groups, I am also aware of having left many questions unanswered. It remains unclear how the subjugating third can be transcended and the shared third restored. Many authors usefully address how the analyst or consultant can facilitate this transition. However, if we assume that he is mutually embroiled in the chaos, then what enables *him* to break out of it, so that he can be of use to others who are embedded in it? I believe that this issue merits further attention. Finally, my case illustration reflects the difficulty inherent in demonstrating theoretical concepts through material reported by a theorist/director of a more traditional Tavistock orientation. Additional case material is essential for the project of extending an intersubjective perspective to the study of group relations.

Notes

1. Bion called this the basic assumption mode of functioning and posited three types of basic assumptions: dependency, fight/flight, and pairing. In each case, psychotic anxiety leads to projective identification, which, in turn, gives rise to irrational behavior and distracts from the rational task-oriented activity of the work group. Due to space limitations, I will not discuss the various basic assumption groups in detail. For a full description, the reader should consult Bion's (1961) *Experiences in Groups and other Papers*.
2. My critique of the Tavistock model draws on criticisms previously articulated in the intersubjective and relational literatures. For a more extensive discussion of intersubjective and relational critiques of classical psychoanalysis, the reader is recommended to the work of Stolorow and Atwood (1992), on the one hand, and to that of Mitchell (1988), Aron (2001), and Wachtel (2008) on the other.
3. It should be noted that I have chosen to focus on what some might consider "the early Bion" (see Ogden, 2004b), namely, the Bion of *Experiences in Groups* (1961). Based on the central role of this text in the foundation and development of the Tavistock approach to Group Relations, this seems to be the most relevant Bion for my argument. Nonetheless, one might argue justly that a more nuanced reading of Bion emerges if one considers also his later work—for example, *Attention and Interpretation* (1970). In Ogden's reading, this later work struggles to convey that "psychoanalysis is most fundamentally an enterprise involving the emergence into the realm of knowing (K) of unsymbolizable, unknowable, inexpressible experience" (p. 291). The unknowable and unsymbolizable dimensions of experience (O) are, in turn, "highly specific to the emotional situation generated by a particular analyst and a particular patient at a given moment of analysis" (p. 292). In this way of reading Bion, his work can be seen as developing toward a systemic, context-specific conception of experiencing and knowing that anticipates contemporary intersubjective and relational approaches. The analyst or group consultant's task, in this later paradigm, consists of making himself as open as he can to experiencing the inexpressible aspects of the analytic or group experience and attempting to find words that make these dimensions of experience accessible for reflection.
4. A number of contemporary theorists describe a similar capacity to recognize the other as a separate subject and to accept being influenced by someone who is "other-than-me" as a feature of mature selfobject relating (e.g. Stolorow & Atwood, 1992; Kieffer, 2007).
5. The implication is that, under certain circumstances, any apparent "work-group" functioning might be coercive; the members essentially act like good little boys or girls in order to please the consultant so that he will show them more affection. Similarly,

some children engage in displays of good behavior in order to help a preoccupied parent respond to them with the level of emotional attunement that the children need.

6   Ogden (1982) elaborates: "the recipient experiences himself in part as he is pictured in the projective fantasy. In reality, however, the recipient's experience is a new set of feelings experienced by a person different from the projector. They may approximate those of the projector, but they are not identical: the recipient is the author of his own feelings. Albeit feelings elicited under a very specific kind of pressure from the projector, they are the product of a different personality system" (p. 17).

7   Ogden (1994, 2004a) describes the jointly created intersubjective bond between the analyst and analysand as "the analytic third." It can be characterized as a "third" area of experience, because it is the product of a dialectic generated between the two distinct subjectivities of the analyst and analysand within the analytic setting. Winnicott (1959) hinted at this way of thinking in his claim that there is a third area of living, which corresponds to the transitional space between the separate subjectivities of the mother and infant. Whereas other theorists have used the concept of the third to describe the symbolic father who constitutes a part of the Oedipal triangle (e.g., Lacan, 1977; Britton, 1988, 1998), the term is used in this context not to describe a real or symbolic entity, but to refer to a shared experience that is generated in the interaction between separate subjects.

8   Other theorists have suggested similarly that a group can function as a "transformational object"—that is, an object that is sought out because the members identify it with early maternal provision and the metamorphoses of the self (Bollas, 1979; Hazell, 2005).

9   Some readers have argued that by introducing the concept of emergence, I might be contradicting the claim that the group experience is co-created by mutual participants. For them, the idea of co-creation implies that two or more actors contribute in a relatively direct way to the shaping of a given experience. The idea of emergence, by contrast, seems to imply that there is a random factor, or perhaps a "ghost in the machine," which accounts for the experience that develops; therefore the experience is not strictly co-created, because it results more from impact of this ghost in the machine than from the direct contribution of the participants. I feel, by contrast, that there is no inherent contradiction between the ideas of co-creation and emergence. The participants in a group each contribute to their shared experience; however, as the concept of emergence implies, there is no direct correlation between their input and the systemic output. They can be compared to players at a pinball machine who each shoot a ball at the same time. Each player contributes something, but there are additional systemic variables that impact what happens next.

10 The use of non-linear dynamic systems theory (NDST) in psychoanalysis raises a number of epistemological questions. Stern (2009) calls for analysts who use concepts from the NDST literature, which spans the physical and social sciences, to be explicit about whether they are using the concept in a literal or in a metaphorical sense. He is concerned that, while the NDST literature provides an array of useful metaphors that can further our conceptual understanding of the analytic process, the literal application of NDST methodology to the empirical study of psychoanalysis would presuppose a positivistic orientation to psychoanalysis. If an author chooses this route, according to Stern, he should be explicit about his choice and should be prepared to furnish an analysis of empirical data that is consistent with his approach. Moreover, I would add that he should be prepared to accept the limitations inherent in the approach to psychoanalysis as a positivistic science, rather than as a human science of meanings that must be interpreted. The metaphorical use of non-linear dynamic concepts, however, can be a rich source of new thinking in psychoanalysis, without the need to apply NDST concepts or methods in a literal sense. Its positive contribution is already evident in the way in which the NDST movement in psychoanalysis has made us more sensitive to the significance of self-organizing

patterns in the analytic process, sudden qualititative shifts in mental functioning, and multiple developmental pathways toward the attainment of mental wellbeing. To give NDST the status of a metaphor in psychoanalysis is not to downplay its significance. As Lakoff and Johnson (1980) argue, conceptual thinking is fundamentally metaphorical in nature, and the history of psychoanalytic theory reveals our inability to think about the mind without metaphor.

11 Grossmark draws here on Bromberg's conception of self-states. For Bromberg (1996), the human experience of authenticity and self-awareness depends on an "ongoing dialectic between the separateness and unity of one's self states" (p. 513). "Self-states" are loosely defined as components of the overarching experience of "me" and are organized through "internal negotiation with the realities, values, affects, and perspectives of others." Bromberg views dissociation as an adaptive process, by means of which individual self-states can function in concert with one another, without any one self-state rigidly excluding the others from emerging into "me" experience. In response to trauma, however, dissociation can become a rigid, defensive way of barring painful, potentially unformulated self-states from subjective experience. In Bromberg's terms, a successful psychoanalytic process often entails a movement from the enactment of defensively dissociated self-states to an interpersonal field in which patient and analyst can "stand in the spaces" between potentially available self-states, as well as experience conflict and repression, as one self-state temporarily gains the foreground over another. While my argument has drawn heavily on contemporary American relational interpretations of Melanie Klein and Winnicott, one could have reached similar conclusions through Bromberg's approach, whose emphasis on multiple self-states, dissociation, and enactment in the interpersonal field places him more firmly in the camp of relational–Sullivanians (along with Donnel Stern). Future conceptual work on the relational theory of group dynamics might address the often unspoken tension between relational–object–relations theorists and relational–Sullivanians, with a focus on the implications for our understanding of groups. For instance, Stern (2009) now argues that the concept of repression is irretrievably bound up with Freudian metapsychology and must be replaced by the concept of dissociation in relational–interpersonal psychoanalysis. Would relational–Winnicotian and relational–Kleinian authors endorse this position, and if not, what different views of group dynamics might result? Although relational psychoanalysis is often conceptualized as a unity, which integrates Kleinian/Bionian, British independent, Sullivanian, self-psychological, infant research, and some progressive ego-psychological perspectives, it might be interesting to look at *different* potential versions of relational group theory, depending on the unique emphases of the relational analyst who is attempting this integration.

12 McRae writes, "My mentor and I were split, with her representing Whiteness, and me Blackness."

13 "Her [Kathy's] behavior was not questioned, at least to my knowledge, by the executive committee, while my behavior was under constant scrutiny" (McRae, 2004, p. 231).

References

Aron, L. (2001) *A Meeting of Minds: Mutuality in Psychoanalysis*. New York: Routledge.

Aron, L. (2003) The paradoxical place of enactment in psychoanalysis. *Psychoanalytic Dialogues*, 13 (5): 623–631.

Benjamin, J. (1995) *Like Subjects, Love Objects*. New Haven, CT: Yale University Press.

Benjamin, J. (1999) Afterword to recognition and destruction: An outline of intersubjectivity. In S. Mitchell & L. Aron (eds.) *Relational Psychoanalysis: The Emergence of a Tradition* (pp. 201–210). Hillsdale, NJ: Analytic Press.

Benjamin, J. (2004) Beyond doer and done-to: An intersubjective view of thirdness. *The Psychoanalytic Quarterly*, 73: 5–46.
Bion, W. (1959) Attacks on linking. *International Journal of Psychoanalysis*, 40: 308–315.
Bion, W. (1961) *Experiences in Groups and Other Papers*. New York: Routledge.
Bion, W. (1962) *Learning from Experience*. New York: Basic Books.
Bion, W. (1970) *Attention and Interpretation*. London: Tavistock Publications Ltd.
Bollas, C. (1979) The transformational object. *International Journal of Psychoanalysis*, 60: 97–107.
Britton, R. (1988) The missing link: Parental sexuality in the Oedipus complex. In R. Schafer (ed.) *The Contemporary Kleinians of London* (pp. 242–258). Madison, CT: International Universities Press, 1997.
Britton, R. (1998) *Belief and Imagination*. New York: Routledge.
Bromberg, P. (1996) Standing in the spaces: The multiplicity of self and the psychoanalytic relationship. *Contemporary Psychoanalysis*, 32: 509–535.
Chodorow, N.J. (2004) The American independent tradition: Loewald, Erikson, and the (possible) rise of intersubjective ego psychology. *Psychoanalytic Dialogues*, 14: 207–232.
Coelho, N. & Figueiredo, L. (2003) Patterns of intersubjectivity in the constitution of subjectivity: Dimensions of otherness. *Culture and Psychology*, 9 (3): 193–208.
Fonagy, P., Gergely, G., Jurist, E., & Target, M. (2002) *Affect Regulation, Mentalization, and the Development of the Self*. New York: Other Press.
Freud, S. (1911) *Psychoanalytic Notes on an Autobiographical Account of a Case of Paranoia (Dementia Paranoids)*. Trans. J. Strachey. New York: W.W. Norton.
Galatzer-Levy, R.M. (2004) Chaotic possibilities: Toward a new model of development. *International Journal of Psychoanalysis*, 85: 419–441.
Galatzer-Levy, R.M. (2009) Good vibrations: Analytic process as coupled oscillations. *International Journal of Psychoanalysis*, 90: 983–1007.
Gallese, V., Eagle, M., & Migone, P. (2007) Intentional attunement: Mirror neurons and the neural underpinnings of interpersonal relations. *Journal of the American Psychoanalytic Association*, 55 (1): 131–176.
Gerson, S. (2004) The relational unconscious: A core element of intersubjectivity, thirdness, and clinical process. *Psychoanalytic Quarterly*, 73: 63–98.
Gertler, B. & Izod, K. (2004) Modernism and postmodernism in group relations: "A confusion of tongues." In S. Cytrynbaum & D. Noumair (eds.), *Group Dynamics, Organizational Irrationality, and Social Complexity: Group Relations Reader* 3 (pp. 81–98). Waldorf, MD: McArdle Printing.
Ghent, E. (1990) Masochism, submission, surrender—Masochism as a perversion of surrender. *Contemporary Psychoanalysis*, 26: 108–136.
Gill, M.M. (1984) Psychoanalysis and psychotherapy: A revision. *International Review of Psychoanalysis*, 11: 161–179.
Greenberg, J. & Mitchell, S. (1983) *Object Relations in Psychoanalytic Theory*. Cambridge, MA: Harvard University Press.
Grossmark, R. (2007) the edge of chaos: enactment, disruption, and emergence in group psychotherapy. *Psychoanalytic Dialogues*, 17: 479–499.
Hayden, C. & Molenkamp, R. (2004) Tavistock primer II. In S. Cytrynbaum & D. Noumair (eds.) *Group Dynamics, Organizational Irrationality, and Social Complexity: Group Relations Reader* 3 (pp. 137–157). Waldorf, MD: McArdle Printing.
Hazell, C. (2005) *Imaginary Groups*. Bloomington, IN: Author House.

Kieffer, C. (2007) Emergence and the analytic third: working at the edge of chaos. *Psychoanalytic Dialogues*, 17: 683–703.
Klein, M. (1946) Notes on some schizoid mechanisms. In R. Money-Kyrle (ed.) *Envy and Gratitude and Other Works, 1946–1963* (pp. 1–24). New York: Free Press.
Klein, M. (1959) Our adult world and its roots in infancy. In R. Money-Kyrle (ed.) *Envy and Gratitude and Other Works, 1946–1963* (pp. 247–263). New York: Free Press.
Lacan, J. (1977) *Ecrits*. New York: W.W. Norton.
Lakoff, G. & Johnson, M. (1980) *Metaphors We Live By*. Chicago: University of Chicago Press.
McRae, M. (2004) Class, race and gender: Person-in-role implications in taking up the directorship. In S. Cytrynbaum & D. Noumair (eds.), *Group Dynamics, Organizational Irrationality, and Social Complexity: Group Relations Reader 3* (pp. 225–237). Waldorf, MD: McArdle Printing.
Meissner, W.W. (2009) Toward a neuropsychological reconstruction of projective identification. *Journal of the American Psychoanalytic Association*, 57: 95–129.
Mitchell, S. (1988) *Relational Concepts in Psychoanalysis: An Integration*. Cambridge, MA: Harvard University Press.
Mitchell, S. & Black, M. (1995) *Freud and Beyond*. New York: Basic Books.
Ogden, T. (1982) *Projective Identification and Psychotherapeutic Technique*. New York: Aronson.
Ogden, T. (1994) The analytic third: Working with intersubjective clinical facts. *International Journal of Psychoanalysis*, 75: 3–19.
Ogden, T. (2004a) The analytic third: Implications for psychoanalytic theory and technique. *The Psychoanalytic Quarterly*, 73: 167–195.
Ogden, T. (2004b) An introduction to the reading of Bion. *The International Journal of Psychoanalysis*, 85: 285–300.
Orange, D., Atwood, G., & Stolorow, R. (2001) *Working Intersubjectively*. New York: Routledge.
Stolorow, R. & Atwood, G. (1992) *Contexts of Being: The Intersubjective Foundations of Psychological Life*. New York: Analytic Press.
Stern, D.B. (2003) *Unformulated Experience: From Dissociation to Imagination in Psychoanalysis*. New York: Routledge.
Stern, D.B. (2009) *Partners in Thought: Working with Unformulated Experience, Dissociation, and Enactment*. New York: Routledge.
Stern, D. (1985) *The Interpersonal World of the Infant*. New York: Basic Books.
Stern, D. (2005) Intersubjectivity. In E. Person, A. Cooper, & G. Gabbard (eds.) *Textbook of Psychoanalysis* (pp. 77–92). Washington, DC: American Psychiatric Publishing.
Terman, D. (2009) An exploration of paranoid leadership and paranoid leaders. *The Psychology of Leadership Conference*. Chicago: Chicago Institute for Psychoanalysis.
Wachtel, P. (2008) *Relational Theory and the Practice of Psychotherapy*. New York: Guilford Press.
Winnicott, D.W. (1959) The fate of the transitional object. In *Psychoanalytic Explorations* (pp. 53–58). Cambridge, MA: Harvard University Press, 1989.
Winnicott, D.W. (1967) Mirror-role of mother and family in child development. In *Playing and Reality* (pp. 111–118). London: Tavistock, 1971.
Winnicott, D.W. (1969) The use of an object and relating through identification. In *Playing and Reality* (pp. 86–94). London: Tavistock, 1971.

Chapter 13

Relational Experiences in Large Group
A Therapeutic and Training Challenge

Rosemary Segalla

> The central dynamic struggle throughout life is between the powerful need to establish, maintain and protect intimate bonds with others and various efforts to escape the pains and dangers of these bonds—the sense of vulnerability, the threat of disappointment, engulfment, exploitation and loss.
>
> (Mitchell, 1988)

> What I have in mind here is the psychoanalytic study of (more or less large) groups: their formation, cohesion, fragmentation; or, stated in more specific terms, the circumstances that favor their formation, the nature of the psychological cement that holds them together, the psychological conditions under which they begin to manifest regressive behavior and begin to crumble, etc.
>
> (Kohut, 1978)

Introduction

Large groups can be, and often are, difficult to comprehend. Moving beyond the small group of seven to ten members to groups composed of thirty or more members can provide unique learning experiences both about the individuals in the group and about the large group process itself. The Mitchell quote captures our ongoing struggle to maintain connection with others. The dyad, our earliest experience, prepares us for larger groups such as the family. School may introduce us to yet larger group settings. Nothing, however, can fully prepare for large group experiences. Le Bon (Kreeger, 1975, p. 23) defined the larger group as potentially a mob in which individuality blurs and more primitive aspects of the self emerge, characterized by a lack of ethical consciousness. Large groups have long fascinated us, primarily for the danger that may ensue as a result of unleashed primitive forces. Thus, the study of large group within psychotherapy and psychoanalysis has a long history. It is a model often employed to train mental health professionals and others about group dynamics. In the United States, the most prominent study takes place under the auspices of the A.K. Rice Institute, which has promoted the large group for many decades. Study of large group behavior, however, also occurs in many other venues as discussed in several books (Kreeger, 1975; Schneider & Weinberg, 2003).

The purpose of this chapter is to explore the large group through the theoretical perspectives offered under the umbrella of self-psychology as well as other relational theories (Harwood, 1995; Segalla, 2001; Grossmark, 2007). Much of what has been written about large groups has been done from Freudian and Kleinian perspectives. While this has proven useful in understanding some of the regressive and aggressive behavior of large groups, it has not offered enough about the more health-seeking behavior also present in the large group as it is in each individual (Kohut, 1984). What has been substantially absent in this literature is an exploration of the positive ways in which the large group overcomes barriers to connection and engagement. This was explored in my 1996 paper but was not the primary goal of that paper. My current interest is in understanding the presence of more positive forces within the large group as well as recognizing that our primary emphasis on the individual has caused us to overlook our inevitable embeddedness in systems. Fosshage (2011), exploring contributions of systems theory, states:

> A nonlinear dynamic system refers to independent and interdependent elements that over time mutually influence and transform each other in a relatively unpredictable fashion. An inherent property of any system ... is that it becomes self-organizing; that is, it establishes patterns that in turn, become more predictable features of the system. This property to self-organize is inherent in each individual and between them.
>
> (p. 98)

This description aptly captures what happens in the large group. One of the many struggles faced by large group members is to maintain a sense of self while also experiencing some sense of a potential loss of self. That can be very daunting. This may be reflective of our intense emphasis on the individual, often loosing contact with our inevitable embeddedness with others from birth. This challenge to individuality and its implications are being explored by Orange (2011b) and others. She has suggested we consider that by primarily focusing on the individual and ignoring larger contexts, we inevitably promote individuality without adequate consideration of the other. This focus on individuality, a very American concept, does not foster mutuality nor does it address what may be a more ethical stance, that of putting the "other" first (Orange, 2011a). Frie puts this very well:

> In contrast to the individualism inherent in the Hobbesian and Freudian world of self-preservation, a dialogical stance is grounded in our social nature. However, neither can this stance overlook the capacity for aggression and domination. As Nussbaum (2007) wrote, 'We all have tendencies that can lead to narcissism and the domination of others, and we all have tendencies that can lead to compassion and acceptance of other's reality' (p. 335). It is

> the ambiguity of experience, the potential to be violent toward or accepting of the Other, that is at the heart of the issue.
>
> (pp. 463–464)

Recognizing our capacity for both love and aggression as seen in both individual and group work has been a topic that has engaged me for the decades I have served as a leader on a large group team and observed many efforts by large group members to reach across barriers, attempting to connect with others in the group. These positive efforts can lead to experiences of transcendence in which group members reach a profound level of compassionate engagement with others in the large group. Moving away from a focus on projections is not to ignore that these are plentiful but to emphasize that the human desire to be part of the tribe (Wilson, 2012) requires positive efforts and that these efforts exist along side more negative projective forces. My emphasis on these more positive efforts at connection is also a reflection of a shift in psychoanalysis, from a hermeneutics of suspicion to a hermeneutics of trust (Orange, 2011a). Orange states her view succinctly: "Freud's hermeneutics, his theory of meaning, assumes that consciousness always disguises and negates truth. He therefore had to approach the patient via a tangled theory of underlying and hidden motives" (Orange, 2011b, p. 27). Her offer of a hermeneutics of trust opens new areas of exploration for therapists. She states:

> This kind of hermeneutics rests on the assumption that we share with the other, for better and for worse, a common inherited world (Dostel, 1987) within which we attempt to understand ... it is a kind of faithfulness to the other and to the therapeutic task.
>
> (p. 35)

Her perspective is considerably different from what Wachtel (2008) describes of that Freudian position: "The mainstream of American psychoanalytic thought emphasized neutrality, anonymity, caution about 'gratifying' the patient's infantile needs and the primacy of insight" (p. 5). Shifting our study of the large group using both self and relational theories, guided by a hermeneutics of trust, opens new possibilities for those endeavoring to study behavior in this setting, bringing to this study a vision reflective of the cultural drift within psychotherapy and psychoanalysis.

Self and Relational Theories in Large Group Behavior: Shifting Emphasis, Shifting Theory

Understanding our inevitable embeddedness in systems that go far beyond the family group to larger groups in the culture is an essential part of the training of therapists, especially those who aspire to becoming group therapists. In recent years, the evolution of psychoanalytic theory has progressed to a deeper understanding of the co-creation of all human behavior (Stolorow, Atwood, &

Orange, 2002; Beebe & Lachmann, 2002; Benjamin, 1998). This brings with it fresh perspectives both about complex systems in which we all exist and the implications for understanding our impacts on the system as well as the intricacies of intimate connections and our inevitable need for the other in developing our own subjectivity. Benjamin (1998) states:

> The confrontation with the other's subjectivity and the limits of self-assertion is a difficult one to negotiate. The need for recognition entails this fundamental paradox: in the very moment of realizing our own independent will, we are dependent upon another to recognize it. At the very moment we come to understanding the meaning of I, myself, we are forced to see the limitations of that self. At the very moment when we understand that separate minds can share similar feelings, we begin to find out that these minds can also disagree.
> (p. 190)

This beautifully captures how the dilemma of mutual recognition, the experience of two subjects, is often a hard one to comprehend. What then happens to this process of recognition as we enter large group experience? How do we hold on to ourselves while also retaining the capacity to engage empathically with the other, trying to experience their subjectivity? What happens when we lose the face-to-face of the dyad or small group? In the absence of seeing the other face-to-face is there an anonymity that allows a regressive pull toward individual omnipotence, disallowing recognition of the other? Does this foster a regressive pull toward undifferentiated states? Can one experience one's subjectivity as well as one's tendency to feel fractured by the large group because of the inevitable lack of recognition inherent in the large group? For example, Rebecca makes a clear statement about what is happening to her in a large group and states that she thinks this group is useless, that she cannot learn anything here. She may be met by silence, which increases her sense of isolation and increases her feeling that the group has nothing to offer or she may be responded to by one or several people who share her feeling, thereby securing a sub-group in which the members share similar feelings, or someone may instruct her, stating that learning to appreciate what happens to her in the large group can help her better understand what can happen in groups and that this is important. These are all examples of relational experiences that can usefully encourage the large group members to struggle with their feelings, respecting that each member of the large group is dependent upon every other member to create a relational atmosphere in which true dialogue can occur and the large group can begin to develop its own culture.

If, however, the group becomes too overwhelming, if there is too much chaos, members will be unable to remain relational and regressive pulls may dominate. It is here that the leader, operating from a hermeneutics of trust, can make an intervention by observing how difficult it is to be in a setting in which one feels a lack of moorings and expresses appreciation for the efforts being made to form connections that may provide those moorings. This statement is both an empathic observation as described by Kohut (1959) and a leading edge statement (Tolpin, 2003) in that it provides both recognition of the experience and appreciation of efforts being made to improve mutual recognition and connection. The implications of this are that the leader both recognizes the truth of Rebecca's feelings, going no further than Rebecca does in her statement, an example of the hermeneutics of trust. She engages empathically with the obvious statement thereby opening a space of trust in which Rebecca and others may find their voices and perhaps be freed to expand on her statement. The assumption is that this young woman, not unlike others, is having a difficult experience, not unusual in a large group, and by speaking to her experience she has both made connections with others, thereby reducing fear, as well as feeling recognized by the leader's statement. Even though the leader's comment may have been made to the entire group, it spoke to Rebecca's dilemma. This kind of recognition has the added benefit of both diminishing empathic ruptures as well as providing an experience-near opportunity to the entire group. It is a somewhat idealized example in that it focuses on the moment-to-moment experience of one large group member when there are perhaps thirty to fifty or more others. The larger context is one in which the voice and experience of the individual can be lost. It is here where I wish to address the large group experience. But before considering new ways to study large group action, it is important to understand some of the earlier history of the study of large groups. Looking through the lens of self/relational and systems theory allows us to recognize that the group is composed of unique individuals and that something new emerges when these individuals are placed in group. I will attempt to expand thinking beyond the perspectives of classical theory but in order to do this effectively, we may wish to consider that current self-psychological and relational theory is in fact rooted in classical ideas. Therefore, exploring some of the earlier evolution of large group theory may prove informative to the reader.

Early Development of Large Group Theory

Freud's examination of group behavior was instrumental in formulating ideas about what happens in groups. His paper "Group psychology and the analysis of the ego" was published in 1921. Though this paper did not initially have a big impact, it gained considerable attention when group therapy was being recognized in the 1930s (Kreeger, 1975, p. 17). Though group treatment was also being explored in the United States, it took the impetus of World War II to formulate large group theory in Great Britain, in an effort to create treatment modalities for a sizeable number of traumatized military populations. Many of the new formulations came from physicians and others who were working with these war-traumatized people on a daily basis.

Beginning in the late 1940s, there were several ground-breaking papers addressing large group experiences (Main, 1946; Foulkes, 1948; Jones, 1953; Rappaport, 1960; Rice, 1965; Bion, 1961).

Schiff and Glassman (Kreeger, 1975) directly described what were some potential difficulties resulting from large group experiences:

1. An increased tendency to sub-grouping, with more rigid hierarchies.
2. Less opportunities for individuals to speak.
3. Dilution of affectional ties.
4. Decreasing familiarity with others as individuals, and, the tendency to stereotype.
5. Skewing of participation—the leaders being more active and the less active members more silent.
6. The greater threat to the individual.

(p. 21)

This straightforward list did serve to describe what was concretely seen. What was also being described was the unconscious aspects of large group membership. A focus on the Freudian unconscious became a primary way in which to understand large group behavior and there were many influences from the Kleinians as well. Perhaps significant is that most of the efforts to understand large group behavior grew out of theories developed clinically in a dyadic relationship. This has often been the case in developing group theory. While this is somewhat inevitable, we must consider the possibility that this transfer of theory from a description of an individual's personal dynamics to group phenomena can severely constrict the field of group psychotherapy as it is impacted by ideas belonging to another realm of discourse. The large group has also been investigated by sociologists (Hopper, 2002) and others, particularly after World War II, in order to aid the numerous veterans requiring treatment, adding to a body of information that was an attempt not only to broaden information about large groups but also to grapple with the most effective use of the large group. There were those who believed that psychotherapy could occur in the large group and, out of this view, arose the therapeutic community still in use in many psychiatric hospitals (Jones, 1946). Since many of the early large group theorists were Freudian analysts (Foulkes, Pines, Main) or Kleinian analysts (Bion, Turquet), there was considerable emphasis on processes such as projective identification, and other aggressive and regressive mental processes. An example of this theory building was the work of Wilfred Bion (1961), formulated as a result of his work with veterans. He described basic assumption groups that arose in these group settings. A.K. Rice advanced this work in the United States, where the task of the large group to study its own behavior advanced this work. This model along with group analysis dominates large group work even today.

This focus on traditional theoretical ideas was the primary way in which to view the large group in the post-World War II era. These perspectives, well presented in the book *The Large Group* (1975), edited by Lionel Kreeger, persisted well into the 1970s and 1980s and continue today, relatively unchallenged. But the adherence to these particular theoretical positions has shifted somewhat as theory has become more influenced by the development of self and relational ideas that offer a view of human engagement that has emerged from investigations of healthy development of the individual. This is reflected in the book, *The Large Group Revisited* (2003). In their introduction, Weinberg and Schneider suggest that:

> The large group awakens feelings of anxiety much sooner than we find in smaller groups. This is probably due to the weaker container function of the large group, fluidity of boundaries, and the seemingly chaotic structure which awakens regressed, primary anxiety formation of feelings of fragmentation, disintegration and loss of reality.
>
> (pp. 18–19)

Though these descriptions do not sound significantly different from earlier writings, there appears to be a less rigid embracing of traditional theory. For example, Jarrar (2003), writing from the personal perspective of a large group consultant, suggests that large group members can "become aware of their internal dialogues with the imagined other and transform them into an external and authentic dialogue with the real other. This is, in my view the essence of large group work" (p. 31). She goes on:

> The large group provides members with opportunities to explore and learn about difficulties we all have, as subjects, in recognizing other subjects as "Equivalent centers of experience" and enabling a move toward enhancing capacities for mutual recognition in the group. The daunting task of the consultant is to create a culture such that "Where objects were, subjects must be" (Benjamin, 1999, p184).
>
> (p. 31)

Thus, we see an expansion of ideas beyond traditional theory to more relational perspectives that offers large group theoreticians an alternative that addresses the more altruistic potential of the large group.

The recent growth of theoretical ideas has had relatively little to say about group behavior, much less large group behavior. It nonetheless offers a new direction to those who continue to do work with large groups, despite the fact that these more current theorists (Mitchell, Aron, Beebe, Bromberg, Kohut, Benjamin, Lichtenberg, Lachmann, Fosshage, and so on) do not study large groups and, for the most part, rarely address group behavior. Though this study of the group is occurring within self psychology (Harwood, Shapiro, Stone, Segalla), further expansion of theory is needed. The case in relational theories is similar. The work of Billow (2003) expands the work of Klein to include more relational ideas. Grossmark, writing about relational group therapy, includes ideas from the work of Donnel Stern and others (2007). Wright has brought an eclectic sensibility to group work, tuning into the current trends in self and relational theories that influences the formation of new theories of group behavior.

The fact remains that the application of these ideas from dyadic treatment is very much a part of how we attempt to understand group action. Perhaps in our efforts to apply these newer theoretical ideas to group therapy and large group behavior, we will begin to formulate a model that is reflective of the individual and the dyad but which understands, as these early theorists realized, that what happens when people are in groups, much less large group, is something new and often unusual. It is not within the scope of this chapter to explore these very interesting observations. But it would be useful to explore more fully the development of self/relational group theory as it attempts to understand what is happening both for the individual and for the group as a whole. Returning to the theme of this chapter, I want to reassert that what I wish to explore is whether large group is experienced differently and has different outcomes when the group leaders offer observations and interpretations from experience-near theories that not only speak to defenses or other more traditional mechanisms but also attempt to explore and expand on evidence of many affective efforts to engage relationally.

I am suggesting that interpretations based in more traditional theories, while often quite accurate, create an atmosphere permeated by the more negative aspects of human engagement. I am further suggesting that by not giving sufficient recognition to the positive efforts at engagement in the complicated setting of the large group, we are doing a disservice to the members, who, despite their discomfort and perhaps disequilibrium, continue to make efforts to cross boundaries in a manner that conveys an ardent desire to truly know the other. While recognizing that this task is increasingly difficult as the group numbers increase, it is important to use another, more experience near lens, that will aid us in filling in the picture of large group behavior. In an effort not to create a binary picture of group action, I would like to acknowledge that though my emphasis is on the more relational aspects of the large group, it is with full awareness of the regressive and aggressive pulls that are also present. In fact, one of the reasons to study large groups is to support efforts to create experiences in which people become accustomed to working across the many barriers to communication among groups across all cultures. Returning to Orange's hermeneutics of trust, we have an opportunity to consider that in addition to self-serving and diminishing behavior that may arise out of experiences of anxiety over a threatening sense of a loss of self, we are all capable of more altruistic aspects of the self that need to be both observed and supported in the large group. Exploring this further may provide us with some new directions in which to study the large group.

Large Group: A New Look?

What follows is based on my work as both a co-leader and member of a large group team that has been operating for over twenty years in the Washington School of Psychiatry, Washington, DC, Group Psychotherapy Institute. In this setting, a training institution, the purpose of the large group is to study its own behavior, aided by the observations of the faculty conductors. There are six weekend conferences over a two-year cycle. Members usually attend all six conferences. Each of the weekends has, as a part of the program, three large group experiences. We, therefore, have the opportunity to observe the large group evolve over the three meetings of a conference weekend as well as the evolution that occurs over the two-year cycle of the institute. Because this large group leader team has remained essentially the same for most of the two decades, it has been interesting to see our evolution as a team. As I consider our shifting perspectives over these decades, I am most interested in how the conduct of the leaders has subtly changed. It is a lovely example of how the cultural shifts, and theory expansion that has been occurring within psychotherapy and psychoanalysis, have simultaneously been incorporated into our work as group conductors. Using ourselves as an example of how we have gradually absorbed the cutting-edge ideas, I will attempt to explore how we have begun to express these ideas in the interpretations that we, the team, make when we are conducting a large group. My primary observation is that our comments and interpretations in the large group have moved away from an emphasis on the regressive, projective, and aggressive aspects of the group interactions toward what Lichtenberg et al. (2003) describe as a more "user friendly approach." Again, I stipulate that I have not lost sight of the presence of a variety of forces nor do I wish to create a binary picture between our attempts to be relational and the more negative feelings expressed in the large group. The complex interplay of all human behavior is perhaps even more pronounced in the large group.

My focus, therefore, is on how self-psychological and relational theories have had an important impact on large group experiences perhaps because the group leader's gradual and subtle shift has led to somewhat different responses in the membership. I am suggesting that the cultural context current in the field is changing which impacts both leaders and members, demonstrating the complex interaction between culture and theory. Like many experiences in the field, we did not set out to change our approach but rather we reflect what has been a loosening of the hold of classical Freudian and Kleinian theory in psychoanalysis.

An additional focus has arisen out of what seems to be a gradually unfolding trend in psychoanalysis. It is my observation that there has been, as an outgrowth of the development of these theories that directly address the mutual influence system of therapist and patient, the necessity of ongoing attention to the relational field. This I believe has prompted closer attention to our values and ethics. Therefore, I am also suggesting that this move toward a more humanistic position has also had significant and subtle impacts. The ethical values of therapists and analysts are no longer closeted but are becoming part of mainstream dialogue.

In the next section, I will explore the impact of the relational and self-psychological influence on large group interpretations, attempting to explicate how leaders' observations from these perspectives have created opportunities for dialogue that supports efforts at connection in the large group. De Mare et al.

(1991) call these efforts "impersonal brotherhood." They arise out of leaders' comments and the comments of large group members.

Following that, I will address the trend toward a deeper appreciation of the other, evolving perhaps out of what E.O. Wilson (2012) describes as social evolution. It is my hope that both leaders and members of the large group will experience a kind of freedom from focused negativity as we absorb what it truly means to put the other first (Orange, 2011a) and to expand our capacity for mutual recognition in this evolving context.

Shifting Emphasis in the Large Group

In an effort to crystallize what is meant by these shifts, I will describe the parameters of my observations. This shift in the culture of the large group is reflective of the cultural shift within psychoanalysis already outlined. In the large group that I discussed earlier, I am one of five consultants or leaders.

The more personal perspective comes from decades of experience as both leader and member of large groups. Having attended many large groups as part of the A.K. Rice Institute during my tenure in the field, I believe I have experienced the fear and terror so often described by various authors and other members of these groups. I remember being completely blank, without a thought in my head. I also recall speaking out and having my comments ignored, experiencing a diminishment of self. "Wasn't that a good observation? Does anyone know I am here?" Over time and with many exposures to this setting, these difficult feelings have gradually dissipated, but not completely. That is, they can also occur when I am working as a group leader. Some of my observations fall flat. "Did I miss the mark completely?" What I am suggesting is that being in the large group requires a deep appreciation of the power of the group as well as an understanding that one can have experiences that can feel deeply threatening whatever role you occupy.

My years of experience have created a wish to explore the large group more deeply. Being a consultant/leader and watching the evolution of my own thinking as well as that of my fellow leaders has led to a reconsideration of the guidelines used for so many years by large group consultants. Therefore my remaining comments will be made based on both a long tenure as a large group leader and an appreciation of the vast evolution in psychoanalytic theorizing over the past decades.

The mitigating circumstances are twofold. One, the large group of which I am a part as a faculty member and leader convenes for two-year cycles at the Washington School of Psychiatry. It is composed of members who are in the mental health field and are working to increase their skills as group therapists. The program, know as the National Group Psychotherapy Institute, has from twenty to thirty-five members and eighteen faculty members. In addition, each weekend conference, of which there are six, is part of a two-year cycle that may also include from eight to fifteen attendees who come just for one weekend. These can include people who are interested in the particular conference topic or as a requirement of a clinical training program that is also part of the Washington School. This offers a somewhat novel experience each conference weekend. For example, this can include the existing group having difficulty integrating the weekend members. This provides the large group the opportunity to deal with this subgroup that can be characterized as "other." It is not difficult to imagine that the new members can become the object of desire, hate, envy, love, or any emotion, positive or negative. How the work is done can be the source of significant insight into large group behavior. It is at these junctions that we see the activation of the desire to connect with these members as well as the desire to kill off these members. It is here that a more relational approach aids the group in their efforts at inclusion and connection. If, however, the consultants attend primarily to the negative emotional expressions, they may miss opportunities to also observe and comment on the efforts at bonding and inclusion. This two-year institute cycle offers a degree of homogeneity in that the population remains essentially the same for the duration. The attendees being members of small groups that remain the same for the two-year cycle further reinforce this stability. Therefore, the members enter each large group as a member of a sub-group. This provides a kind of familiarity that supports a sense of belonging, reducing the isolation of being in a large group. So rather than entering as a singleton, these attendees join as sub-group members. These circumstances, the continuity provided by the two-year program as well as the support of each member's process group create a somewhat predictable environment. This can lead to more stability in the large group that is conducive to feeling more relational with other large group members with greater opportunity to appreciate the subjectivity of the other.

The second aspect of large group work that has shaped my view of the large group has been the work of the large group team of which I am a member. This team has remained essentially the same for over two decades. During these years, as part of every conference weekend, the team meets several times to discuss, postulate, and share feelings about how they functioned while in the large group session. We offer encouragement and support as well as observations that might feel critical. The discussion among the five of us is open, honest, and sometimes painfully direct. This has led to an evolution of this team in which there is a freedom in our discussions, an openness to the experience of each other. This is what I would characterize as relational knowing, an appreciation of our subjectivity, extended beyond the dyad that Benjamin so eloquently addresses. We see each other as subjects and are responsive to each other's vulnerabilities. When we have difficulties, we feel safe in working them through to a better understanding. The intimacy that has developed over time has also been nurtured by the presence of an observer. This is a faculty member who is not on the team who offers observations about the team's interactions, often spurring us on to deeper and more meaningful work. This emphasis on open and constant attention to our relational needs supplies necessary selfobject experiences to each of us.

The team's relational work sets the stage for new kinds of opportunities for large group members. It is, I believe, by providing relational experiences to large group members that an important culture begins to emerge. That is, by having access to our own relational needs on the team, we bring to the large group a particular sensibility that fosters efforts at connection. We enter each large group with a desire for compassionate understanding for the work of both the team and the membership. Once again, I wish to point out that there are also experiences that may feel damaging to particular group members. One of the important parts of the work is the effort made, by group members, to heal the inevitable empathic ruptures. These ruptures, as they are worked through, often lead to deeper connections among group members and also add to the intimacy that can occur when people successfully reconnect. We enter each group with a sense of compassionate understanding. This position has created an atmosphere of a particular sensitivity about the potential impact of group experiences signaling a sense of safety to the members. The sociocultural field of large group is also reflective of the inner world of each member and consultant. This will be explored in greater detail in the following section.

Expanding Self and Relational Theories: Large Group Experiences

Returning to influences from self and relational theories as they have impacted my large group work, I will explore these ideas in more detail. As I have indicated earlier, these theoretical ideas emerged out of dyadic clinical experience; therefore application to large group work is an effort to expand the efficacy of the theories with recognition that they lose some of their explanatory effectiveness, as they become less experience near in regard to larger entities such as large groups.

What has emerged from the study of large groups that parallels in an uncanny way the development of these theories is the work of Patrick de Mare and colleagues (1991). Writing at about the same time, his ideas about large and median groups appear to be somewhat congruent with these dyadic theories. His emphasis is on the sociocultural dimensions most apparent in larger groups. He states, "The large group now shows us the other side of the coin to the inner world, namely the socio-cultural dimension in which these interpersonal relationships take place" (p. 3). He distinguishes between the inner world of the individual and the outer world of the culture:

> The problem for the individual is the intrusion into the individual situation of the repressed unconscious. For the large group on the other hand, it is consciousness that is in jeopardy, both for the individual and for the group's equivalent of consciousness, namely communication and organization. The problem for the rudimentary large group is its mindlessness: not how to feel, but how to think.
>
> (p. 13)

He views the purpose of the large group as that of "humanizing the group as opposed to socializing the individual" (p. 25). Going on he states: "We are troubled by the discrepancy between individual mind and culture; how effectively to hasten mutuality between them? We pose the possibility that culture can be explored more adequately in a setting that is larger than the small group" (p. 25). His position reminds us of how our efforts to be relational, to establish intimate connections in the dyad or small group, become something different when we consider larger groups.

In the Foreword of *Koinonia*, Pamela Pomerance Steiner writes:

> At a large group conference, De mare stated: "It is aimless," as the session came to a close. Therein lay his message. Only in seemingly aimless discussion could a higher aim be realized: to understand large group dynamics, and to learn to communicate more freely with others.
>
> (p. xvii)

This mirrors Gadamer's (1998) important observation about dyadic conversation:

> We say that we "conduct" a conversation, but the more genuine a conversation is the less its conduct lies within the will of either partner. Thus a genuine conversation is never the one we wanted to conduct. Rather, it is generally more correct to say we fall into conversation, or even that we become involved in it. The way one word follows another, with the conversation taking its own twists and reaching its own conclusion, may well be conducted in some way, but the partners conversing are far less the leaders of it than the led.
>
> (p. 383)

We can see from these quotes that both dyads and groups must deal with the unpredictability of human engagement. As Benjamin points out, the task of the dyad is to come to the recognition of the subjectivity of both members of the dyad. The struggle of a small group compounds the efforts to appreciate the subjectivity of each member of the small group. The large group's task is somewhat different. It is here that the demands of the culture are paramount. De Mare sees large group as frustrating, leading to hate, and that it is a necessary task of the large group, through dialogue, to transform hate into "impersonal brotherhood."

This idea of impersonal brotherhood offers to large group theorizing what relational and self-psychological theories offer to dyads and small groups. Appreciating our inevitable embeddedness in the larger culture is an ongoing issue for all therapeutic endeavors. The implications for not attending to the larger culture are that we ignore the reality of the many cultural differences that are always present. As Sperry (2013) suggests: "Psychoanalysis will be limited in appeal and so will our ability as to work effectively with culturally diverse populations, if we fail to reflect on our embeddedness in systems that support Western perspectives and values" (p. 89). This problem is also significant for large groups in which members from different races and cultures become victims of the large group in which the majority of the members have similar backgrounds. It is in the large group that the damage resulting from this obliviousness to cultural issues can be most destructive for the members who do not share the same values as their fellow group members. Sperry goes on to suggest that: "Cultivating cultural dialogue requires a willingness to be exposed but offers the hope that by expanding our 'horizons' (Gadamer, 1991) we may discover human similarity while learning from our differences" (p. 89).

Returning to self and relational theories, how can these ideas be effective in understanding and working with larger groups? Is it necessary to attempt to consider the effectiveness of these theoretical structures in a setting so unlike individual and small group treatment? The large group is made up of individuals so it seems useful to make some effort at importing and expanding self and relational theory in considering large group experience. What has been most influential in my own thinking about dyadic, couple, and group treatment is the work of Kohut, Stolorow, Atwood, Brandchaft, Orange, and Lichtenberg et al. as well as many relational theorists such as Benjamin, Mitchell, and others.

Beginning with Kohut (1959), his emphasis on empathy as the primary tool of observation in clinical work as well as his selfobject theory has had a significant impact on psychoanalytic work. His ideas were quickly applied to group theory as I indicated earlier. Therefore, when I enter large group, I am sustained by my wish to remain empathically connected to each member as well as to the group as a whole, a more challenging task. This requires appreciating that each member and leader has a need for mature selfobject experiences, mirroring idealizing and twinship as well as other selfobject experiences. I can see these needs being expressed in various encounters among group members. It is understandable however, that having these met in large group is very difficult. Therefore, it is essential that the large group supply something akin to selfobject experiences. I have called these needs, to feel a part of something larger than the self, groupobject experiences (Segalla, 1996). That is, the group itself provides a sense of being a member of the tribe, a social need inherent in all of us. The need to be part of a community, to be embedded in something larger than the self, I call the need for groupobject experiences. This emphasis on affiliation mirrors the work of Lichtenberg et al. (2011), who describe as one of seven motivational systems, the need for affiliative experiences that exist quite apart from the need for basic attachment to others. It is also necessary to keep in mind the inevitability of the intersubjective field in which every engagement is constantly being co-created by all those present. Again, it is not easy to imagine co-created experiences in the large group. Does it mean members in this large group are each and everyone, part of each and every unfolding group event? Or can we generalize and suggest that the complex field of large group is the product of all present? Thus, when we refer to "the group," we are noting the inevitable interconnectedness of every person present. Orange (1995), writing about holding our theories lightly, provides a wonderful incentive to viewing large group as a non-fixed entity that defies full description, offering us the opportunity to view group action in a fluid way without being held to a theoretical structure which limits how we engage with the large group.

Moving on to the relational theorists, their influence further frees me from any idea of creating a theoretical perspective that defines and thus ultimately limits large group experiences. The work of Mitchell (1988), making his own efforts to understand the vast array of psychoanalytic theories, offers the view that we selectively integrate theories and traditions that may expand and enrich psychoanalysis. The large numbers of psychoanalysts offering unique contributions to the field capture the imaginative opening of the field, the product of the past quarter-century of creative expansion and redefinition. We can expand further by examining the large group culture of psychoanalysis. It is in this large group that we can see what exists in any large group: competition, envy, hate, as well as collaboration, caring, goodwill, and thoughtfulness. There are trends in our field that examine our attitudes, our values, our sensitivity and vulnerability, encouraging greater openness. As we open the space for more of these experiences, we offer hope not just for the individual but also for each individual existing in the larger culture.

Though self-psychology and relational theories have had a profound impact on my own thinking and have had, almost inevitably, been incorporated into my practice with individuals, couples, and groups, they have still not been sufficient to explain large group action. This requires that as psychologists and mental health practitioners it becomes increasingly clear that we must look to other fields to help us to better grasp cultural impacts. It is essential to consider as our world becomes more connected and continues to be troubled by the vast and endless array of cultural issues and problems.

Large Group: A Sampling

> The group, second of three occurring at the end of year one of a two-year institute cycle, opens in silence. The chairs, arranged in a spiral, are filled except for two in the center, indicating that two members are missing since there are enough chairs for five consultants and the group members. Thomas breaks the silence: "Well, why are there empty chairs? Who is missing and where are they? There was no announcement about any absences!" This is indignantly stated. Jane, speaking from the center of the circle responds: "If the empty chairs disturb you, why don't you come up here and fill one of them?" Barbara interjects: "I don't think his concern is about filling the chairs as much as who is missing." "I know," Jane rejoins: "but he always sits in the back row, I was just giving him the chance to get a different perspective." Matt enters the conversation: "Hey, let's not get lost in the details here. I want to know where Alicia and Rosie are, they were here this morning, and does anyone know

> where they are?" Matt's question begins a group discussion with several members saying that they had seen them talking after lunch. Elizabeth picks up the question of the absence more directly. "I am annoyed! We were discussing something pretty important this morning and now everyone is happy to focus outside the room about where the missing people may be. I think we are avoiding talking to each other right now." Tom joins in, "Yeah, that's why I was concerned about the empty chairs. We were really into important things and Alicia was a part of that conversation so I want her here." Sally responds, "So why did you talk about empty chairs instead of expressing concern about where Alicia and Rosie were? You can be so indirect." "That's true but I was being direct. I didn't know who was missing because I couldn't see who was missing!" Tension begins to build, the group lapses into silence once more. Consultant One states, "There is an urgency about missing members. We can speculate about why that is." "Well," responds Lee, "Alicia and Rosie are important members. I want to hear what they have to say. They help move things forward in here."

In a relationally influenced group, a consultant may observe that the anxiety over the missing members is reflective of the group's fear of a loss of the cohesiveness that has developed over the first year of the institute. The anxiety over the loss of attachment may have been engendered by the fact that the group would not be meeting for five months. It is interesting to consider that groups develop attachment needs as well as attachment styles as is seen in the child and its caregiver.

> The group dialogue continues, Alicia and Rosie enter twenty minutes late and go to the center of the circle, filling the empty chairs. Once again the group falls silent. Neither Alicia nor Rosie offers an explanation for the absence but it is obvious that Alicia has been crying. Edward breaks the silence, "It looks like you are feeling bad Alicia. We were wondering where you and Rosie were." The silence continues. Louise Ann, a member who rarely speaks states sympathetically, "Did something happen Alicia, was it anything to do with this morning's group?" Alicia begins to cry, "I didn't want to come back. Rosie convinced me. When Mary Lou started telling us about her car accident and her severe injury something happened to me. I can't explain what it was but I felt really frightened and wanted to jump up and run out of the room and not come back because this is our last Institute until next October." Four or more people urge Alicia to continue to speak. The group seems on high alert. Consultant Two interjects, "The tension suggests that members may be ambivalent about focusing on Alicia's difficulty. Is there an unaddressed need

to explore why the group feels so disrupted?" Alan, sounding angry, states, "We were getting close to some important things this morning, with the whole group really working together. Now we're spending all our time on one person's issues. I think we'd rather hear about Alicia's story than talk about this group not meeting for five months. Why are tears so compelling anyway? Is anyone else feeling impatient? I'm afraid we're losing the spark we had this morning." Consultant Three suggests, "The group disruption is reflective of some anxiety stirred up by the talk of trauma and loss in this morning's meeting. This is demonstrated by the chaos occurring in this session." His comment is met by more silence. The end of the session is fast approaching. Consultant Four adds, "There has been little reference to trauma yet it is being alluded to by several people. What might the group be avoiding?" Members glance at each other but no one speaks. The group ends with members streaming out of the room except for a small group gathered around Alicia who begins to cry again. There is one more session, occurring the following day, before the institute ends until next October.

Consultant's Meeting

The five consultants retire to another room to discuss the group. "Wow, what was going on in there, it was so fragmented!" Consultant Four exclaims. Consultant Five adds, "I felt so caught up in the process, I couldn't think of anything to say. The emphasis is on thinking but I think I was feeling really blank. Nothing felt available to me, I was having a hard time staying involved." Consultant One states, "It feels like there is some big secret or something. I wonder if something happened in one of the small groups that hasn't been brought into the large group." "And I wonder," Consultant Two adds, "If Alicia is carrying something for the group. Her tears certainly captured everyone's attention." "Does anyone else feel disorganized besides me?" This is stated by Consultant Three. "I am feeling that there is something traumatic operating here. I know I was caught up in Mary Lou's accident story this morning. It is clear that she is physically impaired. I wonder if people are avoiding talking about that and I wonder about the shooting spree in Colorado too. It is pretty amazing that there were absolutely no references to that even though it only happened last week." Consultant Two agrees, "It is unusual that there was no comments about either situation. It certainly reinforces my feeling that Alicia is carrying the trauma for the group. We were trapped in silence too. I think there were only four or five observations made by us. I'm concerned that whatever is going on will not be addressed tomorrow and that we will go into the long break with things being really chaotic." Consultant Four questions, "So are you saying that we need to get more active or something? So what if the group continues to be disrupted? Don't forget, this is the middle session. We often see this disruption, whether or not there is trauma in the air." Consultant Three states, "I agree, we seem as fragmented as the group! What is everyone feeling and are we carrying something that belongs in the group? We know that there is no one thing going on. I am sure Mary Lou's accident and impairment is part of the picture but it isn't the only thing happening. I am much more interested in the absences rather than what is present. Why hasn't Colorado been mentioned by them or by us?" The discussion continues to unfold with consultants becoming more personal about their feelings about the trauma both in the group and in the larger culture. Consultant Two says "I am feeling disrupted. Talk about auto accidents feels too close for me. It certainly stirred up my own distress from last year when I was hurt." "Do you need to talk about that?" asks Consultant Three. "No, no, that isn't necessary but I am sure that I am not the only person activated. I don't feel like I am avoiding talking about it—you all know the details. My point is that there seems to be a lot of undisclosed feelings and I think the Colorado disaster is the big bomb, so to speak. No one wants to feel vulnerable before we break for the summer and talk about that is sure to stir people up—including us."

The observer is asked for her comments both about the large group and the consultant's group before it winds down. "I agree that the comments about the impact of trauma both in the large group and on the team are very important. The large group was rather chaotic, but as you pointed out, that is often the case in the middle session. The anxiety about the loss of support of the group because of the long break is a part of the picture but I think the fact that the group continues to avoid Colorado is being unconsciously supported by all of you. You need to ask yourselves why it is that you did not pick up on the allusions in the group about Colorado. It seems to me that there were enough indirect references that you could have explored. So, I think that the avoidance is possibly emanating from all of you. In our next session, I think we need to open this issue up for further examination. Is there some trauma operating right here with all of you? M. comes to mind—that was a trauma the team suffered as well as the loss of L." "Thanks B. I think you are right on—back to the big issues," states Consultant One. The meeting comes to an end.

Another Example

Re-emphasizing the importance of relational approaches to large group, I recently led two large groups, one in the morning and one in the afternoon, that were a new experiment for Institute of Contemporary Psychotherapy and Psychoanalysis. These large groups were part of an annual conference in which the discussion portion of the day usually follows a format in which audience members, using a mike, direct comments or observations to the guest presenter. This change reflected the topic, race, and culture. The large groups began almost immediately with lively exchanges among many audience members who had received directions to address their comments to fellow conference members. I was initially amazed at the level of discourse occurring in the group in both the morning and the afternoon sessions. As I analyzed the events, I explored why this readiness to openly discuss rather delicate issues was so actively embraced. My conclusions have supported the usefulness and importance of relationally driven approaches to group work. This organization has many members who have had a long history of involvement in the organization. Many of the conference attendees also had long histories with other ICP&P members. This served to create a trusting atmosphere of attachment and recognition among conference members. It also allowed others, non-members, to be supported by the open engagement that was present, thereby encouraging them to add their voices and important comments. These large groups were reflective of the importance of developing a relational atmosphere in any organization, thus facilitating open dialogue in which people can feel trusting and connected to each other. This conference group had over one hundred attendees who because of the trust that had been built in the organization over time (a major stated goal of the organization) were able to conduct themselves in a large group in such a way as to make it feel more like a small group. It demonstrates that people in large groups can come together, given a safe and caring container to, in fact, begin to experience "impersonal brotherhood."

Summary and Conclusion

Though I am hopeful that the shift in psychoanalysis and psychotherapy will ultimately also prove useful for the study of large groups, it has become more apparent to me that we may need to venture into new fields such as conflict resolution to deepen our understanding. The words of de Mare and colleagues (1991) offer the most optimistic conclusions for me. I will end with two quotes from his writings:

> The miniculture of the large group emerges as a result of dialogue. This emerging miniculture then provides the group with a perspective from which it is able to view socio-cultural and subculture assumptions that are being taken for granted. The large group minicultures have the effect of expanding consciousness and so provides an ethicocultural springboard that can distance itself from the unconscious biological and sociological cultures; these can then be demythologized.
>
> (p. 19)

Speaking ideologically de Mare goes on:

> the larger group is a microculture of society, with the distinction that we can address it and be answered by it. It is the watershed between the world and the personal, individual experiential mind. It has features of the unconscious mind, with the unique distinction of being like a dream in dialogue; it offers us the opportunity to humanize both the individual and society concurrently.
>
> (p. 21)

Acknowledgments

This chapter is dedicated to the memory of Marvin Skolnick, MD, and Lamis Jarrar, PhD, large group leaders par excellence. It is also dedicated to fellow members of the large group team: Mary Dluhy, MSW, Mary Ann Dubner, PhD, Leon Paparella, MSW, Michael Stiers, PhD, and Ayana Watkins-Northern, PhD.

References

Beebe, B. and Lachmann, F. (2002) *Infant Research and Adult Treatment*. Hillsdale, NJ: Analytic Press.
Benjamin, J. (1998) *Shadow of the Other*. London: Routledge.
Billow, R. (2003) *Relational Group Psychotherapy*. London: Jessica Kingsley.
Bion, W.R. (1961) *Experiences in Groups and Other Papers*. London: Tavistock Press.
De Mare, P., Piper, R., & Thompson, S. (1991). *Koinonia*. London: H. Karnac Books.
Fosshage, J.L. (2011) How do we "know what we know"? And change what we "know"? *Psychoanalytic Dialogues*, 21 (2): 55–74.
Foulkes, S.H. (1948) *Introduction to Group–Analytic Psychotherapy*. London: Heinemann.
Freud, S. (1921) Group psychology and the analysis of the ego. *Standard Edition*, 18: 67–143. London: Hogarth Press, 1955.
Frie, R. (2010) Compassion, dialogue, and context: On understanding the other. *International Journal of Psychoanalytic Self Psychology*, 5: 451–466.
Gadamer, H.G. (1998) *Truth and Method*. New York: Continuum.
Grossmark, R. (2007) The edge of chaos: Enactment, disruption, and emergence in group psychotherapy. *Psychoanalytic Dialogues*, 17 (4): 479–499.
Harwood, I. (1995) Toward optimum group placement from the perspective of self and group experience. *Group Analysis*, 29 (2): 199–218.
Hopper, E. (2002) Aspects of aggression in large graoups characterized by (ba) I:A/M. In S. Schneider & H. Weinberg (eds.) *The Large Group Re-Visited*. London: Jessica Kingsley.
Jarrar, L.K. (2003) A consultant's journey into the large group unconscious: Principles and techniques in the large group revisited. In S. Schneider & H. Weinberg (eds.) *The Large Group Revisited: The Herd, Primal Horde, Crowds and Masses*. London: Jessica Kingsley.
Jones, M. (1946) In Kreeger L. (ed.) *The Large Group*. London: Karnac Books (1975).
Jones, M. (1953) *The Therapeutic Community*. New York: Basic Books.

Kohut, H. (1959) Introspection, empathy, and psychoanalysis. *Journal of the American Psychoanalytic Association*, 7: 459–483.

Kohut, H. (1978) The search for the self, creativeness, charisma, group psychology: Reflections on the self-analysis of Freud. In P. Ornstein (ed.) *The Search for the Self*. New York: International Universities Press.

Kohut, H. (1984) *How Does Analysis Cure?* Ed. Arnold Goldberg. Chicago: University of Chicago Press.

Kreeger, L. (ed.) (1975) *The Large Group*. London: Constable.

Lichtenberg, J.D., Lachmann, F.M., & Fosshage, J.L. (2002) *A Spirit of Inquiry: Communication in Psychoanalysis*. New York: Routledge.

Lichtenberg, J.D., Lachmann, F.M., & Fosshage, J.L. (2011) *Psychoanalysis and Motivational Systems, A New Look*. New York: Routledge.

Main, T.F. (1946) The hospital as a therapeutic institution. *Bulletin of the Menninger Clinic*, 10: 66.

Mitchell, S.A. (1988) *Relational Concepts in Psychoanalysis*. Cambridge, MA: Harvard University Press.

Orange, D.H. (2011a) *The Suffering Stranger*. New York: Routledge.

Orange, D.H. (2011b) Persons in context, beyond individualism: Philosophical contributions of Buber, Gadamer and Levinas. In R. Frie & W.J. Coburn (eds.) *Persons in Context: The Challenge of Individuality in Theory and Practice*. New York: Routledge.

Orange, D. H. (1995) *Emotional Understanding: Studies in Psychoanalytic Epistemology*. New York: Guilford.

Rappaport, R. (1960) *Community as Doctor*. London: Tavistock.

Rice, A.K. (1965) *Learning of Leadership*. London: Tavistock.

Schneider, S. & Weinberg, H (2003) *The Large Group Re-visited: The Herd, Primal Horde, Crowds and Masses*. London: Jessica Kingsley.

Segalla, R. (1996) The unbearable embeddedness of being: Self psychology, intersubjectivity and large group experiences. *Group*, 20 (4): 257–271.

Segalla, R. (2001) Hatred in group: A rewarding challenge. *Group*, 25: 121–132.

Sperry, M. (2013) Sameness and difference: Cultivating cultural dialogue. *International Journal of Psychoanalytic Self Psychology*, 8: 77–91.

Stolorow, R.D., Atwood, G.E., & Orange, D.H. (2002) *Worlds of Experience: Interweaving Philosophical and Clinical Dimensions in Psychoanalysis*. New York: Basic Books.

Tolpin, M. (2003) Doing psychoanalysis of normal development: Forward edge transferences. *Progress In Self Psychology*, 18: 167–190.

Wachtel, P. (2008) *Relational Theory and the Practice of Psychotherapy*. New York: Guilford Press.

Wilson, E.O. (2012) *The Social Conquest of Earth*. New York: Liveright.

Wright, F. (2000) The use of self in group leadership: A relational perspective. *International Journal of Group Psychotherapy*, 50 (2): 181–198.

Index

Note: Page numbers followed by 'n' refer to notes.

Adult Attachment Interview (AAI) 174
affiliative experiences 171, 255
agency 32–3
Ainsworth, M.D.S. 173
Alanso, A. 198
Aledort, S.L. 117
alien group self 227–9
alien self 227–8
Alonso, A. 45, 54, 171
alternate group meetings 20–1
Alvarez, A. 70
amygdala 179
analyst's self-perspective 130, 137
analytic groups 29, 30, 31–2
analytic third 125, 215, 224, 227, 238n
"animate object" 70
Aristotle 3
Aron, L. 17, 18, 28, 30, 31, 38, 47, 71, 77, 108n, 215, 237
"assignment" 204–5
asymmetry position 20, 130
attachment theory: attachment styles 173–4; insecure attachments 173; limitations of 173; neurobiology and 169; neuroscience and mandate for 41, 168, 169–72, 176; primary functions of attachment system 172–3
attachment theory informing therapy: and ability to establish healthy relationships outside therapy 172; in confluence with neuroscience 175; emphasis on experience over explanation 178–82; group attachment needs and styles 257; and non-linear relational system theory 177–8; and prediction of successful treatment outcomes 171–2, 175; strong group attachment bonds priming the brain for change 176
Attention and Interpretation 237n
attunement 147, 172, 180; parent–child 41, 154, 228, 238n; therapist–patient 39, 41, 46, 49, 126, 154, 161
Atwood, G.E. 41, 129, 131, 132, 147, 151, 153, 156, 188, 222, 237n, 244, 245

Bad Fit concept 117
Balint, M. 86, 115
basic assumptions 9, 99, 103, 104, 107, 237n
Beebe, B. 17, 18, 19, 41, 245, 248
Benjamin. J. 2, 17, 20, 32, 41, 43, 48, 77, 215, 221, 222, 223, 224, 226, 227, 245, 248, 254
Bertalanffy, L. von 61, 190, 199, 202
The Bible 113–14
Billow, R.M. 34, 35, 44, 92, 97, 98, 99, 108n, 188, 201, 248
Bion, W.R. 6, 9, 44, 46, 60, 71, 88n, 91, 92, 99, 100, 103, 104, 108n, 216, 217, 224, 237n, 247
blank screen approach 27, 33, 151
Bollas, C. 70, 92, 231, 238n
Bonnefoy, Y. 59
Borges, J.L. 77
boundaries 191–2
boundarying 192
Bowlby, J. 141n, 169, 170, 171, 172, 173, 179, 184
brain plasticity: and change in group, six factors for promoting 176–83; changes while receiving psychotherapy 168
breast, good breast bad 216, 221

Bromberg, P. 3, 17, 62, 63, 77, 78, 81, 84, 85, 87, 133, 225, 239n
Burke, W. 20
Burston, D. 17, 21

caring and cooperation 182–3
Carr, A.W. 189
causality and nature of change 222
central nervous system 170–1, 176, 177, 183
Coburn, W. 17
Cohn, B. 189, 190, 191, 198, 199
common tensions 102, 103, 104, 105, 107
complementarity 35
complexity theory 61–2, 70–1
conflict, group: clinical example of therapist involved in 49–50; "co-created" conflict 52; relational approach to clinical example 51–3; task of group leader in 47–9; traditional analysis of clinical example 51
container-contained 44; nuclear ideas as 101–2; roles in group 216, 217, 220; symbiotic interactions 102, 108n
containment, group leadership role of 70, 72
context, social/economic and influence on group 204–6
conversation, dyadic 254
cortisol 177
countertransference 15, 19, 39, 40, 45; and empathic listening stance 131–2; from a relational perspective 30, 31; – transference in group work 225, 226, 235
creative work of groups 83–4
culture 208, 249, 250; embeddedness in larger 254–5; group 57, 92, 104, 107, 208; individual inner world and outer world of 253–4; large group 245, 248, 253, 254–5, 256, 260

Davies, J.M. 29, 88n, 108n, 200
De Mare, P. 10, 250, 253–4, 260
death instinct 216, 217, 221, 229
depressive position 115, 116, 117, 118, 119
Derrida, J. 204
description intervention 220
determinism 13
developmental trauma model 153–4
"difficult patients" 44–5, 53–4, 198
direct experience approach 22

disruption 61, 62; clinical study of enactment of disruption and emergence in group session 63–9
dissociation 40, 239n; as distinct from repression 40, 78; shifts to reflection and creation of meaning 62; strong and weak 78, 80; and trauma in group therapy 77–81, 84, 85; undoing 83–4
doer/done to relations 223–4, 234
dopamine 177
dreams 82, 87–8, 134
Durkin, H. 61, 75, 76, 86, 128
Durkin, J. 191, 192, 193, 194, 202
dynamic systems theory 61, 69, 71, 72, 202

Eagle, M.N. 200, 204, 215
"edge of chaos" 58, 61–2, 63, 64, 71
ego 115, 116, 216, 221
ego psychology 131, 134
"emergent" phenomenon 226, 238n
emotional: availability of therapist 124, 125, 145–6, 150, 151–2; communication, wordless 179–82; experience of treatment 13–14; learning 179; thinking 34–5
emotions 180
empathic bonds 148, 151, 152
empathic listening 131–5, 136, 137, 139, 140, 141; concerns over being 'nice' and avoiding confrontation in 133–4; focus on unconscious processing in 134–5; subjectivity of analyst in 131–3
"empathic responsiveness" 133, 151
empathy 182, 223, 255
enactive engagement in group therapy, flow of 75, 85–7
"enactive witnessing" 85, 87
enactment 19, 81–2; allowing free-flow of enactive engagement 75, 85–7; analyzing a painful enactment from two approaches 49–53; analyzing one's part in 35; complexity and multiple self-states in group 61–3; defining 30, 40; disentangling with help of group from 45; of disruption and emergence in group session, 63–9; emergence of unformulated experience in group 59, 60; group finding way out of 69–71; and implications for group analytic technique 71–2; loss of mutual recognition giving way to 223–4; meaning-making and creativity arising

out of 82–4; moving from one to next 29–30, 44, 58, 60; mutual experiences of merger forming new forms of self-experience in 215, 225–7, 229, 236; and repeating of trauma 29, 54, 75, 86, 87; role of therapist in group 19, 46–7, 60, 63, 70–1, 87–8, 227; and shared third space 227; Tavistock conference model and example of "twoness" kind of 224–5; work of group and 58–9
envy felt by therapist 36
Ettin, M. 102, 103
existential therapy 13, 16, 21–2; personal reflections of a therapist of 12–26
experience, unformulated 22–3, 59; and hermeneutic circle 59–60; revealed in enactments 78–9, 86
Experiences in Groups and Other Papers 217, 237n

"familiar chaos" 60, 61, 64
fathering process 34
financial aspects of treatment 204–5
flow of enactive engagement in group therapy 75, 85–7
focal conflict and nuclear ideas 103–4, 105, 107
focus 152–3, 190; and using a systems view in group work 190–1
Fonagy, P. 57, 59, 170, 173, 174, 178, 179, 227–8
Fosshage, J.L. 130, 131, 132, 133, 134, 135, 140, 141f, 243
Foulkes, S.H. 5, 6, 41–3, 57, 58, 75, 76, 86, 92, 103, 200, 246
frame and boundaries, group 71
free association 75–6, 86, 134
Freud, S. 75–6, 86, 129, 134, 216, 244, 246; Mullan's questioning of 13, 15
Frie, R. 13–14, 17, 18, 21, 203, 243–4

Gadamer, H.-G. 3, 60, 83, 203, 204, 254, 255
Gans, J. 45, 54, 171, 198
General Systems Theory 61, 191, 202, 211f
"genuine psychological use" 104, 226
Gergen, K.J. 43
Ghent, E. 48, 53, 61, 94, 224
God, relationships with 113–14
Grossmark, R. 44, 47, 75, 86, 103, 188, 202, 203, 212n, 227, 243, 248

group culture 57, 92, 104, 107, 208; large 245, 248, 253, 254–5, 256, 260
group matrix 57, 200
"Group Psychology and the Analysis of the Ego" 246
group themes 103, 104
groupobject 255
guilt of therapists 35–6

Hayden, C. 217, 218, 220
Heisenberg, W. 129
"here-and-now" in group therapy 30, 46, 59, 200, 201, 204
hermeneutics 58, 63, 83; of Freud 244; hermeneutic circle and unformulated experience in group 59–60; of trust 244, 245, 246, 249; value of hermeneutic thinking 203–4
homeostasis 61, 177, 202–3, 210; / heterostasis 192, 203
Hopper, E. 54, 108n, 188, 202, 247
How Life Imitates Chess 179

"I" and "not-I" 224, 225–6, 232
I experience 230–1, 235
impasse: anecdotal example of overcoming 165–6; clinical examples 154–60, 164–5; interventions at moments of 153–4
"impersonal brotherhood" 251, 254, 260
implicit domain and limbic resonance 179–82
"Inherent Moral Practice in Group Psychotherapy" 14
Institute for the Psychoanalytic Study of Subjectivity 63
Institute of Contemporary Psychotherapy and Psychoanalysis 259–60
insurance companies 204–5
interpretation and change 39–40; Foulkes' understanding of 42
"the interpretive stance" 189
intersubjective approach: advantage of group in 43–4; to analysis of group conflict 48–9, 49–50, 51–3; clinical example combining systems view and 208–10; clinical example of psychodynamic process group 195–6; differences in terminology between traditional psychoanalysis and 38–41; difficulties integrating Tavistock model with 215–16, 221–2; impact on psychoanalytic technique 188; literature

review of groups and 44–5; place of systems thinking in 202–3; vs. relational approach 40–1; role of group therapist in 46, 48–9, 216
intersubjectivity 2, 3–4, 18, 19, 43, 58, 129; development of nuclear ideas out of group 92, 93, 106; importance in shaping our subjective experiences of self and others 222–3; integration into different approaches 222–3; mutual experiences of merger forming new forms of self-experience 215, 225–7, 229, 236; mutual experiences of merger forming new forms of self-experience case illustration 230–6
interventions: combining intersubjective and systems view to prioritize therapist 208–9; at moments of impasse 153–4, 154–60, 160–4, 164–5; Tavistock consultant 220–1
Ionesco, E. 22
isolation 177
isomorphy 192–3, 197

Jarrar, L.K. 248
Joseph, B. 63, 87

A.K. Rice Institute 242, 247
Kasparov, G. 179
Kauffman, S. 58, 61, 62
Kay, J. 168
Kieffer, C. 103, 200, 222, 226–7, 237
Klein, M. 71, 141n, 216, 239n
Kohut, H. 128, 129, 130, 131, 132, 133, 147, 148, 165, 170, 172, 184, 242, 243, 246, 255
Koinonia 254
Kreeger, L. 242, 243, 246, 247

Lachmann, F.M. 19, 41, 130, 141n, 245, 248
The Large Group 247
The Large Group Revisited 248
large groups 242–4; case study of ICP&P 259–60; De Mare on 253–4; early development of theory 246–9; self and relational theories 244–6, 253–6; shifting perspectives 250, 251–3; theories emerging from dyadic clinical experience 253–4; trust in 259–60
large groups in Washington School of Psychiatry training for therapists program 249–51, 251–2; case study 256–9; consultants' meeting 258–9; group leader team 250, 252–3; observer 252, 258–9; program 250, 251–2
LBGT group 208–10
learning, non-linear relational theory to enhance 177–8
Leszcz, M. 20, 23, 171, 201
Levenson, E.A. 29
Lewin, R. 61, 62
libido 151, 220, 221
Lichtenberg, J.D. 72, 130, 131, 132, 135, 250, 255
limbic resonance 180; and implicit communication 179–82
listening/experiencing perspectives 128, 138–40; additional 135–8; analyst's self-perspective 130, 137; clinical vignette demonstrating oscillation between different 138–40; empathic 131–5, 136, 137, 139, 140, 141; evolution of 129–30; oscillation between different 128, 130, 135, 137–8, 140–1; other-centered listening 130, 135–7, 138, 139; of patients and group members 137–8, 138–40, 141; quality of therapist's 152; self listening perspective 130, 138, 139
Living Groups 191, 199
Livingston, L. 146, 153
Livingston, M. 146, 153, 188, 190
Loewald, H. 59
long-term potentiation (LTP) 183

MacKenzie, K.R. 197
Main, M. 173, 174
manuals, therapy 15
Maroda, K. 19
McKenzie 199
McRae, M. 229, 230, 231, 232, 233, 234, 235
McWilliams, N. 34
meaning-making in groups 35, 59–60, 63, 82–4
memory: focus on procedural 178–9; limbic resonance and implicit 179–82
mentalization 173; linking thinking to feeling 173–4; secure attachment and capacity for 173
metaphors for system states 199–200
Metaphysics 3
metapsychological: nuclear idea and extension into 105–6, 107; significance 93, 95
mind–body dualism 172

mirror neurons 182
mirroring 42
Mitchell, S. 28, 36, 63, 71, 129, 216, 237n, 242, 256
Molenkamp, R. 217, 218, 219, 220
"moments of meeting" 39–40, 178
mondo 221
money transactions 35
mothering process 34
Mullan, H. 12–26, 15, 18, 19, 21–2; background 12; example of self-disclosure by 27–8; on mutuality/status denial 18–21; on non-relational/non-teleological 21–4; on subjectivity 14–18
mutual recognition 18, 20, 32, 41, 245, 248; loss of 223–4; restoring 226–7
mutual regulation 18
mutuality 18–21, 32, 47; appropriateness of 20; defining 18; different facets of 19–20

narcissistic personality disorder 45
narratives 174
National Group Psychotherapy Institute 251
negentropy 193–4
neural pathways 183, 184
neurobiology: and attachment theory 169; "interpersonal" 184
neuroscience 23, 168; mandate for attachment theory 41, 168, 169–72, 176; and understanding of psychotherapy 23–4, 168, 175, 177, 184
neutrality of analyst 3–4, 14, 71, 180
non-linear dynamic systems theory (NDST) 2, 227, 238–9n
non-linear relational systems theory (NLRST) 178
non-linear relational theory of therapeutic action 23, 177–8
non-rational/non-teleological 21–4
"not me" 79, 80, 82, 85
nuclear ideas 91–111; "Checkpoints" clinical vignette 97–9, 102, 105; connection to focal conflict 103–4; as container/contained 101–2; and established group theory 102–5; extending discourse to the metapsychological 105–6; key qualities of 92–3; "Not Being Missed" clinical vignette 99–101, 102, 105; summing up 106–7; "Two Groups" clinical vignette 93–5, 101, 105; "Uncomfortable Role" clinical vignette 95–7, 101–2, 105, 106

object-relating and object use 223
object relations theory 170, 197, 220
object relationships 108n, 115, 116, 125, 229; subject/ 221, 223
objectivism transition to constructivism 129–30
Ogden, T. 17, 104, 106, 125, 215, 222, 223, 224–5, 226, 232, 235, 237n, 238n
"the one and the many" 3
open systems theory 188, 202
orality, theory of 171
Orange, D.H. 10, 22, 59, 83, 131, 132, 200, 203–4, 243, 244, 245, 251, 255
Ormont, L. 7, 46, 59, 112–13, 125, 171
other-as-object 223
other-centered listening 130, 135–7, 138, 139
"other than me" 226, 232

perspectivism 30
"phase transition" 62, 69, 71, 227, 234
Pines, M. 2, 42, 57, 59, 83
political context of therapy 52, 54, 97–8, 102, 105
Pollack, L. 32, 33
positivism 129–30, 238n; Mullan's rejection of 13
"process commentary" 30, 46
process observation 220
projective identification 216–17; and alien self 228; Bion's understanding of 44, 217, 247; and conflict 47, 51; and difficulties with integration of Tavistock model and intersubjective approach 221–2; as distinct from projection 216; Ogden's approach to 224–5; personality obliterated and elicited 224, 236; in study of irrational group phenomena 217
psychoanalytic objects 91–2
psychotic anxiety 217

rebellions, group 95, 97, 102, 107
reflexive self function (RSF) 174
refusals, group 98, 99, 107
regression 83, 112–27; attributes of 115; building resilience in group 123–4; case study in group treatment 120–3, 125–7; cycles of progression and 114, 115–18;

group as a transformative agent 118–19; group leader's experience with progression and 124–7; occurrence in group treatment 119–20; in relationships 113–14

relational approach: advantages of group therapy 43–5; to analysis of group conflict 48–9, 50–1, 51–2, 53; differences in terminology between traditional psychoanalysis and 38–41; Foulkes as forerunner of 41–3; and group treatment 1–3; vs. intersubjective approach 40–1; to large group behavior 244–6, 253–6; perspective on group leadership 4–5, 27–37; role of therapist in group treatment 45–7

Relational–Cultural Model 19, 32
reparation 70
repetition compulsion 84
repression 239n; as distinct from dissociation 40, 78
resilience building in group 123–4
resistance 39, 81; clinical examples 196, 198–9, 205–6; static 107
Resistance, Rebellion and Refusal in Groups 201
resonance 42; compassionate 133; limbic 180
responsivity 32
right brain activity 23, 189
Rizzuto, A.-M. 151–2, 190
role specialization in systems 197–9
Rubenfeld, S. 61, 202
Rutan, S. 198

safety of the group 8, 49, 70, 71, 72, 85, 135, 148, 150
Sangiuliano, I. 12–13, 15, 17, 18, 19, 21–2
scapegoating 9, 47, 194, 229
Schermer, V.L. 47, 83, 188, 201, 211n
Schneider, S. 48, 248
Schore, A.N. 23–4, 169, 171, 172
Schwartz, M. 145–6, 152
selection of group members 36
self: in context of the group 3; continuity 77; need for recognition by another 20, 32, 43, 223
self-disclosure 15, 20, 151, 164, 226; clinical example 27–8; group therapy and dilemma of 33–4
self-experience: as dual experience 232; of group leader 164–6, 203, 225–6; "here-and-now" experience and exclusion of 200, 201; hermeneutic analysis and 203–4; in infants 228; mutual experiences of merger forming new forms of 215, 225–7, 229, 236

self listening perspective 130, 138, 139
self-narrative 174
self/object 119, 123, 125, 126, 127, 146; differentiation 114–15, 119; group as 200; return to earlier 115, 116, 117, 118; unconscious matching of 117
selfobject 133, 147, 149, 255; transferences 132
"self-perspective," one's 130, 138, 139, 140, 141
self-psychology 33, 41, 51, 133, 148, 170, 248; and relational theories in large group behavior 244–6, 253–6
self-states 77, 239n; in group multiple 43–4, 61–3; regression as evocation of different 83; regressive 116–17, 120; shifting in clinical example 66, 67–8, 69; standing in the spaces between 62, 87, 88; systems view and 201–2
shame 84
Shapiro, E.R. 189
shared third space 227; case study and emergence of 230, 233–5
Slavin, J. 30, 31, 32, 33
Slochower, J. 20, 33
social difference replication within the group 206–8
social/economic context and influence on group 204–6
social unconscious 54, 188
specificity in treatment 184
Sperry, M. 254, 255
splitting 47, 48, 52, 197, 221
status denial 18
Steiner, P. P. 254
Stern, D.B. 4, 5, 19, 23, 39, 41, 58, 59, 60, 63, 75, 77, 78, 83, 85, 100, 103, 130, 134, 135, 141n, 169, 178, 188, 189, 189–90, 195, 200, 203, 221, 222, 223, 225, 238n, 239n, 248
Stolorow, R.D. 17, 19, 41, 129, 130, 131, 132, 135, 147, 151, 153, 188, 222, 223, 237n, 244
Stone Center, Wellesley College 19, 32, 46
stress levels and brain change 177
subjectivity 14–18; empathic listening stance and analyst's 131–3; and group conflict 48–9; and incorporation in a

nuclear idea 105; and need for recognition by the other 43, 223; in small groups 43, 254; of therapist in group therapy 29, 30, 31, 33–4, 71–2
subjugating third 224, 227, 229, 232, 236; case study on emergence of 230–6; dialectic between shared third and 227
submission and surrender 48
Suchet, M. 54
supervisor, group as good 45, 53, 54
sustained empathic focus 146, 152–3, 161, 165, 166
symbiotic container-contained interactions 102, 108n
synapses 183
system meaning 198–9
Systems Centered Therapy (SCT) 211n
systems theory 188–214; and animation of system 199–200; boundarying 192; classical 190–1; combining with an intersubjective view to prioritize therapist interventions 208–10; general understanding in group work of 188–9; and group field 191–5; helping to ground clinical meaning in contextual truth 200–2; holding system of group in mind 195–7; homeostasis/heterostasis 192, 203; in inpatient units 189; in intersubjective world 202–3; isomorphy 192–3, 197; and large groups 243; metaphors for system states 199–200; negentropy 193–4; as part of a relevant focus 190–1; in private group practice 204–8; role specialization 197–9; social context and creation of group resistance 205–6; social difference replication within the group 206–8; value of hermeneutic thinking 203–4

Tavistock model 217; alien group self in 227–9; case study of staff meeting between director and staff 230–6; characterization of group consultant 215, 236; consultant's task and interventions 220–1; and difficulties with integrating intersubjective approach 215–16, 221–2; emergence of a usable third 227; example of "twoness" kind of enactment 224–5; linear approach to causality and nature of change 222; members' anxiety at start 218–19; mutual experiences of merger and new forms of self-experience 215, 225–7, 229, 236; project identification and understanding of 216–17; subjugating analytic third 224, 227, 229; typical events 218–19; "work group" 229
Teicholz, J.G. 17, 20, 33
thematic development 220–1
theory and practice, relationship between 145–6
therapist: as Bion's "bizarre object" 44; as a blank screen 27, 33, 151; clinical vignettes concerning leadership of group 93–4, 195–7; combining intersubjective and systems view to prioritize interventions 208–10; defensive reactions to group therapy 34–6; emotional availability of 124, 125, 145–6, 150, 151–2; enactment, role in 19, 46–7, 60, 63, 70–1, 87–8, 227; envy felt by 36; experience with progressing while regressing 124–7; in Foulkesian terms 42; group as supervisor of 45, 53, 54; as group leader in times of conflict 47–9; group leadership, containment and complexity 70–1, 72; guarding against patient impact 33; guilt of 35–6; holding group in mind 195–7, 225, 229; intersubjective approach, role in 46, 48–9, 216; interventions at moments of impasse 153–4, 154–60, 160–4, 164–5; neutrality of 3–4, 14, 71, 180; "observing participation" 30; personal reflections of an existential 12–26; relational approach, role in 45–7; relational perspective on group leadership 4–5, 27–37; self-disclosure see self-disclosure, self-experience of 164–6, 203, 225–6; skills for group leadership 46; subjectivity of 14–18, 29, 30, 31, 33–4, 71–2; Tavistock model characterization of 215, 236; therapeutic process and change in 14, 16–17, 19; as unobtrusive analyst 86; unwitting/unconscious participation 29
The Therapist's Contribution to the Treatment Process 12–13
time 59
transference 20, 39, 46, 59, 151; from a relational perspective 30–1
transformational object, group as 231, 238n

trauma: developmental 153–4; and dissociation in group therapy 77–81, 84, 85; enactments and repeating of 29, 54, 75, 86, 87; group interactions as expressions of early 58; and healing power of witnessing 85, 87; impact in a group 258, 259; of military populations 249; and retraumatization 148, 149; shame and enactments of 84; therapist's dream 87–8; vulnerability and evoking memories of early 147

truth: emergence of 189–90; emotional 6, 100, 108n; meaning as a static 83; objective 48, 212n; systems analysis to ground clinical meaning in contextual 200–2

twelve-step programs 119

Uncertainty Principle 129
unconscious 23, 222–3; aspects of large group membership 247; assessment of motivations 136–7; empathic listening stance and accessing 134–5
unobtrusive analysts 86
unwitting/unconscious participation 29
usable third space 227; case study and emergence of 230, 233–5

Valery, P. 60
vulnerability, therapist interventions for: clinical study of affect and 154–60; emotional availability of therapist 150–2; focus on affect and 147–50; and group leader's use of self-experience 164–6; interventions at moments of impasse 153–4, 160–4; safety within the group for emergence and processing of 148, 150; sustained empathic focus 152–3, 161, 165, 166

Wachtel, P. 78, 237n, 244
Washington School of Psychiatry 249–50, 251–2, 252–3
Weegman, M. 44
Weinberg, H. 38, 48, 54, 188, 243, 248
Wilke, G. 42–3
Wilner, W. 22
Wilson, E.O. 244, 251
Winnicott, D.W. 70, 223, 227, 228, 238n
witnessing 85, 87
Wolstein, B.J. 29
"woolly mammoth" hypothesis 78
"work group" 229
Wright, F. 17, 19, 40, 44, 45, 103, 188

Yalom, I. 5, 20, 23, 30, 38, 45, 46, 59, 103, 171, 201